Daily Devotionals for **JUNIORS**

CURIOSITIES

Little-known Facts
of God's Creation

Charles C. Case, Sr.

REVIEW AND HERALD®
PUBLISHING ASSOCIATION
Since 1861 | www.reviewandherald.com

Copyright © 1985, © 2007 by Review and Herald® Publishing Association

Published by Review and Herald® Publishing Association, Hagerstown, MD 21741-1119

All rights reserved. No portion of this book may be reproduced, stored in a retrieval system, or transmitted in any form or by any means (electronic, mechanical, photocopy, recording, scanning, or other), except for brief quotations in critical reviews or articles, without the prior written permission of the publisher.

Review and Herald® titles may be purchased in bulk for educational, business, fund-raising, or sales promotional use. For information please e-mail SpecialMarkets@reviewandherald.com.

The Review and Herald® Publishing Association publishes biblically based materials for spiritual, physical, and mental growth and Christian discipleship.

The author assumes full responsibility for the accuracy of all facts and quotations as cited in this book.

Unless otherwise noted, Bible texts are from the King James Version.

Bible texts credited to Amplified are from *The Amplified Bible.* Copyright © 1965 by Zondervan Publishing House. Used by permission.

Scripture quotations marked NASB are from the *New American Standard Bible,* © The Lockman Foundation 1960, 1962, 1963, 1968, 1971, 1972, 1973, 1975, 1977.

Texts credited to NEB are from *The New English Bible.* ©The Delegates of the Oxford University Press and the Syndics of the Cambridge University Press 1961, 1970. Reprinted by permission.

Texts credited to NIV are from the *Holy Bible, New International Version.* Copyright © 1973, 1978, 1984, International Bible Society. Used by permission of Zondervan Bible Publishers.

Texts credited to NKJV are from the New King James Version. Copyright © 1979, 1980, 1982 by Thomas Nelson, Inc. Used by permission. All rights reserved.

Scripture quotations marked NLT are taken from the *Holy Bible,* New Living Translation, copyright © 1996. Used by permission of Tyndale House Publishers, Inc., Wheaton, Illinois 60189. All rights reserved.

Bible texts credited to NRSV are from the New Revised Standard Version of the Bible, copyright © 1989 by the Division of Christian Education of the National Council of the Churches of Christ in the U.S.A. Used by permission.

Bible texts credited to RSV are from the Revised Standard Version of the Bible, copyright © 1946, 1952, 1971, by the Division of Christian Education of the National Council of the Churches of Christ in the U.S.A. Used by permission.

Verses marked TLB are taken from *The Living Bible,* copyright © 1971 by Tyndale House Publishers, Wheaton, Ill. Used by permission.

This book was
Edited by Penny Estes Wheeler
Copyedited by James Cavil
Cover design by Trent Truman
Cover art by iStock Photo
Interior design by Heather Rogers
Typeset: 10/12 Grotesque

PRINTED IN U.S.A.
11 10 09 08 07   5 4 3 2 1

Library of Congress Cataloging-in-Publication Data
Case, Charles C., 1931-   .
  Curiosities: Little-known facts of God's creation

"Published in collaboration with the Review & Herald Publishing Association as an enrichment of the Morning Watch devotional plan."
Includes index.
  1. Youth—Prayer books and devotions—English. 2. Devotional calendars—Seventhday Adventist.
I. Title.
  BV4850.C37 1985 248.4'8673202 858249

ISBN 978-0-8280-1916-3

To my wife, Millie,
for her counsel, encouragement, and love;

To my daughter, Jackie,
for her faithful typing
of the original manuscript;

To my son, Charlie,
for his encouragement;

To my father, Asa, now deceased,
for instilling in me a love for the out-of-doors.

To order additional copies of
Curiosities, by Charles C. Case, Sr.,
call 1-800-765-6955.

Visit us at
www.reviewandherald.com
for information on other Review and Herald® products.

Hi, Friends!

As we begin this new year together I want to turn your attention each day to the marvelous things that God created for you and me to enjoy. After He created everything, He looked and admired the beauty and perfection that existed. And "God saw that it was good." He must have been thrilled and excited about His new world! Although now marred by sin, the beauty of God's creation still shines in thousands of different ways.

As God created Adam and Eve He carefully thought out every little detail. He gave them the ability to see, hear, taste, touch, and smell. As descendants of Adam and Eve, we also have the blessings of the senses. If we didn't have them we would miss out on many enjoyments in life, because "nature speaks to [people's] senses, declaring that there is a living God, the Creator, the Supreme Ruler of all" (*Patriarchs and Prophets*, p. 48).

This year we will be studying many different aspects of nature from around the world. We know that "there is a simplicity and purity in these lessons direct from nature that makes them of the highest value. . . . The children and youth, all classes of students, need the lessons to be derived from this source. In itself the beauty of nature leads the soul away from sin and worldly attractions, and toward purity, peace, and God" (*Counsels to Parents and Teachers*, p. 186).

My desire is that daily you will see and experience that "the character and power of God are revealed by the works of His hands. In the natural world are to be seen evidences of God's love and goodness. These tokens are given to call attention from nature to nature's God, that His 'eternal power and Godhead' may be understood" (*Medical Ministry*, p. 103).

Join me as we investigate God's world through these daily devotional readings. Look at and learn from the inspiring and interesting lessons from the Creator's first book and His handiworks in the natural world. I hope that by reading these devotionals you will be drawn closer to the Creator, your loving friend Jesus. This is my prayer for you this year.

"Uncle Chuck"

If you desire more information, go to an Internet search engine (such as Google), type in the key word(s), and get more.

AWESOME CREATOR

Now the Lord had prepared a great fish to swallow up Jonah. And Jonah was in the belly of the fish three days and three nights. Jonah 1:17.

It is amazing how Jesus, the Creator of everything on and around the earth, learned lessons from His own creation and taught His disciples lessons from the natural world. Look at this: "And day by day [Jesus] gained knowledge from the great library of animate and inanimate nature. He who had created all things was now a child of humanity, and He studied the lessons *which His own hand had written in earth and sea and sky*" (*Fundamentals of Christian Education*, p. 442; italics supplied). The child Jesus learned lessons from His own creation.

Notice how God controlled nature. "God prepared a plant and made it come up over Jonah, that it might be shade" (Jonah 4:6, NKJV). It immediately grew large.

Jesus was sleeping, and a storm blow up. "Then He arose and rebuked the wind, and said to the sea, 'Peace be still!' And the wind ceased and there was a great calm" (Mark 4:39, NKJV). He spoke, and the wind and waves obeyed His voice.

Jesus cursed the fig tree, saying, " 'Let no one eat fruit from you ever again.' . . . Now in the morning, as they passed by, they saw the fig tree dried up from the roots" (Mark 11:14-20, NKJV).

Other Bible texts record Jesus extending the daylight (Joshua 10:12-14), dividing the Red Sea (Exodus 14:21), and turning water into wine (John 2:1-9). He led the children of Israel with a cloud by day and a pillar of fire by night (Exodus 13:21). He controlled the plagues on Egypt's hard-hearted Pharoah (Exodus 7-12). But I'm thrilled by the last power of God over nature that I cite here. We see God's power demonstrated to Moses by the burning bush. "And the angel of the Lord appeared to him [Moses] in a flame of fire from the midst of a bush. . . . *But the bush was not consumed*" (Exodus 3:2).

Jesus, the Creator, is a mighty God, and He has all the power in the world. Each day throughout this year we will read about our awesome Creator. Let us give honor, glory, and praise to Him every day for what He has done and will continue to do.

LAMP OF THE BODY

The eye is the lamp of the body. Matthew 6:22, RSV.

Our eyes, a marvelous part of our bodies, are made up of different parts, including the cornea, iris, pupil, lens, retina, and optic nerve. These parts, all functioning in harmony, allow us to see in living color what God has created. The light waves that the eye receives are transmitted to the brain along the optic nerve, and the brain quickly translates them into images. It is impossible for us to comprehend the great thought and care that God took in creating both us and other creatures, and especially the sense of sight.

The ability to see is one of the greatest physical gifts God has given us. It is sad to think that the presence of sin has ruined sight for so many people, making them partially or totally blind. Some people are color-blind—they cannot distinguish certain colors. God's world is beautiful! He spoke, and everything He made sprang into existence in living color.

Through our eyes pass images that are stored in our computer-like brains. After returning from a vacation trip, you may say, "I can still see those tall mountains covered with evergreen trees. It was beautiful." You are recalling what your eyes had seen and recorded in your brain. Scientists tell us we remember about 85 percent of what we see.

Satan knows that our eyes are one of the most important organs of our bodies, so he puts vivid scenes on TV and in videos, books, and magazines to capture our attention. We put them into our computer—our mind and brain. "If he [Satan] can control minds so that doubt and unbelief and darkness shall compose the experience of those who claim to be the children of God, he can overcome them with temptation" (*Gospel Workers*, p. 161). Satan wants to pervert our sight, captivate our minds, and take control of our lives. Reconsecrate yourself to God and ask His help to overcome Satan and his deceitfulness.

THE SENSE OF HEARING

January 3

He that hath an ear, let him hear. Revelation 2:7.

A second important God-given sense is hearing. The system of hearing that God created in our bodies is fantastic. Radio, telephone, television, and satellite have all tried to imitate this system for receiving messages.

The human hearing system has three major parts: the outer ear, the middle ear, and the inner ear. We see the outer ear, which picks up the sound waves and sends them through the ear canal to the middle ear. In the middle ear the sound waves first hit against the eardrum and then against the three little bones called the hammer, anvil, and stirrup. As the sound travels from the outer ear funnel to the eardrum, the hammer hits the anvil, which passes the sound through the stirrup. The different vibrations send different impulses through to the inner ear, where the semicircular canals and cochlea are situated. These pass the sound vibrations on to the brain by means of sensitive nerve endings that unite to form the auditory nerve. Our brains help us identify what we hear.

Sounds are measured in loudness by decibels. Absolute silence is zero decibels. A whisper is about 20 decibels, an automobile horn about 85 decibels, a jackhammer about 118 decibels, and an airplane engine about 130 decibels. Music has regular vibrations, whereas noise has irregular vibrations.

God gave us hearing so that we could hear the pleasant and melodious songs of birds and the voices of other animals, as well as to listen to one another. Satan will try to divert your sense of hearing from the good things. He will also try to captivate your hearing by immoral talk, swearwords, unkind words, and unhealthful music.

What we hear, like what we see, is put into our mind computer and recorded there. Take a moment to thank God that He gave you hearing.

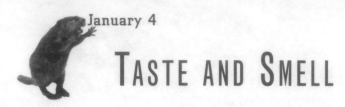

TASTE AND SMELL

[Some] worship man-made gods of wood and stone, which cannot see or hear or eat or smell. Deuteronomy 4:28, NIV.

Idols of wood and stone cannot use any senses, as God gave these only to His created beings. God's gifts of taste and smell are very closely related. Here is an experiment for you to try. It will demonstrate the close relationship between taste and smell.

Hold your nose shut with one hand. Then put some food that you really like into your mouth with the other hand. Notice that it is almost impossible to taste it. Why? Because taste and smell go together. The sense of smell has saved many lives, as people have smelled smoke, gasoline, and other harmful substances. God wanted us to enjoy the sweet aromas from the blossoms and flowers, so he made our sense of smell to be very sensitive. Most animals also have a keen sense of smell.

Taste is a different sense, but as we saw above, it is definitely related to smell. On the tongue are our taste buds. Taste buds on the tip of the tongue detect saltiness and sweetness. At the side we taste sourness, and at the back, bitterness. Try another experiment. Put a few granules of sugar in the palm of your hand and lick them with your tongue. Now try a few grains of salt. Notice how quickly the taste buds notified the brain? It didn't take long, did it? Taste varies, of course, from one person to the other, so not everyone likes the same thing. For that matter, not everyone likes the same scents. Some like one kind of perfume and some another, so life is different for everyone.

Satan tries to pervert the senses that God has given us. Heavy smokers cannot smell or taste as well as they would if they did not smoke. Satan tries to get us to taste and eat things that are harmful to our bodies. God has given us the gifts of taste and smell so that we can more fully enjoy life. Thank God today for these unique gifts that make your life more enjoyable.

The Power of Touch

They brought young children to him, that he should touch them. Mark 10:13.

Touch is another sense that God gave to us to help us enjoy His creation. The sense of touch, or feeling, involves the use of nerve endings in the skin, especially in our hands and feet. A microsecond after you touch an object, nerve impulses jet to your brain. Your brain instantly tells you that the object is hot or cold, prickly or soft, wet or dry, smooth or rough, and so on.

God gave us the sense of touch so that we can enjoy nature to its fullest. Perhaps you've knelt on a beach and let the sand fall through your fingers. Or maybe you've enjoyed the gooey feeling of getting your hands into mud. Maybe you like taking off your shoes and letting your toes feel the coolness of a small stream, or perhaps you've lightly touched the petals of a rose and were amazed at its softness. We can experience real emotion by touching. The sensation of touching the bark of a tree doesn't give us the same emotion as the softness of grass or plush fur of a cat. The itchy feeling that you get from peach fuzz brushing your arm doesn't give the same feeling as the touch of a friend's hand on your arm.

Touch, perhaps more than any other sense, gives us an emotion. It can even give us the sense of belonging. The mothers in Jesus' day brought their children to Jesus for Him to touch them and give them a blessing. The sick woman wanted only to touch Jesus' garment, and she knew she would be healed.

Jesus again demonstrates His love for us in the importance of the power of touch. Thank God today for the feelings you receive by touch. On this first Sabbath of the new year, maybe the touch of your hand on the hand of a sick or elderly person in your family, church, or neighborhood would bring the love of Jesus to them through you. Touch someone today with your life for Jesus.

"Let There Be Light"

God said, "Let there be light"; and there was light. Genesis 1:3, RSV.

A s God began to create the world, on the very first day He simply said, "Let there be light," and the Bible story of Creation reports, "There was light." God spoke, and there it was—light.

Light is composed of all the color rays coming together. If you have access to a prism (a three-sided glass object), you can use it to separate light into its different colors. We see different colors because God created each color with a different wavelength as it travels through space.

Light travels at 186,282 miles per second. That is really traveling! That's more than 11 million miles in one minute, or 670,615,200 miles an hour. Because of the vastness of space, scientists measure distances in light-years, not miles. A light-year is the distance that light travels in one year.

The expanse of the heavens is so vast—and we'll talk about that tomorrow—that if God shut off the sun's light rays, we would still have light for about eight and one third minutes. You see, it takes about 500 seconds for light to travel from the sun to the earth. Light travels nearly 6 trillion miles in one year, and that is difficult for us to comprehend.

Light is vitally important to all life on earth. Without light most vegetation cannot grow. Over time people created artificial light in clay oil lamps, candles, kerosene lamps, matches, and lightbulbs, but only God could create the light that lights up the universe.

We cannot understand how, but God spoke, and the light was there, with all of the color waves. God had an orderly plan in His creation, so the light came first. Aren't you glad that our God of love thought ahead about how to have His children enjoy the outdoors! He gave us light to see by. Thank Him for this light He has given you.

HE CREATED THE SKY

And God said, "Let there be a firmament in the midst of the waters." Genesis 1:6, RSV.

On God's second day of Creation He commanded the firmament to separate from the waters. This is the space above us that we sometimes call atmosphere, or sky. The sky was put there by God for a specific purpose. It contains the weather system, and helps keep the temperature in balance.

As you look up into the sky on a clear day, you see the color blue. There have been many different ideas or theories as to why the color of the sky is blue. Some people said that the atmosphere was made up of tiny water bubbles and that the light passing through these thin bubbles caused the blue color. The most commonly accepted theory is that the atmosphere, up to about 100 miles above the earth's surface, is composed of oxygen, nitrogen, carbon dioxide, several other gases, water vapor, and suspended particles. As the light rays pass through this atmosphere, these various molecules scatter the light. The shorter the wavelength of the color, the more it is scattered. As blue color wavelengths are the shortest, and therefore are scattered more, they cause the blue-sky effect. The sky may appear intense blue overhead and lighter toward the horizon because of the angle at which you are looking at it.

When the sun sets, the color waves must pass through more atmosphere than when the sun is overhead. With the dust particles in the atmosphere and the longer color wavelengths (red being longer) the deep-red, yellow, and orange sunsets are produced.

Astronauts tell us that in outer space, where there is no atmosphere to reflect the color waves, there is no color, and all one sees is black.

God created the atmosphere that made possible the blue sky. Have you ever stopped to think what this earth would be like if that blue sky was not above us? Thank Him for the blue sky today.

FOOD AND BEAUTY

And God said, "Let . . . the dry land appear." . . . "Let the earth put forth vegetation."
Genesis 1:9-11, RSV.

On the third day of Creation God told the waters to divide and let the dry land appear. He called the dry land earth, and the waters He called seas.

Then God told the earth to grow all types of vegetation—trees, shrubs, flowers, grains, grass, and vegetables. The Bible says that within each of these different kinds of plants and trees were seeds so that they could reproduce.

Can you imagine what a thrill it must have been for God simply to speak into existence the many different flowers covering vast fields, swaying with the breeze? My mind just goes wild as I think of all the varieties of beautiful flowers I have seen in different parts of the world.

And what about the trees? The fruit trees, palm trees, nut trees, evergreen trees, and so many others. Can you imagine God speaking, and suddenly trees are everywhere? We wait years for trees to grow from seeds or small plants, but God spoke, and around the world appeared the many different kinds of trees. What a powerful God!

God created the grass as a covering for the earth, to make it beautiful and provide a soft carpet. He created wheat, barley, oats, corn, and other grains. And also springing forth from the earth were the vegetables and all other vegetation.

It must have been exciting for God to see all the different kinds of vegetation cover the soil, making the earth colorful. God demonstrated His love in a magnificent way on the third day of Creation. He was preparing the earth for something else. He had in His master plan the creation of creatures that would need food to eat. So on this third day He created all the food that they would need.

God will provide for all your needs today, if you trust Him, because "my God shall supply all your need according to his riches in glory by Christ Jesus" (Philippians 4:19). Thank God today for His provisions for your physical needs.

GOD'S LIGHTS

And God said, "Let there be lights in the firmament of the heavens to separate the day from the night." Genesis 1:14, RSV.

Light, sky, vegetation, and now lights in the heavens. God knew what He was doing, and He did it in perfect order. In living color God had beautified the earth. Then God made two great lights, the greater light—the sun—to rule the day, and the lesser light—the moon—to rule the night. The Bible adds, "He made the stars also."

The sun gives light and heat, and its rays are very beneficial. It is impossible for most vegetation to exist without sunlight. The sun's rays cause the plants to produce the food they need to stay alive, and the plants provide food for humans and animals. Sunlight is also healing. It also enables our bodies to produce vitamin D, essential for the human body to function properly.

The object of the moon is to light up the night and influence plant growth and produce tides in the oceans. The moon is called the lesser light. It receives its light from the sun, acting as a reflector of sunlight. Thus it provides moonlight for the growth of plants at night.

I'm sure you have gone outside at night and looked up into the sky and seen hundreds of stars. Yes, there are stars, stars, and more stars. Millions and billions, actually. It makes a person wonder how God could create so many stars, but He spoke, and there they were.

For centuries physicists and astronomers have studied the stars. They have made telescopes of high magnification, enabling them to study better. Though they've learned much about the stars, they know very little compared to God's knowledge.

If God could do such marvelous things at Creation, creating the planets and stars in harmony, don't you think He could do great things in your life if you'd just let Him? Ask Him to help you with any problem you have. He will help you overcome it.

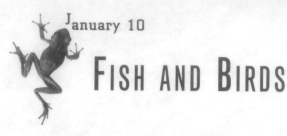

FISH AND BIRDS

And God said, "Let the waters bring forth swarms of living creatures, and let birds fly above the earth." Genesis 1:20, RSV.

On the fifth day of Creation God broke the silence of His world when He created the sea creatures and the birds of the sky. Up until then it was a silent world.

Picture yourself standing by God's side and hearing Him say, "Mammals of the sea, come forth!" and the whales and porpoises begin to dive and splash around. "Now I want fish," you hear, and the marlins, swordfish, sharks, angelfish, guppies, goldfish, trout, salmon, bat rays, bass, yellowtails, barracudas, cods, halibuts, and others churn the water. Next: "Come forth, other sea creatures!" So the octopuses, starfish, sea horses, crabs, lobsters, rays, and all the other kinds of moving creatures suddenly swim in the water. "I want some more beautiful things in the water," and the sea anemones, sand dollars, sea urchins, corals, mollusks, and other sea creatures appear. I would suppose that by this time your eyes would be really bulging as you hear God speak and see all these creatures come to life and the waters swarming with this new life.

He speaks again, and birds appear in the sky—canaries, cardinals, eagles, hawks, vultures, crows, ravens, macaws, and many more. Strutting around on the earth, the ostriches, emus, peacocks, and flamingos spread their wings. Ground birds such as the quail, grouse, pheasants, chickens, and turkeys begin scratching the earth's surface. Singing birds, including the robins, sparrows, meadowlarks, whippoorwills, and bobwhites, begin their songs. Paddling around in the water and flapping their wings are the many varieties of ducks, swans, coots, and geese. Little birds, such as the hummingbirds, chickadees, wrens, titmice, and nuthatches, float through the air from tree to tree.

The newly created sea creatures and birds were created perfect and tame. Fear did not exist. Thank God for the beautiful birds and sea creatures in your world today.

ANIMALS AND HUMAN BEINGS

And God said, "Let the earth bring forth living creatures according to their kinds. . . . Let us make man in our image, after our likeness." Genesis 1:24-26, RSV.

Five full days of Creation had passed, and God must have had a great time. It would have been fun to see all of the different creatures on the face of the earth. Now God was ready to start the sixth day. Only He was wise enough to decide what to create today. According to His master plan He created land animals. God spoke, and the massive elephants, rhinoceroses, and hippopotamuses came forth. Then lions, tigers, giraffes, deer, antelope, zebras, horses, cattle, baboons, monkeys, kangaroos, and many other animals responded to His voice.

God wanted other creatures, so the amphibians (such as frogs, toads, and salamanders), the reptiles (alligators, crocodiles, lizards, snakes, and turtles), and many others suddenly ran and hopped and swam. Insects (such as dragonflies, ladybugs, and grasshoppers) and thousands of other tiny creatures crawled forth at the Creator's voice. As God looked over the earth, it was abuzz with moving and flying creatures. But one thing was missing. His master plan was about to be complete.

God saved the best for last. He formed a human out of the dust of the earth and breathed into his nostrils the breath of life. Then God saw that it was not good that man should be alone, so He caused Adam to fall asleep. He opened Adam's side, took out a rib, and made Adam's side like new. Then He formed a woman from that rib. Adam called her Eve. Then God performed the first marriage.

His creation was complete. The earth was full. His new friends in the Garden of Eden would now take care of things on earth for Him.

As God looked over all that He had made, He saw that it was very good. He had given Adam the privilege of naming all the creatures. Then He turned the earth over to Adam and Eve to take care of. That demonstrates that God is loving, caring, and trusting. Thank Him today that He trusts you with His world, and ask Him to trust you as you tell others about Him.

GOD'S DAY

And on the seventh day God finished his work which he had done, and he rested on the seventh day from all his work which he had done. So God blessed the seventh day and hallowed it. Genesis 2:2, 3, RSV.

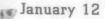

God had had a very eventful six days creating this world. He had ended His work with the creation of a man and woman, and His master plan was complete. Well, almost, anyway. His work was finished, so on the seventh day He made the Sabbath. The Bible says He rested on the seventh day. He blessed that day and made it holy. He set it apart for a special purpose.

God set the seventh day of the Creation week aside for rest, but He did not rest because He was tired. He was resting because He had accomplished His goal of Creation. God blessed and made holy the seventh day of the week. It is a sacred day. No other day of Creation week received this kind of treatment.

God set an example for us. He worked during the six days of Creation then rested on the Sabbath day from His labors. The fourth of the Ten Commandments (Exodus 20:8-11) tells us to do the same. During His ministry on earth Jesus healed, taught, and visited people on the Sabbath. He went into the synagogues and led out in worship, too. Luke 4:16 records, "And as His custom was, He went into the synagogue on the Sabbath day, and stood up to read" (NKJV).

Jesus created the Sabbath to be a blessing to us. It is a day to rest from all our labors. A day to worship God and show love for our Creator. Jesus told His disciples, "The Sabbath was made for man, and not man for the Sabbath. Therefore the Son of Man is also Lord of the Sabbath" (Mark 2: 27, 28, NKJV). That message is for us, too.

God loved us enough that He didn't expect us to work all the time. He set the Sabbath aside to be a special and happy day. It is to be a day of worship, a day of helping the needy, a day for sharing the love of Jesus with others, and a day of real enjoyment.

Thank God for the Sabbath, the day you can leave your work and study behind. Ask Him to help you have a good day today and always, as you rest, worship, and help others.

Stop! Look! Listen!

Make me to understand the way of thy precepts: so shall I talk of thy wondrous works. Psalm 119:27.

Two men were walking down a busy street in New York City. One of the men stopped and said, "Did you hear that?"

"Hear what?" replied his friend.

The first man said, "Listen." Again the noise came. He led his friend down a couple of stairs. Over between two bricks they found a cricket singing his song.

The second man said to the first, "How did you hear that?"

"Watch," replied his friend. He went back up onto the sidewalk and dropped a coin. Many people heard the coin fall and stopped walking to look for the fallen coin.

There are people today whose ears are tuned to the sound of money but are not tuned to the sound of a cricket. There are also people whose ears are tuned to the many sounds of nature. I have suggested to boys and girls that they sit down outdoors and cover their eyes with a blindfold and just listen to the sounds of nature. Try it yourself sometime. You'll be surprised at what you hear. Listen for only the sounds of nature, not the sounds that are artificial.

God's world has so much going on in it that we sometimes hear or see very little because we are caught up in the busy life we are living. We miss many melodious sounds because we are too busy to listen. There are many beautiful sights to be seen if we will just take time to do so.

The back porch on our house faces east, and we stop many mornings to watch the beautiful sunrises that take place over the trees. So many people miss these beautiful sights because they refuse to take time to look. They are too busy!

God wants us to take time for both of His books—the Bible and nature. We can learn many lessons from God's Word, and we can learn many lessons from God's *world*. God can teach us spiritual lessons from His physical world, because He stopped to learn the lessons Himself.

Ask God to impress you to take time to stop, look, and listen to His Word and His world.

MIKE WAS MY MACAW

A merry heart maketh a cheerful countenance: but by sorrow of the heart the spirit is broken. Proverbs 15:13.

One day as I was walking with another missionary at the outdoor marketplace in Iquitos, Peru, I saw a large red macaw that called to us. The vendor motioned to us too, and we stopped. As I came close to this macaw, he put up his foot to take my arm. Knowing that these birds have a strong beak that could clip off a finger in one bite, I refrained from putting my finger too close. The owner said, "Go ahead; he won't hurt you." Hesitantly and cautiously I put my arm over toward this big, beautiful bird, and he put out his big foot and climbed onto my arm. He shuffled sideways up my arm until he could put his head and body against my chest. Then he began to move his head back and forth. I rubbed the feathers on the side of his head, and it seemed that he and I struck up a special friendship. I had always wanted a macaw; now was my opportunity. I gave the man the $7.50 he was asking for the bird and carried him home on my arm. I named him Mike. Mike was my bird. However, he loved my children, too.

When I was home I'd take Mike out of his cage and walk around the mission compound with him on my arm. He liked that! Once I had been traveling for two weeks and arrived home late on Friday. On Sabbath I had a full day with church duties, and went by the cage only to say hi to Mike and rub his feathers through the wire with my finger.

My wife, Millie, said that Mike seemed sick. He hadn't been acting the way he usually did. On Sunday I had to leave again, so I didn't take Mike out of his cage. Tuesday I called home, and Millie told me that on Monday Mike had died. I talked to a veterinarian and asked why Mike had died. He said, "One reason could be that Mike died of a broken heart because he missed you, and you showed him little attention while home that last time." Do birds really die of a broken heart? I don't really know, but I doubt it.

However, on the cross Jesus died of a broken heart. He didn't want sin to separate you from Him. He loved you, and He died for your sins. Thank Him today for His great love toward you.

20

WHITE AS SNOW

Come now, and let us reason together, saith the Lord: though your sins be as scarlet, they shall be as white as snow. Isaiah 1:18.

I like snow. I like to wake up in the morning after a night-time snowfall and see everything covered with snow. It is so beautiful. I don't like to see the beautiful snow covered landscape marred by animal or human tracks, but once it is, I enjoy being in it myself.

I'm sure many of you have had the privilege of waking up and seeing the ground white with snow. You may have gone outside and played in the snow, and even watched the snow get dirty. Then you may have watched it snow again, and as the snow covered everything it became clean and white again. The old dirt cannot be seen. It's a wonderful and picturesque scene—white and clean. Those of you who have not experienced snow can only imagine what it's like.

In today's text God is speaking through the prophet Isaiah. He says, "You have sinned. I know you have sinned. You have been disobedient to Me, but I still love you. Sit down, and let's talk about it." Have you ever had your mother or father say that to you? If so, you and your parent then talk things out. That is exactly what God is saying: "Let's talk about it." Since sin entered this world, we cannot talk to God face to face, so we use the method of prayer. We tell God our troubles. We tell him what makes us happy. And we confess our sins. John writes, "If we confess our sins, he is faithful and just to forgive us our sins, and to cleanse us from all unrighteousness" (1 John 1:9).

We have all made our lives ugly with sin. Jesus accepts our confession of sin, and with His robe of righteousness covers up those ugly sins and makes our lives clean again, as pure as snow. We are cleansed from sin. That is exactly the way God's plan of salvation works for us. We mess it up. God cleans it up.

That is the promise God speaks of in today's text. "Though your sins be as scarlet, they shall be as white as snow." Claim that promise today in your prayers.

BABOONS

From the lips of children and infants you have ordained praise because of your enemies, to silence the foe and the avenger. Psalm 8:2, NIV.

When I think of amusing animals, I like to include baboons. These creatures from Africa and India are so different, so funny looking, and almost so human that it makes one stop and think about them and their lifestyle.

Baboons usually live on the ground during the daytime and sleep up in the trees at night to avoid the lions and leopards that prowl around looking for food. After a night's sleep the baboons come down from the trees and begin to look for breakfast. It's not easy to find the roots and other vegetable matter that they eat, such as fruits and grass seed, so many times they have to search around for food. Once in a while they will pounce on an insect, but their diet is largely vegetarian.

After breakfast they often sit down in pairs and begin to clean each other's fur by picking off the pests and dirt. This is called grooming. They spend a great deal of time in grooming, probably more than in doing any other thing. The babies ride around on the backs of their mothers, or hang like a swinging bundle underneath the mother's chest. The "teenagers" run and chase each other around, screaming and yelling. They may chase each other up a tree, going clear out to the end of a narrowing branch. Then the one being chased has to drop to the ground to get away.

Young baboons must stay with their mothers for a long time until they grow up. Scientists have said this is one of the reasons they believe humans evolved from other primates. But would a loving God make us evolve from an animal when He has the power to create us?

Be glad that He created you and gives you strength and help to resist the devil. Thank Him today that He indeed did create you, and that you didn't evolve from the baboon. Thank Him that He is by your side and gives you strength to overcome Satan.

RAINBOW

I do set my bow in the cloud, and it shall be for a token of a covenant between me and the earth. Genesis 9:13.

If you have the sun at your back just after a rainstorm, many times you can see a beautiful rainbow. We can see only half of it because of the earth's surface. When seen from an airplane, a rainbow has no end; it is a complete circle. Rainbows are caused by drops of moisture in the air, each drop acting like a tiny prism when a ray of light strikes it. As these droplets refract—bend and separate—the white light that God created on the first day, the beautiful colors are seen. You probably learned in first grade that the seven colors of the rainbow are red, orange, yellow, green, blue, indigo, and violet.

Perhaps you've seen rainbows as you were watering your lawn or playing in the sprinkler. You may also see rainbows around waterfalls. Once I was flying over a cloud bank, and all of a sudden I saw the shadow of our plane completely encircled by a beautiful rainbow.

It is interesting to note what others have believed about rainbows. The ancient Greeks thought the rainbow was the bridge of Iris, a messenger goddess who carried news of war and discord. Africans saw it as a great serpent that came out to eat after a storm, and ate anyone under either end of the bow. Some Europeans thought it was a snake that sucked up the water from the lakes and rivers and then redistributed it as rain. A Germanic myth said that God was using the rainbow as the bowl of colors to paint the birds. When I was a child, I was told that at the end of the rainbow was a pot of gold. I looked for it, but someone always beat me to it.

It's strange what different people think about different things, but the rainbow is not something we have to speculate about. God promised His people that He would never destroy the whole earth again with a flood, and the rainbow is the memorial of His promise. It is comforting, as you see the multicolored rainbow, to know that God will keep His promise. When you pray today, thank God that He keeps His promises.

LEOPARD OR PANTHER

Can the Ethiopian change his skin, or the leopard his spots? then may ye also do good, that are accustomed to do evil. Jeremiah 13:23.

One of the keenest, smartest, and most patient hunters in African countries is the leopard. It is probably the most adaptable of all the cat family. It can survive in grasslands, arid areas, thornbush, scrublands, rain forests, in semidesert zones along the coasts, and on mountains.

Little is known about leopards, because they are loners and sly. They do not rush to make a kill in a hurry. They may wait for up to a couple of hours until the right moment to pounce or chase to make a kill. They are known to be nocturnal creatures, but away from the business of life they have been seen quite a bit in daylight.

The pigmentation of their hide that is seen as markings is called melanism. This phenomenon is not fully understood, but the leopard's usual light background coloring seems to have been dyed black or brown in spots.

The panther (often called a black panther) is a leopard that has not colored out. A female leopard may give birth to four or five cubs, one of which may be black. Scientists speculate that in some areas of dense rain forests the lack of daylight may give advantage to the black leopards and allow them to be more abundant.

The leopard cannot change his spots, and you and I cannot effectively change our lifestyle alone. We need help to change our lives and put them in harmony with God's plan for us. We can't do it alone no matter how hard we may try. Only God can change a life through the power of the Holy Spirit. I know people who have held grudges against someone for years. But then their lives changed, and they learned to love the person they had hated. What made the difference? They allowed the Holy Spirit to work in their lives.

Ask God to perform a miracle in your life today and help you feel good about someone you've disliked. God can change your feelings. You may even make a new friend. God will do this if you allow Him to.

REFLECTIONS

Remember the sabbath day, to keep it holy. Six days shalt thou labour, and do all thy work: but the seventh day is the sabbath of the Lord thy God: in it thou shalt not do any work, thou, nor thy son, nor thy daughter, thy manservant, nor thy maidservant, nor thy cattle, nor thy stranger that is within thy gates: for in six days the Lord made heaven and earth, the sea, and all that in them is, and rested the seventh day: wherefore the Lord blessed the sabbath day, and hallowed it. Exodus 20:8-11.

Reflections in nature are so lovely. I enjoy going out beside a lake and just sitting there watching the beautiful reflections mirrored in the lake's surface. As I notice the tall mountains or trees or grass or wildlife rippling upside down in the lake's surface, it naturally makes me think of a mirror, and that helps me to remember many things.

As a teenager I used to go up to Yosemite National Park in California with my parents. We enjoyed camping, so we went often. Several times during our camping trip I would hike up to Mirror Lake to see if I could see the famous Half Dome rock mountain mirrored in the lake, as well as some of the other rock formations. I would hope for a smooth lake, and many times I'd get what I had hoped for. The reflection reminded me of the Rock, Jesus.

Then I would think about things He said in different places in the Bible, and would ponder His words. The only commandment that tells us to "remember"—to reflect back on Creation and the magnificent things He did that week—is the fourth of the Ten Commandments. It's our text today. Jesus said to remember what had been done on that day and what was not to be done on that day. It is difficult for a Christian to look at a reflection of some object of nature and not think of God's creation.

I enjoy going to Wawona Camp, a Seventh-day Adventist youth camp in Yosemite National Park. You can sit on a bench in the campfire bowl and watch the sun go down on Wawona Dome. It is a peaceful place to go and think about what God has done for your life. Ask God today to continually allow you to reflect back on what He has done for you, then thank Him.

SEEDS TELL THE TRUTH

The seed is the word of God. Luke 8:11.

Seeds are very interesting little things. Did you know that seeds tell us a very important story? Suppose you plant some seeds and you don't know what they are. When they produce plants, you can see what kind of seeds they were. Seeds come in all sizes. The Bible talks about the mustard seed (see Mark 4:31, 32) as being the smallest of the seeds, yet it grows into a big plant.

When I was a boy, my grandmother asked me to help her plant some seeds in our garden. I said OK, so she gave me a package of squash seeds and asked me to plant these seeds in hills, three seeds in each hill. Then I was to cover them lightly with soil. So I started down the row. I mounded up the dirt, dug a hole, put in three seeds, lightly covered them, then went on to make another little hill. It was a loooong row! By the time I reached the end of the row I was tired of bending over. I still had quite a few seeds and should have started another row, but instead I just dumped the rest of the seeds into a hole and covered them up, thinking, *Grandma will never know.*

Days went by. With Grandmother's watering and the sunshine, the seeds began to sprout. You can imagine my surprise when she asked me to come to the garden and showed me that hill where I'd dumped the last of the seeds. Instead of just three little plants I saw a whole bunch all struggling to grow. She scolded me and told me that these little plants told her the whole story. She knew what I had done, and she told me to always be honest in whatever I did.

God's Word is like seeds. If we put only a little of God's Word into our lives, people will be able to tell, because only a little will show. But if we put a lot of God's Word into our lives, much will show. Friends and family will know that we spend time with God and His Word. Pray today that God's Word will grow in your life, and you will know which path to take—the one that leads to heaven.

SYRUP TREES

The trees of the Lord are full of sap. Psalm 104:16.

God made trees full of sap because sap is the life of the tree, just as blood is life to the bodies of animals and people.

Through experimentation, people have found that the sap of some trees is sweet and can be used for food. Sugar maple trees are best known throughout the United States and Canada as syrup-producing trees. Long before White settlers arrived, the Native Americans of the Great Lakes and St. Lawrence region knew how to extract the sap (sweet water) from sugar maple trees. Black maples also have this sweet water, but it is not as commonly used as the sugar maple's sap. You might think that taking this sap from the sugar maple would kill it, but apparently the sweet water that is extracted from the sugar maple is different from sap that makes the tree grow.

Sometime between January and April, depending on the area, the sap starts to flow up the tree. It flows the greatest when a thaw follows a freezing spell, with warm days and cold nights. Holes are drilled into the trees, and the sweet water flows out of the holes through pipes placed in the tree and into awaiting buckets. The sap is then boiled in large vats over open fires to evaporate the water. Normally 30 to 50 gallons of sap will produce about one gallon of maple syrup. Did you ever wonder why pure maple syrup is so expensive? Now you know. If the syrup continues to boil, it becomes maple sugar.

Just as God made all trees with life-giving sap, He made us with life-giving blood. However, He also has given to us a life that doesn't require blood, and that is the spiritual life. It requires power from Jesus to live it correctly. Don't let Satan tap into your life. Ask Jesus to guard your life so that Satan cannot tap into you for that spiritual "sweet water," because if he takes this from you, your life will be nothing.

Thank Jesus for His protection today.

SAFETY IN NUMBERS?

For many are called, but few are chosen. Matthew 22:14.

There are more than 3,000 species of aphids in the world. They are considered to be the highest reproducers of all insects. They may even be the most abundant creatures on earth. Aphids reproduce at a very rapid rate. A French biologist estimated that if all the offspring lived, the number produced from one aphid and its offspring in one summer would amount to more than 6 billion.

To explain how the aphid lives and reproduces, let's use an example. One species, the green peach aphid, lives exclusively on peach trees. The offspring from the green peach aphid may live on some 70 types of plants and ferns. There may be more than 15 generations (different families) of offspring in one year from a single female.

Aphids have both friends and enemies, besides humans. The ladybird beetle known as the ladybug will devour aphids. She may lay up to 400 eggs, and the larvae from these could eat more than 140,000 aphids. Parasitic wasps will sting an aphid and lay an egg inside it. When the egg hatches, the larva eats the aphid from the inside out. That kills the aphid, naturally, and the larva uses the body shell of the aphid as a shelter. The aphid has a real friend in some kinds of ants. The ant protects the aphid because the aphid produces a "honeydew" substance that is part of the ant's diet. The ant strokes the aphid with its antennae. This causes the "honeydew" to flow, and the ant eats it. The aphid is known as the "ants' cow." Like cattle, the aphid is more productive when continually "milked."

You may have heard the saying "There is safety in numbers." That's often true, but it isn't true concerning salvation. Each of us is saved individually. However, God wants *all* of us to be saved, not just a few. We should thank God that we are numbered among those Christians who know and love Him.

PRECIOUS PEARLS

The kingdom of heaven is like unto a merchant man, seeking goodly pearls: who, when he had found one pearl of great price, went and sold all that he had, and bought it. Matthew 13:45, 46.

As far back as history goes, pearls have been precious. Pearls are in short supply, and that is part of the reason that their value is so high. Pearls are made by mollusks, water creatures that have shells, such as oysters and clams. Most often pearls occur in saltwater oysters, but some of the most expensive and beautiful pearls have been made by freshwater mollusks. However, this is rare. The most famous freshwater American pearl was found near Patterson, New Jersey, in 1857. It is called the queen pearl.

Pearls are begun when a foreign object such as a grain of sand gets into the shell. The mollusk feels the irritation and tries to eliminate it by coating the grain of sand with a pearl secretion that helps to smooth it. If the object is in the inner part of the body, it produces a round or pear-shaped pearl. If it is attached to the inner wall of the shell, it forms a flat-bottomed pearl. If it is in the muscle of the mollusk, the pearl will be oddshaped.

"We are to seek for the pearl of great price, but not in worldly marts or in worldly ways. . . . There are some who seem to be always seeking for the heavenly pearl. But they do not make an entire surrender of their wrong habits. They do not die to self that Christ may live in them. Therefore they do not find the precious pearl. They have not overcome unholy ambition and their love for worldly attractions. . . . But Christ as the precious pearl, and our privilege of possessing this heavenly treasure, is the theme on which we most need to dwell" (*Christ's Object Lessons,* pp. 117, 118).

If you want to find the Precious Pearl for your life, you must be willing to pay the cost. You may have to give up some things that you like. Ask God to help you find Jesus, the precious "Pearl," and tell Him you are willing to give up your will for His will in your life today.

PACIFIC SALMON

Fear none of those things which thou shalt suffer: behold, the devil shall cast some of you into prison, that ye may be tried; and ye shall have tribulation ten days: be thou faithful unto death, and I will give thee a crown of life. Revelation 2:10.

To me, one of the most fascinating and yet saddest stories is the life story of the Pacific salmon. There are five species of Pacific salmon: chinook, sockeye, coho, pink, and chum. Their life stories are about the same. The word "salmon" comes from a Greek word meaning "hooked snout," which the male salmon develop when they go to spawn. Spawning actively involves both the male and the female salmon.

Let's look at spawning and the life of the Pacific salmon.

These salmon are born inland in little streams or lakes along the Pacific coast of the United States and Canada. When they've grown to about five or six inches long, they leave the waters where they hatched and head downstream toward the Pacific Ocean. At the ocean they go into deeper waters, eating and growing. After being in the ocean for several years, the spawning instinct comes, and they begin the swim toward their place of birth.

By God-given instinct they usually find their home stream and head upstream. They sometimes have to thrash their way upstream, and maybe even climb the salmon ladders built on the face of some electric power dams. Many of them die in the attempt to reach home.

Arriving home, the female swishes her tail around in the sand and gravel and makes her redd (nest). There she lays up to 10,000 eggs. The male comes along and secretes from his body a milky solution called milt, which fertilizes the eggs. After about five months the baby alevins hatch, and the lifecycle begins again with those newly hatched alevins. In the meantime the adults turn around and swim downstream toward the ocean and die.

Jesus gave His life for us, and He promises us a crown of life if we are faithful. The faithful salmon should be a good lesson for us—to be faithful unto death. Pray today that Jesus will help you be faithful to Him, regardless of what happens in your life.

New Tails

And he that sat upon the throne said, Behold, I make all things new. And he said unto me, Write: for these words are true and faithful. Revelation 21:5.

Some little creatures that crawl around on the ground are boys' favorites—lizards. All but two species in the world are nonpoisonous, so kids often have fun with them. There is probably not a reasonably warm place in the world where there are no lizards. To date, scientists have identified more than 3,000 species. Lizards are cold-blooded reptiles that adapt to the temperature around them. They have a dry, scaly skin.

When I was a boy, I delighted in catching and raising horned toads. At times I had cans, boxes, and cages holding my "friends" all over our yard. The day I was told the fable that these toads caused warts on the skin I dropped the horned toad I had in my hand and ran into the house, crying. I asked my mother if it were so. She told me that it wasn't true. I had been handling many horned toads, and I didn't have any warts. I felt better and went out and picked up my friend again. In fact, horned toads are not toads, but shorttailed lizards.

Lizards do not have a built-in temperature control like many other animals, so they have to live in the ground where it doesn't freeze. When the desert and dry areas become too hot for them, they hunt shady areas or burrow into the sand to escape the heat. Most lizards are about four to six inches long, but a few are even smaller. Some very large ones are found in Indonesia. These may be up to nine or 10 feet long and weigh up to 300 pounds. Big ones, huh? These are called Komodo dragons, and we'll talk about these on April 16.

Most lizards have a defense mechanism that helps them escape their enemies. As the enemy grabs their tail they are able to detach it and let the predator have it. Many lizards' tails will continue to wiggle after they have been separated from the body. The lizards can grow new ones.

In our lives we can become detached from sin. That's a good thing, and Jesus will make us new creatures if we ask Him. Pray that Jesus will help you to be separated from sin and be a new creature today.

GREAT BUSTARDS

Consider the ravens: for they neither sow nor reap; which neither have storehouse nor barn; and God feedeth them: how much more are ye better than the fowls? Luke 12:24.

The great bustards live in the country of Hungary on the famous Great Plain. A bustard looks like a miniature ostrich, or as someone described it, "a cross between an ostrich and a vulture." The feathers on its body and wings are speckled brown, white, and gray. Its neck is a solid tan. A bustard has an eerie cry, like a subdued whistling moan.

There are 23 species of bustards in Southern Europe, Africa, Asia, and Australia. They prefer running to flying, but they can fly when necessary. Bustards have been observed at altitudes of 10,000 feet on a migration flight over mountains. They are about three to four feet long, weigh as much as 30 pounds, and are about as large as a good-sized turkey. The female is about half the size of the male.

Bustards prefer dry, hot climates, although there are exceptions. Some can be found living in a variety of habitats—dry flatlands, prairies, wooded pastures, and meadows—but they prefer open savannas and arid plains. They are also extremely shy toward humans.

The nest of the bustard is basically a depression in the ground, scratched out primarily by the female. She lays her one to five eggs and incubates them for 25 to 28 days. When the babies start to hatch, it takes them 12 to 36 hours to break out of the shell. Because the bustards were being hunted so much, the Hungarian government set up a special game reserve for their protection. Poland is following the same program as Hungary.

God provides for His creatures out in the wilds, for He loves them. But He loves us so much more. He not only provides for our needs, but gave His Son, Jesus, to die on the cross for each one of us.

Today, thank God again for His undying love and watch care over you.

PETE AND THE ANTS

Go to the ant, O sluggard, observe her ways and be wise. Proverbs 6:6, NASB.

Pete had been at camp for a week. It seemed he was always showing off. While he and some of his friends were out on the ball field, Pete noticed an anthill. He pulled back his leg and with one mighty kick sent sand and ants flying for a short distance.

Back in the cabin after campfire that night, the boys in Pete's cabin, along with their counselor, were having their talk-over time, telling what they did during the day. Pete couldn't wait to tell how he'd kicked the anthill and how the sand and ants flew all over the place. But Pete's counselor had studied ants in a college biology class, and as soon as Pete stopped talking, the counselor began telling the boys about ants.

"Have you ever seen an ant give up when it couldn't get over an object?" he asked the boys. "Have you ever seen an ant carry something larger than itself? Have you seen an ant helping another ant? Ants will help each other," he told them. "They do not give up easily. They keep trying until they either get over the obstacle or around it, but they rarely give up. They are very persistent and energetic."

Pete listened, then said, "I didn't know all that." He looked a little sad. "I am really sorry for the way I treated those ants. I just didn't think about them other than as pests." The next morning when the counselor got up and went outside the cabin, he looked over to the ball field. There he saw Pete on his hands and knees putting the sand back into the anthill for the ants.

As Pete's counselor said, when an ant comes to a hurdle he doesn't "say" "I can't do it! I can't get over it!" God has given the ant an instinct that says, "Keep trying; you *can* get over it!"

And with God's grace, we can overcome the obstacles of sin that Satan puts in our way. Never give up and say it is too hard. If you ask God to help you, He will show you the way to overcome. Never, ever give up!

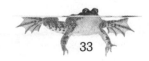

PEAT HEAT

If then God so clothe the grass, which is to day in the field, and to morrow is cast into the oven; how much more will he clothe you, O ye of little faith? Luke 12:28.

Some years ago our family was traveling along the country roads of Ireland. We saw interesting fields that had been cut like steps. Other fields had straight up-and-down cuts, as if they had been cut with a knife. That night as we stopped at a tourist house we found that they were burning a sweet-smelling bricklike substance called peat in their fireplace.

We found out that peat is formed over many years when plants such as mosses and sedges partially decompose in water. For about $7 a year the Irish lease from the government the space they need in a peat bog. They go there and cut out the peat bricks to burn. The peat bricks are cut with an L-shaped tool called a slave, which is sharp on the bottom. This part is pushed down into the bog like a shovel or spade. As it is pushed down, it cuts.

The peat bricks, weighing about 15 pounds each, are taken to the owner's house and put out to dry. A dry brick weighs from four to five pounds, and drying takes about two months. The dry bricks are stacked against the house on the end that has no gable. The peat acts like insulation, helping to keep the heat in. A family may cut several thousand peat bricks in a week. Many households will use up to 15 tons of dried peat a winter, so 50 or 60 tons of wet peat must be cut.

Peat bricks are used for heating and cooking. Food that is cooked with peat has a special sweet odor. It's similar to the way potatoes fried over a hickory fire pick up a special flavor. Water is also heated for bathing and washing clothes by burning peat bricks.

God takes care of all our needs if we will just trust Him. For years H.M.S. Richards, Sr., used to end his radio broadcasts of the Voice of Prophecy with "the longest unfinished poem": "Have faith, dear friend, in God."

We must have faith in God. As you pray, tell Him how much faith you have in Him as your God. And with His help, practice it throughout the day.

LIGHTNING

For as the lightning comes from the east and flashes as far as the west, so will be the coming of the Son of Man. Matthew 24:27, NRSV.

Lightning is all around us in this world. The National Weather Service reports that at any given time there are more than 4,000 electrical storms in the world. That may be hard to believe, but if you have done much traveling by airplane you may have seen the weather changing every little while. It is also reported that every second of the day 100 to 300 bolts of lightning strike the earth somewhere.

The distance you are away from lightning can be estimated by the number of seconds it takes from the time you see the flash until you hear the thunder roll. Since sound travels about 1,088 feet a second at sea level, if you count the seconds between the flash of lightning and the clap of thunder and find it to be five seconds, you know you are about 5,400 feet away, or about a mile.

Lightning is not a trifling matter. It can be very dangerous. My father tells of the time he was in a violent thunder and lightning storm. The wind was so strong that it blew down the high power lines. Over the radio, authorities told everyone who was in a car to stay in their cars and not touch anything metal on the car. Dad saw the power lines come crashing down upon a car with a young woman in it. Several cars immediately stopped and shouted at her to stay in her car and away from all metal. Dad said she stayed there until the power company men arrived and cut the power. Then they were able to remove the high-tension power lines and set her free. The rubber tires saved her life. She was insulated, or she might have been killed.

The coming of Jesus is not a trifling matter either. Jesus has told us that He will come when we least expect Him. We should be ready today and every day so that we will not be caught unprepared. Ask Jesus to help you today to be ready for His lightning-like appearance. Ask Him to help you not to be afraid on that day, but to be ready and waiting to meet Him.

GOOD NEWS AND BAD NEWS

Like cold water to the throat when it is dry is good news from a distant land.
Proverbs 25:25, NEB.

Today we introduce you to some interesting animals that live in Africa: gnus, or wildebeests. These large animals somewhat resemble moose, except they do not have large, flat antlers. Wildebeests' horns are relatively short and curl over their heads. Actually, wildebeests are antelope. They roam the African countryside in larger herds now than ever before.

It is estimated that in one national park reserve there are more than 300,000 wildebeests. The government leases the land for them to roam on for their protection. But the landowners are unhappy with the wildebeests because they eat everything in sight, including the grass for the landowners' own cattle.

At present the largest herds of wildebeests are in Tanzania and Kenya, in reserves called Serengeti and Tsavo, respectively. It is estimated that more than 1.5 million wildebeests live in these national park areas. One of the dangers to the wildebeests is that the human population is expanding, and that is threatening their grazing land. Wildebeest are very particular in what they eat. They like only a few kinds of grasses. When these types of grasses run out, the herd moves on to another area.

The male wildebeests have a very interesting ritual for claiming their territory. They will square off, then run at each other. Just before hitting heads, they drop to their knees, then hit their heads and tussle. They seem to like the eyeball-to-eyeball tussle. After a few minutes they do it again. It seems that about 10 minutes is long enough for the argument. Then one of them gets up and walks away, and the territory belongs to the winner.

Just as there is good news from a distant land about the flourishing of the wildebeest, so there is good news from a distant land that God loves you. Thank Him for His love and care.

DRAGONFLIES

Surely he shall deliver thee from the snare of the fowler, and from the noisome pestilence. Psalm 91:3.

Dragonflies are very interesting and helpful to us. They have four crystal-clear wings with veins running through them. As tiny as these veins in the wings are, there is a blood supply in each. (Remember, blood brings life.) With these four wings the dragonfly can zip along at speeds of up to 50 miles per hour. It can climb straight up, dive straight down, and hover like a helicopter. Each dragonfly has its own territory. It flies back and forth to protect its territory and keep other dragonflies from entering its domain. Mosquitoes are the dragonfly's favorite food, and that is the reason dragonflies are so beneficial. They keep down the number of mosquitoes.

Dragonflies have two large eyes, and their threadlike neck permits the head great freedom of movement. These two eyes take up almost the entire head. Each eye has from 10,000 to 25,000 facets (small seeing units). No wonder it is difficult to catch a dragonfly. However, if you can sneak up on it directly from the back, and if it doesn't turn its head, it cannot see you. It has a blind spot in the back of its head. From the front to the sides it can see everything.

Satan knows that each of us has at least one blind spot or weakness. It is through this blind spot that he tries to tempt us. With some kids it's satanic music, violent video games, comic books, or other things. With others it might be anger and hatred. It may be clothes, jewelry, or appetite. Today's text reminds us that God can and will deliver us from Satan's snares.

Pray today that God will take charge of your blind spot, whatever that may be, so that you will not fall into temptation. Without His help, you might think you can do it by yourself, but when Satan tempts you, watch out!

God will watch your blind spot for you today if you ask Him to do so. Ask Him right now. Don't wait.

February 1

KILLER WHALES

So God created the great creatures of the sea and every living and moving thing with which the water teems, according to their kinds. Genesis 1:21, NIV.

Killer whales, also known as orcas, are the largest members of the dolphin family. They grow to about 30 feet in length and weigh around nine tons. Their dorsal fin can grow to about six feet in height. Like the dolphins, they have a sonar system that helps them in their navigation and communication with each other.

These whales are said to be very sociable. When one pod (group of whales) meets another pod, they will swim directly toward each other. When about 30 feet away, they will stop, regroup, dive down deeper into the water, and swim toward each other, touching as many as possible as they swim past. One researcher said that he had observed this ritual on nine different occasions. It happened the same way each time. Female killer whales that do not have calves (baby whales) of their own will help take care of the other calves in the pod. Researchers who have studied killer whales for the past decade have come to the conclusion that they are playful and gentle creatures.

A group of them were observed taking bunches of seaweed down into the deep water. The whales released the seaweed, and the air bubbles on the seaweed caused it to rush to the ocean's surface. It would pop out of the water, making a sound and turning the water to foam. The whales seemed to think that was fun.

You may have seen an orca or killer whale at a marine park. These whales are black with white trim. It is fascinating to find out that God gave to seemingly every creature He created a desire to play. God certainly is a God of love, and He thought of everything.

It will be great to get to heaven and find out more of the personalities God created in every one of His creatures. Thank God today that He filled this world with so many interesting creatures for you to learn about. It never gets boring. Thank Him that He created an interesting world.

HORNBILLS

And seek not ye what ye shall eat, or what ye shall drink, neither be ye of doubtful mind.
Luke 12:29.

The question is asked, "What sounds like a locomotive, sports a bizarre beak, and seals itself up to hatch its eggs?" It's the hornbill. There are 44 different species of this peculiar-looking bird, ranging from Africa to the Solomon Islands in the Pacific Ocean.

These birds have black feathers on the top side of their bodies and wings, and white cottonlike feathers on the underside. They have long beaks similar to that of the toucan. On the top side of the beak is a casque (helmetlike growth) that is shaped differently according to the species. Some researchers agree that the casque helps the bird dissipate the heat from the body, while other researchers think that it is strictly an adornment for attracting females. The casque consists of a honeycomblike tissue with numerous blood vessels running through it. It *does* help in the release of heat, thus keeping the bird comfortable in the hot tropical forests where it lives.

The helmeted hornbill is the only species with a solid casque on its beak. This characteristic has caused Chinese artisans to hunt the birds for the casque. They carve it into beautiful artifacts such as belt buckles, pen holders, decorative miniatures, and snuff bottles.

Hornbills live principally on fruits. During the nesting period the female seals herself in the nest using a mixture of mud, droppings, and saliva. Only a small opening remains, through which the male brings her food. One male was observed making 10 trips to his mate in one day, and another male was observed bringing a total of 24,000 pieces of fruit to his mate.

We are admonished by Scripture not to be concerned about the food and drink we need. If we trust in God, He will provide, just as the male hornbill provides for the female.

Thank God today for His provisions for you. Tell Him again today that you trust in Him. He'll love to hear that from you.

February 3

New Antlers Every Year

Put on the new man, which after God is created in righteousness and true holiness.
Ephesians 4:24.

More than 50 different species of deer, elk, moose, caribou, and other wild animals grow antlers. Each of these animals has a different kind of antler. Some of the antlers grow straight up above the head. Others have many branches called tines or prongs and may spread as much as six feet across, such as on the moose.

The antlers of the deer family are grown new each year. You may have seen antlers that looked as though they were covered with velvet. They are! In the early stages of growth the antlers are covered with a soft brown-haired skin called velvet. Just under the surface of the velvet is a network of tiny blood vessels and nerve fibers that provide the necessary elements to help them grow. During the velvet season the antlers are tender. If the animal hits a tree limb or some other object and scratches off some of the velvet, it is similar to you scraping your skin—it bleeds.

The antlers are used for protection, but their main use seems to be for mating. As the velvet sloughs off the antlers, they get tough and hard. Then each buck or bull sets up his domain. Any other animal coming into that domain is considered an intruder. As they fight for the females, they use their antlers, and the bigger, stronger animal is usually the winner.

After the mating season is over, the males shed their antlers. In the spring the procedure starts all over again. You may wonder why you rarely see antlers lying around in the forests and mountains. It seems that the antlers contain a great deal of calcium, phosphorus, and other minerals needed in the diet of many animals. Therefore mice, chipmunks, porcupines, squirrels, and others gnaw away on the antlers for physical nourishment.

As the animals grow more antlers, they once again become like new creatures. God has promised to help us become new creatures. Ask Him to help you to be a new creature today.

TUBE WORMS

Look, He scatters His light upon it, and covers the depths of the sea. Job 36:30, NKJV.

It wasn't until 1977, when two men went down deep into the ocean near the Galápagos Islands off the coast of South America, that the first deep-sea tube worms were discovered. The scientists were looking for thermal vents. When the temperature shot up on the thermometer of their research instruments, they got inside their little minisubmarine named *Alvin* and went down almost 9,000 feet. There they saw a whole community of life. Tube worms and other creatures lived all around the thermal vents.

Deep-sea tube worms had never been seen before, and marine biologists were not even aware that they existed. This opened up some new theories and speculations. It was first thought that this was the only area in which they lived. Since that time they have been located in six or seven areas. In March of 1984 *Alvin* took a crew of two to the bottom of the Gulf of Mexico. There they sighted tube worms that were not living near a thermal vent. This led marine biologists to speculate that there may be tube worms living all over the world at the bottom of the sea.

How do they eat and stay alive, you ask? Scientists have discovered that bacteria living in the tube worms provide the food for them. The bacteria, in turn, by utilizing certain properties in the blood of the tube worm, manufacture food for themselves from chemicals in the water. So the tube worms and bacteria help each other.

Just as scientists are still discovering new creatures in nature, so many are discovering new truths in God's Word. It's not that God has hidden anything from us. It is just that in both His natural world and His spiritual world there are many things that haven't yet been discovered.

Ask God to help you find some new truths in His Word today, and that He will help you believe them when you find them.

PENNSYLVANIA INFERNO

Where their worm does not die, and the fire is not quenched. Mark 9:44, NIV.

For a long time in Centralia, Pennsylvania, there has been uneasiness among its 600-plus citizens, because a coal-burning fire has been burning underneath their town for 46 years. The fire started in a garbage dump over an open coal mine seam in the ground in 1962. Because of this, there is a hot spot in Centralia. For more than 40 years people have tried to extinguish the fire, but it has been impossible. (On February 12 we will discuss the buried trees and coal deposits from the Flood.) This mine seems to have a lot of coal burning; it is only a guess as to how many acres the fire covers underground. Estimates range from 350 to 400 acres of surface land.

The first families moved out of Centralia on May 2, 1969, and the U.S. government bought up most of the property to help the residents. In April of 1979 there were still 44 people braving it out in Centralia. There may be fewer today.

On Valentine's Day in 1981 a 12-year-old boy was running across his grandmother's yard when a 150-foot pit opened up in the ground, and he fell in. Fortunately for him, a tree root stopped his fall, and he was rescued. It is estimated that the temperature of the burning coal reaches 1,000°F (537.8°C) With heat that intense, no system of pumping water can be effective enough to quench the fire, so it has continued to burn.

God has told us about a hell that will have a very hot fire. This is not the type of hell that we commonly hear people talk about today, a fire that keeps burning forever. At the end of the 1,000 years in heaven, when the wicked are destroyed on this earth, the fire will be so hot that it won't take long for those who rejected God's love to be burned to ashes.

God has given us the opportunity to escape that hot fire. He told us that if we are faithful we will receive a crown of glory and be with Him in heaven. Pray for that today in your life.

TINY FOOD FACTORIES

I will meditate also of all thy work, and talk of thy doings. Psalm 77:12.

I am amazed at the numerous varieties of shapes and sizes of leaves. Leaves may resemble such objects as sewing needles, human hands, arrows, and feathers. One of the smallest leaves known is about one sixteenth of an inch long and belongs to the walffla plant that grows In ponds. Then while traveling in South America I saw the large *Victoria regia*, a giant water lily that has floating leaves more than six feet across. Some banana plants have leaves up to 10 feet long and two feet wide. The gunnera herb tree has an umbrellalike leaf about eight to 10 feet across, and there's a large palm tree with leaves 26 feet long and five feet wide. The leaves of the African raffia palm tree are up to 40 feet long.

All leaves have one thing in common. They are all food factories for the plant. When the Creator covered trees with leaves, He put a small food factory into each leaf. Even the pine needle has a small food factory inside it. Leaves take carbon dioxide and water to make food for the plant. This provides energy for seeds to sprout, flowers to blossom, and the fruits to form. These food factories are operated by solar energy, using the sun and chlorophyll to form sugars from the water and carbon dioxide.

God created in you and me a small factory to provide energy for our bodies. The brain produces impulses for the nerves, which stimulate the muscles, which in turn allow us to perform all the many things we do. God gave us minds to use, and a sure way to keep the mind useful is to expose it to the great object lessons In God's natural world. E. G. White wrote, "In itself, the beauty of nature leads the soul [mind] away from sin and worldly attractions, and toward purity, peace, and God" (*Counsels to Parents and Teachers,* p. 186). If the light of God's Word penetrates our minds and fills them with good things, we will have the opportunity to live forever. Let us pray that God will help us meditate upon good things in preparation for eternity.

LIGHT FOR GROWTH

Seek ye first the kingdom of God, and his righteousness. Matthew 6:33.

Yesterday we discussed leaves and their importance to the life of the plant, because of the small food factories within each leaf. Did you know that it takes about 50 apple leaves to make one apple, about 30 peach leaves to make a peach, about 15 grape leaves to make a bunch of grapes, and about 12 large banana leaves to make a bunch of bananas? That is why there are so many leaves on the different fruit trees!

Most leaves have three parts: the blade, the petiole, and the stipules (although some leaves don't have stipules). The blade is another name for leaf, and it is the part that houses the food factory. We know the petiole as the stem. This stem plays a very important part in the life of the tree. If the leaf blade did not have the stem to attach it to the limb of the plant, it would not be possible for the food manufactured in the leaf to be absorbed into the plant. When you look at a cross section of a stem under a microscope, you'll see that it is made up of many tiny tubes resembling a handful of drinking straws.

The purpose of the stem is to help the blade manufacture food and to always ensure sunlight for the blade. If the leaf is shaded, the stem will grow longer to allow the blade to take in the sunlight it needs for energy. As you look up in a tree you will notice that all leaves have some sunlight during the day. The stem allows the sugars manufactured by the blade to enter the plant and the water from the plant to enter the blade. Thus the stem is the connecting link between the plant and the leaf.

Jesus is our connecting link to God the Father. Jesus said, "I am come that they might have life, and that they might have it more abundantly" (John 10:10). He is interested in each of us having the light from heaven through His Word, that we might have life through Him. As the stem pushes the blade up to receive the maximum sunlight possible, His Holy Spirit will put you in the light of heaven so you will live forever.

Ask God to send the Holy Spirit into your life.

WHISTLING SLEEPER

Watch therefore, for you do not know what hour your Lord is coming.
Matthew 24:42, NKJV.

Have you ever felt as if you'd like to just sleep and sleep, but someone made you get out of bed? How about sleeping for seven months? Does that sound good? Maybe that's too long for you to enjoy sleeping, but the marmot is a five- to seven-month sleeper. These creatures go into a hibernating sleep in late September or early October, when there is still vegetation and grains around, and wake up from their sleep when there may be snow on the ground. Marmots have a short mating period of 40 to 60 days in the northwestern United States and southwestern Canada.

Marmots, of which there are five species in North America, are the largest of the squirrel family. They spend their time in the ground or among rocks. In the eastern and midwestern United States they are commonly known as woodchucks. They are about 20 inches long and weigh up to 20 pounds. Marmots are vegetarians, eating only grasses, herbs, and grains. They have a long, furry tail, and some people have even mistaken them for beavers.

Marmots are great lovers of community living. They always have a watchman looking for enemies when the colony is out eating or playing. As soon as an enemy is spotted, the guard makes a whistling noise, and all the other marmots scamper into holes. One day a coyote approached a colony of marmots, and the signal was given. Down the holes all the marmots went. The coyote began to dig in one hole when from another hole a marmot stuck up its head and whistled. The coyote ran over there and began to dig, and another marmot stuck its head out of another hole and whistled, and so on. The poor coyote was so confused that it finally left, defeated and hungry.

God tells us to watch and be ready for Jesus' second coming.

Ask God to help you be ready from this day forward, so that you can joyfully see Jesus come in the clouds of glory.

SUCCESSION

For I am the Lord, I change not. Malachi 3:6.

God has worked things in such a marvelous way that the natural world pretty well takes care of itself through God's sustaining power if people just let it alone. God had planned that all be perfect, but when sin entered the world God needed to make some adjustments to take care of the problems it caused.

In its natural state the world has ways by which it continues to live on that people cannot understand. At times a swamp or small lake just disappears. We also see, especially in desert areas, where large lakes that used to exist, but are no more.

There are times that plants do something interesting that we call succession. As the plants grow and the atmosphere, climate, and soil change, the plants change too. Eventually the soil and climate may become unsuitable for some plants, and so they die out. When they're gone, usually other plants take root and fill the void, and soon a whole new group of plants dominate the area. When the plant world changes, the animal world changes too. Certain animals live on specific plants, and as these plants die out, the animals move on to "greener pastures." Succession in nature is an orderly process, a series of changes. These changes occur until there is a stability of plant life. This is called a climax community, meaning that they have arrived.

After a fire, volcano, or flood, certain plants come in and seem to grow immediately. These are called pioneer plants. They must have the ability to withstand hot sun, infertile conditions, and sparse soil. In Hawaii the beautiful pink fireweed grows after volcano eruptions, and the willow herb blankets the blackened earth after a fire has destroyed all vegetation.

Although the earth's vegetation changes because of the circumstances, God says that He never changes. He is always the same. Thank Him today because He is a changeless God.

Leucaena Trees

And my God shall supply all your need according to His riches in glory by Christ Jesus. Philippians 4:19, NKJV.

The leucaena tree is called "the tree that does everything." About 20 years ago a very rare find was made when a crop specialist from Hawaii went to Guatemala and El Salvador and noticed trees that resembled a Hawaiian bush. He took some seeds back to Hawaii and planted them. To his surprise, in their first year these trees grew higher than a two-story building. In two years they were 60 feet high, and the wood was as hard as oak. This tree not only grows fast but also improves the soil, needs little water, and resists fires and winds.

What makes this tree so fantastic? Twelve reasons: (1) the tree yields more lumber than most trees; (2) the wood fiber makes excellent paper; (3) animals can use the nutritious leaves, which are high in protein, as food; (4) small pods and leaves are also good food for humans; (5) it is good for firewood; (6) it adapts well to many environments and fixes nitrogen in the soil; (7) it has a deep taproot, which helps to control soil erosion; (8) it is a good umbrella tree for other crops; (9) it shades undergrowth to the extent that it dies, thus cutting fire hazards, and it has frilly leaves that make it nice for landscaping; (10) its seeds, pods, and bark are used for yellow, red, brown, and black dyes; (11) it makes excellent charcoal; and (12) it is excellent for reforestation because of its rapid growth.

The Hawaiian crop specialist and those working with the leucaona are afraid that people may expect too much from this tree, because it does have shortcomings. Frost kills it, and it grows poorly in high altitudes and in acid soils.

Many people depend on the leucaena trees to answer many of their needs, but we can depend on Jesus, who never fails. He has no shortcomings and will really be the answer to all our needs. Present your needs to Jesus, the same one who created the leucaena tree. He will take care of them. Ask Him today.

MONARCHS AND MILKWEED

They were helped in fighting them, and God handed the Hagrites and all their allies over to them, because they cried out to him during the battle. He answered their prayers, because they trusted in him. 1 Chronicles 5:20, NIV.

Monarch butterflies are probably the most popular and most populous butterflies in the world, especially in the United States.

The flowers of the milkweed plant produce a sweet nectar, and years ago Native Americans made a brown sugar from this nectar. The monarch butterflies have also discovered this nectar, and they flock to the milkweed plants to suck up this natural sweetness. One might think that as these black-and-orange creatures suck this nectar they would attract predators, but most birds have learned that monarchs taste bitter.

Adult female monarchs usually deposit their eggs on the underside of the milkweed leaf. When the caterpillars come out of the eggs, they begin to eat the milkweed plant. If all the milkweed plants were consumed, many monarchs would perish. So the monarch caterpillar turns this milkweed-plant food into a heart drug called cardiac gylcosides, or carenolides, which gives any creature that eats it violent stomach upsets.

Once the caterpillar gets through its growing stage it spins a cocoon, attaching it to the milkweed plant. From the cocoon it emerges as a full-fledged monarch butterfly. As winter approaches, the monarchs migrate by the thousands to the southern United States and Mexico.

The milkweed plant can survive on its own, but monarchs cannot survive without it. One day the many people who are living without Jesus will *not* be able to live without Him. One day soon, those who think they don't need Him will be very sorry.

As the monarch trusts for life in the ever-present flow of sweet nectar from the milkweed, you and I must trust in Jesus for life today and forever. Tell Jesus today that you trust Him.

Black Gold

And every living substance was destroyed which was upon the face of the ground.
Genesis 7:23.

God caused a great flood to come upon this earth. The water came with such force that the mountains were moved, and large majestic trees, along with other living things, were buried under the dirt and rocks. These large trees, forests of them, have fossilized, forming enormous deposits of coal. Oil and natural gas are also products of the fossilization process.

We use these large deposits of coal, gas, and oil to meet our needs for heat and fuel. Refined oil has many uses: gasoline for automobiles and airplanes; heating oil and kerosene; diesel for trains, trucks, and ships; fuel for power plants; lubricants, waxes, asphalt, plastics, synthetic rubber, paints, perfumes, dyes, vitamins, medicines, detergents, fertilizers, insecticides, film, photographic chemicals, inks, and numerous other items. As you see, much of life today depends on this fossil fuel—oil that is pumped from the earth, a result of the Flood.

Natural gas was discovered under the property of Union Springs Academy in New York State. It is used to heat the academy buildings and houses. Another Christian church group found themselves heirs to a deposit of oil under their property. The royalties from the sale of this oil are used to help needy and disabled people in their church, provide education for the children in their church school, and pay for the upkeep on their buildings and property. If there are any funds left over, they are used in community service outreach. To this church the oil is considered black gold to help them meet their needs. They say, "God is taking care of us."

As you think about what God has done, thank Him that He cared enough about you that He made provision for you, supplying many of your needs with the oil that is in the earth. He is a loving God and takes care of His children.

Thank Him for that today.

PHYTOPLANKTON

And the peace of God, which transcends all understanding, will guard your hearts and minds in Christ Jesus. Philippians 4:7, NIV.

The oceans, which cover about two thirds of our earth, teem with tiny microscopic plants called phytoplankton (fi-toe-plank-ton) and microscopic animals called zooplankton. These plankton are very important to life in the seas as well as to life outside the seas.

Scientists estimate that the phytoplankton are responsible for producing about 80 percent of earth's oxygen, and that they also produce as much new plant material as do land plants. Each of these phytoplankton is a masterpiece of engineering. It was not until the 1960s, when the electron microscope was introduced, that scientists were able to see in detail the intricate and interesting forms of the phytoplankton.

One phytoplankton resembles a ball composed of pineapple slices with holes in the center, all wedged together. Another one looks like a miniature pillbox. These phytoplankton are mined in masses, and the shells are used in swimming pool filters and in highway lane stripes to give them the reflecting sparkle. Others add red color to the water and are very toxic. Some early Native American settlers saw in the water some mussels and clams that had a red glow and cooked them and ate them. They became sick from the toxic poison. Many shellfish that are contaminated by the red tides are toxic when eaten by humans.

One scientist speculated that a humpback whale could have 5,000 herring in its stomach and that there may be up to 7,000 larval shrimp in the stomachs of each herring, and each shrimp may have up to 130,000 phytoplankton. Many scientists are predicting that plankton may soon be a very vital source of food for humans also.

The future is in God's hands, and as you confide and trust Him, you will have peace that only He can give. Thank God today for His provisions and peace that you receive from Him, and ask Him to give you peace through your day today.

CAN ANIMALS REASON?

What do you think? If a man owns a hundred sheep, and one of them wanders away, will he not leave the ninety and nine on the hills and go look for the one that wandered off? Matthew 18:12, NIV.

How do you think? Right. With your mind. Our minds were given to us by our Creator. Then how does an animal think, or does it? Scientists are studying much into animal behavior, and there is confusion as to whether an animal thinks.

God may have given many of His created creatures the possibility of thought, but it is not the human mind. That is one difference that humans have from other creatures. Now let's look at some things other creatures do.

A German horse named Clever Hans was said to understand arithmetic. His owner could write 2 + 5 = ? and the horse would tap its foot seven times. It was later discovered that the horse did not actually know arithmetic, but it was nevertheless intelligent. It watched the owner, and when it noticed him relax a bit—which somehow the horse had learned that happened when it had tapped the correct number of times—it stopped tapping. A pigeon was taught to look at slides, and when slides showing people appeared, it was taught to peck for food. At one time the pigeon was shown 1,200 unfamiliar slides, and it pecked for food only at the slides with people in them.

Then there's the interesting story about scientists who were working with bees, trying to coax them to go farther from their hive than they were used to going. They used a bowl of sweet water that they'd move about five feet at a time. After a while the bees seemed to sense what was going to happen, and they would fly on ahead. When the men got there with the bowl of sugar water, the bees were waiting for them.

This all sounds strange, but God gave some degree of intelligence to His creatures. However, He saved the best for last—the human brain. Your brain, and mine! Thank God today that He created this particular brain for you, the "crowning act" of His creation, so you can think, understand, and reason. For a human being that is very important.

LIZARD DEFENSES

My defense is of God, who saves the upright in heart. Psalm 7:10, NKJV.

Lizards have many defenses against their enemies. One is letting go of its tail (autotomy), which in some cases wiggles, distracting the enemy and allowing the lizard to race away. I don't know if the lizard feels pain when it loses its tail, but it doesn't seem to.

The glass snake is a prime example of this type of defense. The glass snake looks like a snake, but it is a lizard. It doesn't have any feet to walk on, but slithers around on its belly like a snake. One difference between the glass snake and a real snake is that it has a tail twice as long as its body. When in danger the glass snake lets part of its tail go. The tail will grow back, but not as long as before. When let go, the tail may flop around for three or four minutes. This often distracts the enemy, and the glass snake can escape.

Other lizards use different methods of defense. The horned toad squirts a fine stream of blood out of its eyes for a distance of up to three feet. Some lizards can change their color for protection. Some lizards just bluff their way through life—that is their defense. The Australian frilled lizard will stand up like a frog and blow out from each side of its neck a roll of skin that looks like an umbrella draped around the back of the head. It opens its mouth wide and hisses. This makes it look and sound bigger than it really is, and most predators will leave it alone.

I am glad that we don't have to worry about fighting the enemy with our own power. We can give him the knockout blow by calling on the power of Jesus. David realized that he needed God for his protection. Call upon Jesus and His angels to look after you today, to defend you against the old devil, Satan. God will defend you if you ask Him to do it. Now is your opportunity to thank Him.

SANDHILL CRANES

And be ye kind one to another, tenderhearted, forgiving one another, even as God for Christ's sake hath forgiven you. Ephesians 4:32.

In the early 1900s the sandhill crane almost became extinct. Several reserves were set up to offer protection to these birds, and today sandhill cranes are making a slow but positive return. There are several wildlife reserves in Michigan for their protection; conservationists count about 200 breeding pairs.

There are six subspecies of sandhill cranes, three of which are migratory. The migrating birds go to the southern United States and northern Mexico. They are the lesser sandhill crane, the cavallion sandhill crane, and the greater sandhill crane. The other three species are the Mississippi sandhill crane, the Florida sandhill crane, and the Cuban sandhill crane.

Sandhill cranes grow to be three to four feet tall. Where I live the most common ones have a bare, red, wrinkled-skin forehead with a few scattered black hairlike feathers. In the fall the birds molt their feathers and turn a beautiful gray. However, when they return from migration they have a reddish-brown or deep-brown plumage.

Both birds of a mated pair participate in the raising of the young. The female will lay one egg and about two days later lay a second egg. Both the male and female tend the nest during the daylight hours, but the female cares for it during the night. The male roosts close by her, standing on one leg in shallow water. After 29 to 32 days the clutch of eggs hatch. The new chicks stand eight to 10 inches high and weigh three to four ounces. The chicks cannot fly for 75 to 90 days, so the family spends time together in the water in a remote area. Sometimes the chicks quarrel.

God intended for us to do things as a family and do things for one another's good. Sometimes, like the sandhill crane chicks, you may not get along with your brother or sister. If that is your situation, ask God to help you love, to be kind, and to get along with them today. He will help you.

SOLAR ECLIPSE

And the sun stood still, and the moon stayed, until the people had avenged themselves upon their enemies. Joshua 10:13.

An interesting natural phenomenon that physicists and astronomers fly all over the world to see and study is a solar eclipse. This happens during the daytime when the moon passes between the sun and the earth. For a few minutes the sun is darkened by the moon. Strangely enough, the moon, which is in orbit about 240,000 miles from the earth, appears to be the same size as the sun, which is about 93 million miles away from the earth.

Most of the time the moon misses the eclipse position as it passes around the earth. But every 18 years or so, the moon passes directly between the earth and the sun, causing the solar eclipse. On June 11, 1983, the longest solar eclipse of the decade was best seen across the Indonesian islands. Hundreds of scientists spent millions of dollars to go see this natural phenomenon and study it for five to seven short minutes.

The rays from the sun that can be seen around the edges of the moon at the total eclipse stage are what intrigues scientists, because this corona, as it is called, is lost when the sun is not shielded. Scientists are studying the corona, trying to understand the nature of natural gases. They keep studying to understand the nature, causes, and effects of God's natural world.

Our Creator, no doubt, created some things that we as humans may never understand. God made the sun stand still in Joshua's day. Science will never understand how God did this. He allowed the dark day of May 19, 1780, across the eastern United States, too.

When you pray today, ask God to help you radiate the light of His love to your friends instead of blocking it.

A HAND FOR DADS

As a father has compassion on his children, so has the Lord compassion on all who fear him. Psalm 103:13, NEB.

There is a great difference among animals and birds as to what the males may do, but in many species the "dad" spends more time with the "kids" than "mama" does. Let's look at a few.

When a fox comes along the male plover will risk its life, fluttering along the ground, pretending to be injured, to lure the predator away from the nest. Small sea horse dads carry the eggs laid by the female until the young are born. Male giant waterbugs may have up to 150 eggs glued to their back by the female with a waterproof glue. They carry these eggs until they hatch. And male ostriches spend up to two years with their offspring, teaching them about life.

Among more than 90 percent of all birds, the fathers are involved in raising the babies. Only about 10 percent of mammal dads, but a surprising number of fish and amphibian fathers, are involved in babysitting. Some prepare the family "home," while others are actively involved in child rearing.

The male pipefish carries the eggs in a pouch on the abdomen. After hatching, a blood supply provides fresh oxygen and food for the young. After three weeks the young leave the pouch and are on their own. Male marine catfish carry the eggs in their mouth. After they hatch, they still gather the young into their mouths for safety. Mongoose males protect the family from predators while the female is out getting food.

The behavior of males among God's creatures may or may not demonstrate the role of the human father, but one thing is sure. We have a heavenly Father who protects, feeds, and helps His children mature with His love. God loved this world so much that He gave His Son to save it. He longs to have His children in His heavenly home.

Thank God for His fatherly care and love today, and tell Him how much that love means to you.

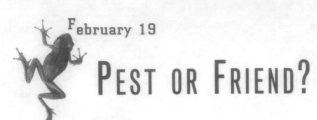

PEST OR FRIEND?

If we confess our sins, he is faithful and just to forgive us our sins, and to cleanse us from all unrighteousness. 1 John 1:9.

While it may be beautiful to behold, some people call it a pest, others a plague, and some even a friend. South Africans call it the Florida devil, and in India it is known as the Bengal terror. How could one thing have so many bad names yet possibly be useful?

The water hyacinth is a native plant of tropical America. Because of its beauty and rapid growth tourists have carried it to more than 80 countries around the globe. Now many millions of dollars are spent every year to eradicate this pest from lakes and waterways. Just the three states of Florida, Louisiana, and Texas spend more than $11 million a year to control this pest.

The water hyacinth has what is termed an explosive-growth pattern. Under normal growing conditions, in about eight months 10 hyacinth plants can multiply to more than 600,000 plants and take more than an acre of water. As these plants grow, their root systems mesh into a thick mat. Years ago in Indonesia the water hyacinths were so thick that they actually dammed up a waterway and caused flooding throughout the province of Kota Bharu.

But water hyacinths are useful, too. They take their nutrients from the water and have been found to be quite biologically beneficial to polluted waterways and lakes. The nutrients that they absorb for life are the common pollutants: nitrates, phosphates, and potassium. Hyacinths are also being credited with absorbing toxic wastes, pesticides, and heavy metals from the water.

Jesus has promised to be our filtering system. He has said that He will take our sins from our lives and make us clean and new creatures. He wants a pure and holy people. Ask Jesus to come into your life today and filter out the pollutants of sin, cleansing you in preparation for heaven. He has promised He will do that if we ask Him.

Tsunami Waves

You are a forgiving God, gracious and compassionate, slow to anger and abounding in love. Therefore you did not desert them. Nehemiah 9:17, NIV.

The word "tsunami" comes from the Japanese word meaning "harbor wave." These large waves are sometimes called seismic waves or tidal waves. Tsunamis are the result of earthquakes or volcanic eruptions in the ocean, and there is no way of stopping them. When a quake is deep beneath the floor of the ocean, tsunamis move very rapidly—up to about 450 miles per hour. While in deep water the height of the wave is not very high, but as the waves get to the shallow water near the beach they may reach 100 feet high, but with much slower speed.

On December 26, 2004, a large tsunami hit many islands in Indonesia and Malaysia, and in just minutes more than 100,000 people were missing. Families were picnicking at the beach and enjoying the water, when the water receded back into the ocean. They walked out to see the phenomenon, and high waves washed back to the beach with tremendous force and swept them all away. All were drowned. This was the worst tsunami ever to take place on earth.

In our lives, some of us set off "tsunamis." When something doesn't go our way, we have an earthquake in our lives and let go with our temper and words. Usually someone else, often someone who is innocent, gets the brunt of our rampage. Should our lives cause tsunamis?

Right now, why not get down on your knees and ask God to help you not to lose your cool today, fly off the handle, or say anything unkind? If you want to be a good person today, ask Jesus to help you. He will, I know, because He gave me victory over my temper. He will help you if you ask Him.

TERMITES

And they said, Go to, let us build us a city and a tower, whose top may reach unto heaven; and let us make us a name, lest we be scattered abroad upon the face of the whole earth. Genesis 11:4.

The Tower of Babel was a tremendous engineering feat. In the animal kingdom, the accomplishments of termites come the closest to this achievement. I did not know much about termites until I went to South America and lived in the jungles of Brazil and Peru. They are extremely plentiful in these tropical regions.

In the termite colony there are three castes or social levels. The largest caste, about 95 percent of the million or more insects in one colony, are workers. These workers are blind, wingless, and move around by touch, taste, and smell. They build the large colony homes. Soldiers make up the second caste. It is their job to protect the colony. Some are also blind and wingless. The colony's third caste are the reproductives. Each termite colony has a king and a queen, and it is their job to continually reproduce more termites. A queen may lay up to 30,000 eggs a day. In Africa one species has a queen that is 2,000 times larger than the other termites. She is huge!

Termite nests can be *big*. Some look like a chimney, towering up to 30 feet in the air. They may be built like pyramids, or dome-shaped. Some have pinnacles. The outside of the nest is built with soil and a cementlike substance that the termites produce, so as to make a hard shell. An inner lining is made of softer fiber called carton. This is a compound of chewed-up plant material mixed with saliva and other substances.

Just as when they built the Tower of Babel, people have tried to outdo God and surpass what He had intended for them to do. God is patient, but He will let us go only so far; then He calls a stop to evil. He did it at the Tower of Babel and soon He will do it again—for the whole world. Ask God to help you understand His will and help you put your life in harmony with His will.

FOSSILIZED WOOD IN INDIANA

Be a good worker, one who does not need to be ashamed and who correctly explains the word of truth. 2 Timothy 2:15, NLT.

Geologists, miners, and hobbyists have found many types of plant fossils. These range from microscopic in size to about 15 feet in diameter. The state of Indiana has an area with tree fossils from one to two feet across. Geologists have found only tree trunks, with no traces of bark, branches, or leaves. It is interesting to note that apparently these trees never grew in Indiana and that none of the trunks have been found in an upright position. They have all been lying down.

Scientists say that these trees floated into the area from New England or southern Canada where trees of their species grow today. These scientists believe that they landed in what is now Indiana sometime during a 50-million-year period called the Devonian period.

We, of course, know from the Bible that God caused a great flood to cover this earth and that everything was destroyed. The large trees were uprooted, deposited, and covered with soil. Some turned into what we know today as coal. Have you ever wondered why coal burns so well in a stove? It has many of the same properties as wood because it once was wood.

Scientists are somewhat puzzled about how all of this was done in the past. We, as Bible-reading Christians, know that there was a worldwide flood. Someone once said, "It takes more faith to be an evolutionist than a creationist."

We should be happy that we have God's book to help us understand what happened in the past and what will happen in the future. We have a God who loves us and gave us a Guidebook to guide us in this life here on earth. Pray today that as you open His Word God will guide your mind to help you live a Christlike life, one that will not lead to destruction but to eternal life.

SALT

You are the salt of the earth. But if the salt loses its saltiness, how can it be made salty again? It is no longer good for anything, except to be thrown out and trampled. Matthew 5:13, NIV.

Salt is a very precious commodity, and our lives depend on it. Problems do occur when we use too much of it, but some salt is necessary for our survival. Salt is obtained in several ways. First, salt is mined from large underground deposits. Next it is taken from salt wells in which a hole is drilled into the salt deposit. Fresh water, pumped in under pressure, dissolves the salt, which is pumped out in liquid form. A third method is to allow sea water to flow into specially prepared holding tanks, or evaporating beds. When the water evaporates, salt is left. Most salt for the United States comes from salt wells.

It's estimated that there are 140,000 uses for salt. Less than five pounds out of every 100 pounds of salt is used for seasoning food. Salt and its by-products are used by meat packers to preserve meat, by chemical companies to make chemicals, and by tanners for the tanning of hides for leather. Fisheries use salt to preserve fresh fish; food and dairy processors use it in their processing. Millions of tons of salt are used in making soda ash, which is used in making soap, glass, and washing compounds.

When salt is broken down by passing an electric current through salt water—a process called electrolysis—caustic soda, chlorine, and chlorine products are made. Salt is fed to cattle in their feed or in blocks set out for them to lick. Salt is used to melt snow and ice on sidewalks and highways to ensure safety. And because of the lower freezing point of salt water, salt is used in ice-cream freezers to melt the ice and freeze the cream.

Jesus told us that we are the salt of the earth, which could melt cold hearts and put His love in them. We are to make the earth a better place, but sin has put a real damper on this. Jesus will help you and me provide the needed "salt" on the earth if we allow Him to. Pray today, asking Jesus to help you melt that cold, icy disposition and to flavor someone else's life today with warm love.

THE OTTER

And when her days to be delivered were fulfilled, behold, there were twins in her womb.
Genesis 25:24.

How often do you hear anything about otters? There are two kinds, river otters and sea otters, and while they're a lot alike, there are some differences. For instance, river otters are about four feet long; sea otters grow up to five feet in length. The female river otter usually gives birth to two or three pups; the sea otter gives birth to only one pup. The river otter eats a lot of fish and some crayfish, snails, frogs, and insects. The sea otter lives on octopuses, squid, sea urchins, abalone, and other shellfish.

Both species of otter have a tapering tail, a large flat head, strong teeth, large nostrils, and small ears and eyes. They have webbed toes and a flexible body, which allow them to have great speed in the water.

The fur of otters is considered very valuable, the sea otter's being the more valuable. It is used for coats, cuffs, and collars. The sea otter's fur varies in color but is usually brownish black with some silvery hair mixed in. Otters are very intelligent, and have even been trained by fishermen in China and Bengal to fish for them.

We have described two creatures from the same family that are somewhat alike, yet different. Maybe you have brothers or sisters, or both, in your family, and you've probably been told you are each different.

When God made each of you, He "threw away the mold," as no two people are alike, even though they come from the same family. Each person has his or her own characteristics.

Esau and Jacob were twins from the same family, but they were very different. Thank God for your uniqueness. You are who you are because God made you to be who you are. Thank Him for that today.

LOONS

The Lord our God has shown us his glory and his majesty, and we have heard his voice from the fire. Today we have seen that a man can live even if God speaks with him. Deuteronomy 5:24, NIV.

Loons live in the lakes of the North, but winter in the South. Both males and females look alike. They are shiny black with white spots. Because of their territorial claims, only so many loons live in a specific area. The males stake out their claim, then the females move in. Three species of loon live in the United States and Canada.

The common loon is the most numerous. Unlike most birds, its leg bones are solid, not hollow. Also the legs are toward the back of the body, which helps them in their diving for food. They can dive to depths of 160 feet, following fish or searching for aquatic organisms, their main foods. Loons have dense body feathers, well lubricated during the preening process (see March 31). This keeps their bodies dry and insulated from the cold waters of the north.

Both parents take an interest in raising the young, incubating their eggs on a nest of heaped-up vegetation that may be used year after year. The one or two eggs hatch in 28 to 30 days. The young will either swim or ride on the backs of their parents. In order to fly, a loon must flap its wings and run along on top of the water until it is airborne.

Loons have interesting calls. Once heard, they are never forgotten. They can yodel, laugh, talk, and produce tremolos (eight to 10 notes repeated loudly). Each sound has a meaning. Tremolos are created when the loon is excited or threatened. Male loons yodel when they encounter another male. Laughs are used to locate other loons or the young, and the talking is used to communicate between pairs or flocks.

As we see above, loons communicate in different ways, and so does God. He tries to communicate with us in many ways under differing circumstances. Invite Him to speak to you today, and He will, in His own way—and you will understand. Ask God to help you hear His voice, whether it is through Scriptures, nature, or even the words of a friend.

LIFE UNDERGROUND

Anyone who claims to be in the light but hates his brother is still in the darkness. 1 John 2:9, NIV.

Although we don't pay much attention to it, the underground world is a world all of its own. Most of us aren't aware of what takes place under our feet, but if we could just see it we'd discover that life there is very interesting. Most of us are so engrossed in our own little world of activities that we don't take time to look.

Many animals make their homes in the ground. There are prairie dogs, chipmunks, ground squirrels, badgers, turtles, toads, some bees and wasps, lizards, salamanders, moles, earthworms, ants, and many other insects. However, millions of little creatures that we cannot see without a microscope also live in the soil under our feet. In just a spoonful of dirt you may find thousands of microscopic protozoans, minute spiderlike mites, tiny nematodes, roundworms, hookworms, and many other creatures. They creep and crawl among the grains of dirt or sand and spend their time eating decaying plants and animals, and sometimes each other.

Many of the creatures that make their home underground are equipped with legs capable of digging. A groundhog is a good example of this. Some, like the chipmunk, don't have strong digging legs, but they use their front feet to loosen and pull the dirt, then kick it out with their back feet. Some underground animals can throw dirt quite a distance with their hind feet. For example, the spadefoot toad digs backward into the ground to build its home. It remains underground during the day, but goes out at night to hunt for food. Earthworms, all 2,000 species of them, do much to enrich our soil. Of course, the ants with their complex underground colonies are probably the creatures we notice most.

Just like the underground animals and insects, some people live in what we could call total darkness. Without the light of God's love in their lives, their worlds are dark indeed. Some of them may be your relatives and friends. But God doesn't want anyone to live in darkness. Ask Him to help you find someone in a spiritual darkness situation and help that person by giving the "light" of the gospel. Just share what God has done in your life.

63

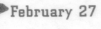

VICUÑAS

And all they that were about them strengthened their hands with vessels of silver, with gold, with goods, and with beasts, and with precious things, beside all that was willingly offered. Ezra 1:6.

One of the most beautiful animals in the world is the vicuña (vi-CUN-ya) It has lovely soft, dense wool that protects it from the harsh Andean cold. Millions of vicuñas used to roam the highlands of Peru, Bolivia, and Chile, but they were hunted for their meat and soft fur, and about 95 percent of their population was killed.

The vicuña is the national animal of Peru, and its picture is on most of the Peruvian coins and in much of the national art. The vicuña is one of the species of South American camels, but it does not have a hump. It looks a lot like the llama (LA-ma) and the alpaca (al-PAK-ca).

In Peru and all over the world the vicuña is protected. It is against the law to buy or sell vicuña fur. The Peruvian government has several herds of vicuñas. Occasionally, because of the lack of grazing land, some must be killed to preserve the others. Even though the government has the skins in their warehouses, they cannot sell them for fur coats and other items, because of the conservation agreement to protect them.

It is now estimated that Peru has about 45,000 vicuñas. These are guarded by about 70 guards. Vicuña wool is so expensive that it's sold for about $600 a kilo (2.2 pounds). Cashmere wool sells for only about $100 a kilo. Once a year in Peru's national roundup, these smaller, wilder cousins of the llama are caught and sheared. Thankfully, they are no longer in danger of extinction, but the government continues to protect them.

The vicuñas were around when the early Inca Indians roamed the mountains of Peru. Drawings of them can be seen on ancient pottery and other art treasures.

The Peruvians and others want the smooth, warm, lightweight wool of vicuñas because it is so valuable. We should want to have Jesus in our lives because He is precious. He will bring to us the opportunity of eternal life. Thank Him today for the life eternal that He provides.

EARTHQUAKES

At that moment the curtain of the temple was torn in two from top to bottom. The earth shook and the rocks split. Matthew 27:51, NIV.

At the time of the crucifixion of Christ there was a violent earthquake, and the ground opened up. Quite an event! I'm sure that the earthquake at the death of Jesus was the same type that we feel today. However, this was induced directly by God. Some scientists estimate that some of the large quakes release energy equivalent to about 200 million tons of TNT, or 10,000 times more energy than the first atomic bomb in 1945. The rocks in the outer layer of the earth are continually being squeezed and stretched by forces within the earth. When this force is more than the rocks and elements can stand, the rocks rupture and are displaced, causing an earthquake.

Have you ever experienced an earthquake? One time I was walking down a street in southern California when the asphalt began to roll under my feet like sea waves. Another time I was in our Inca Union Conference office in Lima, Peru, when a large earthquake struck. Our building leaned and rocked. People ran to the streets and cried and yelled. At the moment the quake hit I was meeting with fellow workers in a Welfare Services committee, known then as SAWS. I immediately went to work with my staff, and we went to the north of Lima, where the center of the quake had been. More than 60,000 people had been left without homes there. Many had been taking their siestas (naps), and were either hurt or killed. We fed more than 10,000 for many months.

Earthquakes produce much damage. While the Bible does not tell us about all the damage that happened at Christ's death, the earth did open up, and some damage was done. The shock waves must have been felt for a long distance. Think of it: even the earth quaked at the death of the Creator!

Today, think about the importance of the death of Jesus. When you pray, ask God to help you better understand its significance. By dying, Jesus paid the price for your sin even though He had never sinned. He died for you, and He died for me. Take a moment to thank Him.

POLLINATION

Yes, I am the vine; you are the branches. Those who remain in me, and I in them, will produce much fruit. For apart from me you can do nothing. John 15:5, NLT.

God planned everything just right when He created this earth. If you'd been the creator, would you have included pollination? You and I probably wouldn't have even thought of it, let alone knew it would be a good idea, but God did.

Pollination is what keeps this world going. If it weren't for pollination, fruits, flowers, and plants would soon cease to exist. Also, a lot of the insects necessary to maintain life would die too. Believe it or not, without pollen there probably would be no hay fever, either! Many of you might rejoice for that.

The main reason for pollination is to enable plants to reproduce, and it occurs in several different ways. A few plants depend on the wind to spread their pollen from one plant to the other, but most plants depend on insects for pollination.

You've seen bees wiggling down into the hearts of flowers. You may have seen the pollen from zinnias sticking to the legs of bees after they've walked around on its flat surface. Some insects use their tongues or probe to dig down into the plant to reach the nectar and pollen. And some plants sprinkle insects with pollen the moment they touch them. One single catkin (a taillike growth) on a birch tree, which depends on wind pollination, may send out 5.5 million grains of pollen to other birch trees, and there may be hundreds of catkins on a single tree. You've probably seen yellow pollen covering the ground under a tree or maybe on a car that's parked under a tree. This pollen was usually spread by the wind.

Jesus said that it is impossible to do anything without Him (John 15:5). Just as reproduction in most plants cannot take place without pollination, so a new spiritual life cannot take place without Jesus. For us to succeed spiritually, our relationship with Jesus must be as closely entwined with Him as the vine is with the branch. If we fail in trying to live a better life, it is because we try by ourselves, and don't rely on Jesus. Ask Him for His help today.

ANIMAL REMEDIES

Go up to Gilead and get balm, O Virgin Daughter of Egypt. But you multiply remedies in vain; there is no healing for you. Jeremiah 46:11, NIV.

Some years ago a shipyard fire in Singapore claimed the lives of 70 men. It left one man alive but badly burned. When Western medical methods failed to alleviate his pain, the family took him to a Chinese doctor. He prescribed powdered cyst from a porcupine brain. The man drank the concoction and took two other treatments, then claimed his suffering was gone.

Witch doctors and native healers have used different concoctions for many years. Today there is a tremendous market for animal parts to treat physical ills. Crocodile scales cooked in butter to cure toothaches and boils. Pieces of tortoise tied on the head is supposed to relieve malaria. Monkey bones are boiled for 10 days to make a tonic to improve circulation and cure severe rheumatism. Scales of pangolin are used for many skin disorders. Whiskers of golden cats are burned and mixed with opium to relieve pain from snakebites.

Parts of the tiger are used for many ills. Just to name a few: some grind up the bone from the tail and mix it with soap to make an ointment for skin diseases. The leg bone is said to make a healthful tonic when added to wine. Tying the small bones from a tiger's foot to a child's wrist is said to prevent convulsions. Sitting on a tiger skin is supposed to reduce fevers caused by ghosts. (If this treatment is used too often, it is said, the patient may turn into a tiger.)

Mix the brain with oil, rub it on the body, and it is a cure for laziness and acne. Roll the eyeballs into rolls and take to avoid convulsions. Wear a claw on a bracelet or carry it in the pocket to give courage and protect from sudden fright. Eat the heart to give strength, carry a rib for good luck, and add honey to ground-up gallstones for a cure for abscesses on hands and feet.

Desperate people will try many different remedies but will not be healed. Jesus is the only remedy that will "cure all." Try Jesus. This morning, ask Him to give you health and strength for today.

COMET DUST

Immediately after the tribulation of those days shall the sun be darkened, and the moon shall not give her light, and the stars shall fall from heaven, and the powers of the heavens shall be shaken. Matthew 24:29.

Scientists are still trying to explain the why of some things. They do not understand falling stars. They do not understand how meteorites—often called falling stars or shooting stars—are formed. And why are they floating around in outer space? Scientists ask many questions concerning these stars.

Researchers are trying to find answers to comets. Where do they come from and where do they go? In about October of 1985, scientists from France, Japan, the Soviet Union, and several European nations started their search for Halley's Comet. They expected it to pass Earth again in early 1986 (see Nov. 21 for an update). The purpose was to scrutinize the material that makes up the comet's tail such as the type of gas, the type of dust particles, and the icy head.

Some years ago the United States Space Agency attached little plates onto the ends of the wings of two U-2 spy planes, which can fly to extremely high altitudes. The pilot could project out these plates in an attempt to catch particles of comet dust. On the first flight they got one speck of dust. The second flight they got nine. But these particles couldn't tell them much. Other methods were tried, such as attaching a vacuum cleaner-like object to a balloon, but none of their methods were effective.

Men continually try to figure out what God has done. One researcher said, "Only God can tell us more. And God ain't talking." But God is talking through His Word, and we only have to read and believe. No, God hasn't told us all the details, but He did say He made this world, and while it would be interesting to know how comets are formed, that God made the universe is good enough for me. Tell God today that you believe His Word, and that you will trust in Him and His promises.

NATURAL ANTIFREEZE

O Lord, thou art my God; I will exalt thee, I will praise thy name; for thou hast done wonderful things; thy counsels of old are faithfulness and truth. Isaiah 25:1.

Fitteen species of poplar trees live in North America. Many of these are well known, usually by other names, such as quaking aspen, lombardy poplar, white poplar, bigtooth aspen, eastern cottonwood, swamp cottonwood, and balsam poplar. Interestingly, all poplars belong to the willow family.

Some of these trees, such as quaking aspen and eastern cottonwood, have long leafstalks that are flat or twisted so that the leaves are able to flutter. In the breeze they look green and flutter as they shiver back and forth. Poplars are fast-growing. Some of them grow up to eight feet a year. The wood is good for making paper and for firewood.

Poplars can live in areas where the winter temperatures go down to –40°F (–40°C). They can even survive in –100°F (–73°C). How? Through what is called the freeze-dry process. In the fall the trees draw out most of the water from their living cells, and this water freezes between the cells. This moisture that freezes contains sugar, which acts as an antifreeze. In the spring, when the warmer weather comes, the ice melts, and the moisture is absorbed back into the cells.

Poplars provide food for more than 40 species of animals. Rabbits and beavers depend on poplar trees for more than 50 percent of their diet. Where poplars grow, worms abound, so the base of poplar trees is a good spot for many animals and anglers to get earthworms.

Yes, we serve a wonderful God. His creation is so complex that scientists continue to be amazed at all the new things they are discovering. Thank God today because He is a magnificent God and has done so many wonderful things for you.

GOLDEN-EYED LACEWING

Ye shall eat, and not be satisfied. Leviticus 26:26.

The golden-eyed lacewing is a beautiful creature, with its golden eyes and four light-green transparent wings that allow the delicate wing ribs to be seen. These insects are about one inch long and very beneficial to those who raise flowers and gardens.

The female lacewing usually goes to a plant that is full of aphids. There, from her abdomen, she will expel a stringlike substance onto the leaf. Waiting a few seconds until it dries, she then lays an egg on the end of it. She continues on until she has many eggs on the end of these little sticks.

After six to 14 days the eggs mature, and out of each comes a small, pale creature with hair all over its body. It has pinchers out front to eat with. As this larval lacewing crawls down the leaf or stem of the plant, it stops to suck the body liquids out of aphids, scale insects, leafhoppers, thrips, mites, and other plant pests. The larval lacewing has been named the aphis lion, because it constantly eats aphids. As the aphis lion grows, its skin becomes tight, cracks, and is cast off. This happens four times in the larval stage of the lacewing.

After about 10 days the full-grown larva spins a golden cocoon around itself. It passes two weeks in this stage. Finally it opens, and out comes the beautiful, graceful lacewing. The females then begin the process all over again, and there are more lacewings. If you see lacewings, don't hurt them, because they will not hurt you, and they help kill many insects that bother, injure, or kill plants.

Jesus told the people of Israel that if they disobeyed the laws He gave them to keep them safe and happy, they would eat and not be satisfied.

Thankfully, many people in today's world are so hungry for God's Word that they constantly read it to become more familiar with the promises He gave His people. Ask God to give you a great desire for His Word so that you will be spiritually satisfied.

FISH WITH THE GOLDEN EGG

To them God chose to make known how great among the Gentiles are the riches of the glory of this mystery, which is Christ in you, the hope of glory. Colossians 1:27, NRSV.

The sturgeon fish that live in the Great Lakes of the United States and Canada, and in Russia, were exploited to the point that they were almost extinct. But modern technology in Russia and laws regulating the catching of these fish in the Great Lakes has started the sturgeon on the comeback trail.

Sturgeon grow to eight to 12 feet long and weigh up to 300 pounds. The largest fish in the Great Lakes, they live near the bottom and eat insect larvae, snails, and clams. These fish have slender bodies covered with rows of bony plates that early settlers to the U.S. used as rasps and graters.

Russians and Eastern Europeans valued the sturgeon considerably more than did people in the United States because they discovered that its eggs tasted good to them. Thus the Russian caviar industry was born and became a great business, especially for weddings and special meals.

Sturgeons grow very slowly. Males take 15 to 20 years to mature, and the female is 24 to 26 years old before she begins laying eggs. Females spawn (lay eggs) only once every four to six years. Because of these factors, laws in the Great Lakes area regulate how long a sturgeon must be before it can be kept when caught. It takes about 25 years for them to grow that size.

Russians have learned how to raise these fish in fisheries so they can gather the eggs for their caviar. Caviar sells for a high amount of money, especially that from the beluga sturgeon, which lives in the Caspian Sea. Once people realized the importance and value of sturgeon, they immediately began to protect them.

Many people do not realize the importance of Jesus. He is our most valuable treasure, but many have not found that out. Some will find it out too late. Others will discover it in time to go to heaven with Him. Tell Jesus how much He means to you as you pray this morning.

March 6

PETRIFIED

Yea, they made their hearts as an adamant stone, lest they should hear the law, and the words which the Lord of hosts hath sent in his spirit by the former prophets. Zechariah 7:12.

What does it mean to be petrified? Sometimes it means scared to death, but in this case it means turned to stone. The children of Israel turned their hearts into stone because they didn't want to do what God wanted them to do. Figuratively they became petrified, although the petrifaction we're talking about today is a real physical change.

Trees can become rock through the process of petrifaction. These can be seen in the Petrified Forest in the Arizona desert and, on a smaller scale, in Mississippi. It is interesting to see trees that have turned to rock.

Scientists say that several things must happen in order for trees to become petrified. It starts when water bearing some minerals circulates through buried fresh wood, then combines with oxygen so that no microorganisms such as fungi or bacteria can get into the wood pores. The moving water carries dissolved calcium carbonate or silica that infiltrates and surrounds the woody tissues. As the water moves out it leaves minute particles of calcium carbonate or silica, which then infiltrate any cavities in the wood cells and replace them. That is the process of petrifaction that hardens over the years.

Some scientists talk about the billions of years that it took to do this, but we understand and believe that this is largely a result of the Flood. As you look at petrified wood you see different colors. Iron oxides produced the fiery reds, yellows, and browns. Researchers tell us that more than 40 minerals are petrifying agents, but only four are common.

As the children of Israel hardened their hearts to God's word, so we, through sin, can harden our hearts to the Savior. He wants to come in, but if we allow sin to penetrate our lives our hearts will petrify, and Jesus will not be able to get in. Pray today asking God to send Jesus into your life so that your heart will become, not hardened and petrified by sin, but softened by His love.

WORKERS OF DARKNESS

Rejoice not against me, O mine enemy: when I fall, I shall arise; when I sit in darkness, the Lord shall be a light unto me. Micah 7:8.

Moles live almost exclusively in total darkness underground. They do have eyes, but their eyes are not very good. Moles are not found in Africa or in Central and South America.

The front legs and feet of these tunneling creatures are well suited for digging, and they can dig up to 100 yards of tunnel a day. (That's the length of a football field!) They have a very soft, short, extremely thick fur that helps reduce friction as they run through the tunnels.

I remember many years ago when I was in the youth tent at a southern Illinois camp meeting, a mole decided to burrow below the ground under the tent right where the song leader was directing the music. Those of us who sat up front watched the mole lift up the sod as it lengthened its tunnel. It passed within a foot of the music leader's foot. When the music stopped, the mole turned its course and burrowed its tunnel out of the tent. Moles do not have external ears, no doubt because of the dirt that they go through, but they are very sensitive to vibrations. If you see a mole digging and try to sneak up on it, you must do so very slowly and cautiously, or it will feel the vibrations and escape through its tunnel.

Of the seven species of moles, one of them is called the star-nosed mole. It has about 22 soft-skin projections on its nose that resemble a star. Moles have two major threats: snakes, and water that can flood their tunnels. A lot of people don't like moles because they dig up the yard and gardens. In fact, I don't like what they do tunneling my yard every spring. But they're also beneficial, eating many insect grubs and other soil-inhabiting invertebrates.

God does not want us to live or work in darkness. His Word will be a light unto our path (see Ps. 119:105), and Jesus will bring light into our life (see John 1:9). Ask Him today to bring His light into your life so that you will never live in spiritual darkness.

CARRIER PIGEONS

And, behold, one came and said unto him, Good Master, what good thing shall I do, that I may have eternal life? Matthew 19:16.

There are many different ways by which animals and birds help people. Today we'll look at the carrier, or homing, pigeon. Long before telephones, TV, radio, and the Internet this special breed of pigeon was effectively used for many years to carry messages.

As a boy growing up I raised many pigeons, but I never had a homing pigeon. But some friends did, and what fun we had! We'd put them in cages and take them miles away from their home. We would then open the cages and let the pigeons out, and then we'd return home as fast as possible. Most of the time the pigeons beat us home, and were waiting for us when we arrived.

During World War I and World War II carrier pigeons were often used to get messages from one place to another. The report is that during World War II the Germans strapped small automatic cameras to pigeons. These cameras were triggered by timing devices as the pigeons flew over the countryside. Thus the Germans could learn the whereabouts of the French military.

A British racing pigeon named Cher Ami may be the world's most famous pigeon. In World War I an American battalion had gotten ahead of its own army and was surrounded by the enemy. Using carrier pigeons, the men sent a call for help. Several of the birds were intimidated by the shelling, but Cher Ami had determination. Even though she was hit by shrapnel and one leg was shot off, she flew for 25 minutes and got the message to headquarters in time to save the battalion. Today Cher's stuffed body rests in the Smithsonian Institution in Washington, D.C. She was a real hero.

In today's text a young man asked Jesus what he needed to do to have eternal life. Jesus told him, but he didn't like what he heard. Oh, that we might heed God's instructions just as the carrier pigeons follow their orders. Ask Jesus today to help you follow the instructions He gives us in the Bible, so that you can be a hero and come through victorious as Cher did.

ANIMALS DO GOOD

Then Jesus asked them, "Which is lawful on the Sabbath: to do good or to do evil, to save life or to kill?" But they remained silent. Mark 3:4, NIV.

Yesterday we talked about carrier pigeons and how they helped a group of soldiers. Today we'll look at other animals that are helpful to people.

Different animals have been taught different skills, making the lives of many people easier and happier. Sometimes they even save lives. An automobile accident left Robert Foster, of Boston, Massachusetts, paralyzed from the neck down. Life was discouraging until he met Hellion—a capuchin (ka-poo-chin) monkey, the type that organ-grinders use. She was trained to help Foster around his house. Hellion unlocks doors, turns on the lights, puts cassettes into a tape player, retrieves food from the refrigerator, and feeds Robert. She also takes a container of juice, sticks a straw in it, and holds it so Robert can drink.

Hellion fetches objects or moves them at Robert's request. How does she understand? She was trained to respond to a light. When Robert holds a light device between his lips and flashes it onto an object, Hellion obediently does her chore. She's rewarded for her good work with banana-flavored pellets released from a dispenser on the back of Robert's wheelchair.

In California the United States Navy uses porpoises to carry tools to the men who are working in a laboratory 200 feet under water. It's much easier than sending a diver down, and a lot faster. Sea lions have been trained to go down and hook grabbers to the tail of rockets that have fallen to the ocean floor, so that they can be raised. In southern Thailand macaque (maa-cock-key) monkeys help the villagers harvest their coconuts from the tallest palm trees.

Animals have been taught how to relate to their master in obedience, and most of the time they do what they've been taught. Jesus has taught us through His Word, and He hopes we will respond positively to Him. Ask Jesus today to help you respond to Him with a "Yes, Lord."

COEVOLUTION

That they all may be one; as thou, Father, art in me, and I in thee, that they also may be one in us: that the world may believe that thou hast sent me. John 17:21.

Plants and animals adapt to pressures from each other in a process called coevolution. A biologist walking along a road in Veracruz, Mexico, saw a beetle land on a bush. As soon as that happened, the beetle was driven away by ants. The biologist discovered that the bush was an ants' acacia bush. The ants were protecting their domain, for they live on nectar from the acacia.

It appears that the ants also protect these acacias. They make a hole in the thorns of the acacia, then hollow the inside of the thorn. There they make their home. The queen ant controls her colony from inside these hollow thorns. The hollowing out of the thorns of the acacia plant doesn't hurt it, and the ants keep away other insects and plant eaters that might eat parts of the acacia for food. They defend the acacia plant, and as a result the plant continues to live and survive. Thus the ants and the acacia are good for each other.

The biologist took a colony of ants away from some acacia bushes in Mexico. He discovered that the ants didn't like any other vegetation so they didn't eat, and they died. They liked only the thick syrupy nectar that they harvested from the acacia's leaf tips. Also, the acacia bushes died, destroyed by various insects and other animals.

You and I need Jesus, and He needs us. When we encounter the storms of life, we can go to Him for comfort and shelter. And He needs us to help spread His love to others so that they will know about His ever-present protection. We need each other, and as we have that close relationship with Jesus, we will have life and safety.

When your friends want you to do something that you know you should not do, just whisper a prayer and Jesus will give you the courage to say "No."

Ask Jesus today to help you keep close to Him, and He will!

Captive Freedom

My God hath sent his angel, and hath shut the lions' mouths, that they have not hurt me. Daniel 6:22.

In many places are wild animal parks that allow visitors to ride in their cars and view the animals in a natural environment. Once I had the privilege of driving through Lion Safari Country In southern California. We were told to stay in our cars and keep our windows rolled up for safety. Driving slowly, we saw many different kinds of animals roaming about in captive freedom. In one large area were ostriches, emus, varieties of deer and antelope, wildebeests, llamas, giraffes, zebras, and many varieties of ducks and geese. They wandered here and there, not fighting with one another—just mingling around together.

Then we entered a high-fenced area with guards by each gate. Here the African lions lived—alone. We saw two ostriches decide they wanted to get close to the lion area. Immediately guards drove up in a jeep. On the other side of the wire fence paced a lion, eyeing the ostriches. Finally the ostriches were driven off by the guards, the lion was driven away from the fence, and all was at peace again.

At 2:30 in the afternoon a jeep pulling a trailer came into the first two areas and poured feed in the center of the paved road. All the wild animals hurried to the road for their lunch. They stood side by side, heads down, eating. I marveled as I saw so many different animals come together, undisturbed by each other. I immediately thought of heaven and of how the lamb and the lion will lie down together and eat (Isaiah 65:25). At the safari park the lions were kept separate from lambs and deer and other animals. God wants all His creatures to be in unity, and heaven and the new earth are the only place that will happen. Lions won't be caged, and humans won't be locked in cars.

As the guards kept the lions from the other animals, so God will keep Satan from you. He protected Daniel from the lions, and He will protect you from Satan. Ask for His protection today.

PLANTS FOR LIVING

And God said, Behold, I have given you every herb bearing seed, which is upon the face of all the earth, and every tree, in the which is the fruit of a tree yielding seed; to you it shall be for meat. Genesis 1:29.

In the beginning God gave Adam and Eve many wonderful things to eat. Then sin entered, and later the Flood came and destroyed all of the vegetation. Immediately after the Flood there was nothing to eat except the clean animals. When vegetation started to grow, Noah's descendants again had vegetables, fruits, and grains to eat.

Since then people have grown thousands of kinds of plants for food. Botanists and other scientists have experimented with many different varieties, improving upon them and developing better seeds for growing bigger and better vegetables and trees.

If you had a garden, what would you plant in it? What would you grow that you really like? I might plant some things I don't care for because my wife likes them. OK, let's plant our garden this morning. I'm going to plant some corn, a nice sweet corn that will melt in your mouth right off the cob. Then I'll put in spinach, Swiss chard, carrots, beets, cabbage, celery, string beans, lima beans, radishes, onions, peas, broccoli, cauliflower, lettuce, rhubarb, asparagus, squash, cantaloupe, watermelon, cucumbers, and there must be some other things I have left out. Oh, yes, tomatoes, potatoes, and lentils. What about okra?

I thank God that He created all of these things for my body to enjoy. God knew what was best for us to eat, so He created these neat foods. Scientists are finding out that when we eat lots of leafy vegetables we don't gain weight so readily, our blood pressure stays normal, and we feel good all over. Did you ever notice that cattle eat green grass and other plants, including corn, to keep healthy, and then they're killed to be eaten? You and I should get our good food firsthand from the plants, as the cow does.

Thank God today that the good food He created is just what you need to be healthy.

STARS

And He [God] took him [Abram] outside and said, "Now look toward the heavens, and count the stars, if you are able to count them." Genesis 15:5, NASB.

Perhaps many nights you've gone outside and looked up at the starry heavens and said, "Wow! Look at all the stars! I can't even begin to count them." God told Abraham to look up and try to count the stars. It is humanly impossible. Astronomers have made many studies of the sky and, by using mathematical formulas, have tried to come up with some type of count, but who knows how accurate it is. The deeper we see into space, the more stars are found. Astronomers tell us that there are more than one octillion stars in the universe. Can you understand that figure? I can't. It's really the numeral "one" followed by 27 zeros. Still can't understand it? I can't either! Let's see what that figure looks like.

1,000,000,000,000,000,000,000,000,000. WOW!

James Snelling, a naturalist friend of mine from Battle Creek, Michigan, says that if the sky began raining green peas, and the lakes, rivers, and oceans froze over so that the peas would stack up, you would need 250,000 planets the size of our earth all covered with green peas four feet deep in order to have 1 octillion peas. That is a lot of green peas! But that's at least how many stars there are. It is hard for our minds to comprehend the greatness of our God and the universe He has created.

Our God created all the heavens and the earth. Psalm 147:4 says: "He [God] determines the number of the stars, he gives to all of them their names" (RSV). On this earth we cannot understand all about the heavens, but we can spend eternity learning about them from the Creator. How long is eternity? My mother used to say, "If a bird came every thousand years and took one peck and carried away one grain of sand, when the earth was all gone, eternity would have just started." How about that? Isn't that exciting?

Don't you want to have that opportunity? Pray today that God will help you on your road to heaven, to trust and believe in Him as the Creator so you can have that eternal experience.

HIMALAYA MOUNTAINS

How beautiful upon the mountains are the feet of him who brings good news, who proclaims peace, who brings glad tidings of good things, who proclaims salvation, who says to Zion, "Your God reigns!" Isaiah 52:7, NKJV.

The Himalaya Mountains, wedged between the countries of Tibet and India, are known as the most inhospitable mountains in the world. Many peaks are more than 20,000 feet high. This vast complex of stone and ice extends about 1,500 miles from Pakistan to Assam and, depending on the location, is from 100 to 200 miles wide.

Naturally, the mountain climate varies depending on the altitude. Temperatures range from the subtropical, with lush plants, to the alpine, where few or no plants grow. In the western sector, forests flourish between 3,000 and 10,000 feet elevation. They include oaks and magnolias, with an undergrowth of bamboo. These give way to fir, hemlocks, and pines at higher elevations.

In these mountains, especially in Tibet, live a variety of game animals. Most are from the goat and sheep families, with antelope, buffalo, and donkeys thrown in. Of course, they do not go by these names, and we would probably not recognize most of their names. Since most of these animals are unusual to us, we'll spend the next four mornings describing 11 of them so that you will understand some of what the young people of Tibet and the Himalayas see.

Tibet is an arid desert, windblown and struggling with low vegetation. Its average altitude is more than 15,000 feet. It sits atop Asia like an elevated island. Temperatures range from 100° F. (38°C) to –45°F –43°C), and the people are very hospitable.

Just like in other parts of the world, there are God-fearing people in this high land, people who love the Lord Jesus and bear good tidings of God's great love to those about them.

Thank God today that Jesus is known in this part of the world and that you too know Him and love Him as your Lord and Savior. What a blessing you have!

HIMALAYAN HIGH WALKERS

The range of the mountains is his pasture, and he searches after every green thing.
Job 39:8, NKJV.

Today's text certainly fits perfectly the three Himalayan animals we'll discuss today. The yak, chiru, and ibex live in the mountains from 12,000 feet to 20,000 feet elevation. The yak lives at the highest altitude, where green food is very scarce.

The yak looks similar to the American bison, though someone has said that it is "an ungainly mass of black-brown hair." It is also called the grunting ox because it makes a grunting sound as it moves along. Grown yaks are about six feet high at the shoulder and weigh about 1,200 pounds. They are quick, sure-footed, and agile climbers. Easily domesticated, they are used as the only means of transportation in the region. They can cope with deep snow and swim icy rivers with a load on their back. They provide milk and meat, and their droppings are used for heating and cooking fuel.

The chiru belongs to the antelope family. It has two horns that protrude about 27 inches straight up from the head. As one looks from the side, the two horns look like one, giving rise to the legend of the unicorn. Chiru usually segregate into herds of males or females and mix only when mating. They stand about 32 inches high and weigh about 100 pounds each. To some they are sacred; to others they are hunted for meat and blood.

The ibex, an agile climber on the precipices, is a true goat. Ibex have long recurved horns up to 50 inches, and are a favorite game animal for hunters. Hunters have found that they must be above them on the mountainside in order to hunt them. They say that when the ibex is in danger it uses its long horns to cushion the bounce as it leaps down the mountainside in long bounds.

These animals live so high up that there is very little food, and they have to spend a lot of time hunting for it. God has provided food to sustain you. Thank Him today for His blessings to you.

HIMALAYAN VALLEY SEEKERS

He sends the springs into the valleys; they flow among the hills. Psalm 104:10, NKJV.

Three Himalayan animals prefer the valleys among the mountains, at an elevation of from 10,000 to 17,000 feet. Two of them, the argali and the bharal, belong to the sheep family. The third, the kiang, is a donkey.

The argali is the world's most desired big-game species because of its tremendously large horns. There are three varieties of these animals, which are considered to be the world's largest wild sheep. They weigh up to about 400 pounds. Their horns may reach a circumference of about 75 inches around the curl. From these horns the shepherds make large bowls to eat from, and they use the horns to set up a night corral for the animals. Hunters pay up to thousands of dollars for a 10-day argali hunt in Mongolia.

The number-two animal from the Himalayan valleys is the bharal, or blue sheep. Zoologists have not yet determined whether the bharal is a sheep or a goat. It does have curved horns like a goat. The horns are about 35 inches around and curl backward over the head. The males weigh up to 150 pounds and are about the size of the Rocky Mountain sheep. Bharal prefer the grasslands and run in large herds.

The kiang is totally different from all of the other animals. It is a donkey that has become very tame. Kiangs are usually found in herds and are real pests, especially to the hunters, as they are extremely curious and inquisitive. They've been known to go right into the hunters' camp and scare the cooks. They sound very inquisitive, don't they?

Springwater runs down through valleys, making them beautiful and green. When the love of Jesus runs into your life, it will water your life with truth, bringing eternal life to your souls. Thank God today that His love flows into your hearts, when we let it. Let His love flow into your heart this morning and throughout the day.

HIMALAYAN CLIFF CLIMBERS

Look! Here he comes, leaping across the mountains, bounding over the hills.
Song of Solomon 2:8, NIV.

Three of the Himalayan animals that we discuss today are high jumpers and live in the mountains between 7,000 and 14,000 feet elevation. These animals are goats or related to the goat family, and are called the tahr, takin, and markhor.

The tahr is a champion among high jumpers. From a standing position it can jump over a six-foot-high obstacle. It is a cousin to the goat and similar to the Rocky Mountain goat in body shape. Tahrs are reddish brown and have a shaggy mane around the neck and shoulders. Their horns are only about 14 inches long. The residents hunt them for meat because it is believed that this meat cures fever and rheumatism.

Takins are among the most unusual and least-known animals in the Himalayas. They look clumsy and are heavily built in the front. They stand about three and a half feet at the shoulder and have bulging shoulder muscles. Their horns are about 24 inches long, and they emerge from the center of the head, then abruptly turn outward, then backward, then upward. Takins inhabit steep terrain and like to be in thickets of bamboo or rhododendrons. In the summer they form into small herds, but in the winter the herds are very large—possibly to keep warm.

Probably no animal has such distinguished horns as the markhor. Their horns are snakelike and may extend to five feet in length. *Markhor* is a Persian word meaning snake eater, but some people think the name really should have been markhar, or snake-donkey, meaning a donkey with snakelike horns. Because of the length of their horns, they have accidentally hanged themselves in trees while reaching for leaves. These goats weigh up to about 200 pounds and are very sure-footed.

As these animals come leaping quickly along the mountains, so Jesus, when He comes, will come quickly. Jesus *will* return, and every eye will see Him. Thank Him today for that certainty.

HIMALAYAN PRECIPICE LOVERS

The Lord is my rock, and my fortress, and my deliverer; my God, my strength, in whom I will trust; my buckler, and the horn of my salvation, and my high tower. Psalm 18:2.

The last two of the Himalayan creatures that we will talk about are the goral and the serow. These two animals enjoy the rocky ledges and precipices, where there is some vegetation. Both are very sure-footed and can climb very fast on the ledges. They live in a wide range of altitudes, from a low of 3,000 feet to 12,000 feet. Since the animals we've discussed the past few days live at such different altitudes, they do not get in each other's way, and there generally is food for all of them.

The smallest of the 11 Himalayan animals we are studying is the goral. It stands about 28 inches tall and weighs about 60 pounds. Its horns extend only about eight inches, and it has a long, coarse, shaggy-hair appearance. Part of the mane of the males stands up. Gorals are buffy gray to rufous brown and have a black streak that extends from the neck to the tail, and a whitish patch of color on the chin and throat. They never wander far from vegetation cover and when in danger sound an alarm, a hissing sound.

The most interesting of all of the creatures is the serow. It looks like the Creator took parts from the cow, the pig, the donkey, and the goat to make it. Serows are about 38 inches high and weigh from 200 to 300 pounds. They have long, shaggy brown hair and 10-inch horns. They are very stocky, have long, pointed ears, and a short, hairy tail. When frightened, they utter a loud call, a combination of a snort and a screaming whistle.

These animals trust in the rocks for their safety, and it is very difficult for their enemies to follow and catch them. The psalmist trusted in God as his rock. We should be happy that we can trust in God. Thank Him for His trustworthiness.

DRIFTWOOD

But let him ask in faith, with no doubting, for he who doubts is like a wave of the sea driven and tossed by the wind. James 1:6, NKJV.

In the forests around the world are millions of trees. Some trees are cut and used for firewood. Other trees are made into boards to build houses or cupboards or objects that are useful or decorative. Many trees eventually die. When that happens, they lie on the forest floor and rot.

However, some dead trees fall into or are washed into a body of water. Most of the time a river carries the tree downstream to a lake or the ocean. As the tree bobs along, occasionally getting stuck on a sand or mud bar or in shallow water, some of the branches break off.

As these smaller pieces of wood break from the tree they too bob with the ripples of the current in the river. They are also rolled along, perhaps over islands of dirt and rocks. Bumping along, they become smooth. The bark and rough edges are worn off. This we call driftwood.

As they float along, these pieces of wood are not able to do anything about how or where they float. They just go along with the current, being carried where the water flows. They are also blown about by the wind. Unless a skilled person picks the wood up, works it over, and makes it into a useful article—which happens a lot of the time—driftwood is good for nothing but to be burned.

Many of us are like driftwood. We just drift along with the crowd. Where they go, we go. We have no purpose, or we don't want to be different. However, we can find a purpose for our lives if we put ourselves into the hands of the Master Craftsman. Jesus is waiting for us to quit drifting and put ourselves into His hands. He will make something beautiful out of us.

I invite you today to put your life into the hands of Jesus—the Master Craftsman. Ask Him to take your life and give you a goal and a purpose. Let Him make something beautiful out of you today.

March 20

SPRING

In whose hand is the soul of every living thing, and the breath of all mankind. Job 12:10.

Today is the first day of spring in the Northern Hemisphere, and new life begins to spring forth. Trees and bushes that lost their leaves in the fall are beginning to leaf out and bloom again. Flowers that have lain dormant will soon be in full bloom, and many people will be planting other flowers, trees, shrubs, and grass, as well as their vegetable gardens.

Fawns are born and butterflies dip and soar, released after months in their cocoons. Bears and some other animals come out of hibernation. In some areas the snow season is almost over. It is a time for all life to say, "This is spring, and I want to enjoy it." And in springtime many boys and girls who know that it won't be long until school is out jump up and down with excitement. It seems that everyone wants summer to come so they can enjoy swimming and all the other fun things to do in the outdoors.

Spring is a beautiful time to be alive. Tulips and daffodils bloom. Birds are building nests. Buds open, and many sweet aromas fill the air, a joy to the senses. This is also the time that farmers go into their fields and prepare them for planting. Yes, spring gives us great promises of the beautiful summer that is soon to arrive.

Have you ever noticed that spring is a time that people go out and really enjoy nature? After the cold days of winter it's great to get out and see all the things that are going on in God's world. And this time of year many young people are finishing plans for a summer wedding. Spring is a delightful time.

In His planning, God didn't leave anything out. Through the springtime God shows us what new life is all about. His creation seems to say, "This, My child, is what I have for you when I come again—a new life in Christ Jesus." Thank Him for spring and life today. It is your life, and Jesus will give you a new life when He comes the second time and for all eternity.

86

GYPSY MOTHS

My little children, these things I write to you, so that you may not sin. And if anyone sins, we have an Advocate with the Father, Jesus Christ the righteous. 1 John 2:1, NKJV.

Gypsy moths first came to the shores of the United States from France in 1869. They were brought to Massachusetts to help in the production of silk, but that experiment failed, and some of the adult moths escaped. Even though they're called gypsy moths, they do not travel very fast. They migrate about one mile per year. Sailing on their silk threads, the wind carries them in different directions to new areas.

Gypsy moths lay their eggs in woodpiles, doghouses, building supplies, bricks, flowerpots, fence posts, and wherever seems to them a good place. As these items are moved, the moths spread. You may have seen a gypsy moth. The female is creamy white and does not fly. She may not travel more than a few yards in her lifetime. Her eggs hatch into caterpillars, and each of the larval stages is called an instar. The caterpillars are grayish brown with rows of red and blue spots.

The male gypsy moth is smaller than the 1½- 2½-inch female, but he can fly.

Gypsy moth caterpillars attach themselves to trees and, if undisturbed, can eat all of the leaves off of a tree. Fortunately they do not kill the tree, at least not at once. Most trees cannot be destroyed unless more than 50 percent of the leaves are stripped for two years in succession. Gypsy moths are a pest and will probably be with us for a long, long time. As one science writer said: "We'll have to live with them as we try to understand nature and its ways."

Unfortunately we have to live with sin in the world, too. Sin will conquer us if we let it. Jesus will help us conquer sin if we ask Him. Pray today that God will help you conquer sin in your life. That is your only safety!

ARMORED NIGHT HUNTER

Therefore put on the full armor of God, so that when the day of evil comes, you may be able to stand your ground, and after you have done everything, to stand.
Ephesians 6:13, NIV.

Lobsters are crustaceans that live on the bottom of the ocean. A full armor covers their body. A lobster's body has 19 parts: the head has five, the thorax eight, and the abdomen six. A soft place between the plates of armor make it possible for the lobster to bend its body. A lobster has 10 legs, eight of which are used for walking. The other two legs, which extend out front, end in claws. With these, lobsters grab and break up their food.

Ranging from 12 to 24 inches in length, and weighing from one to 20 pounds, lobsters hide under rocks or in holes during the day. Because they live in murky water their eyesight is poor. Antennae enable them to feel for food or enemies. Lobsters naturally are dark green or blue. They turn red when boiled for eating.

The male lobster is called a cock, and the female a hen or chicken. The hen lays eggs only every two years. She lays from 5,000 to nearly 100,000 eggs and carries them under her tail for 11 or 12 months. When they are ready to hatch, she shakes the young out of their eggshells. These little baby lobsters—less than one third of an inch long—float to the ocean's surface. There they live for from three to five weeks, prey for birds and fish. Those that survive sink back down to the bottom of the ocean.

Two days after hatching they will molt (shed the shell) the first time. Then they will molt three more times during the first month. During this soft-shell time they have no protection. But if they are not caught by people or other sea life, their average life span is about 15 years.

We are told that we should put on the full armor of God, not just part of it. As the lobster needs its whole armor, so do we—to protect us from our enemy. God has promised to be with us, so let us depend on Him to help fit us up with His armor of protection from sin.

Thank God for His interest today, and ask Him to help suit you with a suit of armor that fits just you.

TOKI

For it is written, he shall give his angels charge over thee, to keep thee. Luke 4:10.

On the Japanese island of Sado lives one of the world's rarest birds. In English it is called the crested ibis, but in Japanese it is the toki. These heronlike pinkish birds are found only on this island and in the Shaanxi province of China. As of July 10, 2003, there were 40 here in captivity, 100 living in China, and now 400 in the Peking Zoo. Ornithologists (bird scientists) from Japan are trying to save these birds. They are hoping to reinstate the beautiful and magnificent toki.

These birds are one of 28 species of ibis in the world. They are about 22 inches long and have beautiful white feathers with a pink tint to them. They have a long black beak with a red tip, and orange legs. Both sexes have the ornate head crest, which has feathers that form a narrow mane down the back of the neck. They have become almost extinct from being hunted for their beautiful plumage and from pesticides in their natural food.

The World Wildlife Fund is working with the Japanese in all-out effort to save these birds. Broken eggs have been found in nests on Sado. New hopes have been encouraged by the find of unknown birds in China to repopulate the birds in the area.

Following the success that ornithologists in other parts of the world have had with ibis in captivity, the Japanese have brought in a colony of Indian white ibis and put them in cages beside the crested ibis. The scientists hope that with the use of mirrors they can make the crested ibis think they are in a large colony, and possibly breed in captivity.

While people are doing all they can to save the crested ibis in Japan, God is working with His angels all over this earth to save boys and girls from eternal extinction. Thank God today for His loving care and interest in you and ask Him for His angel protection today. Angels will be by your side all day and every day, if you ask for them.

March 24

EARTHWORMS

*But I am a worm, and no man; a reproach of men, and despised of the people.
Psalm 22:6.*

The earthworm has been used as a symbol of lowliness because it moves around under the ground. When people don't have good feelings about themselves, they may say, "I feel like a worm." Then there's the little song that says, "Nobody loves me, everybody hates me, I'm going out and eat worms. Big, fat, juicy ones; little, round, gooey ones; I'm going out and eat worms." It's interesting how we as humans see our feelings or behavior in comparison with other creatures. We say "blind as a bat," "sly as a fox," "slow as a turtle," and "low as a worm."

I have asked the question Why did God create the earthworm? Of what good is it? When I was a boy on a small farm in Colorado, I'd dig up worms to fish with. My dad would say, "Chuck, don't dig up too many in one place. Go to several places to dig up your worms. Worms are valuable to our garden."

"Valuable to our garden?" I'd ask.

"Yes," he would reply, "valuable to our garden." Obedient to my dad's wishes, I'd dig my worms in different places, but I couldn't understand why. Years later I did.

As a college freshman, taking a zoology class, I learned that the earthworm has no eyes but has sensory cells on each segment. These make the worm sensitive to light and touch. The earthworm has 10 hearts, or aortic arches. We learned that the earthworm pushes through soft soils and eats its way through the harder soils. It eats decayed vegetation. This passes through the earthworm's body and out the other end. This is called castings and is brought to the surface of the soil. Castings are very good fertilizer, and the soil turnover makes the soil richer so that it produces better crops. The holes and tunnels the worms make are good for the soil too.

Earthworms have an important job, enriching the soil for growing food. How much more important are you to God! He cares for you. Jesus wants to save you. Thank Him.

BEAKED WHALES

My prayer is not that you take them out of the world, but that you protect them from the evil one. John 17:15, NIV.

There are about 14 species of beaked whales. Many of the species vary in size, and they look somewhat different. But they all have one thing in common. The bottom jaw sticks out farther than the top jaw and has from two to four teeth in it. The mouth of beaked whales is quite different from whales that have no teeth; these whales have large fibrous plates sticking down in their mouths. The teethed whales, of which the beaked are only a few, have large throats, big enough that a person could pass through. Those without teeth have very small throats.

Some of the beaked whale species are so rare that no one has actually seen them in the water. However, their bodies have been found washed up on the beach. The largest of the beaked whales is the Baird's beaked whale. These grow to about 42 feet long, exceeded in length—in the toothed class—only by the sperm whales. There are larger whales, but they are in the nontoothed, or baleen, whale category.

Probably the most common of the beaked whales is the Cuvier, or goose-beaked whale. They are globe-trotters, and received the name Cuvier from a nineteenth-century French naturalist. The other name was given for their tapered profile. They are found in both the Northern and Southern Hemispheres and are quite plentiful. They like to swim in groups of 30 to 40. They will spout for about 10 minutes, then dive and stay under water for at least a half hour. Most of the beaked whales are gray, lighter on the bottom and darker gray to black on the top.

God has put these whales in the ocean just as He has put us in this world. He doesn't want us to be a part of the world, but He does want us to be *in* the world. We should be different, but work with the people of the world to complete the mission that we're here for. And that is to save lost souls who do not know Jesus. Ask God today to help you complete Jesus' prayer that you will be in this world to help those who do not know Him, but not part of the world with all of its sinful ways.

DOWN

But what went ye out for to see? A man clothed in soft raiment? behold, they that wear soft clothing are in kings' houses. Matthew 11:8.

Just west of the main island of Iceland is a tiny island called Vigur. On this small island, only about one square mile in size, lives one family, the Baldur Bjarnason family. They share this tiny island with about 4,000 pairs of eider ducks.

These ducks come to Vigur to nest and raise their young. They do not like humans, but they will tolerate them. During the summer the Bjarnason family goes into the ducks' nesting area and gathers the fine down feathers that the eiders use for making their nests. The islanders are very careful not to disturb the setting ducks more than once each year. Since the weather is cold even in the summertime, they leave enough down feathers so that the eggs will be protected and hatch.

The Bjarnarsons gather this down during a six-week period of time. About 35 nests yield a pound of down, and there are about 4,000 nests on the island. The down is placed in piles to dry. After a short time the down is put into a special drum and dried further to make it ready for shipment.

The family also cleans the down of grass and debris, but they can clean only about two pounds a day per person. Eider down sells for about $300 per pound.

Many of you have down jackets and other clothes, and some of you have a nice, soft down pillow. Maybe your parents have a down comforter. Down is as warm as it is soft.

When talking about John the Baptist, Jesus asked the crowd if they'd been looking for a man in soft clothing, meaning someone who had an easy life. Undoubtedly John's tunic was of rough homespun. His whole life was very simple.

The life of Jesus was simple, too, but it was rich in what was most important. He wants us to look for and find the truth in Him and His Word. Ask God to help you as you search for truth in His Word today.

USEFUL PLANTS

For lo, the winter is past, the rain is over and gone. The flowers appear on the earth. . . . The fig tree puts forth her green figs, and the vines with the tender grapes give a good smell. Song of Solomon 2:11-13, NKJV.

There is almost no end to the number of useful plants and trees that God put on the earth for us. In the world's warmer climates, including the southern United States, a large amount of cotton is grown. But cotton has been spun into thread, woven, and dyed since at least 3,000 B.C. For centuries India supplied most of the world's cotton fabric. Cotton was well known in South America, too. I have watched the Indian girls and women in Brazil and Peru spin cotton fibers to make their thread. They make beautiful garments, tablecloths, and other things from the cotton that they spin.

What would we do without rubber? The rubber trees in Central and South America, Southeast Asia, and Africa have greatly improved our lives. In South America the trees are sliced with a sharp knife, and the liquid latex runs down the cut channels into containers. It's interesting that this doesn't hurt the tree. Evidently, latex is a substance that protects the tree from injury. After the latex is gathered, it is wrapped onto a stick and "barbecued" like meat over an open fire until it becomes a large ball. Men carry these balls to the riverbank. From there they are taken by canoe or boat to the rubber peddlers, who ship them to rubber products companies.

Then there's chewing gum latex, which is gathered just like the rubber latex. The chewing gum latex is brought into the processing plant, cleaned, formed into large blocks, and shipped to chewing gum manufacturers. Raw latex has no taste. You've probably enjoyed some flavored chewing gum latex yourself.

I thank God that He put so many interesting plants in our world and that He gave men and women the intelligence to develop from them thousands of products that enrich our lives.

Thank God today for your brain and the ability to think and do.

93

TALL AND MAJESTIC

[Consider] the cedars of Lebanon, that are high and lifted up. Isaiah 2:13.

In the time of Christ the largest trees growing in the Middle East were the cedars of Lebanon. The Bible makes many references to these large trees. However, the people who lived in the Holy Land at that time had never seen the giant redwoods that are found in the United States. Two species are found on the west coast of California and in both Yosemite and Sequoia national parks, also in California. There is one other species (found in China), but it is not an evergreen and not as large a tree.

The redwoods growing along the California coast are the tallest, and the tallest one of them is 368.6 feet high. The sequoias are not as tall, but are much bigger around. The largest sequoia known today is the General Sherman Tree in Sequoia National Park in California. This tree measures 272.4 feet high and 101.6 feet in circumference. It is estimated that this tree would yield more than 600,000 board feet of lumber. Naturalists estimate this tree to be about 3,500 years old, which means that it would have started growing some 1,500 years before Christ lived on earth. (See also April 23.)

Redwoods have an extensive root system. Because of this and the great strength in their trunks, strong winds can scarcely uproot them.

In Psalm 1:3 faithful and loyal people are likened to trees. But God cautions us to beware lest we fall. God wants us to hold our heads up because we are Christians, but not to be proud of what we have accomplished. As Jesus said: "Without Me you can do nothing" (John 15:5, NKJV).

Tell God in prayer today that you want His help so that you will be able to hold your head high as a Christian, and to represent Him today to your friends.

POWER PLAY

For the word of God is quick, and powerful, and sharper than any twoedged sword, . . . and is a discerner of the thoughts and intents of the heart. Hebrews 4:12.

One of the common displays of a power struggle is the rutting behavior of the Rocky Mountain bighorn sheep. The method they use in declaring their domain and exercising their dominance is mind boggling. Two bighorn rams back up some distance, rear up on their hind legs, and lunge forward until they collide with each other, head on. Observers say that when two bighorn rams collide, they are going at a speed of about 30 miles per hour.

The creatures keep this up until one or the other yields to the superiority of the other. This might be accomplished in one collision, or it may take hours. One observer saw a battle continue for 25 hours and 20 minutes, until one of the rams surrendered. During these confrontations the rams not only clash with their horns but will shove with their chests or shoulders, growl, flicker their tongues, and use a variety of kicks. When two bighorn rams clash in the mountains, the resounding noise can be heard for a long distance.

These rams have a double-layered skull. The outer skull is like a helmet. Between the two skulls is about an inch of space, honeycombed with sturdy bone struts. Topping this off is a thick layer of skin. With all of this headgear, the blows are somewhat neutralized, and injuries are not too common.

God's word is even stronger and more powerful than bighorn sheep. He gave us the Bible to help guide our lives. As long as we follow this guidebook, putting our lives in His hands, we will be calmer and more peaceful because we can depend on Him.

Ask Jesus this morning to overpower the devil and sin in your life. With His power He will be the victor in your life, and you will be blessed.

MOUNT ST. HELENS

What manner of persons ought ye to be in all holy conversation and godliness, looking for and hasting unto the coming of the day of God, wherein the heavens being on fire shall be dissolved, and the elements shall melt with fervent heat? 2 Peter 3:11, 12.

May 18, 1980, was a tragic day for birds, wildlife, and even some people. It was the day that Mount St. Helens blew its top. For months scientists had been watching and recording the tremors of that beautiful mountain. Gases were spewing out of the top. Then, with one mighty explosion the mountain spewed hot ash and all kinds of hot materials into the sky.

As the hot lava flowed down the sides of Mount St. Helens it covered many beautiful lakes and rivers, thousands of acres of trees, and millions of wild creatures. The National Forest Service took a census after the first eruption and found more than 67,000 game animals dead. After the ash finished falling, they counted nearly 1.5 million game animals dead and more than 11 million salmon and other fish destroyed. It is estimated that more than 1.5 million birds lost their lives, as well as unnumbered nongame animals (animals not hunted by hunters), amphibians, reptiles, and insects.

Twenty-six lakes were totally destroyed and 24 others partially ruined. More than 1,000 miles of streams were ruined in that they were made inaccessible because of the lava flow. In some areas the ash piled up three and four feet deep. Forestry officials hoped that the rain would not make this ash like cement, which would completely eliminate any future use of the land. But as one ranger said: "Nature has a way of taking care of itself."

Before long, life began to return to the mountain. Bluebirds nested in shattered tree trunks. Elk made their way up volcanic debris, helping to reintroduce plants. God gave our world some marvelous methods of taking care of itself, of repairing what has been partially or totally destroyed. Thank God that He has given this earth this power, and that many ugly places, destroyed either through natural processes or by humans, eventually covered up the scars. God will cover up the scars in your sinful life with the robe of His righteousness. He has promised, so ask and He will do it.

FEATHER ZIPPERS

Do not fear therefore; you are of more value than many sparrows.
Matthew 10:31, NKJV.

Bird feathers are a fascinating example of God's creative ability and thought. Feathers not only cover a bird's body but help birds in many different ways. Feathers serve two primary functions: flight and thermoregulation. The feathers of flightless birds such as the ostrich and emu are used primarily for thermoregulation. The feathers on these birds do the same for them as fur does for an animal. The feathers of penguins are for thermoregulation, too, and they act like the fur on a seal when the birds dive into frigid water.

You've probably seen birds take a bath in dust or water. This is the way they rid themselves of parasites and dirt. After a bird takes a bath, it usually goes to a safe limb and begins preening its feathers—cleaning and putting each feather in place with its beak. The main stem of the feather is called a quill. On either side of the quill are vanes that are made up of filaments or barbs. Each barb has many microscopic hooks called barbules, which have barbicels ending in hooks, and these work like miniature zippers. When the birds start their preening, feather by feather, they zip all these barbules and barbicels into place, so the feathers fit tightly against the body. Most birds have a gland at the base of the tail that produces an oil that makes the feathers waterproof. As the bird preens, the small gland is touched by the bill, and the feathers are zipped into place and waterproofed with the oil. This protects the body of the bird as it flies or as it swims or fishes.

God made the bird feathers to help protect and clothe the birds. The Scriptures say that if God has taken so much thought with the birds, He has taken even more thought with you.

Thank God that He takes care of you and loves you.

SPERM WHALES

O righteous Father, the world hath not known thee: but I have known thee, and these have known that thou hast sent me. John 17:25.

Sperm whales, the largest of the toothed whales, may grow to about 60 feet long. They have a very blunt snout that looks like someone chopped it off. On the left forward part of the head is the blowhole. They're interesting looking, as about one third of their body is the enormous head. The sperm whale has a small, narrow lower jaw loaded with teeth.

There are three species of sperm whales, two of which are called pygmy sperm whales. Sperm whales cruise all the oceans and have been the most hunted whales in history. In fact, the book *Moby Dick* is about a sperm whale. Early whalers have written about the sperm whale. In the early days they hunted and harpooned them from open boats. One man wrote that a whale slammed down on his boat with its head, then backed off and rammed it again, crushing the timbers and sinking the boat. Another report stated that a whale lifted its head out of the water, pitched its whole weight onto the boat, and ruined it, killing the midshipman.

At birth a sperm whale calf is about 13 feet long and may weigh a ton. Its length doubles within about six months, which is the length of time it is nursing. Amazingly, and rather sad, the mother guards her young offspring, even if it is dead. The calf usually stays with its mother for about two years, though it takes eight years for sperm whales to fully mature and about 45 years to grow to their full length. They may live to be 75 years old. Their diet consists mostly of squid and octopus.

Many in the world have known about the sperm whale, but relatively few have known about the God of heaven. He put us here to help the world learn about Him, but He also wants *us* to know more about Him too. Take time in your busy schedule to read and understand more about God. Ask Him to help you understand His Word today. It is a good spiritual diet.

KEMP'S RIDLEY

But be ye glad and rejoice for ever in that which I create. Isaiah 65:18.

Have you ever heard of Kemp's Ridley? Do you even have an inkling of what it is? The Kemp's Ridley is a species of turtle that lives on Rancho Nuevo beach along the Gulf of Mexico in southern Tamaulipas (tom-ough-lee-pas), Mexico.

The rarest and smallest of sea turtles, 99 percent of Kemp's Ridley has disappeared since 1947. Little is known about these turtles, since there are very few of them and they remain mostly at sea. As adults, they weigh between 60 and 100 pounds. Their color is olive green, and they have an oval heart-shaped shell. The female turtles usually arrive at Rancho Nuevo between April and July. After digging a hole, they lay from 50 to 135 eggs the size of Ping-Pong balls, then return to the sea.

In 1947 a Mexican scientist filmed 40,000 females coming ashore, laying their eggs, and returning to the sea. They did this in less than an hour. Today only 500 to 600 females repeat this process each year. The large *arribada* (arrival) seems to be a thing of the past.

Researchers are trying to save the Kemp's Ridley from extinction. They have prepared artificial nests covered with wire. After the females have laid their eggs and returned to the sea, the researchers put the eggs in these nests. Eighty percent of the eggs now hatch with this process. The incubation time, or the length of time it takes for the baby turtles to hatch, is from 48 to 67 days. If the temperature is below 85°F (29.5°C), mostly males will be born. Researchers know that they can live for a minimum of 20 years, but they do not know the maximum. U.S. marine biologists, with special permission from the Mexican government, are transplanting some of these turtles to the southern coast of Texas, hoping for another nesting area.

It is good that caring people do much to take care of many of God's creatures, especially those in trouble. God cares even more for His created children.

Today, thank God that He cares for you, and that He is interested in protecting you from extinction.

Smooth Stones

The waters wear away the stones; the torrents wash away the soil of the earth.
Job 14:19, NRSV.

s there a child who hasn't gone to the water's edge of a small stream, picked up a smooth stone, and tried to skip it across the water? Well, perhaps there is, for many of you live in cities, where there are no streams. But for many years every time I went near a body of water I wanted to pick up smooth stones and skip them across the surface. It is still fun to see how many times I can make the stone skip across the top of the water.

Have you ever wondered what makes stones smooth? A rock hound—that is, a person who collects and polishes rocks—will pick up the ugliest rocks, put them in a tumbler, and after some time take out beautifully smooth rocks. What has happened? As the rocks roll in the tumbler, the sharp edges are worn off, and they become smooth. In somewhat the same way a stream of water, a small river, or even the waves at the edge of the ocean keep rolling rocks, and over a period of time they become smooth. All of the sharp edges are worn off and the rocks become nice smooth stones. They are made smooth not in a day but over a long period of time. Nature's forces are often slow, but because they are steady they have moved mountains, carved new riverbeds, and created underground caverns.

We as sinners have rough edges caused by sin in our lives. The Lord wants to have all our roughness removed, and one way this happens is through the trials that He allows in our lives. Often they help wear down the rough edges and make us a smooth and valuable "stone."

As we meet obstacles and conquer them, roughness is worn off. As we steadily meet trials and conquer them, our character is polished. God does not promise us a smooth life altogether, but He does promise to be with us and help us through the trials.

Ask God today to be with you as you go through the day. As the trials come, with His help you will be able to meet and overcome them.

EVERGLADES

In my Father's house are many mansions: if it were not so, I would have told you. I go to prepare a place for you. And if I go and prepare a place for you, I will come again, and receive you unto myself; that where I am, there ye may be also. John 14:2, 3.

In the southern part of Florida in the United States is a swampy marsh area called the Everglades. This has been home to thousands of species of birds, mammals, reptiles, and amphibians, as well as many species of plant families. More than five feet of rain falls here every year. Until a few years ago the Everglades kept itself in balance. Then housing developers came into southern Florida to build houses so that people could live there. The things they did to make the Everglades livable for people cut its wildlife habitat to about half what it was.

According to one national park biologist, the Everglades are now an area of extremes. There is either too much water or not enough. Engineers have rerouted the flooding from the large Lake Okeechobee so that the "natural" flow of water from this lake is no longer natural. A large canal has been built to handle the floodwaters. This has at times brought drought to the Everglades and at other times, flooding.

The fight has become a real one. Farmers want to raise their crops, and they don't want any more water directed their way. The biologists and conservationists want to protect the wildlife, so the conflict goes on. Because of flooding, many alligator nests have been destroyed; the nesting birds have not had a normal season in a long time, and the wading bird population has dwindled to a small fraction of what it was in 1930. Some say that the Florida panther is also endangered.

It will be great to get to heaven, where there will be no more conflicts over the terrain, water, and the wildlife. God has promised a place for each of us, and all of the wild and tame animals will be there to enjoy it too. Thank God today that He has prepared a place for you in heaven with the tame wildlife.

April 5

IRAS

And they that be wise shall shine as the brightness of the firmament, and they that turn many to righteousness as the stars for ever and ever. Daniel 12:3.

The infra-red astronomy satellite (IRAS) was launched the night of January 25, 1983, with the hope of finding out more about our universe. Dutch, English, and Americans had a part in this program.

The human eye cannot see infrared rays. These are what cause the sunburn on your skin, and even the clouds don't cut them out. Through the use of the IRAS scientists have discovered that the atmosphere has truly a *lot* of dust particles (causing the varying hues of the sunsets), and that some areas are more concentrated than others. The dust particles may obscure infrared rays.

The 22.4-inch telescope that the IRAS carried operated successfully for 300 days, passing around the earth twice daily. The telescope was surrounded by liquid helium, which cooled it so it could correctly relay the images from space. As it passed over Chilton, England, it sent more than 350 million bits of information down to the computers. It may be years before the scientists complete their interpretation.

Although the telescope relayed information for just one year, the whole universe was opened up to scientists by the IRAS. Among its many discoveries were starburst galaxies, five new live comets, and one dead one. It also showed that the Milky Way emits about half of its energy as infrared, and Andromeda about 3 percent. NASA engineers are now working on a new telescope that will find the nearest starlike objects and the brightest galaxies. This mission is named the Wide Field Infrared Survey Explorer, and astronomers say that "a lot of astronomy books will have to be rewritten when all the results are in." Much will be discovered as knowledge increases until Jesus comes.

Thank God today for the knowledge that He has given us, and that you have the opportunity of participating in this knowledge explosion.

SPICE OF LIFE

You have forgotten God your Savior; you have not remembered the Rock, your fortress. Therefore, though you set out the finest plants . . . yet the harvest will be as nothing. Isaiah 17:10, 11, NIV.

Early settlers to the New World discovered and experimented with all types of plants, looking for spices to season their food. Unfortunately, some of the plants they tried probably poisoned them.

We generally think of most spices as coming from dried leaves that are crushed and put into bottles for serving. This is not necessarily so. Some seeds and some dried fruits are also used as spices. Caraway, anise, coriander, and dill are four spice seeds or fruits. Dill is used in the form of leaves as well as seed.

Many of the spices come from the tropical regions, and many of those from Islands. Cloves and nutmegs came from the Moluccas in the East Indies; for many years they were called the Spice Islands. Cloves are made from the buds of a eucalyptus tree of the myrtle family. Nutmeg is produced from a hard nut, and mace is made from the powdered outer covering of the nutmeg nut. Cinnamon is made from the inner bark of the cinnamon tree. Ginger is made from the rhizome of a tropical herb.

For many years herbs have been used by witch doctors and other kinds of native healers to try to dispel a sickness or a devil from a person. How they decided on which herb, I do not know. Each tribe (and in some tribes, even each village) uses a different herb for the same purpose. Anise seed was believed by some to avert an evil eye. Coriander and fennel were used to summon the devils. Din was an herb used in casting spells and was also used to protect against a witch's spell. Sage was thought to give wisdom and life.

God is the greatest "sage" this world will ever know. He planned everything and knows everything. We can go to Him for all of our answers.

Thank Him this morning that He is the all-wise God and that He will listen to you.

April 7

WILD BURROS

Who makes the wild donkeys wild? I have placed them in the wilderness and given them salt plains to live in. Job 39:5, TLB.

Back in the days when horses and donkeys were used for transportation in the United States some of the animals got away or were turned loose. Today their descendants live on—herds of wild mustangs and many wild burros. The little burros are a hardy breed, and have lived in the deserts so long that they seem to be immune to disease.

In their struggle to survive in the dry, barren deserts burros eat just about anything. Nothing is left for farm or ranch animals to feed on. Bare of any vegetation, the overgrazed desert soil erodes easily, effectively destroying the land. Farmers and ranchers, as well as national park rangers, are troubled, and a conflict has arisen. Groups of concerned citizens want the wild herds left intact, while those whose livelihood is threatened by overgrazing want to shoot some of them to reduce the herds. So the struggle continues.

Wild burros have an average life span of 25 to 30 years and need very little water. In fact, they can go for about 24 hours without any water. They can smell water almost as far off as a camel can, and they'll dig for it, which a horse will not do. Because of the hardiness of these creatures, a foal (baby donkey) born to a jenny (female burro) usually survives.

Around 350 burros live in the Grand Canyon. Others live in California, other parts of Arizona, Nevada, and New Mexico. They are not really wild, but domesticated burros gone native. To help with the problems, these burros cause, the National Park Service has started an Adopt-a-Burro program, and approximately 1,600 have been adopted out.

Many of us run around this world just as these wild burros do, tearing up things, especially our own bodies. We can survive for a while, perhaps, but help is greatly needed. Ask God to send His angels to be with you for a good day today.

BIRCHES

Beware of false prophets, which come to you in sheep's clothing, but inwardly they are ravening wolves. Matthew 7:15.

Many birch trees have white bark—the bark that Native Americans used to make their canoes. Birch bark is very beautiful, and these trees are sometimes called the ghosts of autumn.

As the fall of the year comes around, these white-bark trees with their colored leaves are a beautiful sight to behold. One photographer-writer said that as he walked through the woods of Vermont he could classify the different trees by a characteristic. The poplars are opportunists, because they are quick to take advantage of the situation. They grow fast. The maples are selfless providers, with their sugar and good firewood. The elms are autocratic and elegant, but a hard, tough wood to cut. And the birches are elusive and standoffish, he said, because they make you stand in awe as you look at them.

On a Pathfinder Camporee in the Southern New England Conference, two Pathfinder boys helped us find a tree that would serve as a good flagpole. We found a lovely birch, and one of the boys volunteered to go up and string the rope. He was about 20 to 25 feet up when suddenly the tree broke. My heart dropped to my toes, but the Pathfinder hung on to the tree, and it came down gently. We were able to catch him, and he was not hurt. It was then that one of the directors who lived there told me that white birches will rot on the inside while the outside remains unchanged. No one can tell from the outside that the inside is rotten.

Some people look good on the outside but are "rotten" on the inside. Their characters are not what people see. Inside their minds they are selfish, angry, or perverted. They pretend to be something they are not.

Look into your own life today and see if there is any "rottenness" in it. If so, ask Jesus to help clean it up today. Don't wait to do it. Only those whose lives are kept clean by Jesus will reach heaven and be there throughout eternity.

LET YOUR LIGHT SHINE

Let your light shine before others, so that they may see your good works and give glory to your Father in heaven. Matthew 5:16, NRSV.

In a little farming community in the state of Kansas there were only a few stores. As it happened, a variety store and a jewelry store stood side by side on the main street.

The window of the variety store displayed a sample of almost everything it had for sale in the store. What a clutter! There were watches and can openers, candy and clothes. Paper dolls leaned against irons and skillets. Fabric, needles, and thread fought for space with hammers, saws, and nails. The owner wanted to make sure people would see the very thing they wanted and would come into the store and buy it. But so many items filled the store window that it was hard to focus on any one thing.

The display window of the jewelry store was a total contrast. The owner of the jewelry store had carefully thought through what he wanted to display in his window. He took some deep-purple velvet cloth and lined the walls and floor of the display area. Then he took eight pieces of wide white ribbon, and from each of the eight corners, top and bottom, he ran the streamers to the center of the display. In the center, where all the streamers met, he put a small white box lined with purple velvet. In the center of that purple velvet he put a beautiful diamond. Out of sight, he also installed a spotlight. The diamond sparkled as it reflected the light.

As people walked down the street and looked into these two windows they saw a great contrast. One display was cluttered and confusing. The other was simple and beautiful.

Our lives can be like either of those two windows. They can be cluttered with sin, or Jesus can be the center, shining forth from our lives.

Can your friends see Jesus in you? Do they see kindness, truthfulness, thoughtfulness, or a life cluttered by selfishness, dishonesty, laziness, and rebellion?

Ask God to help you be a precious diamond reflecting the light of Him. Let your light shine for Jesus to everyone you meet.

ANIMAL DEFENSES

Thy word is a lamp unto my feet, and a light unto my path. Psalm 119:105.

God created the creatures of nature with many ways of defending themselves. Because of the many varieties it's impossible to consider all of them at one time, but today we will consider a few.

Some insects blend into their surroundings. You might see something that looks like a twig move. But should you touch it, it suddenly *becomes* a twig. In actuality, what you've touched is a walking stick, a master of disguise. You may see a moth fly by and land on the bark of a tree. But when you look for it, you don't see it, for its coloring makes it blend into the bark. Have you been outdoors looking for different things in nature, picked up what you thought was a pretty light-green leaf, and discovered a katydid in your hand?

The ptarmigan bird, arctic fox, short-tailed weasel, and snowshoe hare all turn white for winter, and so camouflage themselves so predators can't see them. Skunks send off an odor to keep their enemies away, and not many animals are interested in getting tangled up with them. You've no doubt heard about the porcupine and its quills. Then there's the opossum and hognose snake, which, as their defense, pretend to be dead. Some moths and butterflies have large eyelike spots on their wings to keep away birds that would want to eat them. An owl will ruffle itself up so big with its wings and feathers that its enemies will leave it alone, thinking that it is much larger than it is.

God gave not only the creatures of the natural world defenses from their enemies; He also gave you and me a defense against our enemy, Satan. He gave us His Word to read and store in our minds. When Satan tempts you, you can say as Jesus did, "It is written," because you will know what the Bible says. Then, too, always remember that the devil flees when you pray for help.

Ask God to help you in your study and prayer to get your defense up against the enemy.

STRANGE PLAYMATES

But I say to you, Love your enemies and pray for those who persecute you.
Matthew 5:44, RSV.

Have you ever heard of the word "mutualism"? This is a scientific word meaning "I'll scratch your back if you scratch mine." In other words, if you do something for me, I'll do something for you.

In Arabia there are several species of butterflies and ants that have an interesting relationship. The butterflies belong to what is called the "blues" family. When a butterfly egg hatches, a small caterpillar emerges. As the caterpillar grows, it changes its skin five or six times. It can do little more than eat and grow.

The caterpillar is vulnerable to many enemies, especially ants, but there is one kind of ant that likes having the blues caterpillars around. You see, these caterpillars have a special gland on their backs that secretes a liquid similar to honey. The ants thrive on this honey. So they look for the blues caterpillars and eat its honey. At the same time these ants protect the blues caterpillars from parasitic wasps and assassin bugs.

These caterpillars actually need the ants. If the honey they produce is not eaten, mildew develops on the caterpillar and kills it. And so it happens that the ants drag or carry the blues caterpillar into their nest. There the caterpillar eats the immature ant eggs, and the ant eats the caterpillar honey.

The caterpillar goes into a cocoon and comes out a beautiful butterfly. These butterflies are all colors of the rainbow, not just blue.

Jesus told us to love our enemies. We are to pray for them. Today I urge you to ask Jesus in your prayer to help you love your enemies. Ask Him to help you treat and talk to them in a nice way. That will be sweet honey to them, and they will not be able to resist you. If you have unkind classmates, ask Jesus to help you love them today.

WALRUS

Which he will manifest in his own time, He who is the blessed and only Potentate, the King of kings and Lord of lords. 1 Timothy 6:15, NKJV.

The monarch of the arctic seas is the walrus. This large seallike animal has two large tusks that hang down from its top jaw. Both the male and female have these ivory tusks.

Walruses weigh from 1,500 to 3,000 pounds and are about nine to 12 feet long. At birth the baby walrus is about four feet long and weigh 130 pounds. The female has one calf every two or three years, and she may nurse each calf for two years. The mother walrus will do anything to defend her calf, even giving her own life to protect it.

These large creatures have stiff bristly hairs on their snouts. They use their large tusks to dig up food from the shallow bottoms of the ocean, usually less than 300 feet deep. When they're not eating, they lie around on ice floes. God created these creatures with very strong back teeth, strong enough to crack the shells of the mollusks that they eat.

Walruses enjoy one another's company. It is not uncommon to find hundreds of them living together, and as many as 2,000 have been counted in one herd. Eskimos hunt the walrus for their meat, ivory tusks, and skin. The ivory brings a very high price in today's market. The skin makes good leather goods and boat hulls because it is almost hairless.

Walrus are not great long-distance swimmers. Though they can swim quite rapidly for short periods, they must then stop and rest, either on land or ice. Otherwise they will drown from fatigue. Swimming in the cold arctic water would be enough to tire anyone out! Polar bears are their only real enemies, and they put up a good fight with them. Usually it's to protect their calves.

As the walrus is recognized as the monarch of the Arctic, so we should recognize Jesus as monarch of the world and of our lives. He will soon be recognized as "King of kings and Lord of lords." Today, recognize Him as your king. Give your life over in service to Him.

ICE

Wait on the Lord: be of good courage, and he shall strengthen thine heart: wait, I say, on the Lord. Psalm 27:14.

You can walk on it, skate on it, suck on it, and preserve foods with it. You can drill a hole in it and fish through it. What is it? Ice! As water temperature gets below 32°F (0°C), it begins to freeze. As ice is formed, it expands and increases its volume by one eleventh. This is one of the reasons ice is lighter than water and floats.

Ice is used for many things today, but chiefly to preserve food. Though in Bible times most people rarely saw it, ice is almost a necessity for modern life. Many years ago American settlers living in cold climates used large saws to cut huge blocks of ice from frozen lakes. These were stored in sheds insulated with sawdust, called ice houses. Besides making drinks cold, ice is used to freeze milk and sugar into ice cream, treat sports injuries, and keep many substances (such as insulin) fresh.

But ice can also be dangerous. When water pipes freeze, expanding ice can break the pipes. Icebergs have sunk ships, the *Titanic* being the most famous. Icy roads cause accidents and death, and ice-covered sidewalks can also be dangerous.

Ice forms on water from the top down, so living things in the water under the ice can survive. Ice actually keeps some warmth in deeper water. If ice formed at the bottom of lakes and froze upward, most creatures in the water would die.

Ice was not part of God's original creation. Sin altered God's plan, but God took these alterations and made them work for the best. In life we make many decisions. Some of them are not wise, and would not have been made had we let God lead. However, God has the power to override bad decisions and bring good things out of them, if we ask Him to do so.

Ask Jesus to come into your life. He will warm you with His love. Invite Him into your heart. Let Him melt the iciness of sin and fill your life with the warmth of His love. Ask Him to help you radiate His love in everything you do today.

ICEBERGS

Do not put your trust in princes, nor in a son of man, in whom there is no help.
Psalm 146:3, NKJV.

We talked about ice yesterday and how it can be good for some things and bad for others. Today let's continue to talk a little more about ice.

Icebergs are found in the Arctic and Antarctic, very cold regions. They are formed where glaciers meet the sea. Immense chunks of ice break off the glaciers and drift away. Icebergs float on the water with only about one ninth of their bulk above the surface. Scientists know of icebergs 400 feet tall, yet only one ninth of them shows above the water. Imagine the massive amount of ice hidden under the water's surface. This is what makes them very dangerous to ships, especially at night, when they cannot be seen.

Radar picks up many things on the ships' receiving units, but icebergs are only frozen water. They have no metal or minerals, so the radar cannot readily recognize them.

On the night of April 14, 1912, a ship named the *Titanic* was near the Grand Banks of Newfoundland. It was the ship's first voyage, a ship said to be unsinkable. It had a strong steel hull and many other features that made it "the safest ship afloat." On that fateful night, as many on board were drinking, dancing, and celebrating, the *Titanic* hit an iceberg, ripping a long horizontal gash in the ship's hull. The *Titanic* sank rapidly, taking 1,513 persons to a watery grave. An indestructible object met an iceberg, which unfortunately destroyed the indestructible.

We cannot put our hope, faith, trust, and confidence in humans and what they make. All that we can make is destructible. Only God can make something indestructible. We must not put our trust in the things of this world. Put your trust in God today. Ask Him to help you be indestructible to Satan.

SNAIL KITE

Man does not live on bread alone, but by every word that comes from the mouth of God. Matthew 4:4, NIV.

In the marshlands of southern Florida lives a beautiful bird called the snail kite. The male is a dark gray, while the female is buff. These birds have been diminishing in number because of the development of southern Florida for houses and industry. The wetlands are being filled in and inhabited by humans instead of birds and animals.

The snail kite has only one item on its menu—the apple snail. These snails live only in the wetlands of Florida and a few other places, such as Cuba and Central and South America. Where the apple snails live, so do the snail kites. The kites must eat about 50 snails a day to stay alive. They go into the marsh and grab a snail with their long narrow talons. Flying up to perch on a limb, they use their pointed, curved beak to pry out the snail without breaking the shell.

The snail kites build their nest among the cattails or on some smaller plant. Male and female work together and build the nest, and both parents will sit on the nest to incubate the three buff-colored, spotted eggs. When the eggs are about half incubated, one of the parents will leave and build another nest. They seem to be saying, "We'll have a spare nest, just in case something happens to this one." So they often incubate two nests of eggs and, if no predator disturbs the nests, on the average they hatch two out of three eggs.

To ensure the diet of the snail kite—and so keep it from extinction—the U.S. Fish and Wildlife Service spent $2 million to build water-filled impoundments in which to raise apple snails. An electric utility company was required to spend $700,000 to reroute one of its high-tension power lines so as not to molest the kites' nesting area.

Snail kites must eat apple snails. To keep us spiritually alive, we must "eat" His Word—the Bible. Ask God to help you with your spiritual diet today.

DRAGONS OF KOMODO

These also shall be unclean unto you among the creeping things that creep upon the earth; the weasel, and the mouse, and the tortoise after his kind, and the ferret, and the chameleon, and the lizard, and the snail, and the mole. Leviticus 11:29, 30.

You may wonder why God said that none of the creatures listed above are to be eaten, why they are considered unclean. After the Flood, when there was no vegetation on the ground, God was very specific concerning the animals people might eat. I do not question God, because He made our bodies and He knows what is best. Unfortunately, many people are not aware that God says that certain animals are clean and others are unclean. Because of necessity, some people eat whatever they can find while others eat whatever they want, ignoring God's command.

The world's largest lizards live on a few small Indonesian islands. One island is called Komodo (koe-moe-doe), from which they get their name. These lizards are members of the monitor family that we talked about on January 25. They can grow to about 12 feet long and weigh 300 pounds. They have very long tails and short, stocky bodies.

They were named dragon lizards because they look like the legendary dragons. Their bodies are covered with small dull-colored scales, and they have large claws used for digging caves in which they hide during the night. They are daytime hunters, feeding on carrion as well as small animals, which they usually locate with their keen sight and sense of smell. Their open mouths look like caverns with big, saw-like teeth. The inside of the mouth is red. Because there is a lot of flesh on their bodies the islanders hunt them for their meat.

God gave us many good things to eat—grains and nuts, sweet fruits, and a variety of vegetables. And while He said that when necessary, some animals may be eaten, God forbade us to eat things that are bad for us. Some people think He was out of line in doing this. Was He? He made us, didn't He? And we belong to Him, don't we? Therefore He has a right to tell us what to eat and what not to. After all, our bodies should be His temple. Thank God today that He took enough interest in you to tell you what is good for you to eat and what will harm you.

LITTLE HAYMAKERS

Take therefore no thought for the morrow: for the morrow shall take thought for the things of itself. Matthew 6:34.

The pika is a small animal resembling a guinea pig. Its back legs are slightly larger than its front ones. Instead of teeth, these little creatures have a series of bladelike enamel plates just right for cutting vegetation. Twelve species of pikas are found only in northern Asia. Two other species live in the western parts of North America, from Alaska south to the High Sierras in California.

The pikas in North America live in rocky areas, but in Asia they live in burrows in the ground. The pika does not hibernate, but lives throughout the winter down under the rocks or in burrows under a lot of straw. It spends the winter eating the grass, herbs, and shrubs that it has gathered and made into hay during the warmer months.

These little creatures are always planning for tomorrow and the future. As soon as the snow melts and the vegetation greens up, the pika, or "little haymaker," begins to gather green grasses and shrubs. It cuts the grass with its teeth, carries it back to the area of its house, and lays it on the rocks or ground to dry. When it's dried, the pika stores it for the winter. Pikas may gather up to 30 different kinds of food for their winter supply. They need to gather large amounts of food to eat since they have little fat on their bodies and their metabolic rate is high. Their main activity in life is to prepare for tomorrow and the winter.

Although we have a greater purpose in life than just preparing our meals for tomorrow, the pika is a good example of our need to prepare for the future. Jesus told us not to worry about the things of today but to prepare for eternity.

He said, "Seek ye first the kingdom of God, and his righteousness; and all these things shall be added unto you" (Matthew 6:33). He'll take care of you if you prepare for heaven. I want to ask you today: Are you storing up in your mind Bible promises that will prepare you for the future? Ask Jesus today to help you prepare for eternity.

SPEWING VOLCANOES

But the day of the Lord will come like a thief. The heavens will disappear with a roar; the elements will be destroyed by fire, and the earth and everything in it will be laid bare. 2 Peter 3:10, NIV.

Although scientists are often aware, long before the blowup, that a volcano is about to erupt, they do not know exactly when it will happen. They can only warn people that live nearby and hope for the best. There is nothing anyone can do to stop the heavy lava flow or ash fall that usually erupts from a volcano.

In Sicily in 1983 pressure in the active volcano Mount Etna could not hold back any longer and blew up. The people in the nearby surrounding towns were terrified and wanted something to be done. The hot molten lava flowed from the volcano at the rate of 50 miles an hour, disgorging more than 2 million cubic yards a day. (A large dump truck can hold from 18 to 24 cubic yards of dirt at a time.) The lava was engulfing buildings, houses, orchards, and wooded areas, turning them into an inferno. Naturally, the farther it flowed, the slower it moved.

Large bulldozers were brought in, and men worked frantically to save three towns. A team of explosive specialists came to see if they could use dynamite to divert the flow of the lava. They tried, but had many problems. The heat of the lava detonated their explosives before the workers were ready to use them. They finally worked out a method, but it did not change the course of the lava flow very much. It seems that once lava begins to flow, it takes its own course. They did save the towns, but it was a very difficult task.

We know that Jesus is coming, but we do not know the exact time. No one will be able to stop His coming. Many will weep or shout in anger. Many will cry to be hidden from His view. Pray that when you see Jesus coming, you will look up in joy and say, "This is *my* God. I have waited for Him, and He will save me."

SNOWFLAKES

All things were made by him; and without him was not any thing made that was made.
John 1:3.

Some of you have never seen snow, and others of you may be glad that it's finally melted. But whether you love it or hate it, I think you'll admit that it can be beautiful. And snow is an interesting phenomenon. Scientists are still trying to figure out exactly what causes snowflakes to form. We do know that an ice crystal forms when dust particles come in contact with water molecules. As more vapor freezes on the crystal, it grows bigger and bigger. And there you have it—a snowflake. Though most snowflakes have six points, no two are alike.

One scientist spent several years using mathematical formulas to figure out how snowflakes form. By analyzing the physical laws that control the process of water forming into an ice crystal, then formulating the mathematical equations of growth for a make-believe snowflake, he created a mathematical model that shows the beautiful hexagonal shapes of snowflakes. Just imagine the time spent just to see how things in God's world are made! Yet these complicated processes happen continually. One scientist wrote, "The structures of nature . . . , complicated or simple, all seem to be controlled by the mysterious process of pattern formation." Where do *you* think this mysteriousness comes from?

Nature can seem mysterious until it's understood, but Christians know that God created this world and everything in it. He spoke, and it came into being. In 1856 a man named Henry David Thoreau put it this way: "How full of the creative genius is the air in which [snowflakes] are generated! I should hardly admire more if real stars fell and lodged on my coat."

God made each of us different from one another. We are all unique. There is no two of us alike. Scientists can't explain it, but God can. Thank God today that He made you a unique person. You are the only one of your kind. Enjoy being you.

JACKRABBITS

And the hand of our God was upon us, and he delivered us from the hand of the enemy and from ambush along the road. Ezra 8:31, NKJV.

Several kinds of hares (rabbits) live in the United States, but the jackrabbits are outstanding because of their very large ears. The black-tailed jack has black tips on the ears, and the top of its tail is black. The white-tailed jack has, of course, a white tail, and is probably the fastest and largest of the jackrabbits.

The jackrabbit's original name was jackass rabbit, named after the long ears of the jackass, or donkey. Eventually the name was shortened to jack. The long back legs of jackrabbits enable them to jump easily over a five-foot object as they run. They are able to dodge very easily also.

Most jackrabbits live on the plains. Years ago, when the early settlers came to the western United States, they killed off the coyotes and other jackrabbit predators. When the increased jackrabbit population began devouring their gardens and crops, the settlers built large corrals and drove the rabbits into them, killing them. On one such drive in southern California more than 20,000 were killed. Even today at the Los Angeles airport many jackrabbits are run over by planes. The carcasses attract buzzards, and the buzzards are very dangerous to the airplanes.

Signs in the state of Wyoming warn travelers to beware of "jack-elopes." The picture shows a huge jackrabbit, a cross between hares and antelopes. Of course it's a joke. There is no such animal. However, in Arizona and northern Mexico is a real animal called the antelope jackrabbit. Its ears are up to eight inches long, and it can make its white underfur move from one flank to another, possibly to confuse predators and give it more time to escape.

Because of their numbers, humans have been one of the jackrabbit's greatest enemies. We have an enemy too. But God will help us avoid him if we will ask Him to. Ask God to help you stay away from the enemy Satan today, and He will.

April 21

MILKWEEDS

Not that we lord it over your faith, but we work with you for your joy, because it is by faith you stand firm. 2 Corinthians 1:24, NIIV.

The common milkweed is well known all over the United States because it is native to America. The early settlers took some of these plants or their seeds to Southern Europe, where the great Swedish botanist Carolus Linnaeus named it. This very common plant has thick, broad leaves that are opposite to each other on stems covered with fine, misty hairs. Milkweed grows to a height of two to six feet. There are about 25 other species of milkweed, but they have somewhat different characteristics.

The common milkweed gets its name from a white sap or milk that the plant secretes. This milk has entertained children and adults alike for generations as a curiosity of nature. Thomas Edison and others experimented with it as a substitute for rubber, but the experiment failed.

North American Indians applied the milk directly on warts and used it in concoctions to control ringworm. It was also used as a remedy for various intestinal disorders, and it was believed that a mixture of milkweed root and marshmallow leaves, steeped in a tea and drank several times a day, would cure gallstones. This same tea was believed to help in cases of dropsy, asthma, and high fever. Most parts of the milkweed plant can be eaten if picked and prepared at the right time. Euell Gibbons in his book *Stalking the Wild Asparagus* tells how to prepare the milkweed plant parts to eat.

I have used the silky seeds that burst from the dried milkweed pod as a background in picture frames in which I mounted butterflies. I removed the seeds and used just the beautiful silk instead of cotton.

God desires that each of us be as useful to humanity as the milkweed. We should look for opportunities to help each other. Ask God to show you ways to be a helper today.

SCARAB BEETLES

"From one New Moon to another and from one Sabbath to another, all mankind will come and bow down before me," says the Lord. Isaiah 66:23, NIV.

Unless you've lived in Egypt or have seen a museum display of items from Egypt, you may not have heard of the scarab beetle. For several thousand years the scarab beetle has been a symbol of the sun, of rebirth, and of life itself. It's associated with the Egyptian god Khepri, who, people believed, pushed the sun across the sky. Much of early Egyptian art shows the symbol of the scarab beetle. It is legendary in Egyptian history.

The legs of scarab beetles are well adapted for digging. These beetles dig a burrow about 12 inches deep near an animal manure or dung pile. When the female is ready to lay her eggs, she rolls up a dung ball, pushes it into a hole, and lays one egg in it. Then she moves on, digs another hole, rolls up another dung ball, and lays another egg. She makes sure that the dung is wet so that when the eggs hatch the larvae can eat the dung and grow to adulthood. The process of hatching to adulthood takes about 30 days. Because ancient Egyptians saw these beetles hatching out of dung they thought they were capable of spontaneous creation.

As the early Egyptians observed these beetles pushing the ball of dung, then seeing the new beetles after a month, they related this process to the sun going down and the moon coming up. Within 30 days there was a new moon and new life! More than 2,500 years ago one Egyptian wrote on a papyrus, "On the twenty-eighth day, which the insect knows to be that of the conjunction of the sun and the moon and the birth of the world, it opens the ball and throws it into the water. From this ball issue animals that are scarabs." Religious and bureaucratic officials used scarab beetles carved from stone to stamp and seal important documents.

From one new moon to another one, we who are faithful will have the opportunity of worshipping the true God, who created life—not a beetle that symbolizes life. Pray that God will help you in your worship of the true God.

GIANT SEQUOIAS

His branches shall spread, and his beauty shall be as the olive tree, and his smell as Lebanon. Hosea 14:6.

As God was willing to bless Israel, so He is blessing the giant sequoia redwoods that grow in California. These trees are interesting. The largest of these trees is in Sequoia National Park in central California. It is called the General Sherman tree and stands 272 feet high. It is about 75 feet to the first limb. Some sequoia are as much as 3,500 years old. Trees this old had been growing nearly 1,500 years when Christ was born. These unusual trees have some natural traits that keep them alive and growing. Their beautiful red bark grows to 12 inches thick. The bark is porous and resistant to decay, disease, and insects. It is also fire-resistant. Because of lightning, fires are inevitable in a forest. Many of the large sequoia have been scarred by forest fires, but they still stand, because their bark saved their lives. It acts as an excellent insulation to protect the tree.

The trees also produce a natural fluid called tannin. This provides the color of the bark and makes the tree insectproof. This is why redwood is so good for outdoor furniture. The redwoods also scatter millions of seeds. God put within seeds the power to germinate and grow when conditions are right, but most of these redwood seeds do not take root.

The roots of these tall redwoods may be 200 feet long, but they lie only about six feet below the surface. Is it any wonder, then, when high winds come, that some of these giants tumble to the ground? These giants also spread their limbs out over many feet in each direction.

God wants you and me to be rooted and grounded in His love and, like the roots of the sequoia, to spread His love widely. Unlike the roots of this tree, we should be rooted deep in His Word. Thank God today for the privilege you have of spreading His love to others. Ask Him to help you study His Word so you will be even more effective.

THE GRUNION RUN

The Lord is good to all: and his tender mercies are over all his works. Psalm 145:9.

It is so interesting that every species of animal life has its own unique ways of doing things. Take, for instance, the grunion fish. These little silvery fish—which grow about six inches long—live in the ocean not too far from the shore. When the females go up onto the beach, in what is called a grunion run, to lay their eggs, the male grunions accompany them. As a female wiggles her tail and digs into the sand to bury her eggs, a male wiggles to the same spot and releases a liquid called milt. The milt runs down through the sand and fertilizes the eggs.

John Olguin, director of the Cabrillo Beach Museum in Los Angeles, says, "We know when the fish will come ashore, but we don't know how they know the correct time. It's possible that grunion have internal clocks—biological mechanisms that enable them to detect minute changes in ocean currents or other aspects of their environment." It happens year after year, from March to August, on certain beaches in southern California and along the Gulf of California. About every two weeks these little fish swim onto the selected beaches to lay their eggs. Some of the grunions lay up to 3,000 eggs at a time.

These eggs must incubate in the sand before the tide can wash them away and break open their transparent membrane sacs. It is only during the nights of the new and full moons, when the tides are the highest, that the grunion run. Interesting, isn't it, to see how God has put His creation in such balance that they work together for each other?

If God can take care of the little grunion, how much more does He take care of you! Pray just now that God will guide you today as He guides the little grunion. Ask Him to help you do what you need to do, just when you need to do it. He guides the grunion, and I know He will guide you, if you will ask Him.

WOODCOCKS

Then many of the Jews which came to Mary, and had seen the things which Jesus did, believed on him. John 11:45.

The woodcock is a plump-looking bird about the size of a robin. Its color is brownish, and it generally lives where there is thick underbrush or in thickets in wooded areas. A nickname for it is the timberdoodler, because it spends so much time in the thickets. Woodcocks are difficult to see. They are described as mysterious, sly, and reclusive. In fact, some people don't even believe that they exist.

A woodcock's bill is quite long for its size, about two and a half to three inches. It's used to get earthworms, the woodcock's principle source of food, out of the ground. A woodcock will sit and stare at a person with its bigger-than-usual eyes, but still it may not be seen. Its coloring lets it blend into its environment.

The male woodcock performs a special aerial dance to encourage a female to accept him. He will fly out into the open and then straight up into the air. He hovers for an instant, makes some musical sounds, then dives straight down to the ground. Once he's on the ground you might hear a "peent, peent, peent" noise. The male and female are talking to each other. At times two woodcocks may be doing their high-flying dance at the same time. At other times two males fly at each other. One dodges and goes on his way, leaving the other to keep on with his ritual aerial dance. This usually occurs at dusk, not during the bright daylight hours.

The female lays a clutch of four brown, spotted, buff-colored eggs. The eggs are difficult to see, so they have about a 60 percent chance of surviving. The eggs of other birds such as quail have only a 33 percent chance of survival. Although woodcocks migrate, they fly low and at night, so very few are seen by humans.

God-given instinct tells woodcocks to hide where they won't be seen. On the contrary, Jesus did all of His work out in the open, never hidden, so that all might see and understand. He wants us to believe in Him. Ask Him to help you in a special way in your life.

SALAMANDERS

Jonathan told David, saying, "My father Saul seeks to kill you. . . . Be on your guard until morning, and stay in a secret place." 1 Samuel 19:2, NKJV.

Salamanders look like lizards with their short legs and long tails, but they are not lizards. They belong to the frog and toad class. Most of these little creatures are just three to four inches long. They are more abundant in the United States than in any other country in the world, but Japan can boast the largest salamander—one that's about five feet long. The most well-known salamander is the six-inch-long spotted salamander, which lives in the United States.

Being cold-blooded amphibians, salamanders adapt to the climate around them. They cannot live where it is too severely cold. They spend most of their daylight hours under moist logs, rocks, bark, and leaves. And while most salamanders are land creatures, a few varieties like the water. Some of the water ones never leave the water, but live in it all their lives. One variety actually lives on the bottom of streams and ponds. Also some salamanders grow to maturity in the egg, and only then hatch and venture out. Others hatch small and grow to maturity.

God created salamanders in such a way that if they lose a tail or a foot they can grow another one. I wish that this were possible in humans, don't you? I wish that some of my friends who have lost an arm, a hand, a leg, or a foot could grow another one, but God did not put that ability in our bodies.

During the years that I was a camp director I think the creatures I saw most in summer camps were salamanders. Boys and girls enjoyed bringing the little creatures back to camp in their cupped hands. They found them when they rolled over rocks and rotten trees and lifted up leaves and other debris.

Salamanders like to hide in "secret" places. God, too, is in a "secret" place, a place we cannot see. But soon He will come to this earth and take us with Him to that "secret place." Ask Him today to help you be ready to go home with Him. And pray that it will be soon.

FROST-FREE

"Then you will know the truth, and the truth will set you free." John 8:32, NIV.

For many years scientists have been going into the Antarctic's icy waters, trying to discover what really makes things that live in that extremely cold water tick. For example, there is the ice fish. This fish puzzled marine biologists for many years. How did it survive in the frigid water under the ice? After much research on these fish, scientists concluded that ice fish have a protein in their blood—a type of antifreeze similar to that used in the radiators of automobiles. They believe this protein is what keeps the fish's blood from freezing.

Scientists are not sure why some of the other antarctic creatures do not freeze to death. One scientist captured a sea spider, small shrimplike creatures called krill, and a giant isopod. In the laboratory he discovered that unlike the ice fish, these creatures do not have the antifreeze protein to prevent freezing, but they have an extra amount of salt in their blood. He believes that this extra amount of salt is what keeps the animals from freezing.

Scientists are still trying to unlock the mysteries of the Antarctic. As one scientist put it: "We could study for a lifetime and never unlock all of the secrets of this ice world."

Since there was no ice or even deep cold in the original Creation, God must have made some adaptations in the creatures that now live in this world changed by sin. It was when sin entered that God placed into action the plan of salvation, which was a change in His original plan.

Jesus died that we might be free from sin. And that freedom would bring a new life throughout all eternity. As Jesus changed His plan and gave life to the creatures in the Antarctic, so He changed His plan and gave to us the plan of salvation, that we might live.

Thank God in your prayer today for that wonderful plan that brings to you a new life in Christ Jesus, free of sin.

PRECIOUS STONES

And the merchants of the earth will weep and mourn over [Babylon]. . . . The merchants . . . will stand . . . , weeping and wailing, and saying, "Alas, alas, that great city that was clothed in fine linen . . . and adorned with gold and precious stones and pearls!" Revelation 18:11-16, NKJV.

Precious stones or gems come in all colors, some more valuable than others. We have already talked about pearls, which come from mollusks, and coral, from sea creatures. Amber comes from the resin of fossil trees, and jet from fossil coal. Today we're talking about gems. These minerals that look like pretty stones are usually found lodged in other rocky substances.

Color determines not only the beauty of the gem but its value. There are two types of color: essential and nonessential. The true color of the gem is called essential. The nonessential is color resulting from some impurity.

The degree of hardness is what determines whether it a colored rock or a true gem. Minerals are classified by hardness on a scale of 1 to 10, with 10 being the hardest. Diamonds are a 10. In order to be classified as a gem, the rock must be a hardness of 7 to 10. At this hardness it cannot be cut with a knife or scratched by glass. Diamonds are rated 10, and are sometimes used as a cutting tool.

Opal and turquoise are found where there is very little moisture— in the southwestern United States and in Tibet. Emeralds, topaz, and tourmaline are found where erosion has exposed the old, once-molten rocks at the surface. Topaz comes from Germany and Russia, but the best specimens are found in Brazil. The best rubies come from Burma, the best sapphires from Kashmir, the best diamonds from Africa, and the best opals from Australia. Value of the gems is determined by color, rareness, demand, hardness, and brilliance.

God tells us that He will build a more beautiful city with even more beautiful and precious stones than we have ever seen. Thank Him for the beauty in the rocks and minerals today.

The Praying Insect

Keep watching and praying, that you may not enter into temptation. Matthew 26:41, NASB.

When I was a boy, my uncle, who was living with us, found some egg cases in the field beside our house. He put them on his windowsill, saying that he didn't know what kind of insect they were, but that maybe we would soon find out. One day he arrived home from work and entered his room. Soon he called me. I went running and saw little green creatures all over his window screen, window, desk, and bed. There were hundreds of them—all over the room.

"What are they?" I asked.

"These are baby praying mantises," he replied.

"What's a praying mantis?" I asked.

"The praying mantis is an insect about four inches long," he told me. "It has funny stilted legs for walking and two spiny jointed front legs that are used to catch other insects for food. They have a triangular-shaped head with large eyes."

"Why are they called praying mantises?" I asked. My uncle told me that these mantids raise their front feet up in a posture of prayer. The mantis will sit quietly for long periods of time. It is not praying, but waiting for food. Mantises are so still that an insect doesn't know it is there until it is captured with the mantis's two front legs. Although the praying mantis is an enemy to other insects, it is a friend to gardeners because it eats many pests. These insects lose their lives because they did not recognize the enemy.

We have an enemy whose name is Satan. As our text for today says, we need to be on guard so that he will not attack us without our knowing it. He will try to bring many things into our lives to trick us into his arms of sin. We must stay close to the Lord so that we can identify Satan when we see him.

As you pray today, ask the Lord to help you recognize Satan and his ways so that you will not be caught as his prey. God will help you identify him if you will only ask Him.

VINES, VINES, AND MORE VINES

Stand fast therefore in the liberty wherewith Christ hath made us free, and be not entangled again with the yoke of bondage. Galatians 5:1.

It seems that the only place that you can avoid vines is in the middle of a desert. Vines are all around us. Some are useful, and some are poisonous. Others are simply pests. I have a cartoon that shows a little boy at camp standing by the nature director with a handful of vines. "Look at these new vines I found," he's saying. But the nature director is backing away, because the vines are poison ivy.

There are always some who find interesting vines that they haven't seen before, and that is probably because there are so many of them. Vines vary from the size of a thread to as large as a person's body.

Vines usually grow on some other natural object, but rely very much on chance on finding something to grow up on. If there is no rock, tree, or other climbable object, vines will grow horizontally on the ground. For many vines, the upward climb to light is what keeps them alive. Some vines spiral around their object while others use barbs, prickles, hooks, thorns, and aerial roots to hang on to the captive object.

The large vines of tropical rain forests that have a woody texture are called lianas (lee-ann-nas). These are the kind that children like to swing on, and grapevines also belong to this group. Monkeys and other animals in the jungles and rain forests use the vines that extend from tree to tree to walk, crawl, and jump on. Some of you have rattan furniture in your house. The rattan is a good-sized vine that climbs partway up the trees, attaches itself with spines, then goes from tree to tree. Rattan palms grow up to 650 feet long and store drinkable water in them.

As the vines wrap themselves around their victims, so sin wraps itself around its victims. Only the blood of Jesus can set you free. Thank Him for that freedom today. Christ came to earth and died so that sinners such as you and me might be freed from the bondage of sin.

SCULPTURES OF TIME

Great peace have they which love thy law: and nothing shall offend them. Psalm 119:165.

Many stand in awe at the beautiful rock formations they see in caves and caverns. It's a totally different world there deep under the ground. Time seems to have stopped. But time does not stand still in a cave. Usually there are ongoing changes.

Many formations grow through the interaction between water and rock. How the specific forms come about depends on the amount of water in the cave and the type of minerals in the water. In standing water within a cave, minerals in the water precipitate out to form clusters of crystals. These clusters of crystals grow into various shapes and forms and are called cave coral.

We've all heard of stalagmites and stalactites. Stalactites grow from the ceiling down, and stalagmites grow from the floor of the cave upward. Both of these columns are formed by the slow but constant dripping of water. The water evaporates, and the calcium carbonate, or calcite, forms deposits. It's fascinating that you'll find many different types of formations in each cave or cavern. One of the prettiest types of stalactite is the soda straw. As the stalactite forms, the carbon dioxide released from the water "fizzes" away, leaving lovely crystals on the stalactite.

Gypsum crystals finer than human hair have been photographed. These grow parallel to each other and appear like the angel hair that people sometimes swirl on Christmas trees.

Many other formations also grow in caves: mothballs, twisted currents, aragonite crystals, calcite chunks, gypsum flowers, cave pearls, gypsum needles, and crystal bunches. Almost all of these form from calcium carbonate, gypsum, and calcite.

Sadly, sometimes even kids have a hard life. Bad things happen to their families and friends. Perhaps they make poor choices. They shut God out of their lives, and their hearts have turned to stone. But God can bring beauty out of hardness, even as shining crystals form on rocks in caves. Ask Jesus to help you live a happy, peaceful, and satisfied life.

SUNSPOTS

The city does not need the sun or the moon to shine on it, for the glory of God gives it light, and the Lamb is its lamp. Revelation 21:23, NIV.

Sunspots. Are there such things? Yes, there are. When I was using radio for communication, sometimes I could reach certain places that other times I could not. I was told that it was because of sunspots. A policeman in West Virginia was calling on his radio for a helicopter to come and take an injured person to the hospital. But a police radio operator picked up this message in Santa Monica, California, some 3,000 miles away!

Normally these radio messages go out only a few miles. What made the difference? Sunspots.

Sunspots are solar activity that are magnetically enhanced regions of the sun. There are not always the same number of sunspots each day, and there may not be the same each week or month. At times they are more intense than at other times. They run in cycles that last about 11 years. Solar flare explosions and other disturbances of the sun are related to distortions of the solar magnetic field.

Some years ago pilots in a Concorde passenger plane, flying at an extremely high altitude, noticed that their radio system was going wrong. They lowered their altitude and found that it had started working correctly again. Sunspots can do interesting things.

The Bible says that in God's New Jerusalem there will be no need of the sun. The brightness of the glory of God will light up everything. We now depend on the sun for much light and heat, but in the New Jerusalem that will not be necessary. It might be well for us to start to depend on God today and every day from now on, so that when Jesus does come our dependence will have been such that we will continue to depend on Him.

In your prayer today, talk to God about your dependence on Him and ask Him to help you be more dependent on Him.

HURRICANE OR TYPHOON

The Lord is slow to anger, and great in power, and will not at all acquit the wicked: the Lord hath his way in the whirlwind and in the storm, and the clouds are the dust of his feet. Nahum 1:3.

What's the difference between a hurricane and a typhoon, or are they the same? It depends on where you live. Storms that develop over the Atlanta Ocean are called hurricanes, while those that develop over the Pacific and Indian oceans are called typhoons. During the summer the warming of the oceans' water causes a patch of warming air to begin to rise, creating an area of low pressure. As the wake trails upward, it sucks in more air. As the air is warmed, it in turn joins the updraft—creating a tropical depression. At higher altitudes the rising column of warm, moist air cools and condenses into huge clouds that spread outward. The chimney in the center becomes the center of the storm, and as the air rushes inward and upward it begins to whirl. As the whirlwind accelerates, the tropical depression becomes a driving storm. Traveling across the ocean's surface, its winds may increase to more than 300 miles per hour even though the storm itself is traveling only about 30 miles per hour.

Mariners have coined a phrase that helps them predict weather conditions on and near the ocean: "Red sky at night, sailor's delight. Red sky in the morning, sailors take warning."

As Creator, God understands when storms develop over the ocean or in our lives, even in the lives of juniors and teens. God longs for us to make Him our protection during stormy times and always. It is not His will that any should perish. That is why He holds back the storms of total destruction. But the day is coming, and I believe soon, that Jesus will return, and the earth will be destroyed.

While there is time He continues to warn us—through His Word, events, and even storms. I invite you to make your decision to be with Him throughout all eternity. Ask Him to help you today. You can trust Him, because He is a God who acts.

May 4

DESTROY THE WEEDS?

The field is the world; the good seed are the children of the kingdom; but the tares are the children of the wicked one. Matthew 13:38.

Destroy all weeds? Are all weeds bad? It certainly seems that way, doesn't it? After all, it's a *weed*. But there is good in everything. Let's find out what's good about weeds. Someone has said that a weed is only a plant that is in the wrong place. A tomato plant in a row of beets might be a weed because it doesn't belong there.

Granted, there are good weeds and bad weeds. However, even the bad weeds can do good. Bad weeds will hold the soil, keeping it from blowing or washing away. Their tough root systems break up the hard ground. Some weeds have such deep roots that they bring minerals up toward the surface of the ground. Other plants use these nutrients to live on. Then some so-called weeds are used for medicines, dyes, and other useful purposes.

Think about the beauty found in many of the plants we call weeds. Look at the thistle's beautiful purple flower and the lovely yellow flower of the dandelion. The blue flower of chicory brightens our roadsides. The yellow flower of mullein and motherwort's pink flower add beauty to our world. And the delicate white lace of Queen Anne's lace reminds us that summer will soon be over. Many weeds have a very deep root. You can chop them down, but they will continue to come back. Unlike most cultivated plants, most weeds tolerate a lack of water and care. For most of us, weeds are just a pest. They serve no purpose. Yet they return year after year.

Have you noticed that shortly after a piece of ground is abandoned, weeds begin to grow? It's evident that weeds need no care to be able to flourish. They can spring up and grow almost anyplace, while cultivated plants need tender loving care to survive.

The devil lets those who follow his leading just grow on their own. But we who follow Jesus are given the tender loving care needed for survival and for eternity. All of us have value in God's eyes. Ask God to help you be a true plant in His love, and not a weed of the devil.

131

May 5

SOME YELLOW JACKETS STEAL

Our inheritance has been turned over to strangers, our homes to aliens.
Lamentations 5:2, RSV.

Yellow jackets are small wasps. They are very aggressive little creatures, and will even buzz over to share your picnic lunch.

Yellow jackets usually build their nests in underground caverns. They attach the nest to the top of the cavern. The nest is made of a soft paperlike material that is—in fact—chewed-up wood mixed with the saliva of the yellow jacket, spit out, and formed into the desired shape.

Yellow jackets live in a colony, made up of one queen and many workers. The new queens mate in the fall of the year, then hibernate throughout the winter. As spring approaches, the new queens fly around seeking new homes for themselves.

Studying the habits of yellow jackets, scientists discovered that there are really two kinds, the *Vespula squamosa* and the *Vespula maculifrons*. For simplicity, let's refer to these as yellow jackets A and B, respectively. In the nests of the yellow jacket A, scientists discovered some yellow jacket B eggs. However, they found no yellow jacket A's eggs in yellow jacket B nests.

As researchers continued their study they found that the yellow jacket A queen let a yellow jacket B queen enter her nest. The yellow jacket B queen took advantage of her welcome and laid a few of her eggs there. Then the daughters of the yellow jacket A queen took over and nurtured the yellow jacket B queen's young along with their own.

As we live a Christian life, doing things the way God would have us do, the old devil, Satan, tries to sneak in and put his pleasures—instead of God's—in our lives. Things that will take us away from God. He tries to lead us into the paths of sin and to entice us into places we ought not to go, trying to kill our spiritual experience. He does not want you and me to have the heavenly home that Jesus has prepared for us. Pray today, asking Jesus to help you keep Satan out of your life. Jesus is waiting for your invitation today. Invite Him into your life now.

QUIET HUNTERS

Now do not let my blood fall to the ground far from the presence of the Lord. The king of Israel has come out to look for a flea—as one hunts a partridge in the mountains. 1 Samuel 26:20, NIV.

Animals in the cat family are many different sizes and colors. For the next few days we will look at several of these silent hunters, those largely from the Asian area, where many of them live. They roam over the southern part of Russia and the northern part of India; throughout the countries of Nepal, Pakistan, eastern China, Java, Sumatra, Borneo, Tibet, Burma, and Thailand; and the island of Iriomote, which is the southernmost of the Japanese Ryukyu Islands.

Twenty different kinds of cats live in this wide area. You are, of course, familiar with the tiger, probably the most famous and the one that receives the most attention. But many other cats live in tiger territory, quietly going about their business. We will look at them from the largest to the smallest.

Asian lions, known as the king of beasts, once made their home from the Middle East to India. Now only a little more than 200 live in the dry teak woods of the Gir Forest in Gujarat, India (another 200 are in zoos worldwide). Lions are the only cats that live in groups.

Three species of leopards live here: the spotted, the clouded, and the snow. The spotted leopard is the most noticeable in Sri Lanka, with the black being more prevalent in the tropical rain forests. There are relatively few snow leopards and spotted leopards left in the world, as they have been hunted for their beautiful fur. Snow leopards live in the Himalaya, Pamirs, Altai, Kush, and Tien Shan mountains. The snow leopard must eat about 2,000 pounds of food a year to stay alive. It has not been known to attack people, as the spotted leopard has.

When David was being hunted by King Saul, he asked the Lord to watch over him.

Probably you don't have a king hunting you, wanting to take your life, but the devil is still silently stalking his victims. Every morning, give your heart again to Jesus. Ask God to help you not to be one of the devil's victims today.

ASIA'S FASTEST AND OTHER BIG CATS

Do you hunt the prey for the lioness and satisfy the hunger of the lions when they couch in their dens or lie in wait in a thicket? Job 38:39, 40, NIV.

The cheetah is the world's fastest animal. It runs at speeds of more than 70 miles per hour for short distances, enough time to catch its meal. The cheetah is nearly extinct now in Asia, but in the olden days the Mogul emperors of India trained it to hunt game animals for the emperor's table. It is a spotted sleek and slender animal, with long legs.

The clouded leopard of Nepal and Borneo lives in the rain forests and is adept at climbing trees. Spots on its lovely clouded coat resemble the mint leaf, so the locals have given it the name mint leopard. These beautiful leopards sometimes slap their prey off their feet with a forepaw before they move in for the kill.

The lynx is brown with a short bobbed tail. It weighs about 40 pounds and has long, distinctive ear tufts. It generally lives in the forests. The caracal is the size of the lynx, but has a longer tail and slimmer body. It has short tan fur and black ear tufts. In the past, like cheetahs, caracals were trained to hunt. They are the fastest and best-jumping cats of their size. Tragically, they are quickly approaching extinction.

The Asiatic golden cat ranges from Tibet to India and Sumatra. These cats are rarely seen because they do not adapt well where there are humans. They are smaller than the caracal and about the same color. In Burma and Thailand the fur of this cat is burned to keep away tigers, so there it has been named the fire cat.

The fishing cat, from Asia, weighs from 17 to 25 pounds. It is gray, with beautiful patterns on the fur. It lies next to streams and waits for fish to swim by. Quick as lightning, it throws the fish out of water with its slightly webbed paw. Considered a timid cat, it can be fierce.

In today's text God threw a challenge at Job because Job was feeling sorry for himself. Yet God took care of him. We may not get all we want, but God still watches over us.

ASIA'S PRETTY CATS

They tracked our steps so that we could not walk in our streets. Our end was near; our days were over, for our end had come. Lamentations 4:18, NKJV.

Today's text shows an interesting situation that we wouldn't want to be in. Yet that is what happens with the prey of various Asian cats. The jungle cat ranges from the Volga River south to Egypt and east to Vietnam. Although the name doesn't tell us so, it lives in high grass, shrubby plains, and thick brush. Not particularly shy of humans, it lives near villages. It has a beautiful grayish-brown fur and is active in the daytime.

The beautiful marbled cat looks something like the clouded leopard. Its fur is yellowish with black markings that merge together like marble. It is confined to the evergreen forests of Nepal, Sumatra, and Borneo. It is scarce and afraid of people.

The leopard cat, a mini-version of the leopard, is found in the Amur Valley of Russia and from western India to Indonesia. It is the only cat found in the Philippines. In China it's called the money cat because its spots resemble Chinese coins. It is one of the few cats that seemingly mate for life, and is probably the most common cat in Southeast Asia.

In 1967 the Iriomote cat was discovered on Iriomote Island. It is the newest cat in the cat family, and very little is known about it. It has long dark-brown fur and rows of black spots that often merge into bands. It is nocturnal. It's said that there are less than 100 of them on the island, making it the rarest of all cats. The native islanders have discovered that the flesh of the Iriomote cat is very good to eat, so that may cut the number further, if the islanders can find them.

Someday soon, maybe sooner than we think, we may be hunted for our belief in God and the practice of our beliefs. Ask God to help you today to be strong for your faith and for Him. That will help you be strong when the time comes to stand up for God.

ASIA'S SMALLER CATS

You stalk me like a lion and again display your awesome power against me. Job 10:16, NIV.

The desert cat, reported to be a relative of the common house cat, is rarely seen by people. These cats live in the drier areas of northern Africa to the central Asian steppes and in central India. They can adapt to drier climates and droughts by eating insects instead of rodents. They have brownish-yellow fur and look like a house cat. The Chinese desert cat is usually found on the deserts, scrublands, and dry grasslands of Mongolia, eastern Tibet, Kansu, and Szechwan, where tigers have not been seen for many years. It is so scarce that little is known about it. It has light-brown fur with black rings on its legs and tail. It is a very striking cat.

Confined to the northern part of the island of Borneo is the Bornean bay cat. It was first discovered in 1856 and has not been seen much since. It has black tips on the ears and is mahogany in color, or it may be a blackish gray. A beautiful little cat. Pallas' cat, in central Asia, is unique in that it has a large rounded head with both eyes facing forward, and small rounded ears. It has long fur underneath to protect it from the cold ground, as well as short stocky legs and a fat little body. It hunts mostly in rocky areas.

Flat-headed cats are one of the smallest and weigh from four to six pounds. These are found in southern Thailand and Borneo. Their ears are low to the head, thus giving the flat-head look. They live along streams and are excellent swimmers. The smallest of all the cats is the rust-spotted cat. It is about half the size of the house cat, has a soft, fawn gray color, with brown spots and bars on the fur. It lives in the dry forests of India and humid forests of Sri Lanka. Very little is known about this animal.

God hunts us only to show to us His love. Unlike Satan, He does not hunt us to cause us harm. Thank God today that He is interested enough in you to want to be with you.

Barnacles

The Lord reigns forever, your God, O Zion, for all generations. Praise the Lord. Psalm 146:10, NIV.

Scientists want to know how to make it. Dentists want to use it to repair teeth. Others want to use it too, but no one can discover how to make it. What am I talking about? I'm talking about the glue that holds barnacles to any object they decide to attach themselves to. Scientists have analyzed the substances that are in the barnacle glue, but no one has been able to get the right proportions so that they can duplicate it.

Barnacles may attach themselves to a rock that is constantly beaten by waves. It is estimated that barnacle glue can withstand forces equal to a human being trying to stand up in a 300- to 400-mile an hour wind. Yet these creatures remain on one spot day after day, year after year, sometimes as long as 40 years or more.

Barnacles attach themselves to different sea creatures, such as turtles and whales. Sometimes these barnacles remain attached to the same whale for its entire lifetime. In fact, they may outlast the whale. According to sea life specialists, barnacles are choosy as to which surfaces they adhere to. Of the more than 1,500 species of barnacles in the world, each has a preferred surface. Many times they stay permanently, although they can move if they want to.

In Florida, coastal engineers have noticed that barnacles attach themselves to dock posts and seawalls at the surface of the water. The engineers claim that during the last few years the ocean water has risen several feet, thus boosting the theory that our earth temperature is warmer and the ice fields are melting and raising the ocean level.

As barnacles hang on seemingly forever, so God will reign forever. There will be no letting up of His reign of love. There is no end.

Pray that God will help you stick to His gospel, and remain stuck to Him for eternity.

THE RAVEN

The eye that mocks a father, and scorns obedience to a mother, will be pecked out by the ravens of the valley. Proverbs 30:17, NIV.

Three kinds of ravens live in North America, but they all share similar characteristics. They build crude nests of sticks, lining them with animal hair, shredded bark, moss, seaweed, or grass. The nests are usually quite large and located on the top of a cliff or at the top of a large tree. Their eggs are greenish-gray with brown spots, and they usually lay from three to eight. Ravens have a wingspan of up to three feet. A strong and hardy bird, the shiny black luster of their feathers makes them look very impressive.

Ravens have good eyesight and are constantly on the lookout for food. They eat a lot of insects, grain, small rodents, and bird's eggs. They also eat dead animals. When ravens come to a fallen animal, the first thing they do is peck at its eye. God has given them the instinct to know that if the animal tries to cover its eye it is not dead. If the animal does nothing, the raven knows that it is dead and so begins to eat the animal.

Sometimes when young people start to reject their parents and others in authority, it is a sign that they are beginning to die spiritually. There may be good reasons a youth rejects certain people, but he or she should think carefully about that choice. If it is the wrong choice, they are leaving themselves open to Satan's temptations. Satan will look into their eyes, as it were, and if he sees spiritual dying he will work hard to cause a spiritual death.

It's not always easy to do what your parents or teachers require of you. Part of growing up is learning to be independent. But another aspect of maturing is to choose to respect those in authority and to do as they ask. Most often, when you are older, you'll see that you did the right thing.

Don't give Satan a chance to pluck that Christian gleam from your eye. Be the kind of person that you know God wants you to be—kind, loving, and obedient.

THE TOAD WORLD

You are to bring into the ark two of all living creatures, male and female, to keep them alive with you. Genesis 6:19, NIV.

Ot all the creatures that came from the ark when Noah landed safely, some were toads. Today many varieties live in almost every country except Australia, New Guinea, New Zealand, and Madagascar. In Mexico and Trinidad lives a giant toad, about nine inches long. South Africa has the smallest toad, called the rose toad—only about one inch long. A popular toad of England is the natterjack. It has short legs, runs instead of hops, and butts with its head. Then there is an African toad that gives live birth to its babies in a stagnant pool of water. Toads eat vast quantities of insects and so are beneficial. Some even eat snails and slugs.

Toads adapt very well to the temperatures and climates in which they are found. The boreal toad of Alaska and British Columbia does well in colder climates, and the green toad of the Himalayan Mountains lives at elevations up to 15,000 feet. The Colorado River toad is at home in the southern deserts of the United States and the northern deserts of Mexico. Its skin is so baggy that when it grows from tadpole to toad it looks like a fat man who's lost a lot of weight but still wears his old suit. It has to grow into its skin!

Found in the waters of Trinidad is the granular toad. It's covered with warts, but fortunately it doesn't give warts to people any more than any other toad does. This toad even sings under water. Toads singing in the tropical rain forests provide a real musical treat. When we lived in the Amazon jungle I used to lie in bed at night listening to the toads singing their songs. One night we recorded a program in our house to broadcast over the radio. The next night when it played, we heard toads providing a background musical chorus to our program.

I'm thankful that God spared the lives of toads during the Flood so that we can enjoy them and reap the benefit of their insect control. Thank God today for His thoughtfulness. Ask Him to help you enjoy His creation more.

NEW JERULSALEM FOUNDATIONS

The foundations of the wall of the city were adorned with all kinds of precious stones: the first foundation was jasper, the second sapphire, the third chalcedony, the fourth emerald, the fifth sardonyx, the sixth sardius. Revelation 21:19, 20, NKJV.

Today and tomorrow we'll look at the 12 foundation stones that God will use in the walls of the New Jerusalem. Some of these precious stones are more common than others.

Jasper is a mixture of quartz and iron oxide. It comes in many colors, such as green, yellow, brown, black, and red. Sapphires come from corundum and are usually blue. The deeper the blue, the more expensive they are. Other sapphires also exist—the pink sapphire, the oriental emerald, the oriental topaz, and the oriental amethyst.

Named after the town of Chalcedon, Turkey, where these gems were found, chalcedony has been called thunder eggs. There are many varieties of this gem, also called the white agate, as it is semitransparent to translucent. Petrified wood has deposits of chalcedony in it.

Emeralds, in larger sizes, are almost as expensive as diamonds, because they are very rare. Emeralds are usually a pale to a rich green and have a six-sided form. They are a type of beryl, which is usually found in a rocky substance with many layers of pegmatites. Sardonyx is a variety of agate that is a form of quartz or chalcedony and is usually cut flat from layers of banded masses of agate. This is the cheapest of the gems and used widely in jewelry.

The orange-red sardius comes from the iron compounds of chalcedony that permeate the colloidal silica, today known as carnelian. It is used extensively in jewelry.

Why will God use these precious stones in foundations, you ask? Why not? They are beautiful, and He made them. He wants the best for His children. The streets of heaven will be pure gold, so why not make the foundations of the New Jerusalem from precious stones? God is a lover of beauty, and these gems are beautiful. Seek Him today, asking Him to help you so that you may enjoy this beauty forever in heaven.

MORE FOUNDAITON STONES

The foundations of the city walls were decorated with every kind of precious stone. . . .
The seventh chrysolite, the eighth beryl, the ninth topaz, the tenth chrysoprase, the
eleventh jacinth, and the twelfth amethyst. Revelation 21:19, 20, NIV.

Today we read about the other six foundation stones. Chrysolite is a type of peridot or olivine, which is a magnesium-iron silicate. The colors are yellow, brown, and green, the best colors being yellowish green to green. The chrysolite that is yellowish-green is the most expensive of all of the peridots.

Beryl are popular crystals because they are among the largest, some of them weighing up to several tons. Within their gem materials are smaller and more valuable crystals that are slightly harder than quartz. They vary in color from bright grass green to a dull bluish green, yellow, pink, or white.

In early days the name topaz was used to designate the colors from yellow to orange. But some of the topaz colors vary from brown to pinkish-red. Topaz is a mixture of aluminum silicate and fluorine, and one of the hardest of the gems. Some of the crystals are colorless. The largest of the colorless crystals weighed nearly 600 pounds.

Chrysoprase, also a chalcedony, is a combination of nickel and colloidal silica. It is easy to get a high luster from polishing this transparent apple-green gem, thereby making it one of the most beautiful of gems. Jacinth is an orange-colored gem that is probably a sapphire, which is also a corundum. It is a very hard mineral and almost transparent.

The last of the foundation gems mentioned by John is amethyst. It is a quartz and gives a show of zones in its purple color. The large crystals are beautiful as they radiate the zoned look. Interestingly, the best of most of these precious foundation gems come from Brazil. It is a country rich in natural resources.

What a privilege it will be to see all of these precious gems in the new earth and have them all around us. Ask God to help you be faithful so that you can live with precious stones.

PALM TREES

The righteous shall flourish like the palm tree: he shall grow like a cedar in Lebanon. Psalm 92:12.

There are many types of palm trees around the world, and many of these are quite useful. In the country of Israel are beautiful date palms with very large dates on the trees. Date palms are also cultivated in California. The majority of the dates eaten in the United States are grown there.

In the country of Peru, in South America, certain palm trees bear other types of fruit. The aguaje (a-GUAW-he) palm produces a barrel-shaped fruit about three inches long and covered with scales for skin. The Peruvians peel the skin off with their teeth and eat the meat of the fruit, which is only about one fourth of an inch thick. They also make a drink and ice cream out of it.

Brazil, also in South America, has probably the largest variety of useful palm trees. There is the carnauba palm with a very large fan-shaped leaf that produces wax. From these trees companies harvest the wax, which is used on automobiles and wooden floors as well as in some furniture polishes.

Then there's the famous chonta or palmito palm. People cut these trees down and harvest the heart of the tree. This is cut up into pieces or strips like ribbon and cooked or served raw in a salad. It is very good.

From a certain type of palm tree in Brazil, people gather the fruit, squeeze the juice, and make a very nutritious drink called assai (as-SIGH-ee). Still another palm tree produces nuts that Brazilians make cooking oil from.

In His creation God created all types of trees for our use, and people around the world benefit from them. As Christians you and I are to grow, with God's nurture, like the palm trees and bear fruits of righteousness to our friends and neighbors.

Ask God to help you bear fruit to someone today as you associate with your friends.

Shamans and Plants

Fruit trees of all kinds will grow on both banks of the river. Their leaves will not wither, nor will their fruit fail. Every month they will bear, because the water from the sanctuary flows to them. Their fruit will serve for food and their leaves for healing. Ezekiel 47:12, NIV.

Shamans, also called witch doctors or medicine men, are a vital link in the indigenous traditions and rituals among most of South American and many African tribes. The shaman is the central figure of the community. As such, he tells his people what he wants them to do, and because of fear or loyalty, most often they listen and obey.

For years shamans have used various plants to drive out the devil or treat some types of diseases. Scientists realized that perhaps they had valuable knowledge about using plants for medicinal purposes, so many researchers have gone and lived with South American Indians. Gaining their confidence, they have learned which secret plants are used to treat different diseases and physical disorders.

Some years ago, when we lived in Iquitos, Peru, we met Nicole Maxwell. She had come to the Amazon to learn about the medicinal plants used by the Indians. Through her friendships with them they shared many of their medicinal secrets. Nicole wrote a book entitled *Witch Doctor's Apprentice,* telling about these natural plants. While there she fell on her machete, badly cutting her arm. An Indian chief quickly made a brew from a common bark. Nicole drank this, and within three minutes the bleeding stopped. About 1,370 different plants are used by these Indians to treat ailments, most of them successfully. Many large pharmaceutical companies now use and sell medicines developed from them.

Through trial and error Indian shamans helped discover plants that are used today to treat heart failure and leukemia. And modern doctors use as anesthetics some of the poisons the Indians use on arrows, because they do not kill, but temporarily paralyze.

In heaven there will be no sickness, and we will eat those delightful foods that God has waiting for us. Ask God today to help you live a healthful life.

143

ALTERNATIVE ENERGY PRODUCTION

By what paths is the heat spread abroad or the east wind carried far and wide over the earth? Job 38:24, NEB.

During the past few years in the United States people have been trying to produce energy alternatives, and some have discovered some real winners.

Have you heard of the rabbit-heated greenhouse? Bill Schultz, of Grants Pass, Oregon, had a greenhouse that was expensive to heat. He knew that rabbits, with a body temperature of about 102.6°F, generated a lot of warmth. So he bought 400 rabbits, and with the heat radiating from their bodies—about 180,000 BTUs, equivalent to the output of one commercial greenhouse heater—he heated his greenhouse. When the outside temperature was 32°F (0°C), inside his rabbit-heated greenhouse it was a nice 56°F (13°C). Schultz not only got the heat from the rabbits, but also had so many baby rabbits that he sold them to local markets.

In Chicago and many other cities in the United States, commercial firms are burning garbage to produce heat and electricity. With the heat from only 22 percent of Chicago's garbage they are able to heat a large candy factory, a large car garage, and the garbage-burning facility itself. Other areas use cow manure to produce methane, which powers generators that produce electricity. In Henniker, New Hampshire, a factory is producing digesters that enable a farmer to use the manure from his cows for heating purposes.

The large Prudential Insurance Company contracted with a man who brought in a large snowmaking machine and built a 60-foot-high mound of snow by their offices. He covered it with an insulated blanket, and all through the summer the company used the melting water to cool the large building. The company said they saved $12,000 in one year on air-conditioning.

God made so many things that creative people use to make their lives better. Thank Him today for being such a great and marvelous God.

Screaming Demons

See, the Lord has one who is powerful and strong. Like a hailstorm and a destructive wind, like a driving rain and a flooding downpour, he will throw it forcefully to the ground. Isaiah 28:2, NIV.

As you know, forces of nature such as wind, fire, and water can be very destructive. This was not in God's original plan, but, as we have said before, sin changed things in God's world.

The Lord didn't create His world to be damaged or destroyed, but that is the result of sin. As storms go through an area, especially thunderstorms, which can bring heavy rain, wind, and hail, there is the possibility of a tornado. Tornadoes may form during the early stages of fast-developing thunderstorms. How this happens is complicated, but they can occur when a warm, humid air mass meets a cool, dry air mass.

You may have seen a tornado funnel in a photo or in real life. The funnel is a part of the cloud that extends down and may even touch the ground. The air speed whirling inside this funnel may reach the speed of a jet plane, and the funnel itself as it travels along the ground may have the speed of an automobile. It has such force that it destroys much of what is in its path.

A tornado acts like a giant vacuum sweeper. It inhales the air as it goes along, so that when it hits a house or building, the air is sucked out, and the house falls in on itself with the force of an explosion. That is why it does so much damage. It is no fun to be in a tornado. There is an area in the midwestern United States called tornado alley. Many of you reading this today will have actually seen a funnel cloud or have been in or near a tornado. You know what we are discussing. It is a frightening experience.

Soon God will send Jesus back to this earth. When He comes, the earth as we know it will be destroyed. No human will live on this earth after that experience until Jesus makes it new. Don't you want to be in the group that will escape the destruction of this earth, then live forever on the new earth?

Ask God today to help you be in Jesus' group that will live forever in heaven.

145

FIRE IN THE SKY

His lips are full of indignation, and his tongue as a devouring fire: and his breath, as an overflowing stream. Isaiah 30:27, 28.

Most of you have seen an extinct volcano, either a photo of one or the real thing. When I was a child, my parents and I saw several extinct volcanoes during our travels. Also, I have seen many pictures of volcanoes, and they've fascinated me.

While I was living in South America it was my privilege to fly over the Andes Mountains and to travel through the Andes by car, train, and horseback. We even went across Lake Titicaca by boat at night. During those seven years in Peru I always wanted to see an active volcano, but did not have such success.

Several years ago when our family went to the Hawaiian Islands we saw results of active volcanoes. We saw how the lava had boiled out over the top of the mountain and run downhill, covering everything as it flowed. We saw trees that had been flattened and destroyed by the flowing hot lava. We saw a bubbling volcano and smelled the sulfurous gas coming up out of the cracks in the ground and from the bubbling mud. And one evening as we looked from our hotel balcony, we saw fire shooting up into the sky. *Now*, at last, I had seen an active volcano. I was happy that the fireworks were not large enough to destroy property, animal and plant life, and possibly human life. However, later the volcano exploded with a very large eruption and did just that.

As the underground gases get hot and expand, there must be a way to release the pressure. There is, and it's called a volcanic eruption. It's the same in life. Many times we develop a lot of emotional pressure inside. Our friends, parents, and teachers aggravate us until we can't take it any longer and we erupt just like the volcano—spewing angry words out all over the place. But our God of love will help us not to explode if we want His help. In your prayer today, tell God you want your life to be changed. If you often explode in anger, ask Him to help you change. He will do it.

FLOWERS OVERHEAD

Verily, verily, I say unto you, He that believeth on me hath everlasting life. John 6:47.

Almost everyone enjoys springtime flowers that we see around us on the ground and bushes. Who doesn't love the gold of daffodils, the reds and orange of tulips, and the bright faces of pansies? But have you taken time to notice the beautiful flowers that bloom overhead on many flowering trees? Springtime is the time to see many of these beautiful flowers.

We may be familiar with the blossoms of the cherry, apple, peach, apricot, and pear trees, but what about all the other trees that have flowers or flowerlike cones? Some the trees that have flowers on their branches are the maples, oaks, and birches. Flowerlike cones are found on the pine, cedar, fir, and tamarack trees. In order to produce seeds, they must have a flower. Of course, some of these flowers are not large. That's why you have to look for them. According to the information I have, there are about 100 different types of evergreens in the United States and more than 650 broad-leaved trees. With this many trees, a variety of flowers are produced. Some are small and dainty, and others are broad and large.

As you walk underneath the broad-leaved trees you may hear buzzing overhead. These trees depend largely on bees and insects to pollinate them. The pollinators work busily, collecting nectar and spreading pollen. Conifers (evergreens) don't need insects to spread the pollen, but depend on the breeze and the wind.

These flowers add beauty to God's world for only a short time. Imagine when God spoke at Creation and all the vegetation came forth! It must have been like spring all at once. I think that we cannot even imagine the beauty of the Garden of Eden.

Today, thank God for your life. And every day thank Him for the new life that He gives you, waking you each morning. As He takes care of the flowers, so He will take care of you and give you everlasting life.

DWARF MONGOOSES

For this cause I bow my knees unto the Father of our Lord Jesus Christ, of whom the whole family in heaven and earth is named. Ephesians 3:14, 15.

Mongooses live principally in the Serengeti area of Kenya and Tanzania, although some live in Asia. There are 31 species of mongooses, and today we will talk about the smallest, the dwarf mongoose. There is a story about a man who wanted a mongoose for a pet. Then he decided he wanted two of them so that he could raise mongooses. But the poor man didn't know if the plural for mongoose was mongooses or mongeese, and he didn't want to show his ignorance. So he sent a letter to a friend in Africa, asking him to send him a mongoose. Then he added, "While you are at it, send me another one."

Dwarf mongooses are very small, not much larger than a rat, and weigh less than a pound. They live together in colonies or communes and have a dominant male and female as the leaders. The selection of leaders is usually determined by age. Dwarf mongooses live largely on termites and other small insects, and will go into the ventilation channel of an unused termite nest to have their young. During the months of November to May each female will have two to three litters, with a total of up to six young. The young stay in the nest with the mother for several weeks, then go out foraging with mama.

At times, a mother mongoose falls prey to another animal. If that happens, other females take over and nurse the orphaned young. Or there may be in the commune a mother that has lost her litter but is still producing milk. She may help feed the young of another female in the nest. It takes from 12 to 24 months for a mongoose to mature. At that time it may have to leave its commune or pack and go to another one, or try to form a new one.

Like the mongooses, we are to help take care of one another. When one is sick, disabled, aged, or discouraged, we should visit and help them. In fact, as members of God's family we should help one another. Thank God today that you belong to His family.

CORK

And when he had gone a little farther thence, he saw James the son of Zebedee, and John his brother, who also were in the ship mending their nets. Mark 1:19.

For centuries people have used nets for fishing. And one of the things that they required to be successful was cork floats to hold up the edge of the net. History tells us that cork floats were in use as early as 400 B.C. The Romans had another use for cork. They wore cork sandals to keep their feet warm. Later, in the 1600s, cork began to be used as bottle stoppers.

Cork is a lightweight, soft, spongy substance that comes from the bark of the cork oak tree. This tree is a live oak, which means it is green year-round and doesn't lose its leaves. Cork trees grow to about 50 feet high and live from 300 to 400 years. They grow mostly in Portugal and Spain, while the third-largest producer of cork is Algeria.

The outer layer of cork oak bark is composed of dead cells whose thin walls have become thickened and waxy. Trees must be about 20 years old before cork can be harvested. Workers strip the cork, or outer bark, off the tree only once every 10 years. Long-handled hatchets are used to cut the cork into long oblong sections, from the top of the lowest branch to the bottom of the tree. The cork is then carefully stripped off so the inner layer of bark will not be disturbed. The inner layer will not grow any more cork if it is damaged.

Next the cork is boiled to soften it and remove the rough, gritty outer layer. Boiling also dissolves the tannic acid in the cork. Then it is cut to whatever size is needed, and shipped. Cork has been used for many years as insulation in freezers. Linoleum is made by mixing cork powder with linseed oil and spread as a paste over burlap or canvas, and left to dry.

Jesus wants to take the rough skin of sin out of our lives and allow us to grow new fresh skin that produces good works. Ask Jesus to help you get rid of the old skin of sin and grow a new Christian skin, soft with kindness and buoyant with love.

FLY IN THE FRUIT

I will send swarms of flies upon thee, and upon thy servants, and upon thy people, and into thy houses: and the houses of the Egyptians shall be full of swarms of flies, and also the ground whereon they are. Exodus 8:21.

Flies have been a plague since before the days of the children of Israel and Pharaoh in Egypt. The many species of flies have made life miserable for the human family as well as for the rest of the animal kingdom. They remind us of sin.

There is a species of fly that likes fruit, called the Mediterranean fruit fly. Recently in the United States it's become better known as the medfly. This fly is a real pest, and has made things miserable for fruit growers as well as for fruit eaters. These fruit flies destroy the insides of many varieties of fruit and vegetables, including apples, apricots, most citrus fruits, nectarines, peaches, plums, mangoes, and tomatoes.

These pests were discovered in Africa in the early 1800s. As the years passed, they spread to Australia, South America, Hawaii, Europe, and other areas, and were discovered in Florida in 1929. The many attempts that have been made to exterminate them have met with little success, so most countries have just learned to live with them. These tiny flies plant their eggs in the ripe fruit and wait for them to hatch.

Although the females' reproductive period is only about a month, one female in hot areas can lay up to 500 eggs and have about 12 to 13 broods of offspring in a season. These eggs hatch into larvae in a day, and begin to eat the fruit. This ruins the fruit and causes it to drop to the ground prematurely. When the larva is about seven days old, it leaves the fruit, bores a hole in the ground, and nine days later comes out a mature fly, ready to begin the process again. Think of the millions of fruit flies that are reproduced this way.

Could it be that God is trying to tell us, as He did Pharaoh, that His people are going to remain and be victorious over sin? He'll take care of the flies eventually. He'll rid this world of all sin. Thank God for that promise today.

GREAT WHITE SHARKS

So, because you are lukewarm—neither hot nor cold—I am about to spit you out of my mouth. Revelation 3:16, NIV.

Ichthyologists (fish scientists) are still trying to unravel the lifestyle of the solitary great white shark. The reason that they are such a mystery is that no one has been able to keep any of these sharks in captivity for a length of time, and scientists have not been able to study them in the ocean. Great whites go to places and depths where they cannot be followed, and they attack anyone who bothers them. They are usually found along the California coast and around the country of Australia. Scientists are still unsure how to tell their age and how long they live.

Only 33 divers had been attacked during 53 years up to 1985, but that number has increased greatly in the past few years. In almost every case, the great whites, after biting humans, spit the victims out and leave them to bleed to death. They can smell blood up to five kilometers away.

When attacking, great whites zoom toward their victim. About seven or eight feet before reaching the target they open their mouth, roll their eyes to the back of the head, and let their electrical sensing device zero in on the prey. Many times they miss, but the great white is quite agile for its size. The top of this shark's body is dark and its underside is white, making it difficult to detect. Scientists can only speculate how large the babies are at birth. They have never seen one born, but they know that these little calves are born live.

The great white shark seems to have a built-in heater that keeps its body six to 18 degrees warmer than the water it is in. With this added heat it is able to move faster, as the muscles respond more rapidly with a higher temperature.

As scientists desire to know more about the great white, so we should desire to know more about God. He does not want us to be lukewarm, but hot in our Christian experience. Pray that He will help you be a hot Christian, and that you will not be spit out of His mouth, which means to be left out of heaven.

THE VULTURE

There is a path which no fowl knoweth, and which the vulture's eye hath not seen.
Job 28:7.

Vultures fly very high and look for food on the ground. They are known for their ability to spot the carcass of an animal at a great distance. Vultures do not kill for food, but they are the world's garbage collectors (or you could call them recyclers). They eat the carcasses of dead animals.

When we lived in Brazil and Peru, it was against the law to kill vultures, and they were everywhere. Many animals were killed on the road by trucks and cars, and the vultures came in by the dozens and cleaned up the carcasses. There wasn't much left when they finished. According to scientists, these birds seem to be immune to poisons that may have killed the creatures they eat.

There are many species of vultures all over the world. In North America are the black and turkey vultures and the California condor. Vultures have about a four- to six-foot wingspan. It is a beautiful sight to just watch them soar in the sky, for they seldom move a wing. They have a special God-given ability that enables them to stay aloft by catching the rising warm air columns produced by uneven solar heating of the landscape.

Have you ever noticed the head of a vulture? Its head and neck have no feathers. Do you think God in His plan thought about the cleanup crew that would be needed after sin entered this world? If these birds were going to be cleaning meat off the bones of animals and reaching into the carcass with their heads and beaks, feathers would get in the way and not be very hygienic. They may look ugly, but this featherless head is very practical for their way of life.

As the miner digs under the ground for precious minerals and the vulture searches for food, you can dig for and find God's wonderful promises in His Word. Ask God to help you find the promises as you search for these precious truths today.

COUCH'S SPADEFOOT TOAD

But God has revealed it to us by his Spirit. The Spirit searches all things, even the deep things of God. 1 Corinthians 2:10, NIV.

About three feet underground in the Sonoran Desert in Arizona live the Couch's spadefoot toads. These are not just any ordinary amphibian. These toads live under the hot desert sands during the day and come out to feed only at night.

These toads have little spurlike projections on their back feet, which they use to dig their way down into the sand. They await the torrential rains to breed, but these come sporadically and only during the months of April to August. God has given these creatures a built-in alarm clock to tell them when the time is right. They await the vibration of the rain on the desert floor, then tunnel up through the sand at night to the water holes that have been made by the rains. There the female spadefoot lays as many as 1,000 eggs, which the male then fertilizes. By morning the toads have eaten and are back down in the ground to escape the heat. When they are out, they must eat enough to last them for the extended dry periods that they remain underground.

The eggs hatch in record time for any amphibian, about 24 to 36 hours. The tadpoles develop and grow in the 100°F (38°C) pools of water lying on the desert floor. In 15 to 40 days they are fully developed. At that point they are too young to dig, but spend a day or two in cracks. Then they begin to dig into the sand. The young toads that cannot find cracks in which to shelter die of the terrific heat. Those that survive eat like there is no tomorrow and prepare for the long stay underground.

There are many things on the surface and in the depths of this earth that people do not fully understand. In God's Word also there are some tremendous challenges that we do not fully understand. But God is willing for us to understand, and if we will ask Him for the wisdom necessary, the Holy Spirit will provide it. Ask Him today for the power of the Holy Spirit to bring you that wisdom to understand the depths of God's Word.

OOMINGMAK

So Christ was once offered to bear the sins of many; and unto them that look for him shall he appear the second time without sin unto salvation. Hebrews 9:28.

Our title sounds strange, I know, but that is what the Inuit call the musk oxen. *Oomingmak* (o-MING-mack) means the bearded ones. Musk oxen are making a comeback in the state of Alaska. The last of the wild musk oxen on this continent were seen 120 years ago. Desiring to have musk oxen back where they'd once lived, the United States acquired 34 in Greenland and transported them to Norway. From there they were taken to New York, Seattle, and finally Alaska. These 34 were put into a herd at the research quarters of the University of Alaska.

Much research has been done on these creatures since they arrived in Alaska. In 1969 the first musk oxen were taken out to the wilds to live. One researcher was watching them when he saw one making a dash for him. Quickly he thought about what he might do to escape the attack, but decided to stand still and, if necessary, sidestep the charging animal. When the musk ox came to within 50 feet of the scientist it stopped, got down on its front knees, and began to back up. It was later realized that all this "pet" wanted was his head scratched.

Musk oxen are fairly short, probably not more than five feet high. They have long shaggy fur that at times reaches to the ground. Underneath this fur is a silklike hair that scientists say is eight times warmer than wool.

For their defense against attackers such as wolves or wildcats, the musk oxen—usually in herds of 20 to 30—pack themselves in a circle, facing out, with the young calves on the inside of the circle. This way they can fend off the attacker. Predators generally work on one animal at a time to fell it. The musk oxen's method of defense does not permit this, which makes them rather safe from predators.

As the musk oxen have returned to their native home of Alaska, so Jesus will return to His home with His earthly family. Ask God today to help you return home with Him.

UNITED THEY STAND

Behold, how good and how pleasant it is for brethren to dwell together in unity!
Psalm 133:1.

The playful penguins, as they are often called, are very intelligent, are family- and society- oriented, and mate for life. Year after year they make the long trek to the same breeding grounds. The males find their nesting place, and as the females begin to arrive at the icy nesting area, the males make a noise that sounds like *gug-gug-gug-gug-gaaaaaa.* The females seem to know the sound of their respective male partner, and they will slide on the snowy ice toward them.

As the arriving female gets to her companion, the two put their heads side by side, their beaks high in the air, and shout over and over. They seem to be saying, "We belong to each other." Two weeks after they mate, the female lays one or two light-green eggs on the stone nest that her mate prepared for her. As soon as she lays the one or two eggs, she, along with all of the other females, goes out into the water to feed on squid, their favorite food fish, and krill (shrimplike creatures).

If all goes well, the females return to the nesting area in about two weeks. During this time the males have been sitting on the nests, or incubating the single egg by holding it on the top of their feet. A blizzard sometimes comes upon them, but the males will endure it to preserve their families. The male loses about one third of his body weight while incubating the egg and awaiting the return of his mate. This ritual is repeated a second time, with the females going out to feed. They do not stay long the second time, because when they return, the egg has probably already hatched. Then the mother and dad penguins take turns going into the ocean, eating, and bringing back food for the youngster.

Thank God that He loved you so much that He called you out of this world and put you into His body, the church. Thank God today that He has called you to be part of His family.

MANGROVES

For he shall be like a tree planted by the waters, which spreads out its roots by the river, and will not fear when heat comes; but its leaf will be green, and will not be anxious in the year of drought, nor will cease from yielding fruit. Jeremiah 17:8, NKJV.

Mangroves, found all over the world, are an important part of the ecosystem and necessary to preserve the lives of many creatures. They are not the nicest-looking things, but they're very important. A mangrove thicket consists of thousands of trees that grow by the edge of water or in the water. Their prop (aerial) roots project into the water and get tangled up with other roots, until it looks like a tangled mess. This is anything but pretty, but enables new land to form as silt catches and stays near the roots, and debris collects around them.

A mangrove swamp can be a forbidding place. It generally has a spongy mud base. Many thousands of creatures live in and around these mangroves. In some areas (such as in the tropics), there may be up to 50 varieties of trees in a mangrove thicket. The leaf coverage is so dense that it is difficult for sunlight to penetrate it. Mosquitoes buzz all around the place. Because they are unattractive and a bother, people have begun clearing them out to make room for housing developments. But scientists have found that this destroys not only the trees but the breeding and living areas for many thousands of wildlife creatures.

How does a mangrove swamp provide life for so many creatures? Let's look. The droppings from the trees, such as leaves and buds, hit the water and are eaten by tiny organisms, such as plankton, worms, crustaceans, and mollusks. These then are eaten by larger creatures, such as shrimp, mollusks, crabs, and small fish. These in turn are food for even larger water creatures, such as certain fish, birds, and more.

Let alone, these mangroves will last for centuries. When we have a personal relationship with Jesus, the Good Book tells us that we will be as a tree planted by the river. We will be in need of nothing and will bear fruit. That is the way the mangroves are. Today, ask Jesus to help you throughout this day to have a good relationship with Him.

WHICH END IS UP?

A land for which the Lord your God cares; the eyes of the Lord your God are always on it, from the beginning of the year to the very end of the year. Deuteronomy 11:12, NKJV.

Have you ever wondered how plants know which end is up? As a boy I often wondered, when I planted seeds, how it was that the seeds opened and the shoot went up and the roots went down. How did the seed know which way to send the shoots and roots?

Biologists have been stumped for many years as to why the shoots go up and the roots go down. They related this to gravity and called this plant reaction "geotropism." Biologists still do not know how the seeds get their directions straight. The scientist Charles Darwin found that on the roots there is a small cap that acts like a helmet that offers protection as the plant sends the roots digging through the dirt. When the caps were removed the roots became confused. He asked, "Is there a brain inside the little cap that somehow directs the roots?"

In the 1920s a hormone called auxin was discovered that causes the shoots to grow but does not do anything for the roots. Calcium seems to play an important part in strengthening the plant cell walls of the roots, making them stiff and rigid, which enables them to grow downward into the earth.

Scientists now are looking at how auxin reacts to gravity within the plants' cells. As the auxin is pooled in a specific area by gravity, the hormone enhances shoot-cell growth and inhibits root-cell growth, which causes the shoots to bend up and the roots to bend down. Scientists speculate that this is a polarity that comes from electrical charges, which are different between upward and downward growth. As one scientist put it: "It's all speculation, but it's tempting to think that, because of this polarity, a plant always knows which end is up."

Isn't it great to know we have a God who knows, who has designed the seeds with the know-how to shoot the shoots up and the roots down? God is a great Creator. Tell God today how thankful you are to Him for His wonderful creativeness and care.

GOD-GIVEN STRENGTHS

The Lord is my light and my salvation; whom shall I fear? the Lord is the strength of my life; of whom shall I be afraid? Psalm 27:1.

It is not possible to talk about all of the strengths that God has placed in the natural world that He created, but it is fun to look at a few creatures and see just how God created them.

Some of the strongest creatures in God's world are very small. A beetle was observed pulling an item about 90 times its own weight. That would be equal to a human dragging about a seven-ton load. Just an ordinary flea has the strength to jump more than 130 times its height. For you to equal that, you would have to jump into the air almost one quarter of a mile. The flea can also jump 13 inches in distance (about 700 feet for a human). A grasshopper can jump over obstacles 200 times its size. An American salmon can jump up to 12 feet in the air, and the killer whale, weighing more than nine tons, can propel itself out of the water more than a body's length.

A four-inch abalone can hook itself onto a rock with more than 400 pounds of force. A bolt of lightning can strike the earth with a force of more than 15 million volts of electricity. A small electric eel can send out a charge of electricity of more than 600 volts, or more than five times that you would feel when you get a shock from a light socket. A tidal wave has the force of nearly 500 miles per hour of speed as it rolls through the ocean.

Then there are the jaws of the crocodile, which come together with a force of about 1,540 pounds, while the jaws of a human can exert about 40 to 80 pounds of pressure. Quite a difference, isn't it? The little ant has the strength to lift a bundle 50 times its weight. The ruby-throated hummingbird can beat its wings at the rate of 90 times a second, and the common mosquito can best that with about 1,000 times a second.

Jesus has told us that we cannot do anything by ourselves (see John 15:5). Our only hope to conquer the devil is through Jesus Christ. Ask Him today for the strength to overcome Satan.

BEARING ANOTHER'S BURDENS

Bear one another's burdens, and so fulfill the law of Christ. Galatians 6:2, NKJV.

Today we look at camels without humps. These interesting animals are called the camels of the Andes, and are divided into two species, the llama (LA-ma) and the alpaca (al-PAK-a). These animals belong to the camel family and work like camels. The larger of the two species is the llama. It has long, stringy fur that keeps it warm in the high altitudes of the Andes. Llamas weigh from 250 to 400 pounds and are three to four feet tall at their shoulders. They are able to carry from 60 to 100 pounds of baggage 15 to 20 miles a day. The llama's head is shaped much like a deer's. It has a long neck, and as it walks along it reminds one of a proud person walking with his head held high. Because of the extreme cold in the high altitude of the Andes, many baby llamas and alpaca die shortly after birth. When that happens, their fur is tanned, and this very soft baby fur is used to make slippers, rugs, and coats.

Alpacas are somewhat smaller than llamas, with heavier, softer fur. Alpacas are also used for carrying baggage, and their fur is used more widely for coats, sweaters, slippers, and rugs than is the llama's.

The camels of the Middle East and South American countries are used to carrying burdens for people. As these creatures walk through the deserts and over the mountains, they do their work very faithfully.

As animals carry another's burdens, so God's children are to bear each other's burdens, and do it willingly and faithfully. In other words, we are to help one another. Maybe you have friends or relatives who are sad or need help with their work. Go to those persons and offer your help. In this way you help to carry their burden.

As you pray today, ask God to help you find someone with a burden today that you can help carry. He will show you just the right person who needs your help.

BRAZILIAN FIRE ANTS

Ants are creatures of little strength, yet they store up their food in the summer.
Proverbs 30:25, NIV.

It's a feisty little creature originating in Brazil. You can't control it, and most people hate it. It's the fire ant. These little red ants are tough on those they touch. People who live in Brazil and in the southern part of the United States have learned that you don't stand very long in one spot if there are fire ants around.

The sting of these little creatures is very toxic. First it burns like fire, then begins to itch. As the spot is scratched a red welt develops that takes up to a week to fade. One scientist wondered what could be done to combat the poison in the sting. So he whizzed a large number of fire ants in a regular kitchen blender. He then took the liquid and used it as an antitoxin against the fire ant bite. It worked, just like snakebite antitoxin does.

If you don't have blended ants, ice helps a little. Keep ice on the sting for 10 minutes, then leave it off for 10 minutes. Do this several times. If you're allergic to beestings you'll also be allergic to fire ants, so keep your beesting kit with you when you're in their territory.

It was in 1918 that Brazilian fire ants entered the southern part of the United States. It is thought that they came aboard a ship. Now they infest more than 230 million acres in many of the Southern states. They are moving northward, but very slowly.

In the South many soybean fields are infested with fire ants. Their nests extend from about three feet underground to more than a foot above. The ants have a hardening liquid in their saliva so that their nests harden like rock and damage the combines used to harvest the beans.

Fire ants spend much time gathering their food for the winter months. Even though these ants are hated and people try to exterminate them, they still carry right on with their business. As we look forward to eternity, God expects us to carry on with our business as single-mindedly as the fire ants do. Ask Him today to help you prepare for eternity, just as the fire ant prepares for the future.

Nessie, the Loch Ness Monster

Look, he is coming with the clouds, and every eye will see him, even those who pierced him; and all the peoples of the earth will mourn because of him. Revelation 1:7, NIV.

Since A.D. 565, reports of a monster inhabiting the now-famous Loch Ness have frightened and excited people. (*Loch* means lake in Scottish.) Many people have claimed to have seen this monster. They say it is about 30 feet long, and occasionally parts of it rise up out of the water of Loch Ness. Many pictures have been taken of it, but none of them are clear. People have given the monster the name Nessie.

The lake is about 24 miles long and one mile wide. At its deepest point, which is directly offshore from the ruins of the Urquhart castle, it is 950 feet deep. For many years divers have gone down into the depths of Loch Ness trying to find Nessie, but no one has ever been able to see it up close.

In terms of the volume of water, this is the largest lake in Scotland. The waters are not only cold and deep, but very dark. Below 50 feet it is impossible to see more than a couple of feet in any direction. Divers have taken large and powerful lights into the depths of Loch Ness, only to come back without locating anything that could be the famous sea monster.

A great amount of vegetation grows in Loch Ness, and some biologists believe that now and then gases released by the decaying vegetation pushes some of it up to the surface. It is this that people imagine to be the coils of the Loch Ness monster. However, even this phenomenon has not been seen for years. Most scientists say that there is no monster in Loch Ness.

We all know that one of these days Jesus is coming back to this earth. We don't know when, only that He will. In the same way that people keep their eyes open for Nessie, we should keep our eyes open, watching for Jesus' return. The apostle writes that everyone will see Him. I thank God that we *all* shall be able to see Him come, no matter where we live. Thank God today that you will be able to see Jesus come back to this earth. It will be no mystery.

THE WOODPECKER

Give unto the Lord the glory due unto his name. Psalm 96:8.

On many occasions as I've walked through woods I've heard a familiar sound—that of a woodpecker drilling a hole in a tree. And I've often wondered how these creatures can drill through hard wood with their beaks and not batter their brains. I continue to marvel at how God thought of every little detail for everything.

Twenty-two species of woodpecker live in North America, ranging from the six-inch downy to the 20-inch ivory-billed. One of the reasons the male woodpecker drills into a tree is to build a nest, but another is to tell any female woodpecker around that he is an available mate.

God created woodpeckers with very strong neck muscles. These act like the motor that drives the head and bill. Then inside the head is a sturdy protractor muscle that controls the upper part of the bird's beak. This muscle braces the bill and acts like a shock absorber as the woodpecker drills the hole.

A study found that an acorn woodpecker's beak goes about 15 miles per hour as it strikes the tree. This means a peck almost every one thousandth of a second. The researchers believe that the way the beak hits the tree—straight on—is probably what keeps the brain from being battered.

A pileated woodpecker, about the size of a crow, pecks out a nesting place about eight inches wide and 24 inches deep. That's a lot of pecking! Red-bellied woodpeckers communicate by pecking, about two to three seconds, with 20 to 40 taps in a series. Other woodpeckers communicate by taps or pecks and find the tree in which they will build their nests. Interestingly, after all that work, woodpeckers don't return the next year to the same nest.

When David the giant killer turned his life over to God, he glorified God and acknowledged His power and majesty. Today, give God the glory due Him in your prayers. We cannot understand His greatness. We can only give Him the praise and glory for what He has done in making our fascinating world and what He does in each of our lives.

Our Rattling Conscience

Keep your conscience clear, so that, when you are maligned, those who abuse you for your good conduct in Christ may be put to shame. 1 Peter 3:16, NRSV.

Today let's look at the greatly feared rattlesnake. There are many varieties of rattlers—34, to be exact—and all but eight species are found in some part of the United States. And though they have a well-deserved bad reputation, rattlesnakes are not altogether bad. Before striking, they gave warning with their rattler, and they bite humans only in what they see as self-defense. They are helpful, too, eating mice, rats, and other small rodents and pests.

When a baby rattler is born, it has what is called a small prebutton at the end of its tail. This is just a rounded tip. After about two weeks, when it first sheds its skin, the first little button of its rattle forms. Each time that the growing snake sheds its skin another segment is added to the rattle. These segments interlock loosely with one another to form a jointed string. It is longer than it is wide, and it vibrates sideways. The rattling noise is made by rapidly vibrating the segments (about 48 times a second). The segments strike each other and, because of the rapid vibration, produce a buzzing sound. The rattling noise is the snake's warning to stay away. The rattle is one of the most remarkable structures in nature. There is nothing remotely resembling the rattle in any other group of snakes.

God did not make us with a rattle, but we do have a conscience. Our conscience is the Holy Spirit (and sometimes our common sense) speaking to us. If we desire to go someplace or do something questionable, your conscience says, "You know you shouldn't go there or do that. You know that's going to get your in trouble."

In your prayer today, ask God to help you listen to the warnings of your conscience. You would not go near a rattlesnake if you heard its warning, would you? Our conscience, guided by the Holy Spirit, should be our guide in our life today. God will send the Holy Spirit to help us, if we ask Him. Ask Him now.

BEWARE: POISON

He has made everything beautiful in its time. He has also set eternity in the hearts of men; yet they cannot fathom what God has done from beginning to end.
Ecclesiastes 3:11, NIV.

The face of the earth is filled with many beautiful flowers and plants. But if eaten by animals or people, some of these are poisonous. God certainly didn't create these. Poisonous plants can be blamed only on sin. Let's look at a few of these today.

Rhubarb is an interesting example. The stalk is good for food, but the leaf is poisonous. Most of us really like the potato tuber that we eat and that is good for us, but the rest of the plant is poisonous. Many mushrooms are poisonous. In fact, of certain look-alike mushrooms, one may be poisonous and the other just fine to eat. Then there are the plants and weeds that cause traumatic body disorders. These plants do not necessarily kill you, but they can make you very ill or uncomfortable. In each of these plants is some chemical substance that kills or harms an organism. (Maybe you've had a close encounter with poison ivy.) This is why it is very important to learn which of the wild plants and berries can be safely eaten (or even touched).

Not all harmful-to-human plants produce the same reaction. Some cause weakness or paralysis, while some interfere with the circulatory system. Some disrupt the blood chemistry, while others affect the mouth and the digestive tract. And some irritate the skin or cause burns. The carrotlike white snakeroot is said to cure snakebites, but if eaten by cows, it can poison the milk. It is reported that Abraham Lincoln's mother died from this type of milk poisoning.

Poison hemlock looks like parsley leaves. This was the plant liquid that was used to execute Socrates, the great philosopher, in 399 B.C. He was sentenced to die for interfering with the religion of the city where he lived. Some people have been poisoned by using oleander branches to grill their meat on.

Thank God today that He has given us the power of our minds. Ask Him to help you use your mind to the best of your ability to keep you safe from eating poisonous plants and from doing other harmful things.

WOLVERINE

I know all the fowls of the mountains: and the wild beasts of the field are mine.
Psalm 50:11.

For many years the youth leaders at Camp Au Sable in northern Michigan wanted a stuffed wolverine for their beautiful nature center, but they couldn't find anyone who owned one. The wolverine is Michigan's state animal, but almost none live in the state except, perhaps, a few in the far north near Canada. Finally they found someone in Montana who had one, and it's now in the nature center representing the state of Michigan.

Wolverines are the largest member of the weasel family. They grow up to three or four feet long and weigh about 40 pounds. They have very rugged-looking teeth and could frighten anyone, but like so many other animals they have been misunderstood. They've been so feared that they have been accused of killing everything in sight, even bears, coyotes, and large game animals such as deer, moose, and elk.

During a five-year study of wolverines in Montana, where there seems to be a sizable group of them, scientists found that wolverines kill and eat smaller animals, but never in the five years of their study did they find any evidence that they had killed large game animals for food.

Wolverines are very shy and rarely come out in the open. They generally stay in areas of uninhabited wilderness. In the study mentioned above it was found that at times they travel up to 100 miles looking for food. But even as they go long distances searching for food, they usually try to stay away from human civilization.

God made many animals so that life here on this earth would be interesting and exciting. As we study His creation we marvel at all great variation of animals He created. Thank God today for creating your favorite animals for your enjoyment.

ACID RAIN

These men are those who are hidden reefs in your love feasts when they feast with you without fear, caring for themselves; clouds without water, carried along by winds; autumn trees without fruit, doubly dead, uprooted. Jude 12, NASB.

Cries are being heard all over the United States and Canada that lakes are being polluted and forests are being destroyed. Something needs to be done about it. Worldwide, it is estimated that more than 20,000 lakes in Sweden have been affected, and the beautiful Black Forest of west Germany may be beyond hope.

What is happening? you ask. The smoke that boils out of the smokestacks from coal-burning power and industrial plants carries large amounts of sulfur dioxide and nitric oxides. As it lands on the water or land it kills many living things. In and around the lakes that once flourished with beautiful fish and wildlife, the fish have been killed off and the chirping tree frogs, loons, and kingfishers have disappeared.

Can something be done to stop this? Scientists hope that by cutting back on the emissions of sulfur that pour out of the smokestacks, the damage done by acid rain can be curtailed. And workers are spreading lime on some lakes in the northeastern United States to counteract and neutralize the acid so that creatures that live in and around lakes and streams will not be killed.

It's frightening to think that the delicate balance that keeps life going in the world is being destroyed because of our selfishness, greediness, and lack of care. Animals and plants that become extinct will never be replaced.

In our Christian experience also there are pollutants that harm our bodies and our relationship with Jesus. With God's help we can overcome the destroyer, Satan. Jesus will take care of the pollutants in your life if you turn it over to Him.

Turn your life over to Jesus today. Allow Him to purify it, taking out all of the sinful pollutants. You'll have a nice clean life.

MUSKRATS

Deliver me, O my God, out of the hand of the wicked, out of the hand of the unrighteous and cruel man. Psalm 71:4.

If there is any animal that would echo the words of David if it could, it would be the muskrat. This animal is trapped for its fur. Trappers are always on the lookout for it.

When I was a boy, two little irrigation streams went through our farm, and they abounded with muskrats. There were far too many of them for their own good. My father and the other farmers did not like them because they burrowed so many tunnels in the banks of the streams that the banks caved in. So my father bought me some traps. I would set a trap by each hole—one den might have two or three holes—and every morning before dawn I'd put on my rubber boots, get a flashlight and a gunnysack, and go to the streams. I always found several muskrats in the traps.

They'd usually drowned, so I would take them back home and skin them. I got 25 cents each for the fur. That was good money in those days. Today muskrats are still being trapped, as the fur is quite valuable.

Muskrats reproduce rapidly, having from two to four families a summer; each litter has from five to seven young. The young are born blind and hairless, but within a month they are gathering food on their own even though they remain with their parents for a month or more.

Muskrats become a problem when their habits interfere with what people are doing. Yet they're not altogether bad. Eating mostly plants, they may thin out vegetation so that it produces better and thus other wildlife and waterfowl have more to eat. In the winter when ice forms on bodies of water, muskrats eat aquatic vegetation and various aquatic animals.

David wanted to be delivered out of the hand of the devil. This should also be our desire. As the muskrat is trapped for its pelt, so Satan tries to trap us for our lives. Ask God today to deliver you from Satan's traps. God will be glad to warn you before you get into the trap, if you will listen.

AN APPLE A DAY

And I went unto the angel, and said unto him, Give me the little book. And he said unto me, Take it, and eat it up; and it shall make thy belly bitter, but it shall be in thy mouth sweet as honey. Revelation 10:9.

You've no doubt heard the saying "An apple a day keeps the doctor away." Apples provide pectins and an acid that help in digestion, as well as bulk and water that help in other body functions. And their natural fiber helps control cholesterol levels too. Maybe that's why this expression came into existence.

Wildlife have discovered that wild apples and apple trees are especially tasty. Deer and grouse like apple leaves, and there is more calcium and vitamin A in the carbohydrate-type food than in the apple itself. Mice, porcupines, deer, and rabbits like the inner bark of the apple tree, which contains more carbohydrate than do the leaves. Apple seeds are enjoyed by birds and squirrels as well as by other animals that eat the whole apple. Seeds have the most concentrated dose of nutrition.

Ruffed grouse, ring-necked pheasants, and bobwhites like the apple buds as well as the fruit and seeds. Years ago in New England, ruffed grouse ate so many apple blossoms that the crops were endangered, since the blossoms turn into the apples. For years in some Massachusetts townships, a bounty of 25 cents was paid for each grouse shot or killed. In New Hampshire a 1915 law required the state to pay apple growers for crops that were damaged by wildlife that were on the protected list. Since farmers were not allowed to harm these protected animals, their crops were affected.

Apple trees provide a benefit for humans and wildlife. Jesus has suggested to us that His Word should be very attractive to us because in it we can find all the elements necessary to live our spiritual life. Ask Jesus to give you an appetite for God's Word today and in the future, so that you may be nourished by it. It is spiritually healthy!

DEADLY OR DELICIOUS NIGHTSHADES

The staff belonging to the man I choose will sprout, and I will rid myself of this constant grumbling against you by the Israelites. Numbers 17:5, NIV.

More than 2,000 species of plants belong to the nightshade family. These range from a small wildflower to some very large bushes and small trees. Diverse as these plants are, they all have five-petaled flowers shaped like funnels or wheels.

Many of the nightshade family plants are poisonous, but not all. Probably the most toxic is the jimsonweed, which got its name from Jamestown, Virginia, where back in 1676 a group of English soldiers were poisoned from eating it. It has also been called the thorn apple. Native Americans have used the seeds from this plant in their religious ceremonies, because of its narcotic effect.

A second deadly nightshade is the Italian-named belladonna, meaning beautiful lady. Italian women once used this plant to dilate the pupils of their eyes, because large pupils were considered attractive. Today eye doctors use belladonna or a derivative to enlarge the pupils of their patients' eyes so that they can be examined.

Edible plants of the nightshade family include potatoes, tomatoes, chili peppers, and eggplant. The Spaniards that overran the Indians of Mexico discovered tomatoes and sent the seeds back to Europe. The round red fruit was called the love apple. In the 1550s the Italians experimented with eating them and later developed the tomato sauce base so popular in Italian cooking. Potatoes—from the highlands of Peru and Bolivia—also found their way to Europe. Chili peppers were discovered by the Aztec Indians in Mexico, and the eggplant was discovered in India.

Because God is the Creator He can make bloom what He wants to bloom. If you want to bloom for God and look beautiful for Him as a Christian, ask Him to help you do that now. He will be glad to help you be a "blooming Christian" today.

THE ANT LION

Be sober, be vigilant; because your adversary the devil walks about like a roaring lion, seeking whom he may devour. 1 Peter 5:8, NKJV.

The ant lion is nothing like the African lion. It is much smaller. In fact, the ant lion is not a lion at all, but an insect similar to the damselfly.

Ant lions have four narrow transparent wings like the damselfly, and they fold their wings over their backs. When the ant lion is alarmed by an intruder of some kind, it raises all four of its wings together over its back. The head has two large eyes and two antennae that resemble those of the butterfly. Ant lions are of different sizes, from the size of a damselfly to less than an inch across the wingspan.

Larval ant lions feed mainly on ants. In their larva stage they are very ferocious for their size. They have short legs and tough bodies and heads, and live in soft sand. Even at this young age the larvae know how to work. With a quick twist of the head, these larvae (which you may know as doodle-bugs) throw grains of sand or small stones. They dig a funnel-shaped hole with steep sides consisting of fine, loose grains of sand or dirt. As ants walk around looking for food they may get near an ant lion hole. The sides are so loose that an ant cannot hold on and it slips to the bottom of the hole where the ant lion larva is waiting, hidden under the sand. The ant lion larva grabs the ant with its powerful fangs and sucks out the body fluids until the ant's body is just a dry hull. Then it is discarded.

I thought about another creature that lies in wait for us. Satan goes around as a roaring lion looking for his prey—you and me. Satan will try to tempt you, maybe several times today, to do or say something you know you should not. Today before you pray for God's help, let's read Psalm 34:7: "The angel of the Lord encamps all around those who fear Him, and delivers them" (NKJV).

Now pray that God will deliver you from the temptations of Satan today.

ELEPHANT SEALS

At that day shall a man look to his Maker, and his eyes shall have respect to the Holy One of Israel. Isaiah 17:7.

Elephant seals are the largest seals in the world. They get their name from the fact that the males have a trunklike snout that extends down like that of an elephant, except it's not as large. Male elephant seals grow to about 15 to 18 feet long and weigh more than 5,000 pounds! Tragically, they have been hunted almost to extinction for their blubber, which contains a valuable oil. Females are about half the size of the males, and they do not have a trunk.

The northern species lives in the waters off the coast of southern California and Mexico. There are several islands to which they go to breed and raise their families. A newborn calf weighs about 40 pounds, and its mother nurses it for six weeks. By that time it will have grown to 250 to 300 pounds. I'd say that mama elephant seal milk is very nutritious if it can put that many pounds on a calf that fast. The calves are black at birth, but as they grow, their color turns to silver-gray.

Adults come to the islands to raise their families from December to March and remain there through most of the summer. During this time they molt (lose their hair), so by day they cover themselves as much as possible with sand to protect their tender skin from the sun. They do their hunting for food at night. During August the adults leave and remain away until the males return in December and the females in January.

When the males return to the islands they do not eat until the females arrive. They're not afraid of humans. If one was sleeping, you could quietly slip up and sit on him. However, when he awakes he might attack. They don't like humans coming too close.

The big bull seals have respect for each other. More important, we should respect the Creator of the universe. Tell God how much you love and respect Him today, then show Him by your actions. One way to show respect is by being careful how you use His name.

RED-WINGED DIVE-BOMBER

But take good care to keep the commands and the law which Moses . . . gave you: to love the Lord your God; to conform to his ways; to observe his commandments; to hold fast to him; to serve him with your whole heart and soul. Joshua 22:5, NEB.

One of the more common birds you'll see after the winter months is the red-winged blackbird. The male is black with a reddish-orange epaulet at the bend of the wings. The female is a brownish color with dark-brown to black stripes or splotches of color.

I have often wondered why the male species of most birds have such pretty coloring while the females are so drab. I think I know why. In most cases the female sits on the nest to incubate the eggs she has laid. Her coloration enables her to fade into the nest and brush or foliage so that enemies have difficulty seeing her. God camouflaged these female birds for a purpose.

It takes the female red-winged blackbird about six days to build her nest. She builds it of cattail, sledge, and swamp milkweed leaves, intertwining them closely so that they are very tight and supportive. When the nest is finished, the female lays three to five eggs. Only after the third egg is laid does she begin to incubate them.

During the nest-building and egg-incubation period the male red-winged blackbird continually guards the area around the nest. You may have been out on a walk sometime and had a male red-winged blackbird sound the alarm several times, then fly out and dive-bomb you. This is his way of saying, "Stay clear! This is my domain."

God's holy angels are by our side day and night. Should any of the devil's angels come into our territory and near us, God's angels protect us and say, "This person is mine." There is a constant battle of the angels over us. Who wins out is our decision?

Pray that God will help you decide and stay on His side.

Open Mouths

The Lord shall preserve thee from all evil: he shall preserve thy soul. Psalm 121:7.

When animals open their mouths, they may just be yawning, but even the yawns take on important meanings in some animal species. Take, for example, the lion family. When a lion opens its mouth, it may just be yawning from boredom or sleepiness, but it may also be a courting procedure or a territorial signal. If the teeth are showing, it may signify that the lion is ready for action.

A yawn seems to gear an animal up for activity. If the respiration is slow, the yawn gets the body working at a greater speed. The sudden intake of air rushes fresh oxygen into the bloodstream. The heart reacts immediately, sending more blood to the sluggish muscles. When the animal stretches, it squeezes the blood veins and the lymph system, speeding up the blood and reducing the amount of carbon dioxide buildup.

A hippo will open its mouth against another hippo for territorial possession. As these large animals come mouth to mouth and lip to lip, they are saying, "*I'm* the boss here." This is also demonstrated by the javelinas that live on the deserts in Arizona and by some species of baboons and monkeys. Then there are the crocodiles that open their mouths and allow birds to go in and pick the food from around their teeth, because they cannot clean them with their tongue. This helps both the bird and the crocodile.

The zebra says different messages by the wideness of its open mouth. The wider open the mouth, the stronger the message. If the ears are straight up, then the message is a greeting, but if the ears are laid back and the mouth very wide open, look out! The zebra is angry.

So the open mouth can mean danger. David said, "Save me from the lion's mouth" (Psalm 22:21), meaning from the devil. Our text says that God preserves us from evil. Only God and His angels can do that. Pray that today you will be kept from the open mouth of danger—the devil.

CURSED BY GOD

So the Lord God said to the serpent, "Because you have done this, cursed are you. . . . You will crawl on your belly and you will eat dust all the days of your life." Genesis 3:14, NIV.

ne of the most beautiful creatures in the Garden of Eden was the serpent. It had wings and could fly. It was the serpent that Satan used, as it sat in the tree of knowledge of good and evil, to tempt Eve. After Adam and Eve sinned, the serpent was cursed by God to crawl on its belly on the ground.

My family and I had been in Brazil only a short time when into our backyard slithered a big red and black snake. Our little maid cried, "Cobra!" so I left my Portuguese-language lesson to go kill the cobra. When I arrived, I saw that it wasn't a cobra, but I killed it anyway because I was afraid of it. As I picked it up I said to Domingas, "This is not a cobra."

"Oh, yes, it is," she said. My wife settled the argument. It was a cobra, because that is the Portuguese word for snake. I'd thought Domingas was talking about the poisonous snake.

God used snakes back in Moses' day in Egypt. You remember that when Aaron and Moses were before King Pharaoh, Aaron's rod became a serpent and ate up the other rods that only looked like serpents (see Exodus 7:12). Also, years later in the wilderness, when poisonous snakes filled the camp of the children of Israel, God told Moses to make a serpent of brass and raise it high on a pole. Moses did, and if the people bitten by a serpent merely looked at the brass serpent they did not die from the venom. They lived (see Numbers 21:6-9). God used the serpents in these and other cases to teach lessons.

Satan disguised himself in the form of a serpent so that he could talk to Eve in the Garden of Eden, and he succeeded in getting her to doubt God's word. Today he disguises himself in many forms, enticing many to sin. He makes sin look attractive and fun—and it may be, until it destroys you.

Pray today that God will help you not to be attracted to the deceptive beauties of sin as Eve was attracted to the beautiful serpent. Pray that you will be loyal to Jesus.

FOODS OF THE WORLD

Nevertheless he left not himself without witness, in that he did good, and gave us rain from heaven, and fruitful seasons, filling our hearts with food and gladness. Acts 14:17.

When my wife, Millie, and I moved to Brazil, my father-in-law told me that I would find some delightful and delicious fruits and other kinds of food there. He said that I might not like them on the first try, but that God had put good food in all parts of the world. Some would be different from what I was used to, but I would learn to enjoy them.

We were served mangoes as we arrived in Brazil. Millie already loved them, but I'd never tried one. I liked them right away. However, when they gave me a papaya, I wasn't so sure. But now I could eat papaya every day of the week. Also in Brazil were custard apple, passion fruit, breadfruit, acerola fruit, aguaje fruit, and more. Then there were the yuca, mandioca, farinha (far-IN-ya), plantains, inguere (in-GEER-ee), and other roots and vegetables. I needed to learn to like these things, or in some instances I might go hungry. (Beans and rice were almost always available.)

In other parts of the world you find tato root, coconuts, bamboo shoots, water chestnuts, Chinese peas, sweet potatoes, and oh, so many other good things to eat. Yes, God has placed in each region tasty food that grows well in the climate. I didn't mention the fruits we found in South America that are well known in North America: bananas, grapefruit, oranges, lemons, limes, and so on.

The native people in each country have ways of fixing their own foods. Sometimes they will mix them together. Other times they use the simple, common fruit or veggie. I believe the reason people in many countries are so healthy and live so long is that they eat good, fresh and healthy food prepared in a simple way.

God wants to fill our lives with food and gladness, and the only way He can do that is if we let Him. God will fill your life with health and gladness if you ask Him to and follow His simple diet. Try it. You'll like it, and you'll feel good.

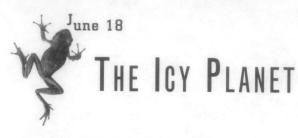

THE ICY PLANET

He was in the world, and the world was made by him, and the world knew him not.
John 1:10.

It was not until 1930 that a 22-year-old Kansas farm boy named Clyde Tombaugh, using his homemade telescope, discovered the planet Pluto. He sent drawings of his sightings to a professional observatory in Arizona that had just acquired a 13-inch telescope but had no money to hire anyone full-time to use it. So they contacted Tombaugh, hiring him part-time to study the heavens.

As Clyde continued to study the stars, planets, and constellations he took photographs and found out more about Pluto. It was the ninth planet discovered in our solar system, and the fartherest from Earth. Eventually others used telescopes to learn more about this little planet. They used the 150-inch telescope atop Mauna Kea in Hawaii, the 200-inch telescope on California's Mount Palomar, and an 80-inch telescope on a mountain in Arizona. They noticed that Pluto rotated on its axis every 6.4 days.

As James Christy studied Pluto with the telescope in Arizona he noticed a smaller celestial body next to it. Further investigation revealed that it was a small moon. Christy named this moon Charon, pronounced sharon, for his wife, Charlene. He also noticed that this moon revolves around Pluto every 6.4 days, the same as the planet's rotation on its axis. For 26 years, from 1953 to 1980, there was much speculation as to the size of Pluto and what type of material it was made of. Then it was discovered that Pluto has a large mass of ice on it, and the moon, Charon, puts out enough heat to melt some of the ice. This releases methane gas that is in the frozen state, and it is this that causes a wispy atmosphere around Pluto. Today astronomers say that Pluto is not a planet. Do they really know?

As scientists have tried to understand the universe, Jesus smiles from heaven, because He created it. The world did not know Him, but He knows you. Thank Jesus for who He is.

"Air Scenting"

And he gave some, apostles; and some, prophets; and some, evangelists; and some, pastors and teachers. Ephesians 4:11.

God not only gave different talents to different ones of us to be able to do different things; He also created many of His animal creatures with different instincts and capabilities. A special training that has been given to German shepherd dogs in recent years is that of air scenting. According to researchers, our bodies are made up of more than 60 trillion cells. They claim that more than 50 million cells are shed and regenerated each day. This exchange causes a scent (not the sweaty body odor) that humans cannot detect but that dogs can smell. Trainers work with these dogs for about a year to make them very effective. With training, a German shepherd can smell a person, not only because of clothing or other odors, but also because of this cellchanging odor.

On March 31, 1982, a 22-year-old ski-lift operator was buried under an avalanche of snow covering the employees' locker room area. Pinned down by the lockers, she remained in this situation for five days. Rescue workers didn't know that anyone was there, but a German shepherd named Bridget was brought in by her trainer, Roberta Huber. Because of her training in air scenting, Bridget smelled Anna under 12 feet of snow. She was the first avalanche victim saved by a dog in North America. Bridget detected Anna's scent through air spaces in the collapsed building.

I am happy not only that God gave each of us talents to be able to do things but also that He gave His creatures special abilities. These astounding abilities have helped save many lives. Anna lost a foot by frostbite, but she could have lost her life. Bridget had been trained, and her God-given instinct saved Anna's life.

God has given you at least one special talent, and probably more. Use those talents for God. Pray in your own quiet way today, thanking God for your talents and asking Him to help you to develop and use them.

June 20

Exploring Ponds

Command those who are rich in this present world . . . to put their hope in God, who richly provides us with everything for our enjoyment. 1 Timothy 6:17, NIV.

Think for a minute about all of the creatures that live in or around a pond. A whole tiny world exists in every pond, as students in outdoor-education classes have found. They get right down into the pond and explore all of the life that is there. And a pond is full of life.

You've probably noticed those little skaters on top of the water. No doubt you've wished that you could skate on the water as these water striders do. Well, there are other pond skaters, too. There's one called the whirligig, which is actually a beetle with a water-repellent body like the water strider's. These beetles usually spin around in circles. Then there are the back swimmers and the water boatmen, which are true bugs. They move along in a kind of rowing fashion. The back swimmer swims upside down.

Looking down into the pond, you will see crayfish, turtles, snails, and other creatures as they rummage around for food. If you put a drop of pond water on a glass slide and put it under a microscope you'll probably be able to see some onecelled protozoans.

Around the pond fly all kinds of birds and insects. This is a place of busy activity. Many creatures build their nests in the broad-leafed trees. Others will use the tall grass nearby. Water lilies will float on the water, giving some support to frogs and small birds that want to rest and sun themselves. In the cool dirt around the edge of the pond you might see salamanders, lizards, and, worms.

God has given us all of nature to enrich our lives. He especially wants us to slow down and enjoy His creation. One way to do that is to sit and watch all the activity around a pond, or even get in for a closer look at the creatures.

Thank God today that He created a beautiful world for your enjoyment, and go out and enjoy it.

BEAVERS

I have therefore delivered him into the hand of the mighty one of the heathen; he shall surely deal with him: I have driven him out for his wickedness. Ezekiel 31:11.

Today's text fits well our subject as we talk about the beaver. We know that beavers have a big flat tail that is used as a rudder when it swims, and that it warns other beavers of danger by slapping its tail on the water. But beavers can also do much damage in areas in which people live and work.

Beavers cut down trees by chewing them close to the ground with their large front teeth. They then cut off the branches and pull them into a stream. By using many small trees, branches, and mud, they eventually dam up a stream, making a nice lake. The lake is handy for beaver swims, and also as the entrance to a nice lodge, or beaver house. While it may seem fun to have a beaver pond nearby so that we can watch the beavers in action, these ponds can be destructive to farmers' crops as well as other wildlife and vegetation.

Many smaller animals have their homes in the same areas as the beavers. Sometimes the homes of these other creatures are destroyed by the rising water, which occurs when the dam is finished. Also, trees and other vegetation can be drowned by the water backed up by the dam. In fact, in many areas having the water dammed up has been so destructive that the dams are purposely broken to let the water flow again. Of course, you've heard of busy beavers, and sometimes the beavers work hard and rebuild the dam. The only way to get the stream flowing freely again is to take the beavers away—or kill them. Most wildlife workers would rather move them to another location to keep them safe, even though they have been destructive.

Pharaoh was a wicked man, and God said that He would deal with him. God drove him out for his wickedness as men have driven out the beaver. God does not want to drive us away from Him for our sinfulness; He wants to forgive us and bring us close to Him. Today ask God to forgive you of your sins and draw you close to Him because of His love for you.

June 22

BULLDOG ANTS

Be glad in the Lord and rejoice, you righteous ones; and shout for joy, all you who are upright in heart. Psalm 32:11, NASB.

Bulldog ants are an inch long. Their sting feels as if a hot needle has been plunged into the skin, and the pain from the sting can last for 10 days or longer. One scientist said that 30 bulldog ant stings can kill a person. The ants are very feisty and aggressive. They're not afraid to tangle with another creature larger than they are. There are 65 species of bulldog ant in the world, and the species I've chosen to talk about today is from Australia.

Like many other ant species, the hub of a colony of bulldog ants is the queen. She is a matriarch of absolute power and may live up to 10 years. Without her tremendous egg output—one egg per hour—the colony would die out.

The devoted workers, all females, are considered midwives. With their antennae they stroke the abdomen of the queen, which stimulates her to lay eggs. As the eggs are laid other workers carry them to a pile, where they are constantly licked with a saliva that prevents fungus growth. Worker bulldog ants are also capable of laying eggs. These are used for food that is fed to the larvae.

When danger approaches, the workers rally to protect the queen. She is put into the safest part, deep down in the nest. Immediately next to her are the teen ants, and then the infants. The worker ants are willing to fight and give up their lives, if necessary, to protect their queen and her colony.

God has placed a value on your life, and the life of every person in the world. That value is the same for everyone, because, unlike these ants, we are all equal in God's sight.

I hope that you will give your life to God today and ask Him to guide you, so that you will be among the righteous who shout for joy at Christ's second coming. Look forward to living in God's colony forever.

FALLING LEAVES

The one who listens to you listens to Me, and the one who rejects you rejects Me; and he who rejects Me rejects the One who sent Me. Luke 10:16, NASB.

Let me share a parable with you. This is not true, only a parable to make a point.

One day a leaf saw other leaves floating from place to place and decided that would be fun. So the leaf said to the tree it grew on, "I don't need your sap anymore. See how pretty I am! I can take care of myself, and I want to be free like the other leaves." The leaf detached itself from the tree and floated in the breeze to the ground. It made many friends with the other leaves as it went from place to place. Life seemed to be very exciting.

One day the leaf noticed that its beautiful color was beginning to disappear and was being replaced with brown spots. A few days later all its surface had turned brown, and life wasn't exciting anymore. Some of its friends had already died, and it was beginning to feel sick. It no longer floated from place to place. It had grown brittle, and now lay in a pile with the other leaves. It wasn't long until it was dead and burned up by fire. It had completely rejected the life-giving sap offered to it by the tree, and now it was too late!

The pleasures of sin are fun for a while, but they are not things that make us truly happy for any length of time. They bring only temporary satisfaction. The leaf in our parable thought it would be great to be free and do whatever it wanted, but it found out that it was fun only for a while and ended in destruction by fire.

Now and again some young people reject help from their parents, teachers, and others. They feel that they are big enough to be independent. They feel that they can succeed on their own. But later they find this was an unwise course, and they return home.

We cannot reject Jesus and expect to live forever. He reminds us, "Without me you can do nothing" (John 15:5, NKJV). We don't need to worry about that fire if we keep a close relationship with Jesus. Ask Him to help you stay close to Him and be a beautiful Christian today.

ARTICHOKES ON LEGS

His scales are his pride, shut up together as with a close seal. Job 41:15.

One of the ugliest creatures that I have ever seen in pictures is the pangolin, called by some an artichoke on legs. These animals have scales that act as their skin, covering their upper body and tail. They are the only animal in their group that has scales. They have no teeth, so they do not chew their food.

Pangolins are nocturnal animals that live in Africa and Asia. With their scales they look like pinecones come to life. These scales grow continuously. They are sharp-edged and can be opened out at will. A pangolin can curl up in a ball for protection. People tell that it takes several strong men to unroll one. This curling procedure is part of the pangolin's defense mechanism.

Pangolins have a long snout, with a small mouth way back underneath. They live mainly on ants and termites. They also have a clear protecting cover over their eyes in case they get into a nest of stinging ants or termites. Their tongue is about a foot long and rolls up in their mouth. A sticky substance on the tongue acts like flypaper to small insects. One dead pangolin was found to have more than 200,000 insects in its stomach, which was a one-day supply. That means that it would eat more than 70 million insects a year. Quite a large diet, right?

There are seven species of pangolins, three living in Asia and four in Africa. Some live in trees; others in burrows in the ground. After birth young pangolins nurse for about a month, then begin to eat insects. Shortly thereafter, they are on their own.

I am thankful that we have a God who looks after us. I am glad also that He has given us earthly parents to love and protect us, as well as provide for us. Thank God today that you have parents, and that your mother cares for you for a long time.

Tree-climbing Lizards

He prays to God and finds favor with him. Job 33:26, NIV.

The intriguing tree-climbing lizard of the Old World is also called a chameleon. They live mostly in trees and shrubs, and even their tails help them climb. A few do spend most of their time on the ground, but even these can and climb.

Tree-climbing lizards look rather odd with their large eyes positioned on each side of their head. Scientists have discovered that each eye works independently of the other, so if the head is held right, they can look forward with one eye and backward with the other. They can see two complete pictures at the same time. Their eyes are protected by fused eyelids forming a coneshaped shield open only at the tip.

No doubt God created these tree-climbing lizards with this special optical system because of their unique way of hunting food. When seeking prey, chameleons' tongues shoot out a distance often greater than the length of their bodies. When they see a small or medium-sized insect, the tongue is quickly ejected. It takes less than a third of a second for the tongue, which has a thick mucous secretion on its surface, to grab the insect and be back in the chameleon's mouth. Yum. Good.

This chameleon has a built-in defense mechanism that lets it adapt to its surroundings. Yellow, black, and white pigments in special skin cells (called chromatophores) enable the chameleon to change colors so that it becomes nearly the same color as the object it is near or on.

God has given us adaptability too. We can go from hot to cold climates, from sea level to high elevations. We can adapt to good friends or questionable friends; to good habits or bad habits; to good motives or bad motives; to good attitudes or bad attitudes. This is the adaptability that God has given to us.

Today, ask God to give you the ability to adapt to good friends, good habits, good motives, and good attitudes. You know which ones are good.

THE CAMEL BIRD

Cast all your anxiety on him because he cares for you. 1 Peter 5:7, NIV.

Many years ago some Chinese people saw an ostrich and called it the camel bird because it was large, had a long neck, and had feet similar to those of a camel. The ostrich has been written about in history for several thousands of years. Early Egyptians used ostrich feathers as a symbol of justice because the vanes on either side of the shaft are exactly equal in width.

Ostriches are the largest birds on earth and are native to the Middle East, Africa, and Australia. They stand seven to eight feet tall and weigh about 300 pounds each. They can run up to about 40 miles an hour, but 30 miles an hour is their usual pace. They can run that pace for about an hour without getting too tired.

The female ostrich lays as many as 15 eggs, and ostriches are good parents. The female sits on the nest during the day, and the male sits on it at night. After the chicks hatch, the mother finds lice, fleas, and worms to feed her young until they start to graze.

In 1960 in the Nairobi National Park, workers recorded a situation in which the male ostrich was sitting on a clutch (nest) of 40 eggs. He was driven off by a pride of lions. The lion cubs played with the eggs as though they were balls, batting them all over the area. When the lions finally left, the male ostrich gathered the eggs back into the nest and sat back down on them. Amazingly, they hatched. Ostrich eggs are so large—with a capacity of two pints—that in earlier times the shells were used to carry water.

As the ostrich parents guard and provide for their young, so God guards and provides for His children. Today as you pray, ask God to take control of your life and to keep you from all harm. He will do it, because "he cares for you."

COUGAR

Where now is the lions' den, the place where they fed their young, where the lion and lioness went, and the cubs, with nothing to fear? Nahum 2:11, NIV.

The cougar, catamount, mountain lion, puma, or panther, as it is called in different regions, can live in just about any terrain. For many years the cougar had the reputation of being a killer—that it lay in wait to kill anything that came along. Probably Hollywood films have done the most to discredit the cougar. In movies the cougar crouches and at the right moment lets out a roar and pounces on a person or animal.

Fortunately, that is not the true story of the cougar. According to wildlife researchers in Idaho, many cougars live in the same area that sheep are pastured, yet each year only two or three instances are reported of a cougar killing a sheep.

Cougars are carnivorous (meat-eating) and therefore do kill to eat. Deer and antelope are their main diet. But they are not on the prowl all of the time. A cougar will stalk an animal when hungry, but usually the ones they catch are the older or sickly animals. This way the cycle of life is kept in balance. An adult cougar may kill a deer or antelope only once every two weeks or so, depending on the climate and the scarcity of food.

Many of those people who for years hunted the cougar to kill it have now become their protectors. They see that cougars are not bad creatures. They also realize that cougars are not really dangerous. In fact, many of these people would be delighted if they could see a cougar out in the wild.

God doesn't desire us to go around in a sneaky way and get the best of people. He wants us to share with them what He has done for us. God wants us to show how His power can work through us. Ask God today to give you "lion" power to overcome the devil when he tempts you.

DRINKS AROUND THE WORLD

Let us eat and drink; for to morrow we die. 1 Corinthians 15:32.

I have always enjoyed different fruit juices. When I went to South America, I found many drinks that I didn't know existed, just as visitors to the United States find drinks such as root beer that they hadn't known before.

Around the world God has given many different things to drink, and people have made others that God didn't plan for. When sin entered, people decided to do some things their way. The price has been poor health and death.

People in Brazil make a drink from the guarana (gwar-ANN-na) fruit. This is kind of a national drink and is usually carbonated. They also mix avocado, sugar, and milk to make a drink called *abacatada* (a-BAA-ka-ta-da). Ice cream is also made out of that mixture. Brazilians make a drink from a palm fruit called *assai* (ah-SIGH-ee). It is usually very thick and a deep purple. Juice is also squeezed from sugar cane. People like to suck the *caña* (CON-ya) right from the stalk.

Coconut milk is a common drink, not only in South America but in other tropical places. Pineapple, guava, orange, grape, grapefruit, passion fruit, and other tropical fruits make nice *refrescos*, as the Peruvians call their drinks. Many people take such grains as wheat, rice, barley, corn, oats, and rye and make cereal coffee from them. They first toast and grind the grain, then boil it to make the coffee. Teas, too, are made from the leaves of many different shrubs and trees. My favorite tea from Peru is *yerba louisa,* made from a sweet grass. Is it good! Apple leaves, lime or lemon leaves, garlic, and many grasses are used to make teas.

I have had many people offer me fermented drinks, but these destroy the brain, and I have said no. Why numb my brain when there are so many good things to drink that are pure and sweet? God doesn't want us to just eat and drink because we are going to die. He has better plans for us—a good life for eternity. Thank Him for that plan, and enjoy the good drinks.

186

BUFFY

Behold, I stand at the door, and knock: if any man hear my voice, and open the door, I will come in to him, and will sup with him, and he with me. Revelation 3:20.

An estimated 60 to 70 million buffalo, or bison, lived in the United States, Canada, and Mexico in the early 1800s. It was not unusual to find herds of up to 4 million in one location, and they roamed an area of about 1,000 square miles. Then the early settlers began to kill the buffalo for food.

In 1889, with only 541 buffalo known to be left alive, conservationists began a movement to save them. Today there are an estimated 60,000 in the United States, Canada, and Mexico in private, state, and federal herds. The state of Kansas has several herds. Each year they must be thinned out, so some calves and older buffalo are made available for sale to the public.

At the SDA church camp in Kansas, Broken Arrow Ranch, we decided we'd like to have a buffalo for campers to observe, so we put in our order to the Kansas State Fish and Game Commission. They honored our request, and on a set day we went to pick up our buffalo. It was a 6-month-old female calf right off the range, and she was wild. The game commission workers vaccinated her and sent her down the ramp into our pickup truck, which had iron cattle railings. She didn't like that at all. When we arrived at the camp, we turned her loose in the large corral next to our Appaloosa stallion, Arapaho. We named her Buffy, and she and Arapaho became good friends. When we took Arapaho out of his pen, Buffy would cry and whine. We could even let her out when we rode Arapaho, and she would follow right along like a colt beside him.

Jesus wants you to trust Him, as Buffy did Arapaho. He wants you to open up your heart and tell Him your joys and sorrows, and let Him know what you need. Take the time and open up your heart to Him. Tell Him how much you love Him, and that you want Him as your best friend. "Prayer is the opening of the heart to God as to a friend" *(Steps to Christ,* p. 93).

BLUEBIRDS

And Jesus said unto him, "Foxes have holes and birds of the air have nests, but the Son of man has nowhere to lay His head." Matthew 8:20, NKJV.

At one time some birds, such as the bluebird, were abundant, but now they are scarce. Many people are trying to help the bluebird make a comeback. They are building bluebird houses by the thousands, hoping to bring these beautiful birds back to the numbers they once were.

Bluebirds were plentiful where I grew up. We enjoyed feeding and watching these birds with their pretty blue feathers. Today all of the three species of bluebirds in the United States have been affected, the eastern bluebird the most. These birds often nested in the wooden fence posts of old. Over the years the posts rotted, and most were replaced with steel fence posts. Male eastern bluebirds have a bright-blue back, blue tail feathers, and a rosy-rust breast. Their habitat is from the Rocky Mountains to the East Coast.

The mountain bluebird, which has more open space, has fared quite well. It lives in the northwestern United States, through western Canada, and as far north as Alaska. The males are all blue except for a whitish belly. The range of the western bluebird extends from the Pacific Coast to the Rockies. The males are blue except for brownish feathers on their backs.

All three of these species have suffered because the hollow trees that they used for nesting and raising their young have been cut down for new developments. It has been difficult for these birds to survive.

As the Bible tells us, Jesus did not have a home of His own. However, back then the large housing developments that we have today did not exist, and so the birds did have places to nest. Although Jesus had no place here to call home on earth, now all of heaven is His home. He longs to return and take His children back to share His home.

Ask God today to help you be a faithful Christian so that you can enjoy the house He has prepared for you and His home with Him forever.

OCEANS

The sea is his, and he made it: and his hands formed the dry land. Psalm 95:5.

As you look at a map or a globe of the world you will notice that about 70 percent of our world's surface is covered with water. And although they are connected, each of the bodies of water has a name. The Pacific Ocean is the largest, and the Atlantic Ocean the second largest. The others are the Indian, Arctic, and Antarctic oceans. The Pacific Ocean covers about 64 million square miles, or about one third of the earth's surface.

Challenger Deep, in the Mariana Trench close to Guam, is the deepest spot in all the oceans. Its bottom is 37,782 feet below the surface. If we could put Mount Everest—at 29,028 feet the tallest mountain in the world—into the Challenger Deep, more than a mile and a half (8,754 feet) of water would cover its top.

The ocean is never still. It is always moving. This movement is caused by wind and earthquakes and by the gravitational pull of the sun and the moon. The moon's pull is so strong that it causes the tides, and that is why you see the breakers near the water's edge on a beach.

Many of the islands in the oceans are nothing more than the tops of mountains that project out of the deep water. Around most continents there is a plateaulike formation called the continental shelf. It gradually slopes down from the shoreline until it is under about 650 feet of water. There the shelf ends abruptly, and the bottom drops away to what is called the abyss.

We should be thankful there is a God who created this earth and all that is in it. Although sin has changed many things, still God is in control, and that should strengthen our faith. God said it, and I believe it, and that is good enough for me!

As you think about these thoughts today, thank God that He is in control.

A PRICKLY WORLD

To keep me from becoming conceited because of these surpassingly great revelations, there was given me a thorn in my flesh, a messenger of Satan, to torment me.
2 Corinthians 12:7, NIV.

Cacti are considered to be all-American plants because all but one of the more than 1,500 species are confined to the Americas from Canada to the tip of South America. The hub of most of the cacti is the near-desert lands of northern Mexico and the southwestern United States.

When we think of cactus, we immediately think of the spines, or stickers, that most cactus plants have. Those spines are the reason different ones of the cactus plants have the visually descriptive names of pincushion, hedgehog, porcupine, eagle claw, prickly pear, and fishhook. But there is a reason for these spines. Not only do they keep away animals that would eat the cacti, but they also play a very important part in the life of the plant.

Spines have the important function of helping the plant live in the hot desert temperatures. Have you ever wondered how cactus plants survive where it is so very hot? Here's how. The spines screen the sun's rays and help keep the plant cool by trapping an insulating layer of air close to the plant. They reduce evaporation by breaking up the drying winds and air currents, and they collect raindrops and dew, gently dropping this water to the ground beneath the plant, where it can soak up the moisture.

Spines come in different sizes and shapes. They always are in clusters, in rows, or in spirals, and grow from spots on the plant called areoles. Some spines are short and stout, while others are long and straight. Some are curved; others are barbed, hooked, feathered, or even hairlike.

The apostle Paul talked about a thorn, a problem, in his life. Some people, like the cactus, just naturally live a thorny life. However, with Jesus in your life it will be less thorny. Not all of the thorns will be removed, because they help us develop a patient character. Thank God for the thorny growing experiences you may encounter, and make the best of them with God's help.

DESERTS

[The desert] shall blossom abundantly, and rejoice even with joy and singing.
Isaiah 35:2.

Deserts are interesting places. Much can be learned from observing nature on the deserts. Ellen White, describing the results of the Flood in the book *Patriarchs and Prophets*, wrote, "Where once had been earth's richest treasures of gold, silver, and precious stones were seen the heaviest marks of the curse" (p. 108). Could she be talking about the vast desert wastes on Planet Earth? I believe that she is.

In the sands of the deserts are millions of little seeds that are doing nothing. Some wait in the soil for several years until they have the right conditions to grow. And when it rains, giving seeds the moisture they need to sprout, the desert floor is transformed by the brightness of plants and flowers.

We know that some animals burrow under the sandy soil to escape the heat, and in a way, some plants do the same thing. Take, for example, the living stone plant, which is a native of southwestern Africa. It grows under the sand, with only a part of the leaves above the ground. These portions are called the windows, because they take in the sunlight. The plant must lose as little water as possible, and living almost totally submerged in the sand helps it do that. In fact, reducing water loss in one way or another is a trait of most of the desert vegetation.

The plants that survive on the desert have become so adapted to their situation that water loss is at a minimum. Some plants have a waxy surface that helps keep the water in. Others have dense mats of silvery hairs that reflect the sun, thus reducing evaporation. As water becomes scarce, some plants shed their leaves, so that they don't need so much water. When the rain comes, the leaves grow again. With moisture and rain the desert blossoms out in a magnificent way.

God is waiting for the time He can see His world in full bloom again. He also wants to see us blossom for Him in a spiritual way. Ask God to help you blossom as a Christian today, and ask Him to come soon so that you can see His new earth in full bloom and living color.

191

THE AMERICAN SYMBOL

They pass by like swift ships, like an eagle swooping on its prey. Job 9:26, NKJV.

Various nations around the world use a mammal, bird, or leaf as a national symbol. On June 20, 1782, the U.S. Congress adopted the bald eagle as the national symbol of the United States. There was some resistance, because the eagle has characteristics that are not honorable. Ben Franklin wrote, "He is a bird of bad moral character. He does not get his living honestly." Richard B. Morris, a historian, wrote that the bald eagle is a "gangster bird, a hijacker . . . a symbol of espionage . . . an image of frightfulness."

Because the eagle often snatches a fish from an osprey that has caught it, or takes prey from other birds or animals that have killed it, some do not look favorably on the eagle. It is reported, believe it or not, that the eagle is a real coward. Yet bald eagles are very good caretakers of their young. As far as research can tell, they also mate for life. The bald eagle does not get the white feathers on its head until it is 5 years old. They are a beautiful and stately bird.

In past years the eagle was used as a symbol of imperial might, swiftness, and brute power. The Persians and Romans carried standards with the eagle symbol into battle. Emperors of Rome bore ivory scepters topped by an eagle, and Native Americans worshipped the eagle because of its beauty.

For some time bald eagles were on the endangered species list because of their fast disappearance. Today it's estimated that there are only about 7,000 breeding pairs in the United States. Still, bald eagles were taken off the endangered list in 1995.

One of the lessons we can learn from the eagles is that they take good care of their families. God is interested in His family and wants to take care of us. The eaglets allow their parents to take care of them. Do we allow God to take care of us? Or do we want to do things our way, by ourselves? God will take care of us if we allow Him to.

Invite God into your life this morning and ask Him to take care of you. Turn your life over to Him today.

FLIERS WITHOUT FEATHERS

Who are these that fly as a cloud, and as the doves to their windows? Isaiah 60:8.

We generally think of birds and insects when we think of creatures that fly. But a number of other creatures, while they do not actually fly, have membranes they use for gliding.

Probably the greatest gliders of all the animals are the colugos of Southeast Asia. The colugo, which looks something like a lemur, is about the size of a house cat. It has also been called the cobego and flying lemur. Colugos can jump from high in a tree and sail up to 100 yards. A baby colugo will tightly cling to its mother as she glides.

In Australia we find a gliding opossum, the smallest gliding mammal. It is only about six inches long, and half of that may be tail. In the jungles of Southeast Asia is the flying dragon, which has folds of skin on its sides. As it leaps from limb to limb it stretches out these folds of skin and can glide up to about 50 feet. It can twist its body while flying and go to the right or left. The flying gecko lizard has webbed feet and skin flaps on its sides that it spreads to glide from tree to tree. Some Asian frogs have tremendous folds of skin between the extremely long toes on their feet that act as a parachute when they jump.

Flying fish are a beautiful sight as they soar through the air. Actually the fish are not flying, but gliding. These fish build up speed, then shoot out of the water and, with extended paired fins, glide for a short distance. At times the wind may help them glide farther, and at times as they begin to come back down they vibrate their tail fin in the water to keep their body above the water so they can glide even further.

One day you too will be able to fly. God will give you the ability to travel and explore through His universe to your heart's desire, throughout all eternity. Pray that God will help you have that opportunity.

FAITHFULNESS AND MODESTY

I want their hearts to be encouraged and united in love, so that they may have all the riches of assured understanding and have the knowledge of God's mystery, that is, Christ himself. Colossians 2:2, NRSV.

In the language of flowers, violets stand for faithfulness and modesty. They have been gathered for their beauty, too. Violets come not only in violet but in shades of yellow, white, and blue. They've been used as food, medicine, cosmetics, and as omens. Children have enjoyed running into the fields and woods and picking handfuls of violets. There are more than 60 different species of violets in the United States, and there may be others in other countries.

According to Greek myth, the god Zeus created violets for his lover Io. Hera, Zeus's wife, found out about it, and Zeus hid Io by transforming her into a heifer. When she complained about the coarse grass she had to eat, he created the white violet for her food. The purple violets are said to have come from the Roman goddess Venus as a symbol of love, since she was the goddess of love. I'm certainly glad we have a true God-Creater, so we don't have to believe in all of this mythology, aren't you?

In the Middle Ages violets were used to make violet syrup, violet sugar, violet jam, and violet greens. Modern wild food enthusiasts proclaim that violet leaves are high in vitamin A and that the leaves and flowers have more vitamin C than oranges. They are also a good laxative.

Violets reproduce in three ways, by self-fertilization, vegetative runners, and open pollination. Usually at least one of these methods will work. The activity of insects and birds around the flowers causes mature seed capsules to erupt. When they do, the seeds shoot up to five feet away. The smooth yellow violets sometimes eject the seeds up to 15 feet away.

Many things that God has done are a mystery to humans, but we can trust Him, knowing that He did all for our good. Thank God that one day you will understand much more. Ask Him for wisdom in your studies today.

NURSERIES OF LIFE

And God said, "Let the water teem with living creatures." ... God blessed them and said, "Be fruitful ... and fill the water in the seas." Genesis 1:20-22, NIV.

When God created this earth, He told all of His creation to multiply and produce more of the same. God gave each species the power to procreate its own kind. He gave this command to the creatures of the sea, and they fulfill God's command in different ways.

Along the coast of many of the world's countries are swamping areas called wetlands. Many feel that these are a waste of space that should be drained and filled in with dirt. In addition to being used for farming, many real estate developers use the former wetlands for cabins and houses. Of the 221 million acres of wetlands in the continental United States in the 1600s, less than half remain.

To protect these vitally important areas for the benefit of sea creatures, birds, and other wildlife, the U.S. government passed the Wetlands Act. The act protects many, but not all, of the areas, and is very important to natural creatures as well as to naturalists. Not only does it preserve the places these creatures multiply, but it enables scientists to study their life cycles and habits. Many creatures that cannot multiply in the open seas come into these marshes and have their families. As the tide goes back out to sea, many small creatures are caught in the ponds. Most of the time this is beneficial to them.

When the wetlands are made habitable for humans, it endangers many species of sea life, birds, and other wildlife. Often one type of wetland creature depends upon other creatures in the wetlands for its food and life.

As Christians we should be good conservationists, doing all we can to preserve these areas. In this sin-filled world there are wetlands that you can enjoy. They can teach many lessons if you take time to observe them. Thank God today for the wetlands and the joy they can bring you.

NO DRINK

For the Lord is great, and greatly to be praised: he is to be feared above all gods.
Psalm 96:4.

The koalas of Australia rarely drink water. In fact, in a primitive Australian tribe the word *koala* means "no drink."

Although koalas are often called bears, they are in fact marsupials, or pouched animals. They carry their young in these pouches for three to six months. After leaving the pouch, the babies ride around on the mother's back until they are about a year old.

Koalas spend most of their lives in trees and are especially fond of eucalyptus, living on the leaves and young shoots. Although there are about 350 species of eucalyptus trees in Australia, koalas eat the leaves from only about 20. Interestingly, koalas in different parts of the country eat different kinds of eucalyptus leaves. These leaves contain substances that affect body temperature. Koalas in the cooler climates eat leaves that contain phellandrene, which increases body temperature. On the other hand, koalas in warmer climates eat leaves that contain cineole, which decreases body temperature. Koalas eat so many eucalyptus leaves—about two and a half pounds a day—that they smell like eucalyptus. They get most of the water they need from the leaves.

Generally koalas will come down from a tree only to walk over and climb another tree. While on the ground they lick soil and gravel to aid them in digestion. These little teddy bears may live to be 20 years old.

Today's kids love the toy teddy bears, the koala look-alikes. Real-life koalas have soft fur and look like lovable little creatures, although they do fight among themselves.

God loves us even though we're not always lovable, and He longs for us to accept His love. Thank Him for His love today and ask Him to help you be a lovable Christian.

THE LADY WITH SPOTS

For thou art great, and doest wondrous things: thou art God alone. Psalm 86:10.

"Ladybug, ladybug, fly away home. Your house is on fire, and your children will burn." I learned this little saying when I was a small boy. I don't know where it came from and I don't know the meaning of it, but maybe I said it just so I could see the bright little ladybug fly away.

Ladybugs are actually beetles, and they are beneficial to the human family. They are found all over the world, with approximately 150 species in North America. These little creatures range in size from that of the head of a straight pin to that of a large thumbnail. They may have no spots or up to 22 spots on their back.

Like many other insects, ladybugs go through a four-stage life cycle. Theirs lasts about 27 days. They pass from the egg to the larva, then pupa, and finally to the adult. The female lays her eggs in clusters on the bottom side of a leaf or in the crotch of a tree. A female may lay as many as 1,500 eggs in a two-month period. When an egg hatches and the larva comes out, it looks like a small alligator with hair. Ladybug larvae will eat all types of small insects, but aphids are their favorite. During the larval stage they shed their skin four times. Ladybugs also vary in color, most of them quite bright.

Ladybugs are so beneficial that gardeners and farmers buy them by the gallon to live on and near their plants to save the plants from many small destructive insects. There are about 135,000 ladybugs in a gallon! Their fame as pest killers was established in 1888 when the vedalia beetle, a species of ladybug, was imported from Australia. This beetle saved the California citrus crops from the cottony cushion scale insect, which also came from Australia and feeds on the sap from leaves and twigs.

God can save you from the enemy too. Thank Him for His care for you today.

HIDDEN IN THE CORAL REEF

Save me, O Lord, from my enemies; I have fled to you for refuge. Psalm 143:9, NRSV.

Among the most interesting and yet misunderstood works of God is the coral reef. Coral reefs are made by colonies of the coral polyp, a tiny sea animal. Reefs grow in shallow seas from the bottom of the ocean upward, and each type of coral polyp depends on some sunlight. Coral grows in warm water areas that have very little change in temperature.

Some oceanographers claim that coral reefs are the mightiest structures ever built by any form of life on this planet. The largest reef known is the Great Barrier Reef off western Australia. It is 1,250 miles long and said to contain more than 5,000 cubic miles of limestone. The little flowerlike coral polyps deposit one molecule of lime, or calcium, at a time, and thus the limestone coral reef is made.

Each type of coral has its own growth pattern that produces a characteristically shaped structure. The brain coral resembles the human brain, and the branch coral looks like small trees and plants. Other types are not so smooth and branchy.

The coral polyps are the architects and landlords of the reef. Coral reefs provide food, housing, and protection for many ocean creatures. More than 3,000 different varieties of sea life have been counted around some coral reefs in the Pacific Ocean. They include shellfish, fish, snails, eels, lobsters, sponges, starfish, and sea fans.

We have a protector, God, who will hide us from our enemy (Satan) if we are willing to stay close to Him and be sheltered by all His love and protection. Ask Jesus today to help you stay close to Him and to put His loving arms of protection around you. He will!

THE SOLITARY STALKER

All our enemies have opened their mouths against us. Lamentations 3:46.

One of the most stately and beautiful birds in the world is the great blue heron. These birds stand up to four feet tall, have a wingspan of more than six feet, yet weigh only five to eight pounds. Their bill strikes with accuracy and force and is usually deadly to their prey.

Great blue herons are found from Canada to Mexico, and they can adapt well to whatever area they are in. They like to fish in shallow rivers or lakes and delight themselves with the crayfish and other small creatures that are found in the water.

As an extremely skillful stalker, the great blue heron can hold still for a long time as it waits for the instant it can strike. One day I watched one in a lake in northern Michigan. It stood still for about a half hour, then bingo, it had the fish in its mouth.

Great blues make their nests high up in the trees. Their nests look quite flimsy, yet hold both the eggs and the parents. The female lays from three to five eggs, and the parents take turns incubating them. After about 28 days the little chicks peck a hole in the shell and appear, saying in bird language, "Hi, I'm here, and I'm hungry." At first it is necessary for the parents to regurgitate food, a little at a time, into a baby's mouth. Later, as the chicks grow, the parents bring in small snakes, mammals, softshell crabs, and fish. It is a real trick for the parents to find and bring all the food their offspring need, as the growing chicks eat about one fourth of their weight daily.

Just as the great blue heron is an enemy to many creatures, there are many evil angels flying around that are enemies to God's children. They want to feed us things that will corrupt our minds and that will harm our spiritual well-being. Pray today, asking God to take control of your mind so that the evil angels have no room to feed you any trash.

July 12

ALLIGATOR OR CROCODILE?

And Peter opened his mouth and said: "Truly I perceive that God shows no partiality."
Acts 10:34, RSV.

As you look at the long, slender, rough body with a huge tail, a big snout, four short legs, and a mouth full of teeth, what do you call it? Some people call it an alligator. Others call it a crocodile. The two are not the same, but people get them confused. One of the easiest ways to tell these two creatures apart is by the teeth. In the crocodile's lower jaw the fourth tooth from the front on either side fits into a notch in the upper jaw. When the mouth is shut, these two teeth protrude out farther than the others. Also, the crocodile's snout usually is longer, more pointed, and narrower than the alligator's.

Crocodiles range in length from 7½ to 12 feet. The record length in the United States is 15 feet, and in South America it is 23 feet. About a dozen species live in Asia, Africa, Australia, Madagascar, and North and South America. They enjoy the shallow water, rivers, swamps, and marshes. With their long, powerful, flexible tails, they are excellent swimmers. As they float along on top of the water, their eyes, which are up on top of their heads, look forward out of the water.

I have had the opportunity of going up and down the Ucayali River in the jungles of Peru and seeing very large crocodiles crawl from the bank or sandbar into the water right underneath our canoe. I can tell you that it gives a person an uncomfortable feeling to wonder where the crocodile went and what it is doing. We saw many of them, and they didn't seem to be looking for a missionary dinner. They were trying to get away from us, for they were just as wary of us as we were of them.

To most people all crocodiles and alligators look alike, but an expert knows them apart. Jesus can tell who we are, too, and knows us all by name. Be thankful you have a God who is the owner of the world, yet knows you by your name. Thank Him today for His expressed love.

THE CAPYBARAS

[He] gave himself for us to redeem us from all wickedness and purify for himself a people that are his very own, eager to do what is good. Titus 2:14, NIV.

Venezuela is the home for the capybaras, the largest rodents in the world. Their front legs are shorter than their hind legs, and they live where the environment is somewhat swampy. Capybaras can weigh up to 120 pounds each, and are neither fast nor enduring runners. They are not aggressive, they grow fast, and they require very little care. Social animals, they live in small family groups, usually dominated by one adult male.

Young capybaras mature quickly, and the females are able to reproduce in about 15 months. They produce three litters of babies every two years. Capybaras live from eight to 10 years, and a female could produce 36 young in a lifetime.

Because their feet are partially webbed, capybaras are excellent swimmers. They can dive and stay submerged for a long time. More than 300 years ago, because of the close association of the capybaras with water, the Roman Catholic Church classified capybaras as fish and so could be eaten on meatless days. No one considers them fish today, but capybaras are still used for meat. In fact, the salvation of these creatures came when it was discovered that they were "good" to eat. Large farms in Venezuela raise them like cattle for their meat, which is said to taste like a combination of pork and beef. These creatures are in abundance now.

As the capybaras are different from all other rodents, so God has chosen to have a people who are different from other people. Different does not mean to be funny or odd, but different in lifestyle and beliefs. God wanted a special people, a chosen people.

Just as capybara are valuable to the Venezuelan cowboys, so we are valuable to God. Thank Him in your prayer today that you have been chosen by Him.

July 14

THE FLYING ARTIST

He adorned the temple with precious stones. And the gold he used was gold of Parvaim. 2 Chronicles 3:6, NIV.

I n New Guinea and Australia lives a bird called the bowerbird. There are 18 species of these birds, which are about the size of a robin. The males of each of the species are artists, some better than others. They express themselves as human artists do, with different designs and colors.

The males of all but two of the species build a nest (called a bower), or a display area of sticks and grass. Each species builds a little differently. The birds take weeks to build a bower, and when it is finally finished to suit them, they go out and find decorations to adorn its entrance. Incidentally, this is no small house. It's usually about a foot high.

The decorations used by the male birds are different from bower to bower. They use different-colored mosses, fungi, fruits, leaves, flowers, pebbles, shells, feathers, and anything else of beauty they can find. Depending on the species and likes of the males, they may use all one color. Some even paint the inside of the bower with chewed-up berries. The adornments are spread out at the entrance, and the purpose of all this work is to attract females.

The males of different species have different coloring. Eleven of the 17 bower-building males have a colorful crest on top of their head, like a rooster. Some of them have beautiful colored feathers, while the females are plain brown. If the female accepts the male, she goes off and builds her own nest and incubates her eggs alone. These artistic guys build only a bower, and then they are through.

Solomon built his Temple with the most beautiful materials and colors to glorify the Lord. He was an artist, I would say, in the use of beautiful materials. Jesus has gone to prepare mansions for us in heaven. We have no idea what they will look like, only that they will be beautiful. Thank God today for Jesus, and that He has gone to prepare a beautiful home for you in heaven.

DEPENDENTS

If anyone asks you, "Why are you untying it?" tell him, "The Lord needs it." Luke 19:31, NIV.

In the context of today's text, Jesus needed an animal to ride into the city of Jerusalem, so He told His disciples to go get a donkey colt.

There are plants that God created that need each other too. It is interesting to see how many plants need each other. We have talked about pollination—how some plants need pollen from other plants like themselves in order to bear fruit. Then there are the plants that depend on other plants for their lives. We call these parasites.

Parasites can grow in several ways. The true parasite grows directly on the plant, attaching itself to the plant and taking its nourishment from it. Now, certain dependent plants grow from the ground and use the host plants only to support themselves. They do not take anything from the host plant, so these are not parasites.

Some common parasites are mistletoe and dodder. Mistletoe attaches itself to the limb of a tree and lives by boring its rootlike tentacles into the tree. Through these it sucks out the water and dissolved minerals necessary for its life. Interestingly, one mistletoe may attach itself to another mistletoe, living off of its own kind. Few other parasites do this. When too much mistletoe attaches itself to a tree, the tree dies. When that happens, so does the mistletoe.

Then there is a tropical parasite that lives inside its host plant. It is called the rafflesia. This plant bores into the host and spreads thin filaments through the host's internal tissues. It literally grows inside of the host, and it is difficult to tell the parasite from the host. Rarely does it come into the open, but when it does it produces the largest flower in the world—about three feet across. The flower is brown and purple, and stinks.

Ask Jesus to help you in your need today. He gives life, and it is free.

BEI-SHUNG

Blessed is he whose help is the God of Jacob, whose hope is in the Lord his God, the Maker of heaven and earth, the sea, and everything in them—the Lord who remains faithful forever. Psalm 146:5, 6, NIV.

What is black and white, fuzzy, and lovable? If you guessed a giant panda, you guessed correctly. The giant panda, a native of China, has been imitated by stuffed-animal creators the world over. Thousands of these pandas are sold each year and cuddled by small children and others.

Bei-shung is the Chinese name for this animal, which is related to the raccoon. The panda is mostly white, with black ears, shoulders, legs, and feet, and black trim around its eyes. Pandas are great lovers of sweet bamboo shoots. They eat 40 pounds or more of bamboo shoots a day. They also like fruits and berries. It is estimated that pandas spend about two thirds of their time eating. Young pandas climb trees, but the adults live mostly on the ground.

Pandas weigh more than 200 pounds and are about five or six feet long. At birth a baby panda weighs no more than three pounds.

It was not until 1869 that a French missionary reported to the Western world about the giant pandas. Before that time, only the Chinese knew they existed.

The Chinese government has desired to keep control of these animals. Any pandas that you see in zoos around the world, including the United States, are on loan from China. At a certain date, determined by the contract China has with that zoo, the pandas must be returned to China.

The Creator fashioned so many things for our enjoyment, and the lovable pandas are just one such creature. Of course, in the beginning all animals were lovable, and will be again in the new earth. Today let us turn our thoughts to the great Creator. Thank Him for creating such wonderful creatures for His and our enjoyment.

Ask Him to help you be kind and loving toward others today.

WATERSPOUTS

Deep calleth unto deep at the noise of thy waterspouts: all thy waves and thy billows are gone over me. Psalm 42:7.

I am curious to know how David knew about waterspouts. Do you suppose there were geysers back in his time? If not, how did he know about them? I'm puzzled. How about you?

There is water under the earth's surface, just as there is oil and other substances. Many homes use water that comes from wells on the property. On some islands, such as Bermuda, rainwater is caught on roofs or in large tanks. Most of us use well water, purified river or lake water, or seawater that has been desalted.

In most areas in which there is underground water, the rocks and sand that hold it are cool. In some areas the water table (the depth underground at which water is found) is shallow, and in other places it is deep. In Colorado our backyard well was only six feet deep. Along the Platte River in Nebraska the water table is just a few feet deep. In other places people must drill down hundreds of feet to find water.

In other areas underground, the rocks are hot and the water is under pressure. As the water runs into these reservoir areas, it heats to a superhot boiling point. Under this pressure, water and steam spout out from cracks or fissures into the air. This is what makes a geyser, something you may have seen in Yellowstone National Park. A famous geyser is Old Faithful, which spouts off at regular intervals. Its routine repeat performance is caused by more water running into the heated area. When it becomes superhot, it spouts off again.

As David recalled his love for the Lord and his desire to serve Him, David realized that his life needed some help. That help could come only from the Lord. Pray as David did, that God will come in and take over in your life. Thank Him today for His everabiding presence in your life.

FLAME FLOWER

And he shall be like a tree planted by the rivers of water, that bringeth forth his fruit in his season; his leaf also shall not wither; and whatsoever he doeth shall prosper. Psalm 1:3.

One of the largest multimillion-dollar plant businesses in the world is the raising and selling of poinsettias. It all started back in the mid-1820s when a man named Joel R. Poinsett, of Charleston, South Carolina, was sent as the first United States ambassador to Mexico. As Mr. Poinsett walked through the hills and valleys around Mexico City, he came across some crimson shrubs that were from six to 16 feet high. The Mexicans called them flame flower. In English they have taken the name of the man who discovered them in Mexico, poinsettia.

What especially interested Mr. Poinsett was their bright crimson color. Botanists tell us that the crimson parts are not really petals but bracts. The bracts surround the real flowers, which are clusters of little yellowish-green buttons.

The flame flower has become a symbol of Christmas. In California is a ranch that grows nothing but poinsettias under 20 acres of fiberglass roofing. If the temperature is not just right, or the soil is too soggy, the plant loses its leaves. Then, of course, the color is gone. This ranch has produced a plant that holds its leaves longer than most varieties.

The Bible writer likens the righteous person to a plant or tree that will not lose its leaves. That person will continue to be a beautiful tree, and others will be introduced to Christ through his or her life. Jesus wants us to show our true color as a Christian and let others know about Him.

It takes a lot of care to make a poinsettia pretty and keep it that way. Jesus is willing to spend time in helping us to remain pretty, if we will let Him. Ask Him today to help you be a true Christian and allow others to see your true color—a life that radiates Jesus.

MY BLACK WALNUT TREE

I pray that you, being rooted and established in love, may have power . . . to grasp . . . the love of Christ. Ephesians 3:17, 18, NIV.

Several species of black walnuts grow in the United States; a smaller variety are in Japan. The eastern black walnut is the largest of all. It can grow to nearly 150 feet tall, and its trunk may have a diameter of six feet.

The black walnut tree is known principally for its beautiful hardwood, which is almost a purplish brown. Cabinetmakers and others who work with wood especially like the black walnut wood because it can be sanded and polished to a very high luster. Not surprisingly, black walnut wood is quite expensive. The tree also bears fruit. Its nuts are embedded in pulplike husks. The aroma of black walnuts can be smelled some distance away.

When we lived in Kansas, a large black walnut tree grew by the master bedroom window. Kansas has many lightning storms, and during the storms it always seemed to me as if the lightning wanted to climb through our bedroom window. One day as I talked with a farmer I told him that I enjoyed having that large black walnut tree by my house, but that every time we had an electrical storm the lightning seemed to want to climb in my window.

"Don't you know why you have that sensation?" he asked.

"No, why?"

"The black walnut tree has a very large taproot," he said. (That's a central root that goes straight down into the ground.) "It acts as a ground for electricity. When lightning flashes, it is conducted through the root of the black walnut tree into the ground."

We are to be a conductor of the radiant love of Jesus. In order to be that kind of person, we must have our taproot grounded deep in Jesus. That comes by study and prayer. If you have your taproot down deep in His love, Satan cannot move you. Ask Jesus to help your root go deep.

THE LESSER LIGHT

And God made two great lights; . . . the lesser light to rule the night. Genesis 1:16.

The moon has been one of the most fascinating objects of our attention. For centuries people have been intrigued by the moon, and in the twentieth century they longed to actually go there. They were almost certain that there was no life up there, yet they continued to search for a way to get there. We know that on July 20, 1969, the United States finally put men on the moon. Did this great feat take away our curiosity about the moon? Some, but not all. Scientists still do not know all about it, and another trip there is possible. God's Word tells us why the moon shines. The moon reflects the light of the sun, and God made it to rule the night.

As we study the moon and God's Word, we see that the moon has a specific purpose. It was created to light up the night. The moon also controls the tides in the ocean. It has a very important part to play in our world.

Just as the moon reflects the sun's light, so we as Christians should reflect the light from Jesus to others, that they might see Him in our lives. But is that all? No, it isn't.

In giving light, the moon plays a secondary role to the sun. Though the moon is number two, it still keeps reflecting and doing its job. In fact, it keeps working even when it cannot be seen. This demonstrates that I don't always have to be the big shot and get all the attention. I should do my assigned job willingly, even if it isn't a task that will give me attention or prominence.

What about you today? Will you follow the moon's example? By beginning the day with God—by reading the Bible, thinking about what you have read, and asking that the Holy Spirit control your thoughts and actions—you are placing yourself where light from the Sun of Righteousness will shine on you. Ask God to help you reflect Jesus in your life today.

FISHERS

"But now I will send for many fishermen," declares the Lord, "and they will catch them. After that I will send for many hunters, and they will hunt them down on every mountain and hill." Jeremiah 16:16, NIV.

In the northern part of the United States lives a furbearing animal called the fisher. One of the larger members of the weasel family, they are known by several other names—marten, pekan, black cat, and black fox. The fisher has a soft, silky, beautiful fur coat. Around its neck and shoulders the tips of its fur are an attractive silver, which gives the fisher a grizzled look. Most fishers also have some small irregular white spots on the throat and underparts.

The males are 30 to 40 inches long, including a 13- to 15-inch tail. They weigh seven to 12 pounds. The females are about one third smaller and half the weight of the male. When possible, fishers are opportunistic feeders and eat whatever is close by—both plants and animals. Baby fishers are called kits, and in each litter there will be an average of three.

Wildlife experts are happy to have the fishers around. The state of Wisconsin imports them from other states because they help control the rabbit and porcupine population. While fishers like rabbit and porcupine meat, they also like squirrels, mice, some fish, and various berries, leaves, and buds. When they are hungry, they've been seen jumping from tree to tree like a squirrel, chasing a squirrel. They are quite agile in the trees, but do not spend much time there. They prefer the ground and like living in hardwood forested areas. They are great hunters and roam over about a 10-square-mile area.

Jesus likened His kingdom to a large net. He wanted His followers to be fishers and hunters of men, going anywhere to find them and teach them of His great love for them. Thank Jesus that He has found you today. Ask Him to help you be a "hunter" for Him, and share His love today with a friend.

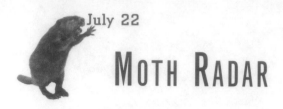

MOTH RADAR

If ye shall ask any thing in my name, I will do it. John 14:14.

Unlike butterflies, which flit from flower to flower and shrub to shrub during the daylight hours, moths are generally nocturnal creatures. Moths and butterflies belong to the same order of insects, but they are different. One of the main differences is the antennae. Butterfly antennae are bare with a small knob at the end, but the moth antennae are like graceful tapering filaments. On some species it looks like a feather.

The largest and most showy is the giant silk moth. Industrialists thought they could raise these to spin silk threads, but that idea caught on only in Asian countries, not in the United States. Giant silk moths have a five- to six-inch wingspan. Their adult life span is very short.

Like butterflies, moths go through a metamorphosis process from an egg to a larva or caterpillar, to a pupa, and finally to an adult. The female lays its eggs on the leaves or twigs of a specific species of plant, according to the species, because only these plants will provide food for the offspring. After she has laid her eggs, she has completed her role in nature and dies of total exhaustion. She may have lived as a moth for only a few short days.

As a female silkworm comes out of either a ground burrow or a cocoon, she emits into the air a chemical known as a pheromone. This transmits a certain message to lonely males. From great distances they pick up the pheromone messages on their antennae and begin to fly in a systematic pattern, homing in on the female moth. And man thinks he created radar! When a male finds a female, they mate. Soon she is ready to lay eggs, and the cycle begins again.

When you are in need of help and call out to God, He will find you. His radar is accurate and exacting. If you desire Jesus to come and live in your life, ask Him today. His global positional system is set, and He can pinpoint your exact location. Isn't that exciting?

SUPERSEALS

Have you not known? Have you not heard? The Lord is the everlasting God, the Creator of the ends of the earth. He does not faint or grow weary; his understanding is unsearchable. Isaiah 40:28, NRSV.

Weddell (WED-do-l) seals are remarkable. Called superseals because they live and survive in the extreme cold of the Antarctic, they live under the antarctic ice for months at a time. How do they survive? How do they get air? They keep breathing holes open by gnawing at the ice with their strong canine and incisor teeth. The upper incisors extend forward and contact the ice before the canines.

During the summer the Weddell seals climb out on top of the ice to sun themselves and give birth to their pups. This time in the warm sun is very limited, because the sun doesn't stay long in the Antarctic. In the winter, temperatures drop to $-80°F$ $(-62°C)$. If they stayed out in this temperature they would freeze, even with their fatty blubber insulation, so they live mostly under the ice, where the water temperature is about $29°F$. $(2°C.)$.

Superseal pups have the shortest childhood of any large mammals. The mother gives birth right onto the ice. The newborn pup begins to shiver because the difference in temperature between its mother's body and the air is more than 60 degrees. The shivering not only shakes off the ice crystals that immediately form on its body, but also warms up the pup. Soon it is drinking its mother's warm milk and starting to grow. At six weeks its stops nursing, and its mother shoves it into the sea. She swims near it and protects it, but soon it is on its own.

God has many secrets that we will probably never know or understand, and there are many questions about the superseals that scientists cannot answer. God knows the number of stars in the unlimited heavens and the number of hairs that you have on our head—because He is the Creator. Thank God today for the knowledge that He has allowed you to understand and obtain through your study.

BLUE-FOOTED BOOBY

*To every thing there is a season, and a time to every purpose under the heaven.
Ecclesiastes 3:1.*

The blue-footed boobies are very comical birds to any person watching them. But of course to other boobies they are perfectly normal. The blue-footed booby has large light-blue webbed feet. That's how it got its name.

There are six species of boobies. The blue-footed lives in colonies on islands, mostly along the Pacific coast of Central and South America. Their main food is fish. When there is an abundance of fish, they begin their courtship dance. The males point their long bills upward, extend their wings, and strut around. Then they begin to dance a little. If a female becomes interested in a certain male, she will join him in the dance, and then the courtship will begin. The birds stay close together, point their bills into the air, touch their bills, bow, and goose-step with their big blue feet.

As the young hatch, the older boobies will catch fish and bring them to the babies. They commonly fly about 50 feet or more above the water until they spot a fish; then they fold their wings and dive into the water. They are so designed by God that just before they hit the water they can readjust their aim, arrange their wings in a streamlined fashion, and pierce the water like an arrow. They seldom miss their prey.

As both the Bible and common sense tells us, there is a time for everything. Boobies have a time for their courtship dance, and a time to fish. Many of us need to learn that there are certain times we do things and other times we don't (see Ecclesiastes 3:1-8). If we are to survive spiritually, every day we must take some time with God's Word.

Ask God to help you take time with His Word today.

KANGAROO RATS

And he said unto his disciples, Therefore I say unto you, Take no thought for your life, what ye shall eat; neither for the body, what ye shall put on. Luke 12:22.

The kangaroo rat doesn't worry about what it will drink. Just as all of the other pocket mice and rats do, it gets its water from the food it eats, which is mostly seeds. Kangaroo rats live in the southwestern United States. They are basically hermits, in that they each have their own house away from other rats.

Kangaroo rats build numerous interconnected tunnels in the ground and have as many as 12 entrances to their house. They go above the ground to gather up seeds, storing them in pouches in their cheeks. They may get hundreds of seeds before coming back and unloading the seeds in the tunnels, where they are continuously moved from place to place. The seeds are not only food but den humidifiers as well, both of which are necessary for survival

These little creatures are about 15 inches long, more than half of which is tail. They have short front legs and long back legs, like a kangaroo. That's where they got their name. Their tail is used to give balance as they jump. It has a nice bushy clump of hair on the tip. They have pale-yellow to dark-brown hair on top, with a white stripe along the side and down the tail, and a white underside.

The female gives birth twice a year. There are from two to six in a litter. Naturalists say that the tunnel house becomes a nursery of infants, mewing like kittens When they get angry, they thump the ground, which is a warning to stay away.

Kangaroo rats put most of their energy into storing up food. God tells us not to worry about our physical needs. If our spiritual life is right with Him, He will take care of the rest, but most of us have so little faith that we don't want to trust Him that far. Tell God today that you want to trust Him. Then really and truly trust Him. Let Him help you make the tough decisions today, and see what happens. You'll be surprised.

July 26

GLACIERS—RIVERS OF ICE

Out of the south cometh the whirlwind: and cold out of the north. Job 37:9.

Glaciers are caused by the buildup of ice and snow in mountains in North America and other parts of the world. The Rocky Mountains in both the United States and Canada have some very large glaciers. Walking out on them might give you an uneasy feeling. I always watch for the ever-present cracks when I walk on a glacier, for I don't want to fall into one.

A glacier is a fascinating formation. They are usually in high-altitude areas that get a lot of snowfall but have a short melting period. I used to wonder why those cracks or crevices were always present; then I found out why. The ice of the glacier moves downhill. As it comes to uneven terrain the top of the glacier continues to move, but the bottom of the glacier slows down. That causes a split to form. Scientists have also discovered that the ice of the glacier moves faster in the center and slower on the edges.

As glaciers move downhill, they flow at different speeds. When the glacier gets to a warmer zone, it melts completely and forms a creek or river. Since the summer is short and the weather is always cool where glaciers form, the glacier usually doesn't disappear entirely. As the snow falls and builds up, it turns to ice, and this accumulates. Many of the North American glaciers may be between 200 and 300 feet deep. They usually form in valleys where they are protected, but they may spill down into open areas as they move and melt.

It is interesting that even in Bible times prophets wrote about the cold coming from the north. In the Northern Hemisphere, cold still comes from the north. The farther north you go, the colder it is. The farther south, the warmer it gets, until you get to the southern part of the Southern Hemisphere. Then it gets cold again.

God's love for us is never cold or hot. It is always the same temperature, and He invites us to take advantage of His love. Tell Him you want to experience His love toward you today.

RUBIES OF THE BOG

I pray for them. I do not pray for the world but for those whom You have given Me, for they are Yours. John 17:9, NKJV.

When the Puritan pilgrims landed on the eastern shores of North America in 1620, the Wampanoag Indians presented them with some small red berries as a goodwill gift. The pilgrims had no idea what these berries were called or how to use them, but they accepted them in good faith and planted them. In June of that year they noticed that the berry vines were covered with pale-pink flowers that made the vines look as if they were sprinkled with powdered sugar. Up close the flowers looked like the head of a bird called a crane. So the Pilgrims named the berries crane berries. It wasn't long until the name was shortened to cranberry, and that is what we call them today. The commonwealth of Massachusetts has many cranberry bogs, especially on Cape Cod.

Cranberries need to grow in a sandy soil, with peat on the surface, where the sun does not get too hot and where some snow comes in winter to cover the vines and keep them from freezing. Unless the plants are well pollinated, they will not produce well. The growers discovered that by bringing in bees to pollinate the plants, they produced better. Of course, the bees liked the cranberry flowers and made good honey.

In 1816 Henry Hall began to take an active interest in farming the cranberries. From that point they really became famous. Many others started farming them, even in the states of Oregon and Washington.

It wasn't until Jesus took a special interest in this world and decided to come here that we were given the hope of a new life. If He had not taken this special interest in the world, you and I would not be here today.

Thank God in your prayer today that Jesus took a special interest in you, so that you could have a new life for all eternity. It will be a life you'll enjoy—living near God, and traveling to other planets to see what they are like. And that will be for all eternity. Forever and ever, without end.

WATER MONITORS

Behold, I will bring it [Jerusalem] health and cure, and I will cure them, and will reveal unto them the abundance of peace and truth. Jeremiah 33:6.

In the countries of China and Malaysia one of the food delicacies of the people is a lizard called the water monitor. The people like the meat; they broil, grill, stew, fry, smoke, and curry it. The skin is much desired for purses and other leather goods, as it is very fine and soft.

Drum heads and small stringed musical instruments similar to the banjo are also made from the skins. Some drums have been used by the tribal people for hundreds of years. The tonal quality of this lizard skin is considered to be very good—superior, in many cases, to other things.

These lizards are also used for medicinal purposes in witchcraft and other healings. People eat the meat because of the superstitious belief that strength and heat come from it. The gallbladder is dried, and a tea is made from it that is supposed to help with heart and liver ailments. The body fat is mixed with herbs and sold as a balm for a variety of illnesses. Because the monitors get few diseases and seem rather healthy most of the time, the natives believe that eating the meat can bring strength and health to them.

In the country of Sri Lanka some people believe that one can be killed by administering a concoction of human blood and hair mixed with monitor oil and flesh.

We should be thankful today that our God of love has given us the proper things with which to take care of our bodies. He tells us that our bodies are His temple and that we should take care of them. As Christians we thrive on the love of Jesus. We get that power, not from eating meat, but from "eating" His Word.

Thank God today that there is power in His Word to give you good health.

Flashlight Fish

But blessed are your eyes, for they see: and your ears, for they hear. Matthew 13:16.

Living among the coral rock in Caribbean waters, between the United States and South America, are fish that have lights on their heads. These have been properly named flashlight fish. The first one of these fish was found in 1907, floating on the water near the island of Jamaica. Mexican fishermen found the second one in 1972.

Scuba divers reported that they had seen these from a distance, but no one came close to them in their natural habitat until 1978. At that time a team of four divers went down more than 200 feet in the Caribbean waters.

These divers dove at night, in total darkness. As they approached the 200-foot mark, they knew they could spend only about 10 minutes at that depth. Suddenly they saw the headlights of a Caribbean flashlight fish. They immediately surrounded it. Using the fish's own tactics, they shone a light on it and began to take pictures.

The Caribbean flashlight fish are very timid. They live at depths of 100 to 600 feet. They can turn the light fixtures on their head off and on, as desired. If in danger, they zigzag through the water, turning on the lights when they zig and off when they zag. The brightness of their lights is about that of a dull pensized flashlight.

In the Red Sea and Indo-Pacific area are two other species of the flashlight fish. During the Six-Day War in 1967 an Israeli night plane spotted a green glow near the water's edge in the Red Sea. Thinking it was from underground Egyptian frogmen, they threw hand grenades into the water. The next morning there were dead flashlight fish all over the beach. A green glow still shone from their tiny eye pouches.

God has given us spiritual eyes as well as physical ones. He expects us to use these spiritual eyes to find His truth and all the counsel He has given to us. Thank God today that He has given you spiritual eyes whereby you can see the light of truth in His Word.

JUMPING KIDS

Let them [false gods] rise up and help you, and be your protection. Deuteronomy 32:38.

The Rocky Mountains, from Alaska southward, is home for the American mountain goat. These white-haired creatures live on the steepest slopes and precipices that exist anywhere. They do this for safety and security.

Except during the birthing season the goats generally move in herds. At that time a female, or nanny, will leave the herd and pick out a crevice in which to stay. Within a day or two she gives birth to her kid. This newborn kid—about the size of a human baby, eight to nine pounds—will soon be up and around, trying to jump and frolic. Its legs aren't that stable yet, but it tries anyway. The nanny stands between her kid and the edge of the cliff so that if it does something foolish she will be there to keep it from falling off the rocks to injury or death.

The kid nurses at first, but on the second or third day it will try to join its mother in eating vegetation. In about a month it is weaned and eats only vegetation. After about two weeks from giving birth the nanny is eager to join the herd, so she takes her kid along with her. Meanwhile it has learned to jump from one jagged rock to another, but the nanny is always near to protect and help.

Sometimes the larger, older adults in the herd try to push the younger ones out of the way, but for their first 10 or 11 months Mother is always nearby. Sadly, during the winter's heavy snows about half the new kids lose their lives, as the temperature and snows are too cold and too deep for them. They weigh only about 40 to 50 pounds, and have very little fat. The first winter is rough on the new kids.

In our text for today Moses indicates that false gods cannot protect Israel. But God can. As the nanny protects her kid, so God will protect His "kids." He loves His family and will go all out to protect them from the enemy. Ask God today to protect you from your enemy.

MARVELOUS EYES

For since the creation of the world His invisible attributes, His eternal power and divine nature, have been clearly seen, being understood through what has been made. Romans 1:20, NASB.

Who could make something as complicated as a human eye? Human beings have tried to duplicate it. A camera lens is similar to the human eye. When bad things happen in an eye, ophthalmologists (eye specialists) can often times repair it or transfer other parts to it, but they cannot create a new eye. When an eye goes completely bad, in many instances it must be removed and replaced with an artificial eye.

God did a masterful job in creating eyes. Sight can be broken down into four parts: (1) ability to detect light from darkness, (2) ability to detect movement, (3) ability to detect and make out forms, and (4) color vision.

It is fascinating to note that not all creature's eyes are the same. An owl has very keen night vision. That is when it hunts for food. The earthworm has two eyespots for sensing light. An amoeba senses only light and darkness. Spiders have a simple eye structure that allows them to see objects at a close distance. Flies have fantastic eyes, and dragonflies probably have the most complex eyes in the animal kingdom. Reptiles see well and have very keen vision. And as a whole, birds have the keenest vision of all. Some vultures can see a "meal" on the ground from 4,000 feet in the air.

Dr. Les Thornburg, an optometrist from Durand, Wisconsin, says, "We will probably never be sure of what other animals see. . . . But one thing seems sure . . . every animal sees exactly what it needs to see." That is just the way God created all of His creatures, different for a purpose.

We have a loving, caring God who created us with tender loving care. He thought of everything. Thank Him in your prayer this day for the way He made you and the life you have from Him. He wants the best for you. Always!

WARMTH FROM THE SUN

Ye have sown much, and bring in little; ye eat, but ye have not enough; ye drink, but ye are not filled with drink; ye clothe you, but there is none warm. Haggai 1:6.

Butterflies are interesting little creatures as they flutter, float, and glide from flower to flower and from tree to tree. Researchers tell us that the different kinds of butterflies react differently to the warmth of the sun's rays.

Most butterflies fold their wings straight up over the thorax (body), so that the wings almost touch. But some hold their wings completely open, and other species hold them at various other angles. The butterflies bask in the sun to absorb the needed heat to be able to fly, and the angle controls the amount of heat they receive in the thorax.

The body temperature of butterflies cools off very rapidly. Some butterflies cannot fly more than about three feet without having to stop and get more heat. The larger butterflies can fly for greater distances because of the larger thorax, which does not cool down so soon. There are some that can fly in the shade, especially in the heat of the jungles of South America.

To be able to fly, all butterflies must have a temperature between 82° and 105°F (28° and 41°C). About 50 species need to have their bodies heated up to about 95°F (35°C).

How many of you have gotten up on a cold morning and, still in your pajamas and with your teeth chattering, have gone over to a fireplace, stove, or heater and rubbed your hands together and said, "This heat feels so good!" After a few minutes of warming you feel that you can function, so you get dressed and go to school.

The butterflies need the warmth of the sun to keep flying, and we as Christians need the warmth of God's love to function properly in our Christian life. This warmth is received by a close relationship with Christ, by studying God's Word, by praying to Him, and by sharing Him with others. Ask God to send the warmth of His love to you today.

SPIDERS

But glory, honor, and peace for everyone who does good. Romans 2:10, NIV.

Many of us react negatively to spiders because we are afraid of them and don't really understand them. But most spiders are harmless and helpful creatures. Out of more than 30,000 species of spiders, only a few of them are harmful to humans. Spiders are useful in that they gobble up insects by the thousands. That saves our health, our crops, and maybe our dispositions.

Spiders are not insects, because they have eight legs and only two body parts. They all have jaws with fangs at the tip. Venom runs through the fangs into the victim's body to kill or paralyze. Most spiders have eight eyes, situated in two rows. Others have fewer eyes, and those living in caves have no eyes at all.

All spiders spin silk, which comes from glands in the abdomen. The fluid passes through little organs called spinnerets at the tail end of the creature and solidifies into tiny threads when in contact with the air. These threads have many uses. Some spiders weave webs to catch food. All spiders put out single strands of silk called draglines that are used as lifelines for them to move from one place to another or to escape from enemies. Many spiders make bags from their silk to deposit their eggs in until they hatch. Spider silk is used by some spiders as transportation. They will let a strand loose in the air until it bears them aloft, then hang from it and drift with the air currents from place to place. This is called ballooning. One report said that a spider was seen floating on a silk strand more than 200 miles out at sea.

God created each of us different. Each of us has our way of doing things. Praise God for your individuality. There are characteristics that all spiders share, and there are characteristics that each of us has. You can be creative and, with the help of God's Spirit, develop your own way of growing spiritually.

Ask God today to help you be creative in your life so that you can be *you*. He will help you be creative in your religious experience.

GREAT THINGS FROM SMALL BEGINNINGS

And the earth brought forth grass, the herb that yields seed according to its kind, and the tree that yields fruit, whose seed is in itself according to its kind. Genesis 1:12, NKJV.

Acorns are the fruit from more than 100 different varieties of oak trees in the United States. Historians tell us that up until the Middle Ages many Europeans ate acorns. Some Europeans still eat them today, but Americans rarely include them in their diet. The Europeans discerned that if the leaves of the oak tree had rounded lobes, which indicated that they were the white oaks, the acorns were sweet. If the leaf lobes were pointed, they belonged to the red or black oaks, and the acorns were bitter.

Acorns come in many sizes, from that of a pea to about the size of a large purple grape. In some species, such as the over-cup and laurel-leaved oak, the acorn can barely be seen in the cap, while in the California white oak the acorn protrudes out of the cap about one and a half inches, with the cap just barely covering the base.

Acorns are eaten by deer, squirrels, woodpeckers, raccoons, wood ducks, turkeys, and bears. The many nutrients in acorns make them a good food for the animals that eat them as the main part of their diet. So many animals and birds eat acorns that most of them do not grow into trees.

God has put into the tiny acorn the entire growth systems necessary for a large oak tree. The tiny acorn has the potential root, trunk, branch, and leaf systems in the embryonic state. God put everything necessary in the acorn for the seed to sprout and make a big tree.

God has equipped us with special senses to help us learn about Him and know Him better. He hopes that we will use these senses to become strong Christians and that we will not be detoured by Satan. Use your senses today to know God and learn more about Him. Remember that with God's help, you too can grow into a big and powerful Christian.

Masked Bandit

Finally, all of you, live in harmony with one another; be sympathetic, love as brothers, be compassionate and humble. Do not repay evil with evil or insult with insult, but with blessing. 1 Peter 3:8, 9, NIV.

In the world of nature today's text reminds us of raccoons. They are playful. They have compassion one for the other and do not seem revengeful toward each other. They are mischievous, but not normally harmful.

Raccoons are found almost everywhere in the Americas. And although many have been killed for their skins, they flourish anyway. If there is anything that they can get into, they will. They can open doors, pull out drawers, get into refrigerators, and into just about anything to get at food or something else that they want. Where we lived in Massachusetts it was difficult to keep them out of our garbage cans. I would tie the lids on, and they would untie the rope with their little hands and get in.

A female raccoon usually has four kits in her litter. She nurses them for a short time, and carries them by the back of their neck until they are able to go on their own. Raccoons may wet their food before eating to wash off sand or grit or unpleasant skin secretions. A female coon will attack her enemies if they try to bother her kits. Coons will eat eggs from nests, as well as crayfish, snails, other small animals, and fruits. Sometimes they playfully bat the food around with their paws before eating it.

God wants us to enjoy life, like the little raccoon. One way to do that is to be kind to one another. I know it's hard when your brothers or sisters tease you and your schoolmates call you names, but be kind to them and see if it doesn't pay. Our text says that you will receive a blessing.

Ask God to help you be kind today. Your blessing may not come immediately, but it will come.

Deep-sea Talk

And when they went, I heard the noise of their wings, like the noise of great waters, as the voice of the Almighty, the voice of speech, as the noise of an host; when they stood, they let down their wings. Ezekiel 1:24.

In the depths of the ocean are many voices and meaningful movements. Sea creatures are communicating with one another. Some of these sounds and actions are addressed to their own kind, and sometimes they form messages for others.

Marine biologists have discovered that fish actually converse with vocal sounds or other noises. During World War II the U.S. Navy developed a device that picked up underwater noises. Its purpose was to track German submarines. To their surprise, when they tested the device they heard a chorus of snapping, barking, grunting, and clicking. And that's how it was discovered that deep-sea fish actually communicate with one another.

Fish do not have vocal cords, but they make a variety of noises by flexing the muscles attached to their swim bladder, causing it to resonate like a drum. The male damselfish makes a staccato chirplike noise in the courtship ritual. Groupers thunder as a warning.

Fish also communicate without making a sound. The way they dart or swim can be a message to nearby fish or intruders. Other fish make a certain movement, and their neighbors know that it's "chow" time. Let's explain this one. Some fish are cleaned by other smaller creatures, such as the small wrasses and cleaner shrimp. When a big fish wants a cleaning, it gives a signal, such as head down and tail up, or the other way around. It could also be by raising the left pectoral fin and holding it straight out, as if the big fish wanted to make a left turn. At these signals the cleaning fish and shrimp rapidly swim to the motioning fish and begin to clear off its dead skin, clean its teeth, and groom off the parasites.

In our text today the prophet in vision heard the sounds of angels. Thank God today that He is interested enough to speak to you through His Word.

PUPFISH

You were bought at a price. Therefore honor God with your body. 1 Corinthians 6:20, NIV.

There is a delicate ecological experiment going on, and the fact that it is God's rather than ours is all the more reason to surround it with barbed wire." This was a statement by Pete Sanchez, a natural resources specialist with the U.S. Department of Interior. Mr. Sanchez was referring to the Devil's Hole pupfish, near Ashland, Nevada.

It seems that some small fish called pupfish have been marooned since the Flood in a little spring-fed pool about 20 miles from Death Valley. According to some ichthyologists (scientists who study fish), this species of pupfish has no commercial or aesthetic value. Because the species is found only in this small pool of water, it has been placed on the U.S. government's endangered species list. A chain-link fence has been erected around the pool to protect them.

In 1977 there were only 350 fish in the pond. They grow to a length of one or two inches long, and they have pelvic fins. After birth, they mature in two to five months, feed on algae, and live only three to six months as adults. However, they may live in a dormant stage until the water is plentiful again. The males are a metallic blue, green, and gold with silver bars. The females are a dull greenish blue.

A group of real estate developers wanted to develop this property and sell the lots, but they were not allowed to do so because that would have destroyed the pools where these and other species of pupfish survive. If they'd gone ahead with the plan, the penalty would have been a year in jail. They had hoped to sell the lots marked out in the development for about $420 million. The U.S. government has spent $5.5 million to develop a wildlife reserve to save these few hundred little pupfish because it was felt they were valuable. Imagine spending $5.5 million to save a few small fish!

There is a high value placed on our lives by Jesus. He gave His life, dying on the cross, that you and I might be redeemed from sin. Thank Him today for that valuable sacrifice for you.

PRAIRIE, PAMPA, SAVANNA, STEPPE, VELDT

And I will send grass in your fields for your livestock, that you may eat and be filled.
Deuteronomy 11:15, NKJV.

What is nicer than a prairie, pampa, savanna, steppe, or veldt? What are all of these places, anyway? They are the same—just different names in various languages for a treeless grassland. Prairie is English, pampa is Spanish, savanna is African, steppe is Russian, and veldt is Dutch. The prairies are in the United States, the pampas in Argentina, the savannas in Africa, the veldts in South Africa, and the steppes in Russia.

People have asked the question for years. What makes a grassland? Why are there no trees? It is believed that the bison had much to do with there being no trees on the prairies of the United States. As the small tender shoots of trees came up, the bison ate or trampled them into the ground, so they didn't grow. But though they ate the grass also and trampled it, it continued to grow. Scientists think elephants are doing the same thing in Africa by pushing down trees to eat the foliage.

Grasslands are homes for many varieties of wildlife. Many birds live in the grasslands. Those that cannot nest in trees (because there aren't any) use the grass or ground as nesting areas. Many rodents and other small animals live in the grasslands too, burrowing into the earth for their homes. Large animals and birds also live in some grasslands. The grass is the main part of their diet. Hundreds of species of insects also claim the grasslands as home. They live on the grass, in grass clumps, and in the ground. These creatures also provide food for the other grasslands inhabitants.

Jesus created the grass on the third day of Creation. It was to be for food and to beautify the earth. Can you imagine how dusty and dull this world would be if it weren't for green grass? Thank God today for the beautiful grass that covers the ground and helps beautify the earth.

PLATYPUS

Lift up your eyes on high, and see who has created these things, who brings out their host by number; He calls them all by name, by the greatness of His might and the strength of His power; not one is missing. Isaiah 40:26, NKJV.

For many years scientists spent time categorizing different types of creatures so that the study of God's creation would be easier. They recognized such categories as birds, mammals, amphibians, fish, etc. When they thought that they'd covered every area and things were well organized, someone called their attention to a creature that lives in the streams of Australia and Tasmania. This animal defied every category. It was the platypus (PLAT-uh-pus), sometimes called a duckbill platypus.

What makes a platypus so different? Well, it has fur like a mammal, a snout and webbed feet like a duck, a flat tail like a beaver, and there are venomous sharp spurs like a rooster on the hind legs of the male. It barks like a dog, but it lays eggs like a bird instead of giving birth to live babies. Actually, the platypus is a mammal, because it nurses its young with mother's milk.

The platypus uses its leathery bill to find crayfish, worms, and other small creatures at the bottom of the streams. Platypuses do not have teeth, so they chew their food with two horny plates on each side of the jaw. They're about two feet long, including the tail.

When the eggs hatch, the mother platypus uses her tail to hold the young close to her, as they have no fur. This helps protect them, and she can nurse them at the same time. They stay hidden in the nest for several months, and if enemies approach, the "daddy" uses his poisonous spurs to scratch and poison them.

God created many varieties of things for our enjoyment, some quite novel. Thank Him today that He created you different from all of the other creatures. You were made in His image.

THE MYSTERIOUS WIND

The wind blows where it wishes, and you hear the sound of it, but cannot tell where it comes from and where it goes. John 3:8. NKJV.

Have you ever wondered where wind comes from? I did, for many years. In fact, I really never understood much about the wind or weather until I was studying to become a pilot. Then I learned that wind is caused by an uneven heating of the air around the earth by the sun.

Yet wind remains mysterious. We can feel it, but we cannot see it. Even though it is somewhat mystical, it still is refreshing to humans and other creatures on a hot day. In its strongest force, wind can bring destruction.

No doubt you have seen the destructive results of wind. Trees have been blown down, houses have been lifted off their foundations and even moved to another spot, automobiles have been blown off streets, and large ships tilted out of the water and sunk into the ocean. High waves caused by strong winds have been very destructive to coastal areas. Wind has blown many airplanes off course, and if the pilot or navigator was not watching carefully, the plane may have missed its point of destination or hit against a mountain and crashed. Hurricanes, tornadoes and typhoons are names given to destructive wind-driven storms. Although wind has caused much damage, scientists have not been able to figure out any way to actually control the winds. Only God can.

In our spiritual lives we feel the winds of temptation blowing. They get stronger and stronger as the devil and his angels tempt us. Jesus invites us to come to Him, and He will calm the troubled sea of our lives with His almighty hand. When He was on earth, a word from Him calmed the wild waves of the Sea of Galilee. Is anything too hard for Him?

Ask Jesus in your prayers to be with you during this day, to help keep you in His love, away from the winds and storms of strife and temptation. He's waiting; just ask Him.

LIVERWORTS

August 10

A people has come out of Egypt; they cover the face of the land and have settled next to me. Numbers 22:5, NIV.

Many areas of the earth are covered with an amazing variety of plants that we call mosses, but actually they are liverworts. Closely related to mosses, the liverwort gets its name because years ago people thought that since the small leaves looked like the human liver, the plants must be good as a cure for liver diseases.

Liverworts usually grow in cool, shady areas or near water. Some varieties actually grow in water. They are valuable to our ecology, especially where there is bare soil, because they take root and prevent soil erosion.

The main part of the plant is called the thallus (or gametophyte). Underneath this leaflike part are tiny rootlets that absorb water and minerals, which the liverwort needs to stay alive. They also hold the plant to the rocks and trees.

On the liverwort thallus, or gametophyte, are male and female organs that help in one method of the plant's reproduction. The male antherozoids swim through the moisture on the surface of the plant to the female eggs. As they meet, the egg is fertilized. The fertilized egg then grows into a tiny new structure called the sporophyte. This lives on the gametophyte and in time begins to produce spores—the tiny seedlike bodies that make new plants. Thus, they alternate. The gametophyte produces sporophytes; the sporophyte produces gametophytes. As these tiny spores grow, more and more bare ground is covered.

As the liverworts cover the ground, so the children of Israel were covering the land of Moab, and King Balak was fearful. The day will come when the world will be fearful of God's remnant church, and some will do what they can to destroy it. At that time, as always, you and I must be ready and faithful to stand up for our beliefs. Ask God to help you stand firm.

A TENTACLED NEUROLOGY LABORATORY

Let this mind be in you, which was also in Christ Jesus. Philippians 2:5.

In early June, as the sun begins to warm the coastal waters around Cape Cod, Massachusetts, a group of Atlantic squid arrive from far out on the edge of the continental shelf. These squid are about 12 to 18 inches long and swim in a darting fashion. There are literally tons of these creatures.

At the same time about 50 scientists also arrive at Cape Cod, to continue their research on this squid. Through scientific investigation scientists have discovered that it has a central nervous system similar to that of higher orders of animals and of humans. The nerve fibers of these squid are larger than those of any other creature, even humans, and therefore are easy to dissect and study. And so researchers—studying these nerve cells under powerful electron microscopes in the laboratories at the Wood's Hole Marine Biological Laboratory on Cape Cod—are trying to find answers to serious human nerve problems.

Many people are afflicted with one of two diseases of the central nervous system, Alzheimer's disease and Lou Gehrig's disease. Alzheimer's causes progressive senility in which the victims forget, get disoriented, and eventually lose their mind. Lou Gehrig's disease involves the deterioration of the motor nerve cells that serve the body's major muscles. The victims lose control of their muscles, usually starting in the feet and working up the body trunk. Lack of breathing muscles usually causes death.

Squid make an excellent resource for researchers who are looking for cures to these two diseases, as they are able to inject drugs and do many other things with the large nerve fibers of the squid. I hope that these scientists find a cure or treatment soon. God wants us to have good, sharp, keen minds. Thank God today if you can think clearly and can move your muscles easily.

CROSSBILLS

For your Father knows the things you have need of before you ask Him. Matthew 6:8, NKJV.

Crossbills are a unique kind of bird. Do you know where they get their name? The bottom and top parts of the beak cross over each other. The bottom part curves up, and the top part curves down. And so the top and bottom beaks cross each other. Unlike the beaks on most nonpredatory birds, the two parts of the beak do not come together and match.

There are five species of crossbills, with two living in North America. All the males are red, and the females are a dull olive gray. The red and white-winged birds live in the northern part of the United States and Canada. The red crossbill also lives in Europe and northern and central Asia, while the white-winged also lives in Russia. A gizzard is a special part of these birds' stomach. Hard foods, such as seeds, are ground up in the gizzard with the help of sand or gravel. A gizzard does the same job for the bird that our teeth and jaws do for us, but they must eat sand and small pieces of rock to help the gizzard do its job.

One person in Montana reported that a whole flock of crossbills flew down onto the chimney on his house and began pecking at the mortar between the chimney rocks. They may have been looking for sand for their digestion and calcium for their bones, as most mortar has calcium in it. The ground was completely covered with snow, and these crossbills probably couldn't find any sand or small gravel except in mortar.

How do these birds stay alive in winter? There are nuts inside the cones of fir, spruce, and pine, and with its special beak the crossbill can pry out nuts that most other birds cannot.

God provides for the needs of the crossbills, and He will also provide for you and me. He tells us that He will supply all our needs. (Philippians 4:19). Tell God what you really need today in your life. Thank Him for His provisions to you thus far.

LARGE ANIMALS

Behold, God is mighty, and does not despise any; he is mighty in strength of understanding. Job 36:5, RSV.

Probably all of you are familiar with the elephant, rhinoceros, hippopotamus, Cape buffalo, and lion. Once everything went great for them on the African savanna, but that is not true today. Except for the lion, all of these animals are herbivores (plant eaters). Plants and grasses are their daily food. As the countries in Africa continue to develop and more and more people are added, the conflict grows between people who need the land to live on and farm and these large animals that need so much land to eat from.

For example, an adult elephant eats more than 500 pounds of foliage a day. That's 80 tons a year! An elephant needs about one square mile of grassland a year to fill its need. In Kenya alone the elephant population needs about 225,000 square miles to feed on. Rhinos also need a lot to eat. If farmers come into their area and plant crops, the rhinos will tear up the crops and maybe even attack the farmer.

Then there are the hippos. They need about 130 pounds of foliage a day, yet they cannot be too far away from water, because if they become overheated they will die. If a farmer comes into a hippo's territory, the hippo just makes itself at home on the farmer's crops and enjoys them. Cape buffalo also eat a lot of grass—about 50 pounds a day, or nine tons a year. All in all, what these four large eaters need is space with foliage, and the humans are taking up that space. There are several game preserves in Kenya, but they cannot accommodate the large populations of these animals. What will the future hold?

Thankfully, we know who holds the future in His hands. God will have many animals in the new earth, and they will have no problems finding food. They will not be carnivorous, either. Ask God today to help take care of the needs in your life. He will be glad to do it if you ask Him.

HYDROTHERMAL VENTS

I know your deeds, that you are neither cold nor hot. I wish you were either one or the other! Revelation 3:15, NIV.

A group of scientists were working from a boat in the Pacific Ocean near the Galápagos Islands, close to the west coast of South America. They were dragging a camera and thermometer through the water, about 8,600 feet down, looking for hydrothermal vents. These are places where hot water comes up out of the ocean floor. They had heard of such, but had never discovered any. All of a sudden the thermometer shot way up. The boat was stopped, and three scientists went down in a little mini submarine called *Alvin*. They found the hydrothermal vent, and around it were strange-looking creatures called tube worms.

Apparently what happens, according to the scientists, is that the cool ocean water is sucked through openings in the ocean's floor. It passes over hot rocks near the earth's core, and this hot water then comes streaming back up through other vents in the ocean's floor. The water takes on a black appearance, and so the hot stream is called a black smoker. It resembles the lava from a volcano.

As this water goes from cold to hot and goes through a portion of the earth, it picks up some chemicals and forms a chemical soup. As it flows upward out of the earth this soup is affected by bacteria in a process called chemosynthesis. In the process the bacteria convert the compounds of the soup from carbon dioxide into the organic molecules that make up carbohydrates and sugars. Did you understand all that? It is just a process of making food by bacteria.

Scientists believe that there is heat inside this earth. "There is fire there," they say. God wants us Christians to have a fire inside us for Him. Unfortunately, many of us are cold and do little to share our love of Jesus with anyone. Ask Jesus to help you be "hot" for Him today.

HALOPHYTES

Salt is good, but if it loses its saltiness, how can it be made salty again? It is fit neither for the soil nor for the manure pile; it is thrown out. Luke 14:34, 35, NIV.

Have you ever heard of pickleweed, Palmer's grass, and saltwort? I hadn't until I read about a project undertaken by the University of Arizona's Environmental Research Laboratory. Researchers there are trying to grow food plants in salt water or salty soil. Such plants are called halophytes.

In the United States about one twelfth of the land is unusable for agricultural because of the high salt content in the soil or because salty water lies close to the surface of the soil. So there are many sandy and salty areas in which different types of halophytes could grow. The researchers who are working on this project say that the output of these plants is from two to three times that of those that grow on regular farming soil.

Some halophytes exclude most of the salt at the roots by means of semipermeable membranes. Some plants absorb salty water, and the salt is secreted by special salt glands on the leaves. Others absorb the salt and deposit it in the stems and leaves. But when the third type absorbs salt water, it clogs up the feeding system.

Pickleweeds can tolerate salt, but they grow better where it is less salty. Palmer's grass, which grows in the northern estuaries of the Gulf of Mexico, drops seeds that are eaten like peanuts, and this grass does not absorb salt. Saltwort traps salt in the cells in the leaves so that it cannot escape. One good thing about halophytes is that their leaves are 14 percent protein, the same percentage as in the alfalfa plant.

God wants us to be the salt of the earth so that we will season our environment with the sweet savor of His love. Ask Jesus today to help you season someone's life with the richness of your life, through the power of the Holy Spirit.

PLAYING AROUND

When I was a child, I talked like a child, I thought like a child, I reasoned like a child. When I became a man, I put childish ways behind me. 1 Corinthians 13:11, NIV.

Researchers are discovering that the younger creatures in many of the mammal and bird families play games. You've no doubt seen puppies, kittens, and other young animals play with each other. One pup will jump and play with the other pup. One kitten will jump at and play with another kitten. And when they don't have one of their own kind to play with, they happily play with another. Surely you've seen a kitten batting at a patient dog.

A few years ago the camp at Broken Arrow Ranch in Kansas was given a baby coyote and a baby raccoon. These two babies were raised in cages side by side. From time to time the nature director would take them out of their cages and put them together. They would run and jump, roll and tumble, and bite each other—all in fun. They were real pals and had many friendly brawls. Shotgun, the coyote, and Ringo, the raccoon, grew up together and were not afraid of each other.

Monkeys run and chase each other. Little lambs and deer run, jump, and twist their bodies. Horses run, kicking up their hind legs. Even birds dive at each other and struggle. All of this play among the animal and birds, researchers tell us, is to help them mature. And as children run and chase each other and play games, they are learning how to get along with one another.

The apostle Paul, in our text today, is saying that when you grow up you put away childish things. Juniors no longer act and play the way little kids do. Soon you will be teenagers, and then adults. With these milestones you continue to mature.

As you become more mature in your Christian life you enjoy reading and studying more difficult biblical passages. As your mind matures you understand and act differently.

Pray today that God will help you recognize the needs for your age, and that as you grow you will be more mature in your decisions for the Lord.

THE RIGHT WHALE

Now the Lord had prepared a great fish to swallow up Jonah. And Jonah was in the belly of the fish three days and three nights. Jonah 1:17.

In the Argentinean waters between Buenos Aires and Tierra del Fuego is an outpost called Patagonia. This is a great place for people to study whales. The whales that come here in most abundance are the right whales. Yes, this is their name. It is not just correct—it is right. These whales grow up to 60 feet long and weight 45 tons, or about 90,000 pounds.

Right whales come to the gulf waters of the Peninsula Valdes, where they mate and have their calves. Whale watchers have counted about 700 coming there year after year, but they have identified only about 500. These have individual characteristics so that they can be picked out as regular yearly visitors. The identifying characteristics are color and irregular growth patterns on the head.

The whales begin to arrive in July and August. They just loaf around, swimming in the gulf waters, until the calves are born and they have mated again. The gestation period is 12 months for these whales. The right whales swim around in the warm gulf waters of Patagonia until about December, when they head out to sea. No one has been able to follow them, so the scientists are not sure where they go, but they think that they go down to the Antarctic waters.

These whales move with a gentle grace in the water. When they wish to rise to the water's surface, they do so with such ease that they display neither speed nor strength. In musical terms, if the dolphin is the staccato (fast-moving and lively), the right whale is the basso profundo (slow-moving and dignified).

God doesn't always move fast to display His speed or strength. He moves in His own way, in His own time, to do that which He knows is best for us. Thank God today that even though He may not move fast, He does show His strength to ward off Satan, the devil.

LIKE A MERMAID

If one of you says to him, "Go, I wish you well; keep warm and well fed," but does nothing about his physical needs, what good is it? James 2:16, NIV.

Many years ago a strange creature surfaced in the water south of Florida and scared some fishermen. They could not imagine what type of animal or creature it was, because it had its baby clutched to its chest. It had only one swimming flipper on each side, and its body tapered into a single large flat tail, with no hind legs or flippers. What the men were looking at was a manatee, a water mammal that lives in the warm waters from Florida to eastern South America. The fishermen said that it looked like a mermaid, and that is what many people have called the manatee.

Manatees are not harmful. Rather they are gentle and can be easily trained, but in the wild they don't like to be too close to humans. They have a long face that in some ways resembles a large dog, but their face is full. They have big cheeks, with whiskers growing out from them. They eat the profusely growing flowers, vines, and other aquatic plants that can clog up the waterways in Florida. The manatee is a natural waterway cleaner.

Manatees seem lazy during the daytime, for they just float in the water with their heads and tails down and only part of their backs showing. They eat mainly at night. The female gives birth to her baby right in the water, then takes it to the surface for about 45 minutes. After that she submerges it in the water a little at a time, until it gradually gets used to the water. Later the baby will learn to eat and nap like its mother, with its head and tail in the water, and to look for food at night. Adult manatees are from eight to 15 feet long and weigh from 500 to 1,300 pounds.

Like the manatees that need warm water to stay warm, we need a close relationship with Jesus to stay spiritually warm. He longs for us to have that relationship with Him, and to join each other in this delightful experience. Ask God to help you feel the warmth of His love today.

PYGMY CHIMPS

So God created man in His own image; in the image of God He created him; male and female He created them. Genesis 1:27, NKJV.

Pygmy chimpanzees are found in only one part of the world, the rain forests of the Democratic Republic of the Congo. Researchers claim that these small chimps are as close biologically to human beings as any animal can be. Bonobos (bo-NO-bos), another name for pygmy chimps, are very playful. They are also intelligent and easily taught. In an experimental zoo close to Atlanta, Georgia, researchers are working with these chimps to teach them to "talk" by means of symbols. They make little grunts and noises, but of course it is impossible for them to actually talk like humans.

Blood tests run on these pygmies show that they all have the same type of blood, type A, like some humans. Their genetic material is 99 percent identical to humans.

Bonobos have rounder eyes, smaller ears, and less protruding jaws and brows than common chimps. They inhabit a rain forest in the Congo that is very difficult to get to. However, developers are starting to bring housing and industry to their habitat.

Pygmy chimps move through the trees with great ease, swinging, leaping, and diving from one branch to another with more acrobatic maneuvers than the common chimps. They are also more sociable. They eat fruit and leaves as well as the stems from some plants, and they like to share their food with each other. They don't seem piggish with their food. They are very protective of each other, especially of the young.

In the beginning God created animals and then humans. Aren't you happy that you were created by our loving God and didn't evolve from an animal? Thank God today that He is a personal God. You have a wonderful Creator!

MIMICRY

And be not conformed to this world. Romans 12:2.

In southern Arabia is a butterfly called the milk-weed butterfly or plain tiger. This butterfly resembles the common monarch butterfly we see in many parts of North and South America. It has rich, honey-brown colored wings on top with jet-black tips on the forewings, slashed by a prominent white bar. These colors and the slowness of flight that leave the wings open for easy visibility are a warning to birds not to eat it. Why? The milkweed butterfly is poisonous. In its caterpillar stage it feeds on milkweed plants, which to most other creatures are poisonous, but not to this caterpillar. As the caterpillar pupates and turns into a butterfly, the poison from the milkweed plant remains in its body. Most birds, through God-given instinct, are aware of the poisonous nature of this butterfly and leave it alone.

A second butterfly in southern Arabia is called the eggfly butterfly or diadem. The male diadem has jet-black upper wings with white egg-shaped spots bordered by brilliant purple. The female is an almost perfect copy of the plain tiger butterfly. Although the diadem butterfly is not poisonous, the instinct of the birds tells them to keep away from it, because it resembles the poisonous plain tiger butterfly. This look-alike trait among animals is known as mimicry.

Today it seems to be the in thing to live a lifestyle and dress like others in the world. Many young people are not interested in being different, but want to live as their non-Christian friends do. After all, why be different? If your friends know you want to be a Christian, they may make fun of you or ignore you, so it is easier for you to mimic their language, lifestyle, and clothes.

But Christians should be different. Our lifestyle should be one of kindness and respect, taking care of our bodies and caring for one another. We are not to mimic the worldly lifestyle. People should be able to tell that we are different, and when we are asked, we can tell them why. Ask God to help you to conform not to the worldly lifestyle but to God's lifestyle.

NATURE'S MURDERERS

Thou shalt not kill. Exodus 20:13.

As we look at God's natural world around us, we are saddened to see how it has been altered by sin. God's original plan was perfect, but jealousy and selfishness have caused all of the problems that we have today. The root cause of many murders is jealousy.

Unfortunately, the natural world has not escaped this terrible ordeal. Many of the lovely creatures that God created have become murderers. This is not a very pleasant subject to talk about, yet we must face the issue, as this is reality. For many years my wife has had a little cartoon on the refrigerator door. It shows a family with all kinds of problems. The caption says, "You can't switch channels, kids. This is real life." So it is.

Except in the search for food, most animals are not killers, but there are a number that are. The reason is usually jealousy. Interestingly enough, in most cases it is the male of the species that does the dirty work. That's not necessarily so in humans.

What a sad state of affairs, that animals cannot be happy either. Some of the most docile animals, such as certain species of monkeys and baboons, will kill swiftly and fiercely. Jealousy is a real threatening situation for the males that have harems. Other males want to be king among the females, so they challenge and fight the dominant males.

God never intended His world to be so upset. All was created in peace and harmony. This world will not get to that state again until Jesus comes back to this earth. In your prayer today, ask God to help you make this world as nice a place as possible to live in.

Ask Him to help you not to be self-centered or jealous today, but to be a peaceful person. Show your friends what Jesus can do in the heart of one who invites Him to come and live within.

CALIFORNIA SEA LIONS

Look on every one that is proud, and bring him low; and tread down the wicked in their place. Job 40:12.

Just off the coast of southern California are the Channel Islands, the special habitat for many thousands of species of ocean creatures. One of the animals that has survived well is the California sea lion.

Adult bulls grow to be about eight feet long and weigh around 500 pounds. As usual, the females are smaller, about six feet long, and weigh up to 300 pounds.

Every summer as the bulls swim into their island paradise, they stake off their territorial claim. Most of them want to be close to the water, so the early comers have the advantage. The reason that beach property is preferable to inland is that as the females come swimming in the bulls can get their early attention. That gives them a good choice of mates. The bulls use their large teeth to fight off other bulls, trying to tear their opponent's skin and drive it away. The bull may bleed profusely, but usually they're not seriously hurt. The thick layer of blubber protects them. As the bulls fight, they raise their heads in the air. Scientists think this is a special act.

In experimenting with a sea lion, a scientist noticed that when he was lower than the sea lion, it attacked. When he stood up and was thus taller, the sea lion did not attack. It is evidently a matter of pride, a status symbol, for the sea lion to hold his head as high as—or higher than—that of his opponent. Sea lions have very poor eyesight and must depend on smell and hearing for safety. When their calves are born, the mothers start to bellow, in sea lion talk, and the others answer back. Mother sea lions swim with their babies, bellowing to them as they swim. This is how the mother keeps the calf safely beside her.

Jesus doesn't want us to be proud of ourselves or our accomplishments, but He does want us to be proud that we are Christians. Thank Him today that you've had the opportunity to know about God and that you are a Christian.

OWLS

For he will repay accordingly to each one's deeds: to those who by patiently doing good seek for glory and honor and immortality, he will give eternal life. Romans 2:6, 7, NRSV.

Owls are most active at night, as their eyes allow them to see up to 100 times more effectively than a human can in dim light. They can also turn their heads nearly 270 degrees, which is three fourths of a circle. However, they cannot move their eyes up and down or sideways in their sockets, as you can. The owl has to move its whole head to see objects around it. A barn owl can hear sounds 10 times fainter than you can; therefore, it can easily catch a mouse in the barn in total darkness.

The flight feathers of the owl's wing are soft, and the fringed edges of these feathers help it fly quietly to unsuspecting prey by muffling the noise of air passing through. An owl will attack a skunk from behind, sinking its razor-sharp talons into the skunk's head. Thus the skunk does not have a chance to spray its smelly chemical on the owl. The skunk's stinky spray wouldn't make much difference to the owl anyway, since it doesn't have a good sense of smell.

There are about 250 different species of owls in the world, ranging in size from the five-inch elf owl of Central and South America to the 30-inch great gray owl. Owls are good to humans in that they destroy many of the small pesky rodents that cause problems for us in many different ways. I enjoy hearing the hoot of an owl when I am out camping in the woods, because I know that a night guard is on duty.

Jesus made the owls, as He did all of the other creatures, and He gave them instincts to know how to survive. God has given to each of us talents. Maybe you could use some of these talents to know and understand Him better.

By sharing Jesus' love with our friends, we are able to give the devil a "surprise attack." Ask God today to help you invite a friend to accept Jesus today as his or her personal Savior.

TOY DEER

Fear not, little flock; for it is your Father's good pleasure to give you the kingdom.
Luke 12:32.

Out on the Keys (small island off the coast of Florida) lives a tiny deer called the toy deer or key deer. When fully grown, these deer are smaller than a great Dane. The hoofprint of one of these fawns is about the size of a human thumbprint. The only place these small white-tailed deer can be found is on the Florida Keys.

Unfortunately, some years ago these deer were being treated roughly by humans and were fast disappearing. An 11-year-old boy decided he would do something about it. In 1949 this lad, named Glenn Allen, wrote a letter to President Truman asking that land be set aside as a refuge to save these toy deer. He also wrote to members of Congress and to newspaper editors, asking for their help. Residents of the Keys didn't want to give up their precious land for deer, so they tried to block the establishment of a deer refuge.

Eight years later, when Glenn was 19, he really went to work on his project. He got others involved, and in 1957 Congress passed a bill creating the National Key Game Refuge. People who live on the Keys today are friendly to the little deer. Presently only about 400 still exist. Surely if this refuge had not been created they would be extinct.

When Columbus sailed to the New World for the fourth time, they landed on a Key, and one of the sailors went exploring. As this man tramped through the thick tangle of palmettos he saw a small deer staring at him. In the ship's journal he described this toy deer as a "great wonder." Glenn Allen and his friends also saw these toy deer as a great wonder and were successful in preserving their lives.

Jesus has promised to give us a refuge too, as we here on earth are His great wonders. Thank Him for that promise we read in today's text. It is His pleasure to give us His kingdom. Trust in Him. He'll never fail you.

SAHARA

The wilderness and the solitary place shall be glad for them; and the desert shall rejoice, and blossom as the rose. Isaiah 35:1.

The Sahara is a desert famous for its great heat and dryness. From 2 to 3 million people inhabit this desert, which covers more than a third of northern Africa. Water is very scarce there, but in this great expanse of land are some beautiful places called oases. Since each oasis can support only a few people, the men of the families who live there travel to the northern cities to find jobs. With the money they earn they buy things and take them back to their homes in the oasis.

Water there comes from deep wells. Donkeys provide the main source of power for pulling the water out of the wells. When the water has been drawn, it is put into animal-skin bags and taken to the house and stored.

In July the sun passes directly overhead, dividing the day into two equal 12-hour periods. With the intense midday heat, the farmers work their farms early in the morning and return home about 10:00 a.m. Then they take a long siesta and rest until the late-afternoon worship time.

These desert dwellers must continually battle to keep the wind from piling up the sand in their oases. Each family has a house made of mud and cement. The houses are built around a courtyard. The family can stay, work, and visit in the courtyard, which helps protect them from the blowing sands. Each room has a door that opens into this central courtyard.

Date palms grow on most of the oases. The dates are eaten, and the wood is used for pole rafters in the houses. The dates are harvested once a year. Each tree may yield more than 100 pounds of dates. All the water used to irrigate the date palms must be carried from the wells.

What a joyful event it will be when Jesus returns and makes these barren and desolate places beautiful again. Thank God for His restorative power for the world and for you.

TRILLIUMS

And after three months we departed in a ship of Alexandria, which had wintered in the isle. Acts 28:11.

Winter is a long drawn-out season to many people, especially those who live in the cold and snow. They have to fight the cold for many months. Of course, there are sports enthusiasts who feel that winter is not long enough for all the skiing and snowboarding they want to do. But to many people around the world, winter is not a welcome season.

During the winter many things in nature slow down and almost stop because of the cold. Many plants and animals become dormant, while some just slow down their activity. Others seem to prepare for the spring and summer that will come. There are many people like that, too.

One of the plants that I especially like to watch for as the snow begins to melt is the trillium. To me trilliums are some of the most beautiful flowers in the world, and they start to bloom as the snow leaves the ground. Trilliums belong to the lily family. I am aware of six or seven varieties of trilliums. The one I was describing, that comes out while the last remnants of snow is still melting, is the snow trillium, with its beautiful white petals. All trilliums bear single flowers with three petals, three sepals, and six stamens, and there are three whorled leaves on the stem.

The reflexed sepal and the sessile flower trilliums have purplish-brown petals. The large flower variety has large white petals that turn pink with age. The Gleason's trillium has a long stem and bends down. Walpole's trillium also is purplish, but has cream-colored stamens.

Trilliums wait out the winter, then perform in all their beauty, demonstrating God's love for life and beauty.

Many times in our Christian experience we run into a winter experience in which all seems bleak and dreary. Ask Jesus to bring the beautiful spring into your life, and He will brighten and beautify your day. Then you will be radiant, just like the beautiful trillium.

CAPE BUFFALO

For what profit is it to a man if he gains the whole world, and is himself destroyed or lost? Luke 9:25, NKJV.

Although the Cape buffalo of Africa like to graze or quietly loll around on the plains, probably more hunters have been killed by this creature than by any other animal in Africa. The Cape buffalo is one large animal that has never been tamed. The Cape buffalo's heavy ridged horns start in the center of its forehead and take a downward swoop, then curl back up in a half circle.

These buffalo cannot exist more than two days without water, so they stay fairly close to ponds and streams. They eat lots of grass, green or brown. In a herd of buffalo there will be several large dominant bulls. Occasionally a young bull will try to take a place in the herd. He will confront a dominant bull, and there will be a lot of clashing of heads and horns, but it lasts only a short time. The loser will just quietly walk away. The females usually stay with a herd all their lives.

The buffalo calves are the beneficiaries of this communal society of the Cape buffalo, because they grow up in the herd and generally stay with it throughout their lifetime. Male buffalo spend hours each day lying around soaking in the mud. They don't toss and move around, as the hippos, elephants, and rhinos do. They just lie there. They do a lot of their feeding at night and do not want to be disturbed. If danger approaches, the males lie in wait and charge at the last minute. Because of this, many hunters have been killed. Lions have a hard time killing the Cape buffalo for food. It takes several lions to bring one down, and even then they may not succeed.

Cape buffalo protect their own and act as though they own the whole world. Jesus has told us that it is possible for us to gain the whole world but lose our own soul.

Ask God to help you put your trust and hope not in the world but in Him. Put your emphasis on God's kingdom and His righteousness today.

THE INSECT WORLD

For I am not ashamed of the gospel of Christ, for it is the power of God to salvation for everyone who believes. Romans 1:16, NKJV.

There is good news and bad news about insects. Let's start with the bad news first. Insects bite and sting, and eat clothing, wooden buildings, and wool carpets. They invade the food and flour bins, cookie and cracker boxes, and so many other things. They sound pretty bad, right? Half right. The other half is good news.

Insects provide honey for us to eat, silk to make clothing from, wax for candles and polish, and shellac for wood finishing. They pollinate many crops, which provide nutritious food for our tables. Much of this would not happen without insects. They are also food for other creatures. Just by existing, they help make our world more interesting and beautiful—some of them, that is—so we take the good with the bad.

More than 800,000 insects have been classified, and every year scientists tell us that they are still discovering thousands more. Someone has estimated that there are still from 2 to 5 million insects to classify. Trying to catch them and classify them as they fly around is a real challenge.

Insects are different from other creatures in that they have six legs, three main parts to their body, and antennae, and many have wings of some sort. Spiders, ticks, centipedes, and mites do not fit into the insect category because they do not have the identifying characteristics. The three body parts of insects are the head, thorax, and abdomen. The head has the antennae, eyes, and mouth parts. The six legs, and any wings, attach to the thorax. The tail section or abdomen is the digestion and reproduction center.

In our world are billions of people, only a small part of whom are Christians. There are so very many waiting to be "classified" as Christians. Someone needs you to share God's love with him or her today. Ask God to help you identify a person in need today, and share God's love with that person.

LEECHES

For the life of every creature—its blood is its life. Leviticus 17:14, NRSV.

For years leeches have been charged as being bloodsuckers, and most of them are. But some of the 650 known species of leeches live on the larvae of different insects, worms, and snails instead. Leeches are found all over the world. Generally we think of them as living only in the warmer climates, but more leeches have been found in Antarctic waters than in the tropics. They are also found from sea level to more than 12,000 feet in elevation.

Roy Sawyer, a research scientist from the University of California at Berkeley, was on an expedition in French Guiana. As he was stomping through the swamps looking for leeches, he found the kind he had been looking for: an 18-inch-long Haementeria brown leech. Ecstatic, he brought two back to the laboratory for experimentation. The researchers named one Grandma Moses because she produced 750 offspring in three years. These large leeches can lay up to 200 eggs three times a year.

In his research Sawyer has discovered that leeches are gluttons. They will fill themselves so full of blood at one sucking that they can live for four to six months without eating again. Four or five good-sized leeches can drain the life out of a rabbit in about 30 minutes. In the Middle East there is a species of leech that attaches itself inside the nostrils. When Napoleon's army entered the Sinai in 1815, they failed to heed the Jewish Talmud, which specifically warned about drinking water from open ponds. The lives of many of Napoleon's men were lost because of the leeches that attached themselves to the nostrils of the soldiers. The British suffered the same fate in World War I, just 100 years later.

God has given us life through the blood that runs in our veins. Jesus gave *His* life so that we might have a new life for all eternity. Thank Him today for His life that gives us life.

GANNETS

In the Lord I take refuge. How then can you say to me: "Flee like a bird to your mountain." Psalm 11:1, NIV.

Gannets have very interesting takeoff procedures and nesting habits. There are six North American colonies of the northern gannet, and 24 colonies in Great Britain, Iceland, and France.

The gannet is a beautiful white bird with black wing tips. The young adults have black specks on their wings until they reach about 4 or 5 years of age. These birds usually mate for life. When they arrive at the colony nesting grounds, they become very excited as they seek their mate. They will dance around with their bills in the air and rub their bills and necks together. The neighbors are easily offended, and they peck the new arrivals with their bills.

The gannets are skilled fishers. With their eyes on the front of their heads it's almost as if they're wearing binoculars, for they can see fish swimming in the water from more than 100 feet in the air. However, they usually fish from about 50 feet up. When they spot a fish they zoom down in a fast dive that plunges them underwater. When they hit the water, it may spout up in a 10-foot spray. For the gannet, the dive is cushioned by air-filled cells beneath their skin. These cells are mostly around the birds' necks and shoulders and are connected to and controlled by the lungs.

Gannets make their nests in the colony and come back to the same nest year after year. After the single egg is laid, both the male and female will sit on the nest to incubate it. The male probably spends more time than the female, though. After 42 days the egg hatches, and both parents take on the job of fishing and feeding the youngster. As the parents come to the nest they open their beaks, and the youngster sticks its head inside and eats the regurgitated fish.

As the young gannets put their trust in their parents, so we, like David, should put our trust in God. He will take care of us, even better than the parent gannets care for their young. Thank God today for His loving care and protection.

REAL FRUITS

Ye shall know them by their fruits. Do men gather grapes of thorns, or figs of thistles?
Matthew 7:16.

One of the joys that we have here on this earth is to eat delicious, juicy fruits. Each fruit has its own flavor, and it is very rare for two fruits to taste alike. However, there are fruits that do taste alike but don't look alike.

Many types of bananas grow in Brazil, including one kind called the maçã (ma-SAH) or apple banana. If you close your eyes and ignore the texture, thinking only of the taste, you would think you were eating an apple.

A few years ago during a family reunion in Hawaii 13 of us traveled in two station wagons. As we were driving down the highway we came around a curve in the road. There we saw large bushes covered with small white flowers. Mingled in with them were big bunches of red flowers. I couldn't believe my eyes. I slammed on the brakes and pulled to the side of the road. Jumping out, I took some pictures with my camera. Then, wanting to take a closer look, I went over to investigate. Guess what I saw? Someone had taken clumps of big red flowers from one bush and wired them among the small white flowers of another bush. What a letdown! But it was still pretty for the holiday season.

Jesus said that people would be known by their fruits. He meant that people who look at the lives of others can tell if they're Christians. People who are Christians will do things that a Christian should do. They will not go to places a Christian should not go. They will not use language a Christian doesn't use. They will not eat and drink things a Christian should not drink. And they will not act like those who do not follow Jesus.

As your friends and teachers observe you today, will they know that you are a Christian? Ask Jesus right now to help you act and talk like a Christian today.

CHESTNUTS

For, behold, I create new heavens and a new earth: and the former shall not be remembered, nor come into mind. Isaiah 65:17.

For many years chestnuts were an important food, not only in the United States but in Japan and Europe. In the early 1900s chestnut wood was used in many industries in the United States, especially for furniture.

Telephone poles and fence posts were made from chestnut trees, because they not only resisted rot but grew tall and straight. Chestnut trees grew from 70 to 100 feet tall and three to four feet in diameter. The northeastern part of the United States was the most populous area for chestnut trees, and more than 25 percent of all its trees were chestnuts.

It is presumed that about 1904 a shipment of Oriental chestnuts arrived in the United States with a blight that spread, until most of the East Coast trees were contaminated with it. The blight later spread to Europe. It is believed that it arrived there aboard a shipment of mine timbers about 1917, but it was not discovered until the 1930s, when blighted trees were found in Italy. By then a large portion of trees there were already infected. Since then, Italian and American scientists have worked to try to stop the blight.

The largest stand of chestnut trees is now in Michigan along the shores of Lake Michigan. The blight continues, but scientists and interested citizens are trying to keep it from spreading. It may be a losing battle, but they won't give up.

Sin has really made a mess of God's creation. Just think how good this world would have been without the blight of sin. Jesus has told us that He is preparing a new world that will be without sin. Ask God today to help you be faithful so that you can see that new world, where everything will be beautiful and perfect.

CAMOUFLAGED

In the shelter of your presence you hide them . . . ; in your dwelling you keep them safe.
Psalm 31:20, NIV.

For many little animals and birds their color is a means of survival. If God had not made them with the colors He did, they would not be able to live very long. God thought of everything as He created this earth, and I am amazed more and more as I continue to study His creation.

The variety of colors that God used was more than accidental. Camouflage was one purpose God had in giving colors to some of His creatures. Let's look at a few today.

The ground-nesting American woodcock blends right into the dead leaves upon which it builds its nest, lays its eggs, and incubates them. It is very difficult to see the hen sitting on the nest. The eggs, and later the chicks, are the same color as the leaves. It's a perfect blend.

And baby deer, as many of you know, are a light reddish-brown color with white spots sprinkled across their backs. As the fawn lies down or meanders through the woods, the colors and spots blend into the light and shadows of its environment.

The American bittern has a long neck. As it stands among the cattails, stretching its neck and pointing its bill straight up, its coloration blends in with the cattails. Neither predators nor the fish it eats can tell it is there. Some moths look just like the leaves or the bark of a tree. It is very difficult to tell them from the tree, they look so much a part of it. The same is true of some lizards and also a number of insects, such as the walking stick, which has the color and looks of a small twig.

God has planned that these creatures use their colors and shapes to camouflage themselves for safety and life. God has promised to protect us from the enemy too. I invite you today to kneel down and thank God for His protection, and ask Him for it especially today.

LEMURS

At the same time came the disciples unto Jesus, saying, Who is the greatest in the king-dom of heaven? And Jesus called a little child unto him, and set him in the midst of them. Matthew 18:1, 2.

Today we'll look at a fascinating little tree creature, the lemur, whose name means ghost. Lemurs are related to monkeys, and there are many species of them, ranging in size from that of a rat to a medium-sized dog. Their faces look like a raccoon or a fox, and they all have a soft fur in various colors, depending on the species. Some of them are white and black, like a skunk. Others are the reddish brown of a small fox, and the fur of others is like that of opossums, monkeys, and koalas. They also make a funny little "oink" noise, like the pig.

Lemurs are native to the large island of Madagascar, but an unfortunate thing is happening there. The dense forests are being cut down for lumber and farms, and that is taking away their natural habitat. Lemurs are tree creatures, eating leaves, fruits, insects, birds, eggs, reptiles, and other small forms of life. Some of them are active at night, and others are active in the daytime.

The lemurs are family-oriented. As soon as the young are born, both the mother and father take care of them. They are very solicitous and guard them carefully. To the parents, the baby lemur is very important. One writer said that the young are the center of their attention.

The disciples of Jesus wanted to know who was the greatest in the kingdom of heaven, because most of them were interested in gaining that position. Matthew tells us that Jesus took a little child and set him in the midst of them. That, my young friend, is what Jesus thinks of you. You are very important to Him and to your family, too.

Ask Jesus in your prayer today to help you be the kind of young person that you know you should be. It's possible that you might hurt Jesus today in something that you do or say, but He will still be by your side. He is there to help you when you stumble and fall into sin. Ask Him for help, and He will fulfill His promise.

NUDIBRANCHS

For the wrath of God is revealed from heaven against all ungodliness and wickedness of those who by their wickedness suppress the truth. Romans 1:18, NRSV.

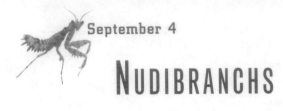

More than 2,500 species of nudibranchs, or nudibanks, commonly called sea slugs, are found in the ocean waters around the world. Although slow in movement, the nudibranchs can be vicious to their prey. They thrive in the sea world that is populated by faster, larger, and better-armed creatures. Nudibranchs are mollusks and are related to snails, oysters, and clams, but they do not have a shell.

Ocean nudibranchs are not a dingy gray like their cousins found in your gardens and yards. They have bright and beautiful colors that vary from species to species. Some of them are a bright orange, purple, red, and yellow. They have been nicknamed butterflies of the sea.

All nudibranchs are predators. They feed on sponges, anemones, jellyfish, and sometimes on each other. As they attach themselves to a yellow or orange sponge, they take on the pigmentation color of the sponge. One species that eats jellyfish will attach itself to the body of the jellyfish and begin to turn blue or purple. It will eat away on the body of the jellyfish until it is all gone. Unlike most predators of the jellyfish, the nudibranch eats the stinging cells as well, and later may use these stinging cells, incorporated into the cells of the cerata, for its own defense against another predator. Scientists have not been able to understand how they do this and have no ill effect.

Jesus warned us not to spend too much time with people who are not good, for we might become like them. He wants us to be, not like other people, but like Him. As His children we should show love and kindness toward others. Although the nudibranchs live to consume others, Jesus wants us to love and live to *help* others. Ask God today to help you not to be like the nudibranch, adapting to someone of the wrong type. Ask Him to help you be a good influence on others, and have a Christlike attitude and character. It will work if you ask Him to help you.

HONEY ANTS

He hath chosen us in him before the foundation of the world, that we should be holy and without blame before him in love. Ephesians 1:4.

There is a species of ants called honey ants. They were given that name because they collect a sweet nectar from galls. Now, a gall is an enlarged ball caused by a wasp laying her eggs on a branch or in a crotch of the tree. A gall forms around them. Droplets from the galls ooze out, and the honey ants greedily suck up this gall sugar.

These ants have a honey stomach in which they carry the gall sugar back to their colony. There it is stored by another amazing group of these ants called honeypots. These are special worker ants whose bodies are actually storage tanks for the nectar brought in by the other worker honey ants. These special tankers hang from the ceiling and act as the pantry for the colony. Their abdomen stretches until they swell to about the size of a grape. Should they fall from the ceiling to the ground, which happens quite frequently, they burst as they hit.

When winter arrives and nectar is not available from the galls or the yucca plants, the other ants stroke the honeypots with their antennae. The honeypots then spit up nectar, a little at a time, until they are empty.

Early Native Americans in the United States and Mexico used to dig down into the nests of these ants, find the honeypots, and use the nectar for food and to treat diseases. In Australia the aborigines dig up the honeypots and bite off the nectar-filled abdomens for the sweet nectar.

No one knows how the honey tankers are chosen to be the nectar tanks. They are called for a very special task, and they fulfill that task.

Jesus has called us to be His children. As all children have tasks at home, so He has given us a task—to share His love with others and to be loving. We have been chosen by Him. What a privilege to be chosen by Jesus. Thank Him today that He has chosen you to be His child.

MALLEE FOWL

Hide them in the dust together; and bind their faces in secret. Job 40:13.

One of the most bizarre creatures in Australia is the mallee fowl. These birds are quite ordinary looking, but they are very different from any other bird in the world. About the size of a chicken, the mallee fowl male rakes thousands of pounds of dirt, leaves, sticks, and sand into a giant nest, probably among the largest of all nests. They are a wonder among animals.

In the Australian desert, where the mallee fowl lives, the temperature may vary as much as 40 degrees between night and day. Therefore the mallee fowl must build a nest that is well insulated because the eggs must be kept at a constant 90° to 96°F (32° to 36°C).

The mallee fowl male digs a hole in the sand about three feet deep and six feet across. Leaves and sticks are raked into this hole, which will become an egg chamber. Next comes the insulating layer; thousands of pounds of sand, twigs, and leaves are scraped over the egg chamber. By the time the nest is built, it may be 16 feet across and three feet high.

Although the nest is ready, the female has to wait for the right time. A tunnel has been made to the egg chamber, but it is temporarily closed.

Then the rain comes. The nest gets wet and begins to ferment, and the debris begins to heat up. In the meantime the male keeps the female away until the temperature is just right. He has a heat-sensitive membrane in his beak, and when all is right the female uses the tunnel to go inside and lay her eggs. The male watches over them to see that they are kept at the right temperature. Seven weeks later the eggs hatch. The chicks have to dig their way three feet up to the surface. They are able to take care of themselves and may never see their parents.

God takes care of His children because He wants them to live forever. At the right time He will come and get them and take them to heaven. Ask God in your prayer today to help you be ready for that right time when Jesus will come back to get you and all His other children.

WOLVES

And in thy seed shall all the nations of the earth be blessed; because thou hast obeyed my voice. Genesis 22:18.

A wolf howl may be a bloodcurdling sound that makes shivers go up and down your spine, but the howl is actually the wolves' way of communicating with each other. A howl is a song of the wolf. It may be a song of reunion, of membership in a pack, the wolf's family unit. The howl often assembles members of a pack before a hunt, provides communication during a hunt, and reassembles the group following a hunt. Howling also serves as a warning to outsiders that a specific area is being occupied by a wolf or pack.

Wolves are the largest member of the canid family. The average wolf weighs from 50 to 75 pounds, and some of the males can reach 100 pounds or more. The largest wolf ever reported was in Alaska and weighed 175 pounds. The males stand two and a-half to three feet at the shoulder and can be four and ahalf to six feet long. Wolves live about 10 to 12 years.

Wolves are highly intelligent and very sociable. They enjoy each other's company and at times depend on each other to help hunt for food. Play activity is important to wolves. They will run together, tumble, bite lightly, and play tag.

In each pack there is an alpha male and female. These are the leaders, and the other members of the pack submit to them. There is also a number two male, called the beta male. He assists the leader, leads the way on hunts, and breaks the trail through the deep snow in the winter. He is a sort of field commander. The beta male leads the way in all activities.

Our conscience is like a still small voice telling us what we ought to do. Jesus talks to us through this still small voice. Do we listen to it and obey it? As the wolves listen to each other, we should listen to Jesus. Tell Jesus today that you are willing to listen to His voice as He guides you in your life. You'll be glad you did. As God blessed Abraham, He will bless you.

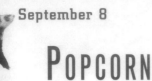

POPCORN

You visit the earth and water it, you greatly enrich it; the river of God is full of water; you provide the people with grain [corn], for so you have prepared it. Psalm 65:9, NRSV.

I can't find anything in the Bible that tells me that the people back then knew about popping corn, but the early settlers in the United States used all types of corn, and they may have even popped corn. Popcorn is different from ordinary corn. Each kernel has a very hard covering. When the kernel is heated, this cover keeps moisture inside, and it turns to steam. When the steam builds up to the right amount of pressure, it bursts, or pops, and you have popcorn! Good kernels will enlarge from 30 to 35 times their original size. Growing and popping corn is big business today.

Popcorn, like apple pie and baseball, has become known as an American specialty. Back in the Depression days of America, the 1930s, there were many people who had very little to eat. Some of them grew popcorn and ate it. They would use it for breakfast cereal and eat it with milk. Some used honey or molasses and made popcorn balls.

Popcorn is produced by the millions of tons in the United States and shipped all over the world. Popcorn experimentation has developed strains of popcorn that when popped leave very few unpopped kernels.

Popcorn is a Saturday night tradition in many homes. It has always been very popular, and probably always will be.

We should be thankful to our Creator as He thought of His created sons and daughters and created fun foods for us to enjoy. Thank Jesus today for the good things He created for your nourishment and enjoyment, because "God saw that it was good."

COLOR CODE

And I said unto you, I am the Lord your God; fear not the gods of the Amorites, in whose land ye dwell: but ye have not obeyed my voice. Judges 6:10.

G od talked to the Israelites, but at times they wouldn't listen, because they wanted to do their own thing. God communicated with them time and time again by voice and other signs, but often they ignored His communications.

God has given fish in the depths of the seas the ability to communicate, and one means of communication is by color. God has given some fish the power to manipulate their color pigments, just as some lizards do. Scientists have discovered that just under the transparent scales of certain fish are color-bearing cells. These cells contain such color pigments as red, yellow, and orange. Some cells are black, and some others have a greenish or yellowish color. When these colors are combined, they may produce a silver, white, or iridescent color.

The small male Siamese fighting fish signals its preparation for battle by increasing its color intensity. When it is backing away defeated, it dims its color. A species of fish from India actually fights with color. These fish will square off with each other, then "fire" with their color by brightening it. When one or the other acknowledges defeat, it dims its color to a very pale hue and swims away. Groupers can use so many different colors in their communication, and change colors so quickly, that the species are very difficult to identify. Some fish can use from eight to 12 different colors to declare anger or fright, show aggression, or court another fish.

Fish take note of the colors they see because the color usually communicates something. God communicates to us with colors. The green grass and beautiful flowers demonstrate life. The rainbow is God's promise. Colored leaves in the fall illustrate death. Ask God to help you understand His communication in living color.

ANOTHER SOLAR SYSTEM?

It is I, Jesus, who sent my angel to you with this testimony for the churches. I am the root and the descendant of David, the bright morning star. Revelaton 22:16, NRSV.

Astronomers say they have discovered another solar system and that there may be others out there, too. They cannot explain the true origin of the heavenly bodies, yet they are finding out many new and interesting things.

Large telescopes such as the one on Mount Palomar in California are good, but now with the new IRAS (infrared astronomy satellite) telescope, astronomers have discovered a large halo around Vega, which they believe to be the beginning of a new solar system.

The IRAS is sensitive to heat. Vega is twice as hot and about 60 times as luminous as the sun. But there was something about it that was puzzling. Then the scientists discovered that there is a halo around Vega with a temperature of –300°F (–184°C). They estimate this halo to be about 15 billion miles across. Vega is only 27 light-years away from the earth, or about 160 trillion miles.

Scientists have used Vega as one of the standard stars to calibrate their instruments by, but they are bewildered by this new discovery. They said that they do not believe this pebbled halo mass will condense and form other planets, yet they feel there are now many other planetary systems in our galaxy.

Millions of dollars are being spent to investigate the world of space. Although the Bible does not tell us much about the universe, we know that God created it—a concept that many scientists do not accept. But as newer and more interesting discoveries are being made about our universe, men and women are becoming more knowledgeable about it.

Thank God today that Jesus informed the world that He was "the bright morning star." Our confidence can be placed in Him, for He has all the answers. Place your confidence in Jesus today.

THE GREENHOUSE EFFECT

While the earth remains, seedtime and harvest, cold and heat, winter and summer, and day and night shall not cease. Genesis 8:22, NKJV.

When God formed the earth during the Creation, He did so with a purpose. Everything in this world had a purpose. Everything that God, the Master Designer, made had a reason for existence. Today's scientists are trying to figure out what some of those purposes are. They are doing all kinds of experiments to find out how and why.

Recently there has been much scientific investigation into what is called the greenhouse effect. Scientists claim that the temperature of the earth is changing, and they believe that it is because of the burning of fossil fuels (coal, oil, natural gas). They say that the burning of these fossil fuels is emitting a lot of carbon dioxide into the earth's atmosphere. As this goes into the air it helps cause clouds, and these clouds are holding in the heat. Some say the earth's temperature may be increased by about four degrees within the next 30 to 40 years. The scientists fear that with the increase of temperature ice in the polar regions will melt, raising the water level in the oceans. That would cause mass flooding and terrible damage. What some scientists don't know is that God is in control of His earth.

Carbon dioxide and water vapor allow the visible light rays to pass, but absorb the infrared radiation. This causes concern to some of the scientists and meteorologists. They foresee this heat causing changes in rainfall patterns, which could upset the crop-raising regions as well as the rain forests and desert areas. What they are saying is that something is going to happen, but we don't know what.

We as Christians know that this old world is not going to last too much longer, and we know that God has control of it all. We need not fear if we have our faith and confidence in God, the Creator. He will protect us and see us through until Jesus comes. Thank Him today for the promises that He has made that He will be with us always.

LEAVING THEIR MARK

Whether you turn to the right or to the left, your ears will hear a voice behind you, saying, "This is the way; walk in it," Isaiah 30:21, NIV.

If read properly, tracks in sand, mud, and snow can tell a story or a situation. Animal tracks are interesting to follow. No doubt you have sometimes seen tracks and said to yourself, "I wonder what kind of tracks those are." Or you may have seen some other types of markings that made you ask, "What did that?"

As you walk through the woods you may notice different animal tracks or signs of some creature's behavior. Holes in trees tell us that certain woodpeckers were there. A large pile of pinecone scales might indicate the presence of squirrels. Lower branches of trees that have been trimmed of leaves would indicate that deer had eaten heartily during the winter, and blackened, peeled-off aspen bark might show that elk had been there, since they like aspen bark. Animal tracks can indicate if the creature that made them was alone, in a hurry, stalking another animal, or just meandering along.

You may have seen a sign in a park or forest that read, "Take only photographs and leave only footprints." That means "Don't pick or take anything from the area, and don't leave any litter behind you."

Each one of us leaves our mark on this earth, more than just a footprint. People can tell that we have been around. People knew where Jesus was or had been because He went about doing good. He left His tracks by the miracles He performed and the people He healed. Jesus set an example for us.

We can follow His example and leave our identifying marks by thinking of others and helping where it is possible. Thank Him for His example and ask God today to help you find someone you can help or encourage. Your identifying mark may be left somewhere today.

BIOLOGICAL TRICKERY

On each side of the river stood the tree of life, bearing twelve crops of fruit, yielding its fruit every month. And the leaves of the tree are for the healing of the nations. Revelation 22:2, NIV.

From what researchers are finding, God has given methods of defense not only to many species of animal life, but even to trees. Some call it biological trickery; others call it the silent battle. Whatever it is called, it is fascinating.

It was noted that among groves of trees, only a few trees in each area had suffered from the gypsy moth caterpillar. These caterpillars chew through every leaf in sight, and strip the boughs clean. Observing that many trees escaped damage, scientists began to restudy what was happening. It had been felt that only weather, predators, diseases, and parasites controlled these insects. Scientists have now discovered that many trees and some plants fight back with an arsenal of toxic chemicals. These chemicals make the foliage almost impossible to digest, or so toxic that it kills the insects outright.

Some plants contain as many as eight toxins. Others change their toxin from year to year. In some groves of trees in Washington and New Hampshire, scientists discovered, by examining the tree leaves every few days, that when one tree was being attacked by some insects, the other trees began producing toxins in preparation for the insect attack. The researchers have almost begun to believe that some sort of silent communication goes on among the trees and plants. One researcher said that "the whole point for the trees is to keep the insect zigging when it should be zagging." What kind of mystical sense did God give the trees and some plants for their protection?

God's tree of life is for His people in heaven. It will have a variety of fruits on it; the leaves will be for the healing of nations, and they won't produce a nasty toxin. No doubt you'll want the opportunity to eat the special fruits from God's tree. Ask Him today to help you live a life like His, and someday you will eat that delicious, uncontaminated fruit forever.

BUILT-IN BABY CARRIER

He tends his flock like a shepherd: he gathers the lambs in his arms and carries them close to his heart; he gently leads those that have young. Isaiah 40:11, NIV.

Animals with a built-in baby carrier are called marsupials (mar-su-pi-al). Most of these animals have a pouch to carry their young, but a few have large folds of skin that do the same job. Australia has the greatest number and widest diversity of marsupials. There are some 250 species around the world, and the opossum is the only marsupial native to North America.

Marsupials are born at a very early stage of development. Then they have to climb, without help, into the mother's pouch, which is quite a job for such a small creature. For example, a baby marsupial mouse is about the size of a grain of rice, a newborn koala is about the size of a bumblebee, and a new birthed kangaroo about one inch long. The rear legs of these tiny creatures are not yet developed. With the sense of smell to give direction, they must use the power in their front legs to make the trip to the mother's pouch. The kangaroo baby, known as a joey, usually stays in the pouch for about seven months before it is weaned.

Marsupials range in size from a five-inch-long mouse to the seven-foot kangaroo. Marsupials with large pouches include the kangaroos, koalas, and larger American opossums. The Australian mulgara (mouse) has folds of skin. The Latin American rat opossums and the ant-eating Australian numbat have no pouches at all.

Some of the more common Australian marsupials are the kangaroo, Tasmanian wolf, marsupial mouse, tiger cat, wombat, and marsupial mole. They do not all move in the same manner, as their sizes and shapes are different. Marsupial doesn't mean that they look and act alike, only that they have a means of carrying their young in a pouch or fold of skin.

Jesus is a lover of His children, and He will carry them through trials and temptations. He is eager to help you in this world of sin. Thank God today for His heavenly care for you.

WORMS IN TENTS

I am come that they might have life, and that they might have it more abundantly.
John 10:10.

If you have cedar trees in your yard you've probably seen hanging in the trees some small pointed webbed bags covered with tiny parts of cedar leaves and twigs. These were made by bagworms. The cedar tree is a favorite of the bagworms, but they make and hang their tents in other trees as well. The female bagworm has special built-in tubes through which she spits out the silklike fiber that makes the tent. The silk hardens when it comes in contact with air.

The female bagworm lays many pale yellow little eggs in her narrow, pointed tent. Each egg hangs inside the tent by a silken cord, and is housed in a cocoon made of a silken fiber also spun by the mother bagworm.

As the winter gets colder, the little bagworm eggs stay nice and warm in their cocoon. In the late spring the eggs hatch into tiny caterpillars that chew their way out of the silk tent and crawl down the tree and onto the ground. Then they invade other trees and begin to make their own little silk bag. As the wind blows, these little bags are blown from one tree to another.

As the fall comes, the bagworms attach their tents securely to a branch and seal up both ends. This is the time for them to change into adults. After three weeks the male bagworms turn into small beautiful brown moths with hairy bodies and clear patches on their wings. The female never becomes a moth. The male flies to seek out a female, which he finds from a scent she gives off. When he finds her tent, he puts his abdomen into it, and they mate. After she lays her eggs in her cocoon she drops to the ground. In a few days both parents die.

Jesus loves us and allows us to live a life full of many activities. The winds of strife come and blow us from place to place, but we can come back to Him and attach ourselves to Him for security. In your prayers today, thank Him for giving His life for you that you might have a more abundant life.

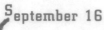

ALL-STAR CAST

I will make your offspring as numerous as the stars of heaven, and will give to [them] all these lands; and all the nations of the earth shall gain blessing . . . through your offspring. Genesis 26:4, NRSV.

Besides the stars we see in the heavens, numerous other stars are found somewhere else. These stars have multiplied so that they are all over the bottom of the sea. They are called starfish, and there are more than 1,800 species of them. They are somewhat similar to each other, yet different. Some of these sea stars are very small, only a fraction of an inch across. Then there is the large Pacific sunflower star, which measures two feet across.

Most of the sea stars have five arms, but some species have as many as 40. Starfish anatomy is very simple. It includes a hinged armorlike skeleton that covers the outside of the body, light-sensitive eyespots, and tiny tube feet carried in each arm. These tiny tube feet are what the starfish uses to move itself over coral reefs and the bottom of the sea. Many species of sea stars were created with duplicate vital organs in each of the arms. If an arm becomes separated, the starfish can grow a new arm, and the broken arm can grow a whole new body if part of the central disc remains. This is also true of the 2,000 species of brittle stars. They not only grow new parts but lay several million eggs into the water, and these become starfish.

Some years ago a group of fishermen, trying to protect their abalone and shellfish beds against the invasion of starfish, which eat them, caught as many starfish as they could and cut them up into pieces. They expected that this would kill them, and their shell fishing grounds would be saved. They threw the starfish scraps back into the water. Little did they know that most of these pieces produced another starfish.

God's promise to Abraham was real. Abraham's offspring, God's people, were to go to ends of the earth. Today we find God's people in all parts of the world. Thank God today that you are part of His family and that one day soon you will be with Him in heaven.

TRUMPETER SWANS

I will call upon the Lord, who is worthy to be praised: so shall I be saved from mine enemies. Psalm 18:3.

The trumpeter swan is North America's largest waterfowl. Trumpeters weigh up to 35 or 40 pounds and have a wingspan of up to eight feet. Once a plentiful species in North America, their native homeland, In the early 1900s trumpeters almost became extinct. The Migratory Bird Treaty of 1918 saved these birds. Today there are about 3,000 trumpeter swans in the contiguous United States and Canada, and 13,000 in Alaska.

The trumpeter swan gets its name from its low-pitched trumpeting call. The swans trumpet as they battle over their territorial domain. Unlike many other birds, a pair of trumpeter swans, which mate for life, requires a 30-acre lake. Some of them, however, desire more area. They don't like to be in close proximity to other trumpeters, and this may cause more problems as their numbers increase.

They prefer to construct their nests on clumps of reeds. If reeds cannot be found, they will pull up cattails stalk by stalk and lay them on the water until they have their floating home. The female then lays her eggs and incubates them until her babies hatch. Baby trumpeter swans are called cygnets.

Many years ago trumpeter swans were hunted for their meat and feathers. The skin was used for powder puffs and clothing. The swans were considered very valuable commercially. Now they are considered a valuable creature to be protected, because they are not plentiful.

Today Christians are in the minority on this earth. Our foundational doctrines must be based on the Solid Rock, Jesus, and our relationship with Him must be for life. Call upon Jesus to help you to be true to Him in your actions today. Ask Him to help you put more trust in Him.

PINE WILT

Think not that I am come to destroy the law, or the prophets: I am not come to destroy, but to fulfill. Matthew 5:17.

Since sin has entered the world, there seems to be no end to the number of things that destroy other things. About 35 years ago a pest called blister rust swept across the United States. It was caused by a fungus transported by a beetle, and it infested pine trees and killed them. During part of their life cycle these beetles were sustained by wild gooseberry plants, so the Forest Service hired young men and women to go into the forest and pull up the gooseberry bushes, thus breaking the beetles' cycle.

Today there is a new pest called pine wilt that is harming the pine trees of North America and Japan. Pine wilt has been a severe problem in Japan for many years, but is relatively new to North America. The pines actually wilt to the point that they die with their needles still on the trees. This disease is caused by a small parasite called the pine wilt nematode. It gets its name from the pine wilt disease in Japan. It was not known by American entomologists (insect scientists) until a visiting Japanese plant pathologist (cell tissue scientist) suggested that they soak a piece of diseased wood in water. They did so, and hundreds of nematodes floated to the surface.

These little parasites attach themselves to the adult pine sawyer beetle—also called the roundheaded wood borer—by entering the breathing pores and moving up to the breathing tubes. When the beetle bores into the bark, the nematodes leave it and enter the tree. They bore into the core of the tree and enter the pitch, cutting the flow of sap to the branches and trunk. When the weather turns warm, they hatch and develop in only five days. When enough of them eat the trunk lining where the pitch flows, the tree dies.

The nematodes are in the destroying business, but Jesus said that He came not to destroy things but to hold up and fulfill.

His law, the Ten Commandments, will show us the way to life. God will help you develop these principles into your lifestyle if you will ask Him today.

TROPICAL FROGS

And Aaron stretched out his hand over the waters of Egypt; and the frogs came up, and covered the land of Egypt. Exodus 8:6.

The Bible doesn't say what type of frogs came up on the land of Egypt and covered everything, but it would be interesting to know. In South and Central America are some of the most colorful frogs that exist today. These frogs vary in color, including red, white, yellow, pink, orange, and many shades of green.

Parenting among frogs is different in each species. There are about 2,000 known species of frogs, and about 10 percent of these frogs take special care in raising their young. The male Darwin's frog waits until the female has laid the eggs, then swallows them into a special vocal sac. There they remain until they are small froglets. Then they leave the father's vocal sac and exit through his mouth, and begin life on their own. The male Fleishmann's frog sits on the eggs for 30 minutes every night, during which time it will wet on the eggs. Other male frogs do not help in the incubation of the eggs but will guard them.

Poison dart frogs, named for their toxic skin secretions that Indians used on their hunting arrows, lay their eggs on damp ground. After the young hatch, the male carries them piggyback to a leaf that is full of water. There the female will lay other unfertilized eggs for food. Another kind of frog is the midwife. The male midwife wraps the eggs around his legs and carries them wherever he goes until they hatch. Then he goes into the water, and the tadpoles just swim away.

Don't you think that God enjoyed making frogs! He surely made many different varieties. I would like to have seen all of the frogs that appeared when Aaron raised his hands, although I'm glad I didn't have to put up with them. God showed His power by using Aaron, and He can show His power through you as people see that you have a changed and different life.

Ask God to show you His power in your life today.

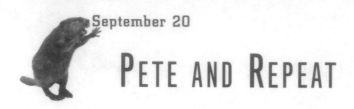

PETE AND REPEAT

You are my friends if you obey me. John 15:14, TLB.

One summer before our youth camp season started, Dave, our nature director, came to me and asked if I'd like to have a couple of crows at camp. I told him it would be great, so he climbed up to the top of a large pine tree and took two baby crows out of a nest. He began to feed them and get them used to a human mother. They were almost full-grown when Dave brought them to camp. He worked with them inside the cage as he fed them from day to day.

One day Dave came to me and said, "I think they will stay around camp now. Is it all right if I let them out of the cage?" I agreed, and out of the cage came Pete and Repeat. The crows would fly and land on the head, shoulders, and arms of the campers as they held them out. The campers had fun with Pete and Repeat. In fact, these characters got so bold that when all of the campers were lined up, they'd fly out to where we were and go down the line and untie some of the campers' shoestrings. They especially liked to untie my shoelaces.

We could depend on Pete and Repeat to be up to something mischievous all the time. Every morning between 5:30 and 6:00 they'd come to a tree close to my cabin and call me. I never needed an alarm clock while they were around. Toward the end of camp Repeat flew away to be with the wild crows. He would come back near the camp with them, but never again did he actually come down to be with us. Pete stayed around the camp for several months until the heavy snows came and very few people were around. Then he too finally went wild. We were happy that God had allowed these two birds to be friends with us during that summer.

Jesus wants to be your friend for a long time. He has been in this world and was a friend of many people, but He went back to heaven to be with His Father. Although we don't see Him anymore, He is still our friend. He wants us to talk to Him often, so kneel down and talk to Him today. Then throughout the day, continue to talk to Him.

ANIMALS IN ARMOR

Put on the whole armor of God, that you may be able to stand against the wiles of the devil. Ephesians 6:11, NKJV.

Armadillos are probably one of the oddest of the North American mammals. They have a head like a lizard, ears like a donkey, claws like a bear, and a tail like a rat. In addition, the entire upper part of their body is covered with armor. There are 20 species of armadillos, most of them living in Central and South America. However, one species lives in the southern part of the United States, the nine-banded armadillo. The name *armadillo* comes from Spanish, meaning "little fellow in armor."

The nine-banded armadillo has shoulder armor, then nine armor bands covering its back, followed by a pelvic shield that covers the rear end. When armadillos cannot dig a hole to escape—and they are fast diggers—they curl up into a ball and let the outside armor be their protection. Coyotes are their feared enemy. The coyote will sneak up on them (and that isn't hard, as armadillos hear and see very poorly; they depend mostly on smell to locate food) and flip them over, attacking them in the belly, where they have no armor.

A female armadillo usually gives birth to identical quadruplets— all the same sex. These four little creatures look just like mama, but they have a soft armor that gets harder as they mature. Though they will be out foraging in a few days, they nurse for about two months. Armadillos are mostly nocturnal creatures and can run quite rapidly, although a human can catch them. They make poor pets, as they are always foraging in the yards and gardens for food, tearing up the ground. They eat mostly fire ants, roaches, tarantulas, scorpions, grubs, grasshoppers, worms, and some berries. To cross a creek, they gulp air to inflate themselves, then float across.

We are told to put on the "whole armor" of God, so that we might be saved from the attacks of the enemy. God will help you with this armor if you ask Him to.

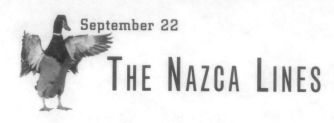

THE NAZCA LINES

Everyone therefore who acknowledges me before others, I also will acknowledge before my Father in heaven. Matthew 10:32, NRSV.

For many years the Nazca lines in southern Peru have baffled scientists. The Nazca lines is the name given about 300 well-drawn figures and geometric lines etched in the earth and rock. Surveyors are amazed at their precision. And as one looks down on these lines from the air they see enormous figures of hands, a hummingbird, a spider, a monkey, a bird, and many other shapes. What intrigues people most is that they can be recognized only when seeing them from high above the earth. Who made these figures on this barren terrain and why they did it is not known.

For almost 40 years a German mathematician and astronomer, Maria Reiche, studied these lines that had been preserved in the gypsum soil, which has hardened like cement. She discovered that the lines in the ground match similar animal figures on Nazca Indian pottery. The Peruvian government was so interested in her work that they gave her food and housing in the government hotel in Nazca.

An expert on ancient irrigation systems was in the Nazca area in 1939 and saw the Nazca lines. He got in touch with his friend Maria and asked her to come and study them. What began as a favor for a friend became a lifework for Maria Reiche. She dedicated herself to this work, receiving only a small salary from Germany.

What a different place this world would be if all of us as Christians were as dedicated to studying and telling others about our find—Jesus—as Maria Reiche was to her project.

When you pray today, ask God to help you be willing to tell your friends what Jesus has done in your life.

SUPERGRAVITY

But thou, O Daniel, shut up the words, and seal the book, even to the time of the end: many shall run to and fro, and knowledge shall be increased. Daniel 12:4.

Albert Einstein had a dream. A physicist, he wanted to discover a single theory that would explain the existence of all matter, all energy, and all forces in the universe. The day before his death in 1955 his calculations were still no closer to answering this puzzle than when he began. After his death other physicists began to study into what Einstein had been studying. They came up with a new theory that they call supergravity, a set of mathematical equations.

Using the formula, they feel they can explain space, time, matter, and the manifestations of gravity and other natural forces. According to the scientists, supergravity explains the gap between gravity, which holds the macroscopic world, and quantum physics, which describes the microscopic world. Einstein studied mostly electromagnetism and gravity. Gravity, as you know, is the force that pulls toward the earth (when you jump up in the air, you come back down). One writer said that the reason that Einstein didn't succeed in the study of gravity was that he simply didn't keep up with the studies others were doing in the field of physics.

Scientists are still baffled by gravity. They really don't understand what it is all about. They know that it exists, but there is much to learn about it. Experimentation with gravity has been difficult, so it has been ignored by most physicists.

Although man cannot explain gravity, God can. Could it be said of us that the reason we don't understand God's love is that we haven't kept up with the reading of His Word? Pray today that even though you may not understand physics and the law of gravity, God will help you increase your knowledge about His great love toward you and give you the desire to read His Word.

LAPLAND

This same Jesus, Who was caught away and lifted up from among you into heaven, will return in . . . the same way in which you saw Him go into heaven. Acts 1:11, Amplified.

Far north of the countries of Norway, Sweden, Finland, and Russia in the Arctic Circle is an area called Lapland. Although the people who live in this area are citizens of the different countries in which they live, they are called Lapps. In Lapland the winters are nine months long and extremely cold.

The Lapland culture has some interesting customs. When a young man falls in love with a young woman and decides he wants to marry her, he puts on his finest clothes and gets on his sleigh. Pulled by a reindeer, he rides his sleigh to his chosen's house and circles it three times. If the young woman is interested in marrying him, she will go out after he completes the third circle. When he stops his sleigh, she goes over and unhooks the reindeer from the sleigh. Soon there will be a wedding.

The Laplanders depend much on the reindeer. They use them to pull their sleighs. They use their hides for carpets in their shelters, and their meat for food. Since they depend so much on their reindeer, they take good care of them. This includes traveling with the migrating reindeer as they move in search of food. These migrations may take them far north, where the sun does not set for long periods of time and where there are no trees. The whole family goes along. The younger boys and girls and the women handle the sleighs. The men, older boys, and the dogs stay with the reindeer to keep them together. This is a long, hard trek, but the Lapps enjoy it.

Someday there'll be a grand migration of God's children as we travel to heaven. God wants us all to come with Him on that migration. We will carry no baggage or belongings, just our character. God has prepared a home for us. I want to be there, and I trust that you do too.

Pray today that God will help guide you into that heavenly migration.

PECCARIES OR JAVELINAS

Some distance from them a large herd of pigs was feeding. The demons begged Jesus, "If you drive us out, send us into the herd of pigs." He said to them, "Go!" Matthew 8:30-32, NIV.

We all remember the Bible story of the demoniacs and how the devil spirits, at the command of Christ, went into the pigs, which then raced down into the lake and were drowned. I had the privilege of seeing that historical place. It was very barren.

In the southern United States and in Central and South America we find wild pigs called peccaries. In the Southwestern states they're called javelinas. Whatever they are called, they are related to the pig family. They have gray hair like a pig and a snout like a pig. The front foot has four toes, and the back has three.

These creatures run in bands. When danger approaches, they back into a circle, like the musk ox does, and defend themselves. They can tear a dog, coyote, or wolf apart with their long tusklike teeth.

The collared peccary that lives in the United States has a white collar around its shoulders. It's been suggested that as it travels it marks its trail with scent from a gland, called the musk gland, on its rump. This gland secretes a musky odor that may rub off onto the shrubs as it goes through them.

Peccaries eat all types of berries, fruits of prickly pear, herbs, acorns, roots, and beans from mesquite trees. There are usually just two piglets in a litter, but there may be more. They are reddish-brown at birth, and within a few hours they can outrun a man. The hide of the peccary makes good gloves and jackets.

On one occasion Jesus cursed the pig as unclean, and on another He allowed the evil spirits to go into the pigs so that they drowned. Thank God that He gave us instructions on what we should and should not eat. He knows best, because He created us.

SUPERPLANTS

Yet I planted you as a choice vine, from the purest stock. How then did you turn degenerate and become a wild vine? Jeremiah 2:21, NRSV.

Botanists (plant scientists) can graft branches from one tree to another so that the tree grows bigger and better fruit. Now researchers are saying that we need bigger and better plants so that we can have bigger and better vegetables. Better seeds bring forth better plants, which produce better vegetables. How far can this process be carried?

A plant geneticist (cell and organ scientist) in Peru is collecting samples of tomatoes that are twice as meaty as the tomatoes available for most of us to eat. They are ugly, green, and berrylike in appearance, yet they are resistant to disease. He has also collected tomato plants at elevations up to 12,000 feet. They don't need so much water for growth, and are resistant to diseases and insects. What he and other scientists want to do is transplant genes from these plants into ordinary tomato plants, the kind that grow the tomatoes we now eat. They expect that this "super" plant would grow healthier, meatier tomatoes. Can it be done? Only God knows.

Other plant geneticists are experimenting with genetic engineering. They are trying to alter the present genetic structure of a plant and make it do something else. This has been done successfully in cloning, which is the growing of identical plants from single cells by a process biologists call tissue culturing. This is being done successfully in a few limited plants such as carrots, petunias, and tobacco. Important cereal grains and beans haven't responded well yet to cloning.

Will people be able to improve plants by manipulating their genes? Only God knows that answer. Thank God today that He is all-powerful, and that He has all of the answers to our problems. We can trust Him.

MORAY EELS

O Lord our Lord, how excellent is thy name in all the earth! Psalm 8:9.

I have often wondered why God created some of the things that He did, but I must trust in Him and His judgment, because I have seen so many wonderful things happen. I must praise Him, even though I don't know why He created the moray eel.

There are about 100 species of the moray eels. According to marine biologists, these eels are fish, but slightly different. Yes, they are *slightly* different! The moray eels have a mouth full of teeth, and they constantly display them. Some divers have thought that the eels were challenging them, and they may have been, but they may have been just breathing. To breathe, the moray eel must open and close its mouth, for it sucks water through its mouth and over its gills, and expels it out through a small circular gill opening.

On rare occasions moray eels have been known to attack divers. They are very nearsighted, but they have a powerful sense of smell. At times that is detrimental to them. In their hunt for food, eels generally do not go more than about 10 feet from the hole in which they live in a coral reef. Many of them stay in their hole, even to hunt. Only part of their body comes out to grab fish, crabs, octopuses, or other food.

Many species are beautifully colored and fit right in with their environment. They come speckled or in solid colors. They range in length from less than a foot to nearly 10 feet. They range in weight from a few pounds to more than 75 pounds.

Very little scientific knowledge about the eels is available. Some divers have been bitten by a moray eel and become deathly sick. No one has yet proved that eels are poisonous, but some species may be.

Even though we may not understand why God created certain creatures, we can trust Him, praise Him, and thank Him for being a God of love and understanding.

NATURE'S PINCUSHION ON LEGS

Above all, taking the shield of faith, wherewith ye shall be able to quench all the fiery darts of the wicked. Ephesians 6:16.

The porcupine comes equipped with a spiny pincushion shield. It works quite effectively against all animals except mountain lions, bobcats, and fishers. When the porcupine is attacked, it puts its head down and sticks up its quills. But mountain lions, bobcats, and fishers have learned how to roll it over, usually without harm to themselves, and attack its unprotected belly.

A mother porcupine usually has only one baby at a time, but on occasion she may have two. The quills on the newborn porcupine become hard and sharp as soon as they are dry. The baby can walk almost immediately, and begins foraging soon. It will nurse for about seven weeks before it starts to go out on its own.

Porcupine quills are difficult to get out once they are in the skin. A tiny barb on the end continues to work its way *in* and makes it difficult to pull out. The natural movements of the victim's muscles keep the quills moving into the body, sometimes even piercing vital body organs. Some poor animals have had the quills work into their throat so that they could not eat, and have starved to death.

Porcupines don't go around looking for trouble. They are principally night creatures and spend their time just looking for food, but other creatures usually disturb their foraging process. Porcupines make nice pets, and they will play with humans the same way puppies and kittens do. But the porcupine has to initiate the play. They can be petted, but they must be stroked in the direction of the quill, not against the way the quills lie. Pet porcupines like to be stroked and do not release their quills unless they are handled too roughly.

As God has given all creatures some type of protection against enemies, He has also given us a shield of faith. Faith is belief. Practice faith in your life, and ask God to help you.

Famous Krakatoa

Watch therefore, for ye know neither the day nor the hour wherein the Son of man cometh. Matthew 25:13.

Have you heard of the small uninhabited island of Krakatoa? It is in the middle of the Sunda Strait, between the islands of Sumatra and Java. Before May 1883 Krakatoa was just an uninhabited island, consisting of an old dormant volcano and ignored by most travelers. But in that month billowing clouds of smoke and booming thunder from the island caused a shiver of terror among the people of neighboring islands. Many asked if the Krakatoa volcano was making a last gasp, but as smoke continued to flow skyward day after day, the islanders grew bored with this natural display and began to ignore it. Then on August 27, 1883, Krakatoa exploded with such force that the sound was heard nearly 3,000 miles away.

Because of the explosion, the port cities of Java and Sumatra were hit by sea waves more than 100 feet high, and the islands were blanketed by almost total darkness from the volcanic ash and the huge waves. When the fury ceased, more than 36,000 people had lost their lives. Although this eruption was not the largest in earth's history, the tsunami waves it created were recorded as the very worst until the tsunami of 2004. Two thirds of the five-mile-long island of Krakatoa had disappeared under the sea.

This volcanic explosion that happened more than 100 years ago in Indonesia may not seem to mean much to us today, but it does have a significant lesson. Jesus has given us warnings all along that His coming is soon. He has given us prophecies in the Bible to clue us in on what will happen. But many of us, like the Indonesians in Java and Sumatra, get bored with the signals, and we begin to ignore them. The coming of Jesus will catch many unawares, and sudden destruction shall come upon them.

Pray today that God will help you heed His promises so that you will not be taken unawares when Jesus comes back to this earth again.

September 30

PRONGHORN ANTELOPE

So he will hoist a signal to a nation far away, he will whistle to call them from the end of the earth; and see, they come, speedy and swift. Isaiah 5:26, NEB.

The fastest of all the North American mammals is the pronghorn antelope. Not a true antelope, it is the only species in its family. The pronghorns, which ranged from southern Canada to northern Mexico, were almost wiped out many years ago. Today they are staging a comeback because they are on the protected list, although some states now allow some hunting of them.

The horns of the male pronghorn go up and curve to the back. These pronged horns consist of permanent bony cores covered with a sheath that is shed each year. The horns of the females are smaller. The males weigh about 115 pounds and the females about 90 pounds. They both are a light tan with a white rump, undersides, and stripes on the throat. They have very keen eyesight and sense of smell, and their diet consists of sagebrush, grasses, and other vegetation which varies from place to place.

The hair on the pronghorn's body is hollow and serves as insulation. That helps them as they range in areas where the temperature may be as hot as 100°F (68.2°C) or –50°F (–45.5°C). The hair grows thicker as the weather cools and thinner as it warms. The pronghorns have muscles attached to the hairs so that they can raise them or lower them, depending on the temperature. When they get frightened, they raise the white hairs on the rump. This bright white spot is visible for one to two miles away and warns others that danger is near. God gave these creatures great speed. They can run up to 60 miles an hour at times.

God will also allow His message of love to go with great speed to those in this world that want to accept it. The day that His message of hope and love will spread very rapidly is coming soon. Ask Him today to allow you to be one of those who take this message of love and hope to others.

BLOOMING MEAT EATERS

See to it that no one takes you captive through philosophy and empty deceit.
Colossians 2:8, NRSV.

Insects are attracted to the amazing pitcher plants, usually found in swamps and bogs in the eastern part of the United States and Canada. They have modified, tubular-shaped leaves that look like upside-down half-closed umbrellas. Each has slippery inner walls and a pool of liquid at the bottom containing digestive enzymes. Insects are attracted by the odor of decay within the pitchers, and the nectar that causes the slippery coating is very attractive to them. As the insect lands on the pitcher, it slides to the bottom of the pitcher. And there it stays! Sharp hairlike bristles on the walls that point downward prevent its retreat. The plant's digestive juices break down the insect's body and decompose it, and it is absorbed for food.

Several different creatures are not affected by any of the 10 species of pitcher plants. The pitcher plant mosquito lives in the plant and moves around it like a helicopter, laying its eggs in the pools in the leaves. The Sarcophaga fly lays its larvae in the plants. When they hatch, they secrete antienzymes that resist the plant's chemical reaction, and they feed on the remains of less-fortunate prey. This harms neither the plant nor these flies. But the Exyra moth lays its eggs at the mouth of the plant. When they hatch and crawl into the plant, they spin a web that blocks all insects that want to enter. And so the pitcher plant starves to death and dries up. It then becomes a special hibernating cavity for the moth.

As the pitcher plant attracts insects and then eats them, the Bible says Satan goes around seeking whom he may devour. He uses deception, sometimes in the form of doctrine that is not according to the Bible. Paul tells us to beware and to know what is true by studying the Bible.

Thank Jesus today that He cared enough for you to give you counsel from His Word.

October 2

PONY PENNING

Let both grow together until the harvest: and in the time of harvest I will say to the reapers, Gather ye together first the tares, and bind them in bundles to burn them: but gather the wheat into my barn. Matthew 13:30.

Just off the Maryland/Virginia coast is a small island named Assateague (ASS-uh-teeg), which is inhabited by wild ponies. It is believed that the ancestors of these animals swam to this island from a ship that wrecked near there many years ago. The ponies thrive on the island, and their numbers multiply. And so every year, during the last week of July, people from the nearby Chincoteague (SHING-kuh-teeg) Island go to Assateague and drive the wild ponies from Assateague to Chincoteague. The water is not deep and the distance is not far, so the ponies easily make this trip through the water. All along the route are small boats loaded with people who encourage the ponies along or just observe.

This roundup has the longest history of any in the East, and it is called Pony Penning. After the ponies reach the island of Chincoteague they are allowed to rest, then are driven down the town's main street to a large corral, where hay is provided for them to eat. Thousands watch the wild horse parade. In fact, many come from far away to watch and be part of this event. As the ponies are eating, men enter the corral on foot and go among the herd, separating the colts from their mothers and putting them into separate pens. The following day the colts are auctioned off. The highest bidders take them home. The proceeds from this annual event help buy firefighting equipment for Chincoteague and contribute to the care of the ponies on Assateague. The rest of the herd is taken back to Assateague, where the Chincoteague islanders carefully watch over them during the next year.

Jesus said that the sinful people will be separated from the righteous and punished, and only the righteous will go into heaven. Ask God to help you today to be in the group that will enjoy eternity with Him.

THE SELFISH SEA CUCUMBER

It is more blessed to give than to receive. Acts 20:35.

One of the most interesting sea creatures I have observed is the sea cucumber. It belongs to the same group of sea creatures as the sea lilies, starfish, and sea urchins, but its cucumber-shaped body is leathery and elastic. Because its body is mainly muscle, it can stretch out quite a ways or pull back to a small size.

The sea cucumber is an adaptable creature. Some species live in shallow water; others live in depths down to 30,000 feet. It eats plankton (small ocean organisms). Amazingly, it eats up to about 100 pounds of these microscopic sea creatures in a year. Sea cucumbers may be black, dark-brown, sky-blue, or orange. It is reported that there are about 500 different species. The sea cucumber usually burrows into the sand, making an arch with the body and allowing only its head and tail to be exposed. Its mouth is located at the head end of the body; it may have from 10 or more branching tentacles with which to eat. As the tentacles float in the water, the plankton are caught like flies on flypaper. One by one the tentacles are inserted into the mouth, and the plankton are cleaned from the tentacles and eaten. This is a continual process. The sea cucumber is always eating. You could say that it has a selfishness about it in that it constantly takes but never seems to give anything away.

We can observe these creatures and learn from their habits so that our lives may be more meaningful and worthwhile. The sea cucumber is like some Christians who only want help from God but are not willing to give up their desires and their will to Him. They want God to answer their prayers, but don't want to let Him lead in their lives. Or perhaps they are selfish and refuse to help anyone else. I hope that you will follow the thought of our text today and not be like the sea cucumber. Truly, "it is more blessed to give than to receive." Many people need a helping hand. You could be just the one to help them out and cheer them up. Ask God to help you find someone today to help.

THE PROUD COCK

So if you think you are standing, watch out that you do not fall.
1 Corinthians 10:12, NRSV.

One of the most beautiful birds I've ever seen is in the jungles of South America. It is the cock of the rock. The male bird has bright-orange feathers all over its body and the comb. The feathers on its wings are black and white. The female is dark, with no orange feathers. The cock of the rock got its name because the male has a comb like that of the rooster, and the female raises her young in sheltered rock niches.

Many Indians in the jungles of South America depend on bird meat to supplement their diets, and the cock of the rock is one of the birds they hunt for food. After they've killed a male bird, they skin the body, eat the meat, and dry the skin with the beautiful feathers. They use the feathers to decorate the large pod necklaces they wear, or they hang them in their houses for decoration.

The cock of the rock is about the size of a pigeon and an interesting creature. At mating time the males expand their tail feathers and march around in what we'd call a proud strut, trying to show off to the females. Once two birds mate, the female usually returns to the same male year after year. Having mated, the female builds her nest, lays her eggs (usually two), and incubates them with no help from the absent dad. She feeds and raises her young alone, too. All the cock does is strut around.

Today's text tells us not to be proud like that strutting cock. We are to put our faith and trust in Jesus, not in ourselves. I invite you to pray today, asking God to come into your life and to help you not be proud and boastful. God will help you be a thoughtful, helpful Christian who thinks of others, as Christ did when He was here on this earth. Ask Him now, believing that you will receive the answer to your prayer.

GOLDENROD

Judge not, that ye be not judged. Matthew 7:1.

Toward the end of the summer many fields turn yellow, and people who are allergic to pollen begin to sneeze. They often blame the yellow flowers called goldenrod. They think that these plants, which are in such abundance in some areas, are what makes them sneeze and wheeze. But the goldenrod is probably not the cause of all this discomfort. The poor goldenrod gets blamed for what its cousin the ragweed is doing. Have you ever been blamed for doing something that someone else did? I'm sure we all have. Well, that's what has happened to the goldenrod, because it and the ragweed bloom at about the same time toward the end of the summer.

There are more than 100 varieties of goldenrod in North America, and they are quite useful to the total environment. During the Revolutionary War George Washington and his troops sipped a substitute tea made from the goldenrod. The states of Nebraska and Kentucky have chosen the goldenrod as their state flower. Related to the daisies, goldenrods are called composites, because each plant's flowering heads are made up of many tiny disk flowers in the center with ray flowers around the outside. There is one species, the silverrod, that has white ray flowers instead of yellow.

More than 1,000 kinds of bees, beetles, flies, butterflies, and moths feed on the goldenrod. On crisp, cool nights many of the creatures take refuge in the feathery fruit heads, which have absorbed the warmth of the afternoon sun. The pollen of the goldenrod does not fly into the air, because it is a heavy sticky type and is spread only by insects. Goldenrod belong to the genus *Solidago*, which means to heal or make whole.

Remember the innocent goldenrod, which is blamed for another's faults. Ask God today to help you not judge or criticize anyone you see do something you question in his or her actions.

THREE WORLDS, ONE COUNTRY

In the mountains, and in the valleys, and in the plains, and in the springs, and in the wilderness, and in the south country. Joshua 12:8.

The children of Israel settled in a land that encompassed all types of terrain. When I had the opportunity to visit Israel, I saw all these different types of land. In addition, I have had the opportunity of living in Peru, a country that has similarly diverse terrain, except that the mountains are higher.

Peru is unusual in that within its boundaries there are actually three different worlds—the coast, jungle, and highlands. My family and I lived in two of these worlds—the jungle and coast. In all three areas the people are friendly, loving, and kind. But each area has their own distinct way of doing things, as about 30 Indian tribes live in the jungle, two large Indian tribes live in the highlands, and many mestizos—those with a mixture of American Indian and European ancestry—live on the coast. Lima, the capital city, is about in the middle of this coastline. It is a very prosperous and bustling city. The majority of the people who live in Lima are mestizos and highland Indians—Quechua and Aymara.

Along the 1,400-mile Pacific Ocean coastline of Peru is a long narrow desert area. Until the Peruvians began to irrigate these sand dunes, they were considered good for nothing. The Peruvians now irrigate them and plant beautiful gardens. Some of the tastiest, most beautiful, and largest vegetables in Peru grow there. The people grow squash so large it takes three or four men to carry one. Sugarcane plantations are very abundant along the coast too. Irrigation has to be used because for more than 200 years it has hardly ever rained on the coast of Peru.

God provides for all His children wherever they live. He has made provision for our physical needs. While all countries do not have the same variety of food, good food grows in each place, usually in abundance. Thank God today for His love and provisions for you and everyone.

PERU, LAND OF CONTRASTS

And I say unto you, That many shall come from the east and west, and shall sit down with Abraham, and Isaac, and Jacob, in the kingdom of heaven. Matthew 8:11.

Going east a few miles from the coast of Peru, the traveler begins to climb into the Andes Mountains. The roads are winding and narrow, and most of the people who live in the small pueblos (towns) are Indian. Let me tell you, they make you feel at home. There are no hotels or restaurants, so you eat and sleep with the local people. Most of them are from the Aymara and Quechua Indian tribes. They shear their sheep, roll their own wool, and knit their own blankets. Since their homes have no heat except for the cooking stoves, they cover with up to eight or 10 blankets at night, which are so heavy that one can hardly move. Their diet is principally meat, rice, beans, and potatoes. They do have a few other vegetables, and they raise chickens, llamas, and some cows.

On the eastern side of the Andes is extensive jungle. There are many pueblos in the jungle, and the people represent some 100 different tribes of Indians. Many of them live off of their little *chacra* (chalk-raa), a small cleared area in which they plant their gardens. They hunt and fish, as well as work in their *chacras*, for a living. Many of the Indians who live in the jungle give fruits, grains, and vegetables for their tithe and church offerings, as they have no cash. They are a happy and contented people, not spoiled by the materialism of this world.

Even though there are three separate worlds in this beautiful country, the desert, the Andes, and the jungle, when church members are brought together for general church meetings they come in harmony. They all belong to the family of God on earth, and they rejoice in that fact. Although members of the Seventh-day Adventist Church are scattered all over the world, we are an important part of the family of God, no matter our race or where we are from. Thank God for His family today.

MOUNT EVEREST

And he carried me away in the Spirit to a mountain great and high, and showed me the Holy City, Jerusalem, coming down out of heaven from God. Revelation 21:10, NIV.

The highest mountain in the world is Mount Everest, situated in the Himalayan Mountains on the China (Tibet)-Nepal border. This mountain was named after Sir George Everest, an early surveyor of India. Formerly it was known as Mountain XV. Its highest peak is 29,028 feet above sea level. The air is thin at the top, and the peak is virtually devoid of any wildlife. There are fierce winds and low temperatures, usually well below freezing.

This mountain peak has lured many climbers since a British expedition party, under the leadership of George Mallory, tried to climb it in 1921. They made it to the 22,900-foot mark and had to turn back. The next year seven of Mallory's men died in an attempt to climb the mountain. Then in 1924 Mallory and a friend were seen at the 28,126-foot mark, but were never seen or heard from again. They were trying to climb the most treacherous east side, which was not attempted again until 1982. That team failed also, but on October 8, 1983, a team of men did succeed in reaching the top by the east route. It took them five and a half weeks. Today we remember that successful climb, 25 years ago today.

The first climbers to reach the summit, as far as anyone knows, were Edmund Hillary and Sherpa Tenzing Norgay. It was May 29, 1953. Mount Everest has enticed and challenged many climbers, and 62 of them lost their lives trying to make the ascent. One hundred forty-nine climbers, both men and women, in 68 groups representing 21 nations, have successfully reached the summit.

Climbers say that the view from the top of Mount Everest is beautiful. The revelator John saw the New Jerusalem in vision from a high mountain and described it as beautiful too. Tell God today how much you want to be in His New Jerusalem. Ask Him to help you be ready and prepared every day with a life that honors Him.

OCELOTS

Thou art weighed in the balances, and art found wanting. Daniel 5:27.

A round the world are small wildcats called ocelots (oss-see-lots). While they are young they are adorable, but the adult cats usually don't make good pets. I have actually seen these little creatures turn on their master. The governor of the state of Amazonas, where we lived in Peru, had one for a while as a pet, but he had to get rid of it. It got very aggressive, and they were afraid it might attack the governor or some member of his family or staff. But after all, it is a wild animal.

In most countries today it is against the law to kill ocelots. Their fur, which is similar to that of a leopard, is considered very valuable, and in Europe an ocelot fur coat costs up to $40,000. But it is against the law to bring the fur into the United States or into many South American countries.

Ocelots used to be very plentiful in the southwestern United States—in Texas, Arizona, and New Mexico. Now they are almost extinct. A few have been trapped and equipped with radio collars so that scientists can study their habits. But those studying them have not learned as much as they need to know about the ocelot's nighttime activities and eating habits. Ocelots shy away from people. It's known that in Texas they hide in vegetation as much as possible during the day and hunt at night. Ocelots require a territory of from 500 to 800 acres to provide food for themselves, and may go beyond that in order to obtain food.

Just as the ocelots are fading from existence, some so-called Christians are letting their faith in Jesus fade away. When Jesus comes the second time, many will perish because they have not kept their faith in Him. Pray today that He will help you believe and have faith in Him so that you will not be in the group who are found wanting and disappointed at Christ's second coming.

HOT-BLOODED PLANTS

Every plant, which my heavenly Father hath not planted, shall be rooted up.
Matthew 15:13.

People, birds, and animals burn fat in their bodies. But plants burn carbohydrates, which are sugars and starches manufactured from water, sunlight, and carbon dioxide. Plants also have fat cells called lipid cells. These lipids must be converted to carbohydrates. This takes place in the cells, where structures called glyoxysomes (gly-ox-e-somes) provide the enzymes necessary for the chemical change before they can be used by the plant.

Skunk cabbage (not related to the animal) is a plant that takes advantage of turning the lipids to carbohydrates by heat-producing cells. No one has yet determined how skunk cabbage and some of its cousins regulate their floral furnaces. Apparently they are operated by some kind of thermostat. Imagine there is snow on the ground and the weather is cold. Yet during the months of February to April the skunk cabbage pokes its head up through the snow into the cold air, and blooms. Its bloom lasts for about two weeks. During that time the temperature inside the center of the blossoms and plant is 72° F (22°C), while outside it may be freezing.

The spikelike bloom of the skunk cabbage is called a spadix, and is covered by an insulating hood called a spathe. The spathe is what helps maintain the temperature inside the plant. The heat intensifies the aroma of the blossoms, which attracts flies and beetles that carry the pollen from flower to flower.

Why would God be so interested in a little skunk cabbage that blooms for only two weeks, that He should put a heater inside it? I can't answer this question, but God can.

Jesus used many outdoor illustrations. In our text today He refers to people as plants. Those who are not God's children will not last in the end. God does take care of the plants, and He will take care of His children. Thank Him today that He is a God of love, and ask Him to guide and take care of you through this day.

Weevils Spoil Everything

The angel of the Lord encamps all around about those who fear Him, and delivers them.
Psalm 34:7, NKJV.

Someone once said that the noslest creatures in the world are weevils, because they always have their noses into something *you* don't want their noses in. The weevil family has more than 100,000 different species. Scientists have said that there are more kinds of weevils than there are kinds of fish, reptiles, amphibians, birds, and mammals put together. That's a lot of weevils! These little creatures have invaded almost every type of plant there is.

A lot of cotton is grown in the southern United States and other warm parts of the world, and the cotton boll weevil is a real pest. They get inside the cotton bolls and lay their eggs. The larvae feed on the cotton seeds and destroy the plant. Then there's the acorn weevil, which drills a tiny hole in an acorn and deposits her eggs inside. When the larvae hatch, they eat the acorn.

Other weevils get into grain and lay their eggs. The hatched larvae eat the heart out of the grain. Then there are the fruit weevils, which damage lovely and tasty fruits. Some farmers have said there is no good weevil—they are all "evil weevils."

But even weevils have a defense from their enemies. In Peru is a weevil that looks like a fast-moving fly, so birds and lizards don't even try to catch it. Other weevils in South America look like bird droppings, so are left alone. Still other weevils look like the tree bark that they feed on, so no one eats them. On the African Kalahari Desert is a slow-moving weevil that curls up and plays dead. African women make necklaces of these.

Just like the weevils, Satan is into everything. Wherever you go or whatever you do on this earth, Satan is there. He is there to ruin everything, although, like the acorn weevil, you never know he is around. He is sneaky and tries to spoil all of the good things God has given to you. Pray that God will help you beware of the devil, and that He will send His good angels to be with you today and protect you from the devil, an "evil weevil."

A COMBINATION OF OTHERS—
AARDVARK

You are the God who performs miracles; you display your power among the peoples. Psalm 77:14, NIV.

An exciting, little-known nocturnal animal that I want to introduce to you is the South African aardvark (aard-vark). These animals combine many of the features of other animals. I've said it before and I'll say it again: God must have had a great and exciting time creating the animals.

Imagine a 140-pound animal with a long snout, the stout body of a pig, the long ears of a donkey, the thick haunches and long sturdy tail of a kangaroo, and a foot-long tongue. Centuries ago the Boer settlers in South Africa discovered this creature. They named it the aardvark, which is "earth pig" in the language Afrikaans.

The aardvark's long tongue is covered with a sticky substance that picks up ants, termites, and small insects, similarly to the anteater. Aardvarks live in large holes and burrows in the ground. The holes are usually hidden in patches of vegetation and are a danger to people riding horses through these areas. It's not unusual for horses to stumble into these burrows, throwing both horse and rider to the ground and injuring one or both of them.

Females give birth to their young in these burrows, and to avoid danger, they move them every seven or eight days to a new burrow. At birth the babies' skin is so loose that it is five or six sizes too large. Very baggy britches! But they grow into their skin in a few weeks. The young stay with their mothers for about six months, then dig their own burrows a short distance away from mama. Aardvarks use their feet for digging, and they can dig faster and deeper than three or four men working together. The holes and tunnels are entwined, and there may be eight or 10 access holes to more than 500 square yards of tunnels. Some of them are 20 feet deep.

Our God created animals with many amazing abilities. Ask Him today to teach you more of the things you can do for Him.

BIRDS KNOW THEIR WAY

Great and marvelous are your deeds, Lord God Almighty. Revelation 15:3, NIV.

One of the mysteries that scientific researchers have not been able to comprehend fully is the migration of birds. It has been estimated that about 20 million birds migrate from the colder climates of the North to the warmer climates of the South every year. Birds as tiny as the small hummingbird and as large as the red-tailed hawk participate in the migration.

Some of the unsolved mysteries are such questions as: How do the birds know which direction to go? How do they stay on course as they travel? How do they find the same spot year after year? During the day when the moon cannot be seen, how do pigeons adjust their course and fly according to the position of the moon? Do some birds recognize such landmarks as mountains? Do others navigate according to the direction of ocean waves? Some researchers even feel that birds navigate by smell and others by hearing. How do birds know when to take off and migrate? Can they tell time with their internal clocks?

Researchers also discovered that pigeons and white-crowned sparrows can be confused by transmissions from a radio tower. They found that these birds have a sort of magnetic detector in their neck that evidently helps them to fly like a pilot using instruments in an airplane. Birds such as loons, cranes, gulls, pelicans, swallows, swifts, geese, and certain ducks travel during the day. Hawks, vultures, and eagles soar on updrafts created by solar heat, so they also travel by day. Smaller birds, such as flycatchers, sparrows, orioles, warblers, thrushes, and vireos, travel at night.

God is a great Creator, and we can put our trust in Him. He created not only the marvelous human body but each creature, with mysteries that we cannot understand. Thank God today for the world He created for you to enjoy.

WHORTLEBERRIES

O taste and see that the Lord is good; happy are those who take refuge in him.
Psalm 34:8, NRSV.

I wanta go up to blueberry hill" was the plea from many of the summer campers at Camp Winnekeag in northern Massachusetts. They knew that about the middle of July the hill in back of the camp would be loaded with sweet little blueberries. They would eat all they could, then pick more and bring them down to the cook for muffins and pancakes. If they had brought sufficient blueberries, she'd get up every morning with her staff and bake blueberry muffins for the campers. The campers looked forward to breakfast, and she never disappointed them.

Blueberries were first eaten by Native Americans. Besides eating fresh berries, they also put them out to dry. When Lewis Cass saw his first blueberries in 1831 outside the Indian lodges he called them whortleberries. The deep blue of the berries has a powdery coating called bloom. That is why they look rather whitish.

There are two basic kinds of blueberries, the wild and the cultivated. The cultivated are larger and not as sweet as the wild berries. The state of Michigan is the largest producer of blueberries in the United States, producing about 50 million pounds each year.

Many people like blueberries the first time they taste them, but others have to acquire a taste. Once one likes their flavor, they are hooked. Blueberries are made into pies, syrups, fritters, fruit soup, pudding, muffins, pancakes, and other desserts. When frozen, they are fun to pop into the mouth and suck. They are good to the taste.

David invites us to "taste" Jesus. He will be sweet and good. When we trust in Jesus and He has all of our confidence, we will benefit from His wonderful sweetness. He is a God of love, and that love is ready to be poured out on you. Ask God to pour out His sweet love on you today.

THE ETERNAL DIGGER

For out of the heart proceed evil thoughts, murders, adulteries, fornications, thefts, false witness, blasphemies. Matthew 15:19.

The badger has been called the eternal digger because it always seems to be digging. Badgers are nocturnal animals. They live in underground tunnels with chambers nicely lined with grass or leaves. These tunnels are from five to 30 feet long, and the nest chamber is two to eight feet deep in the ground. When the nests found at the end of the tunnel become too old or disturbed, the badger takes out the old lining and puts in fresh. They are very neat housekeepers.

In the early days in North America the settlers cleared the land and built houses. Along with their settlements they created cemeteries. As badgers burrowed into the ground, many times they would chew through the pine coffins and get their teeth caught in the clothes of the person buried there. Sometimes they would come to the surface with pieces of cloth in their teeth, so they were nicknamed the "grave diggers," or so I am told.

Badgers are about the size of a Boston bulldog. They weigh about 13 to 24 pounds and grow to about two feet long. The badger has powerful front legs with long claws that enable it to dig tunnels, where it lives and raises its young. The badgers in the far north hibernate during part of the winter in the tunnel, but elsewhere they are active all year. In May or June the babies are born, usually two to five in a litter. In late summer the babies are taken out to hunt. Shortly thereafter, they are put on their own. In fall and winter each badger lives alone.

As we can see from the text today, many people are cruel to others, because every action mentioned in the text is against another person. They look for a weaker person to hurt or rob. They fight and criticize. They hurt others with their false witness and do other things to them. These people don't want others to know their lifestyle.

Ask God to help you to be the kind of person who is the same all the time—loving, kind, gentle, thoughtful, and a forgiving Christian.

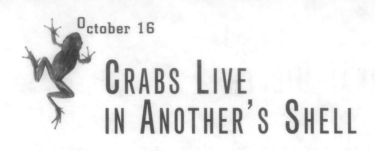

CRABS LIVE IN ANOTHER'S SHELL

They shall not build, and another inhabit. Isaiah 65:22.

You have heard of the hermit crab, haven't you? These are the little crabs that live in the shells of other sea creatures. As the shells are discarded by their original inhabitants, the little hermit crabs find one about its size and climbs into it. As it grows and the shells get tight, it looks for larger shells to live in.

The coconut crab picks up fallen coconuts for food on many tropical islands. Some say it is a cousin to the hermit crab, but it is not a true hermit crab. However, during the first stages of its life it lives like a hermit crab. As the mother coconut crab gives birth to her larvae, they look much like plankton. A month later the coconut crab larvae settle down to the bottom of the ocean and look like the hermit crab larvae. After a period of further maturation and growth, they look for small snail shells and inhabit them, as the hermit crab does. When the small coconut crab has grown to about an inch, it discards the shell and goes on its own without a shell. It is now a land creature with a tough, armored abdomen of its own. It looks for small burrows to live in, because it no longer has protection of the shell to shield it from the hot drying sun. As the coconut crab grows it looks for larger burrows.

The coconut crab can defend itself against any predator. It is reported that it has no known enemies except man. Hunters put out coconuts for the crabs to eat, and as the crabs come out at night to eat, they capture them. But coconut crabs eat not only coconuts but also each other! They are cannibals.

As the coconut crab matures and leaves the protection of the shell, it is responsible for its own defense. When we are small, our parents protect us. As we grow older and are more responsible, we need a relationship with Jesus. Ask Him to be your protector today.

LION'S TOOTH

He said to them, "Go into all the world and preach the good news to all creation."
Mark 16:15, NIV.

If someone came up to you and asked if you would be interested in eating a pot of lion's tooth greens, you might wonder if that person were crazy. But in reality there are many people who eat not only the leaves of the lion's tooth plant but also the roots and the flower. Have you guessed what a lion's tooth is? It is the plain old dandelion. In French the name is *dent de lion*, or the tooth of the lion. That name comes from the toothlike leaves. Dandelion is the English form of the French name.

There is hardly a place in the world where there are no dandelions, because they can grow in almost any soil. Rich in vitamins A, B, and C, the leaves are cooked like spinach, used in salads, or cooked in soup. The taproot, which may be more than a foot long, may be dried, roasted, and ground to make an herb coffee. The Indians named the taproot "strong root." The coffee made from the toasted taproot was drunk to relieve heartburn.

In Europe and England the dandelion was regarded as a medicinal plant. The milky latex was used as a diuretic (to take water from the body) to stimulate the heart and kidneys, thus aiding in digestion and purifying the blood. A paste was made from the leaves and bread dough to heal bruises and skin disorders. The milky substance from the stalk was applied to pimples and warts, supposedly to aid in removing them. A concoction made from the leaves was believed to soothe troubled eyes and strengthen tooth enamel. It seems that the dandelion is good for many things, so it is more than just an unwanted weed in the yard.

Jesus is the answer to our problems. As we reflect Him in our lives, others will note that we are Christians. God wants us to be all over the earth, just as the dandelions are, so that we may be useful to those in need. Christians can bring Jesus' love to many, and that will change the whole world. Ask Jesus to help you to be beneficial to someone today by demonstrating His love.

WATER, WATER, EVERYWHERE

And the spirit of God moved upon the face of the waters. Genesis 1:2.

When God created the earth, water was a very important part of His creation. It would be difficult to have life as we know it without water.

Water is probably the most common substance on this earth. A large portion of this earth is covered with water. Water is all around us—in lakes, streams, and oceans; under the ground; and in the clouds. Even our bodies are made up of about 70 percent water.

Water is very necessary in our world. Just about every living creature needs it. Water helps keep the earth's climate from getting excessively hot or cold. We use water for irrigation, power and energy, drinking, cleaning and bathing, recreation, and industry. Many of us enjoy water for swimming, boating, waterskiing, and just plain getting wet. It is very refreshing to us as well as a cleansing agent.

People in America use an average of 50 to 70 gallons of water per day, either for themselves or to grow the food they eat. Water has a natural recycling process. The clouds carry the water, it rains onto the earth, the water is absorbed into the ground, it filters down underground, and it finds its way to lakes, ponds, streams, and wells. From the open bodies of water it evaporates into the sky by the warmth of the sun's rays, and as it cools, clouds are formed, and the cycle begins all over again.

Water can be a solid, liquid, or gas. As a solid, we call it ice. As a liquid it is known as water, and as a gas it is called vapor, or sometimes steam. There is no other substance that can appear in all three of these natural states. Water is made up of many tiny molecules, and each molecule is made up of tiny particles called atoms. When two hydrogen gas atoms meet one oxygen gas atom, they form a water molecule. That is how it gets the name H_2O.

We should thank God for water and take care of it, because we are dependent upon it.

THE "LONE" COYOTE

The heavens are yours, the earth also is yours; the world and all that is in it—you have founded them. Psalm 89:11, NRSV.

The coyote is a very smart animal, but it has been misunderstood and labeled as a killer. At times it does kill stray sheep and calves, but according to wildlife experts the coyote does not kill for the fun of it. They explain that coyotes are probably more useful than harmful, but ranchers and sheep raisers probably dispute that statement. Coyotes eat many small animals, such as gophers, rats, and rabbits.

Coyotes are very family-oriented and sociable creatures. They are not the loners that many people believe them to be. They may be seen alone at times as they hunt for food, but they are not loners. Several females will help one another when taking care of a litter of pups, and at times a couple of females may even share a den with their pups. In addition, other coyotes will help care for and defend these pups. They are very solicitous of each other's families.

I was often out at our youth camp at night when I lived in Kansas. Out there I could hear the coyotes howling, and it sounded as if they had our scent and they'd soon be upon us. I enjoyed listening to them bark and howl at night, but I was glad they were not close by.

God created the coyote and He created you, but He created each with a different purpose. God loves you because you are made in His image, after His likeness. Jesus died for you, and that is reason enough for you to feel a closeness toward Him. God doesn't want you to be a loner. He wants you as part of His family. I think of the song that says, "I'm so glad I'm a part of the family of God." I am glad. Are you?

Thank Him today that He wants you to be part of His family and does not want you to be a loner. You can be part of His family by accepting Him as your heavenly Father, today.

LAKE TITICACA

And they came to him, and awoke him, saying, Master, master, we perish. Then he arose, and rebuked the wind and the raging of the water: and they ceased, and there was a calm. Luke 8:24.

Lake Titicaca is a most unusual sight. I have stood in awe looking over this lake in the highlands of Peru and Bolivia. It is located about 12,500 feet above sea level and is, according to my understanding, the highest navigable lake in the world. Once I had the opportunity of crossing this lake in a boat during the night. We left Puno, Peru, about 8:00 in the evening, and the next morning we arrived in Bolivia at 7:00.

The beautiful blue water of this lake is very clear. You can see down into the water for a long way if vegetation is not obstructing the view. A giant reed grass grows in the lake, and in one area where this grass is prevalent the Uro Indians have mashed the reeds down and made islands. On top of these islands they have constructed reed houses. They also make reed boats that they use for transportation. For many years the Seventh-day Adventist Church wanted to work among the Uros, but it was impossible, as they didn't trust outsiders. But one day they put confidence in some of our people and permitted us to build a nice metal schoolhouse among their little reed islands. That original schoolhouse was weatherworn, so Maranatha International came in with their volunteers and built a more substantial new one two years ago.

Lake Titicaca has some very large fish in its waters. The water is quite cold, but the fish flourish. Probably the best known is a rainbow trout, a large fish with bright orange-red flesh. When people prepare these fish for eating, they cut them into large steaks—often almost as big as a dinner plate. These fish are tasty and provide a rich protein for the highland Indians. The bones are quite large also.

Because Lake Titicaca is so large, the winds can blow up some tremendous waves, and many lives have been lost from the storms on this lake. This reminds me of how Jesus calmed the Sea of Galilee and that He will calm the storms in your life if you just ask Him.

NANOOK

Oh, sing to the Lord a new song! For he has done marvelous things. Psalm 98:1, NKJV.

A picturesque sight in the Arctic is a giant polar bear on an ice field. The polar bears, known to the Inuit as *nanook* (na-nook), used to flourish by the thousands, but they have been so hunted for their hides that their population has dropped.

A female does not mate until she is 3 or 4 years old. Once she begins mating, she has cubs only every two years. She may have one cub or two, but twins are most common. When the female is ready to have her cubs, she builds a den in a snowbank opposite from the way the wind blows. It is estimated that the temperature inside the den is 40 degrees warmer than outside. She gives birth to her cubs in the den, and these little 1½-pound creatures cuddle into their mother's warm furry coat to keep warm and drink her milk. The cubs are usually born in December or January.

What keeps the polar bear warm in the cold Arctic? Researchers say that polar bears have a thick layer of insulating fat and an extremely dense, oily, water-repellent wool, covered with a coat of long hairs. As researchers looked at polar bear hairs under powerful electron microscopes, they discovered that the hairs are hollow, transparent, and have a reflective inner surface. They speculate that the hair can transmit solar energy to the polar bear's black skin and thereby keep it warm. Did God create the polar bear with a solar heating system? Our guess is yes.

God is a great Creator, and He thought of everything. Would we have thought of putting a solar heating system in the polar bear, even if we could create one? God did. This is another reason it will be so fantastic in heaven, where we can study His marvelous world. Give thanks to God for His marvelous works of creation.

FIDDLER CRABS

Bless the Lord, all his works in all places of his dominion: bless the Lord, O my soul.
Psalm 103:22.

Some 65 species of fiddler crabs are found along the coasts of the United States. These little creatures are only about two or three inches across. The name *fiddler* comes from the fact that the male has a big claw, which is many times larger than the size of the other claw. This tiny crab holds this claw under its chin, much the way a violinist holds a violin. During mating season the claw is moved back and forth like a bow in a movement called waving.

Summertime is the mating season, and the fiddler males stand at the doorways of their burrows, waving their large claw, inviting the females to come. At night a male may beat his claw against the sand, making a thumping noise, to call the females. Each species of fiddler crab makes a different sound. The females listen for the sound that the males of her species make, then heads in that direction.

These little fiddler females are amazing. They have an internal biological clock producing endogenous rhythms, which tell them about the tides so that the female can time the laying of her eggs to the cycle of the tides. Scientists haven't yet found out how this clock works. Once the eggs are laid and safely tucked under the female's abdomen, the male leaves the burrow. The female remains in the burrow for about two weeks, while the egg embryos mature.

At high tide, under cover of night, the female fiddler digs herself out of the burrow and briefly enters the brimming water. On contact with the water the eggs rupture, and hundreds of little microscopic fiddler larvae float away into the marsh, wetlands, or estuary. For the next three weeks they just float and drift through the water, eating while they float.

When you think of the intricate instinct that God has instilled in the lives of these tiny creatures, it makes you realize how much more He has put into your life. Jesus wants to come and live with you. Invite Him into your heart. He will be happy to be there, so ask Him to come in today.

ARABIAN ORYX

And she shall bring forth a son, and thou shalt call his name Jesus: for he shall save his people from their sins. Matthew 1:21.

One of the finest stories that I have heard about how people and organizations have rallied to the preservation of animals concerns the Arabian oryx. In the 1940s there was an abundance of these antelopes in Arabian countries. By the 1960s hunters had practically killed them all off. The last ones in the wild were killed in Oman in 1972. But before the last ones died, a group of people interested in preserving God's creatures captured a few of them and sent them to zoos in the United States and Europe. Those that were sent to the United States were put out on the desert of Arizona. In 1980 some of these antelope were crated and air-shipped back to Oman, where the people wanted to begin to repopulate the area with the oryx. The first group was sent to Yalooni, where the Harasis people pledged to watch over them and protect them from hunters. Rangers were given radios, and several of the antelope wore transmitters around their necks, enabling the rangers to know where they were at all times.

The Harasis people are a very conservative people, and will not even cut down a living tree. They will use only dead wood for fuel. (They would make good Pathfinders, right?)

Millions of dollars were spent to set up and preserve a special fenced area so that the oryx would be protected. The watching and guarding went on for two years; then the first baby oryx was born out there in the new habitat. At that time the scientists said, "The birth of this calf is very important to us, because we feel now that they are beginning a new life, and we feel it will be a prosperous one."

When a Baby was born more than 2,000 years ago in a stable in Bethlehem, the human race did not feel any difference. But when He grew up and submitted to death on a cross, dying for us sinners, many knew that something very important had occurred. Jesus' death and resurrection gave us a new life. His birth on this earth made it all possible. Thank God today for Jesus.

JAPANESE CRANE

And Adam said, "This is now bone of my bones and flesh of my flesh; she shall be called Woman, because she was taken out of Man." Genesis 2:23, NKJV.

The Japanese crane, one of 14 different cranes, symbolizes for the Japanese people happiness, longevity, and marital fidelity, because the birds usually mate for life. It is also a symbol of love. These cranes also live in parts of China, Siberia, Korea, and the east section of Hokkaido. Standing about five feet tall and weighing about 22 pounds, they have a red crown on their heads that makes them outstanding.

Some Japanese cranes winter in Hokkaido. The temperatures go down to about –4°F (–20°C). To keep their long slender legs warm, the cranes stand on one leg while tucking the other leg up under a wing. When the leg they are standing on gets cold, they switch legs. If it is very cold, they also put their head under a wing.

In the early spring the male flies to his mate and begins to court her by jumping and flapping his wings. She joins in the act and does the same things. If there are other cranes around, they too join the aerial dance. This lover's leap lifts the crane high above his mate on the ground. As one jumps into the air the other mate circles on the ground with wings outstretched. When their little dance is finished, the male stands tall by his mate and stretches out his wings, as though to say, "I did it. Now you belong to me." And she does.

The cranes have a call that the Japanese refer to as "the voice of the crane." It is a call of authority, saying, "This is our territory; do not bother us."

Jesus has made us His property. We belong to Him. He has told us how we, both male and female, are to live. Thank God today for the rules that He has given for you to live by, because you are His property.

WEASELS AND MINKS

To this you were called, because Christ suffered for you, leaving you an example, that you should follow in his steps. "He committed no sin, and no deceit was found in his mouth." 1 Peter 2:21, 22, NIV.

The two creatures for today's consideration are not the kind of creature that our text talks about. These two are examples of how Christians should not act. That is why I've chosen to talk about them today.

One naturalist said that the weasel is the symbol of slaughter, the most bloodthirsty of all animals. With a reckless courage weasels will attack anything that comes their way. They take as their motto, "Never Say Die," fighting animals many times their size. In fact, they seem to enjoy picking fights.

Most weasels are brown in the spring and summer and turn white in the winter. Their skins are used for the royal robes of kings, queens, and judges. More than 50,000 of these pelts have been used in British coronation robes.

For a woman, a mink coat is the height of luxury. Fortunately, the mink's disposition has no effect on its fur. Minks have about the same disposition as the weasel, but that has been overlooked because their fur is so valuable for coats and other uses. It takes from 65 to 100 pelts for one fur coat.

In the wild, minks usually live along the riverbanks in muskrat holes, hollow logs, tree root cavities, or old stumps. They feed mainly on small game or water creatures. A newborn mink weighs only about a fifth of an ounce, but grows to about two pounds.

Jesus was not one who went around looking for trouble. He went around looking for people He could help. He is our example, and He recommends this lifestyle to us. What a different world this would be if we were all trying to help someone else instead of trying to get things just for ourselves. Tell Jesus that you want to follow Him and His example today.

FLICKA

You will be betrayed even by parents, brothers, relatives and friends, and they will put some of you to death. Luke 21:16, NIV.

When I first saw her, she was a 6-week-old bundle of black and brown fur. The cutest little German shepherd pup! We had wanted a dog, and my wife, Millie, had the opportunity of getting her. We named her Flicka.

We fenced in the yard so she could not get out, and then we began to train her. She was a family dog, and as she grew she became a real friend to both of our children. One day we decided that she should have obedience lessons. Millie would take her to the lessons, then come home and tell me what Flicka had learned. I would work out with Flicka, training her to do the things that a dog is taught in obedience class. She was very smart and learned fast. I was happy for her progress.

Then came the night of the final examination. I was to take her through her training procedures. We arrived at the park, entered the enclosed tennis court area, and, along with the other dogs and owners, began the graduation exercise. Flicka was doing great. When the other dogs were running around, she was still and obedient. All was going well, and we were proud of her, as she was doing everything right. Then the trainer told us to have our dogs "stand" while we left them. Flicka stood as the instructor went from dog to dog. When she got to Flicka, something seemed to spook her, and she took off running. It was a good thing we had an enclosed tennis court, or she might still be running. She let me down and failed her graduation.

There will be many who will be let down by their parents, friends, and other family members because they have become Christians. Jesus says that at this time we are to remain true to Him. He will never let us down or disappoint us, and we who are faithful will obtain the crown of life. Ask Jesus today to help you be a faithful and obedient friend to Him, because He will remain faithful to you. He will keep His promises!

Chemical Warfare

Bless them that curse you, and pray for them which despitefully use you. Luke 6:28.

We hear much in the world about chemical warfare and how dangerous it is to humans. But in God's natural world chemical warfare goes on every day. We have discussed the trees and their leaves, and how they protect themselves against insects. One researcher said that a tree being taken over by insects is not growing in good ground and getting proper nutrients.

We do not generally think of plants as being aggressors in combat, but in many instances they are. They will go right after the avenger, and usually win. Bay leaves and cucumbers send cockroaches scurrying for the exits. Goldenrod, mushrooms, and marigold plants produce light-activated chemicals that actually burn holes in the insects' cell walls.

Some seaweed in the Caribbean Sea emit a chemical that makes seaweed-eating fish sick, or even kills them. Leaves and roots of black walnut trees, sunflowers, creosote bushes, and wild cherries secrete toxic chemicals that sometimes poison neighboring plants, thus making room for their own seedlings. We've talked about the pitcher plants, too. Of the other insect-eating plants, the bladderwort is unique. Its underwater "trapdoors" open when nudged by a small pond animal, such as a water flea. As this door opens, the water flowing in takes the small creature with it, and the door slams shut. That's the end of the water flea.

The leaves of the Venus flytrap look like an open clam. As the insect lands on it, the plants send electrical impulses that stimulate the leaf cells, which cause the cells to enlarge. With the sudden growth expansion the trapdoor closes—all in a matter of seconds.

How God created all of these wonders we may never know, but we can be sure that He is a God of love. He counsels us to love our enemies, not eat them up. Ask God today in your prayer to help you be a lovable Christian today, and not "eat up" your enemies with gossip.

WAPITI

If any be blameless, the husband of one wife, having faithful children not accused of riot or unruly. Titus 1:6.

Probably the most polygamous (having many mates) of the deer-type animals in North America is the American elk, or wapiti, the name given to these animals by the Shawnee Indians. The English who came to America called them elk because they looked similar to those that they had in Europe. (I have often wondered what happened to the names that Adam gave to all of the animals. Of course, he didn't speak in English.)

Like most in the deer family, the elk lose their antlers each fall and grow new ones in the spring. Bull elk stand five feet tall at the shoulders, with about five feet of antlers, so they are a very striking animal. During rutting season the bulls let out a bellow that sounds like *a-a-a-a-ai-eeeeee-eough! e-uh! e-uh! e-uh!* At that, another bull usually answers back a challenge. They meet and battle until one is driven away. The winner walks away with the females.

Elk have tremendously strong bodies, as though they were made of steel. Their coat is grayish-brown. They have a small whitish tail in the center of a yellowish patch on the rump. A baby elk weighs from 35 to 40 pounds at birth, but it quickly grows to 700 to 800 pounds. They can run up to 35 miles an hour, and are quite quick in a turn. One species lives in North America.

God told us that men should have only one wife and women should have only one husband. But people have altered God's plan since the Garden of Eden, and because of sin, we all suffer. Tell God today that you want to follow His instructions and not have your own way in things. You'll be a lot happier if you follow God's instructions, as He knows what is best.

TOM WAS A STRAY

For I was hungry and you gave me something to eat, . . . I was a stranger and you invited me in. Matthew 25:35, NIV.

Some years ago, when we lived in Topeka, Kansas, my wife was asked to be the Investment leader for the local church. She accepted the challenge and began to work with her committee to lay plans for projects to raise funds for Investment.

They wanted to encourage the church members to choose Investment projects, so they planned an Investment auction. Church members and their friends and neighbors all came, and the auctioneers began. There was a lot to bid on. A stray cat had come to the school, so it was brought into the auction too. No one bid on the cat, so Millie started the bidding at $2.50. Everyone laughed, but no one else bid, so Millie brought the cat home. Millie and our daughter, Jackie, kept calling it a she, so to help them remember that it was a male, I named the cat Tom.

Tom lived with us for several years and was a good cat. He loved attention and petting. Visiting friends couldn't understand why he was so gentle and friendly. He was a model of good behavior.

When we moved to southern New England, Tom went with us. He settled right into the new house and was right at home. He never wandered very far. When we would come home from work, Tom was always awaiting our arrival. He wanted some attention, and he usually got what he wanted. Eventually he died, and two of our neighbors said to Millie, "Let's have a funeral for Tom, because he was a good cat." So they had a little funeral in the backyard, where we buried Tom among the trees.

Tom was a stray, and we took him in. We gave him love, and he responded. We also took in some needy young women to help them, and a close bond of family developed between us as they lived in our home. Jesus invites us to help those who are in need. Ask Jesus to help you find someone who needs your help. You'll feel good about helping someone else.

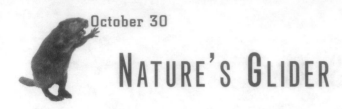

NATURE'S GLIDER

Oh that I had wings like a dove! for then would I fly away, and be at rest. Psalm 55:6.

The flying squirrel does not have wings like a dove, but it has flaps of fur that it extends like wings when it wants to go from one tree to another or from a tree to the ground. As you would expect, flying squirrels live in trees, usually in hollowed-out trees, so that they can hide for safety and care for their young.

Flying squirrels are not large animals. Two of them would fit in the palm of your hand. They can adapt to humans and become very good pets. They have soft brownish-gray fur on the top of their bodies and white fur underneath. As the flying squirrel glides through the air, its extended legs and fur act like wings. Its tail is the rudder. Just before the squirrel lands, the tail makes an upward swing. The squirrel guides itself by raising or lowering its legs. They do not really fly, but glide from above to below aided by gravity and their skill in the air.

Flying squirrels are mainly nocturnal creatures, and they sleep most of the day. They eat mainly nuts and some insects for food. Acorns are their favorite food, and they enjoy the little grubworms in the acorns. They do not hibernate, but will remain in their hollow tree den for long periods of time, especially if the weather is rainy or cold. They usually have acorns stored inside, laid up for their meals in bad weather.

The female will have from two to six babies at a time, and they nurse for five weeks or more, for they develop very slowly. If alarmed, the mother grabs the babies with her teeth and hurries them to safety. In the southern part of their range she may have two litters a year. Among the smaller creatures, they are probably the most docile that exist.

One of these days we will be able to fly away to other worlds and "be at rest," as the psalmist says, with Jesus in heaven. Ask God to help you keep your life in harmony with His will, and you will have that privilege of flying all around the universe. We can't begin to imagine that.

HEAVENS

When I look at your heavens, the work of your fingers, the moon and the stars, that you have established; what are human beings that you are mindful of them . . . ?
Psalm 8:3, 4, NRSV.

As astronomers search through the heavens with their telescopes, trying to understand what space and its celestial bodies are all about, they are making some very interesting discoveries. God could probably look down at us and say, "Ever since this people of Earth began exploring their planetary neighborhood, they have been surprised and awed at what I have created," and He would be right.

First, people looked at the heavens with unaided eyes. Then they built some small telescopes, and later, larger ones. One day scientists decided that they would be able to understand the heavens better if they could build satellites that would carry instruments and cameras into space. Using the spacecrafts *Explorer*, *Mariner*, *Pioneer*, and *Voyager*, we have learned much about the solar system. And when the first spaceship landed on the moon and people walked about on its surface, the world learned more about God's creation.

Using telescopes, scientists discovered a giant canyon on Mars, which they named Valles Marineris. This canyon is 2,800 miles long and four miles deep. That's almost four times deeper and 10 times longer than the famous Grand Canyon in Arizona. A few years ago scientists got a closer look at the complex celestial rings surround Saturn. These beautiful and intriguing rings need a lot more study. Some of them are even braided! Scientists also see a faint celestial ring around distant Uranus. In the ring are frozen moons, three of which have been named Ariel, Umbriel, and Miranda. Astronomers also note that another moon orbiting Uranus, called Titania, has a totally frozen surface—solid ice.

As we consider the complex things that God has created, and especially the heavens, we can only marvel, as did David. God is to be praised for what He has created. He had a purpose in everything He did. Thank Him today for His creation, because *you* are a part of it.

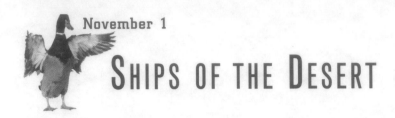

November 1

SHIPS OF THE DESERT

Therefore do not worry, saying, "What shall we eat?" or "What shall we drink?"
Matthew 6:31, NKJV.

There are two types of camels, some of the most versatile creatures living on this earth. They are the Arabian dromedary and the bactrian. Today we'll talk about the dromedary.

Dromedaries provide food, shelter, transportation, clothing, and revenue for their owners. The females give a supernutritious milk. It's said that this milk provides all the nutrients a person needs to live on. I have heard that if travelers crossing the dry and hot deserts run out of food or water and come to a Bedouin camp, they are allowed to milk a camel for nourishment. In preparation for such an emergency they carry a little bowl wrapped in a cloth on their heads, something to hold the camel milk, giving them energy and satisfying their thirst.

Camels can go for several days without drinking water. They get water from the plants that they eat, but contrary to legend, they do not store water in their hump. They have such a keen sense of smell that if the wind is blowing in the right direction, they can smell water a mile away.

For years the best way to travel in the desert was by camel. Freight was carried mostly by the camels, so they became known as ships of the desert. The dromedary does the work its owner requires of it, and does not seem to worry where its water will come from. Camels rely on their owner to care for it. The owners will not neglect their camels, because they depend on them for service.

God has told us not to worry about our needs for the future. He will be more faithful to take care of us than camel owners are of their stock. We belong to God not only because He created us, but because we are part of His family. He will not neglect us.

I invite you not to worry about your future, but to ask God to take care of your needs. He has promised, and He will keep His promise.

MUSHROOMS

Land that drinks in the rain often falling on it and that produces a crop useful to those for whom it is farmed receives the blessing of God. Hebrews 6:7, NIV.

Mycologists. Have you heard of them? They're becoming more and more popular. *Mycologist* is the name given the people who study mushrooms, and they're constantly on the lookout for even more of the fungi. Some even go to the woods and forests to hunt mushrooms—to eat! They feel that wild mushrooms are a treat over those sold in grocery stores, which are grown in hothouses.

Mushrooms need a lot of moisture to grow, and most of the moisture they need comes from rainfall. Approximately 5,000 known species of mushrooms grow in North America, and about 100 of them are poisonous. Only about a dozen are deadly, but some can make you so sick that you think you're going to die. CAUTION: *Never under any circumstances eat any mushroom unless you are positive it is edible.* And that probably means that it should be identified as OK by an authority. Some harmless and harmful mushrooms look very similar.

Mushrooms come in many sizes, shapes, and colors, including red, yellow, blue, green, orange, brown, black, and violet. They range from about the size of your little finger to the size of a shopping cart. They can look like umbrellas, cups, bowls, balls, brains, coral, and other objects. Mushrooms spread and reproduce by spores. The large puffball has the capacity of spreading several *trillion* spores. One mycologist said that if every spore of the mushrooms took seed and grew, we might suffocate in fungi.

God has given us many good things, but Satan has added some counterfeits. Whether it is in the food you eat or in the ideas you entertain, be certain that they are genuine and beneficial—both physically and spiritually. Read your Bible regularly and carefully so that you will not be deceived with wrong ideas or thoughts. Make sure that what you accept as belief comes strictly from the Scriptures and the Scriptures only.

Pray that God will help you distinguish between a genuine life and a counterfeit one.

SILVERFISH

Do not store up for yourselves treasures upon earth, where moth and rust destroy, and where thieves break in and steal. But store up for yourselves treasures in heaven, where moth and rust do not destroy, and where thieves do not break in and steal. For where your treasure is, there your heart will be also. Matthew 6:19-21, NIV.

It is not a very happy sight to go to the closet to get a suit or dress and find holes eaten in the fabric. Most of the time we blame the damage on moths, and often that's the case. But another silent nighttime creature eats holes in clothing too. The silverfish. You may have seen them scampering across the floor or wall when you snap on the light. They work in darkness. They have six legs, a long, slender body with scales, and a three-parted tail.

Most silverfish like to live behind the baseboards, in dark areas such as cupboards, or under the refrigerator or stove. For the most part they like cool, damp areas, though there is one species that likes hot temperatures.

Silverfish lay their eggs behind baseboards, where they hatch and grow into adults. As the baby silverfish grow, they molt (lose their skin) at least three times. Then they get the scales. They continue to molt throughout life, and are the only insect that does this. They may molt up to 50 times after reaching adulthood. That is a lot of changing of skin, especially since they are only about one-half inch long.

Jesus said that we should be preparing our treasures in heaven, where moths and rust do not affect it. But too many of us are excited by and attached to the things of this world, as though *they* had eternal value.

Jesus offers us eternal life; He promises that nothing will threaten or harm, and that no silverfish will eat away at our clothes. Talk to God today. Thank Him for the counsel He has given you, and tell Him of your desire to put your treasures in heaven for eternity with Him.

SLOTH

One who is slack in work is close kin to a vandal. Proverbs 18:9, NRSV.

One of the most interesting animals that I have seen is the sloth. In Brazil and Peru, where we lived for many years, we found that there were two types of sloths. There is the two-toed and the three-toed. These creatures move so very slowly that you have to watch carefully to actually see them move. They average about six feet per minute. However, they can make a rapid slash with the front foot. Their long, curved claws can slice flesh wide open, as with a sharp knife.

Sloths mostly live in the trumpet tree, eating its leaves for food. What most people are not aware of is that sloths—spending most of their lives hanging upside down from the limbs of trees—are the equivalent of hanging zoos. So many different creatures live in their thick fur that someone once joked that sloths are bugged. In their fur can be found nine species of moths, four species of scarab beetles, six species of ticks, and six or seven species of mites. Two species of mites live on the sloth's skin, while the others hitchhike on the backs of beetles. And as many as 978 beetles were found on one sloth. Green algae may also grow on the sloth's fur, giving a greenish color to the natural light tan of its fur.

The sloth needs to make a weekly trip down to the ground for a toilet ritual, digging a hole to bury its droppings. While it is doing this, the piggyback creatures drop off its fur and lay their eggs in the loose soil.

We've been admonished by the inspired Bible writer to not be as the sloth. In fact, some other Bible translations of today's text read "who is *slothful* in his work." Slothful people do nothing, and it takes them forever to do it. God doesn't want His children to be like sloths, so slow that they actually do nothing. He wants His people to be active, to show that they have life in them and that this life comes from the Creator.

Thank God for your life today, and show others that you are alive by what you do.

THE WHITE WHALE WAITED TOO LONG

Therefore be ye also ready: for in such an hour as ye think not the Son of man cometh.
Matthew 24:44.

It is estimated that the white whale population of North America is about 50,000. Only the Inuit are allowed to hunt and use them for food. The Inuit are fond of its thick blubber, and use its oil for lamps. It produces a white flame.

The white whale is quite a singer. The most vocal of all whales, it has a large variety of sounds. They make noises similar to the grinding of teeth, the grunting of pigs, birdcalls, the bellow of a bull, the shrill scream of a woman, a squeaky snore, a baby's cry, a rusty hinge, and a horse's whinny. They chirp, click, cluck, gurgle, grunt, groan, snort, squeak, moo, trill, yap, and mew. They make all these sounds through their nose, which is a crescent-shaped spiracle at the top of their head. Amazing!

The male adults grow to a length of 18 feet and weigh about 3,000 pounds. The female is slightly smaller and lighter. When a white whale calf is born, it is about five feet long and weighs around 170 pounds. At birth the calf is pink. Soon it turns a mottled brown, then yellowish, and about 4 or 5 years of age a glossy white. About 30 years of age the white whale turns a mellow yellow color.

A tragic thing about white whales is that it's easy for them to get trapped behind the fast-forming arctic ice. They like to stay in the warmer bay waters as long as possible, but once ice blocks their way, they cannot escape out to sea. They die there, or are killed by the Inuit.

A lot of people want to enjoy the world's pleasures as long as they can. They say, "When I've had my fun and get older, then I'll become a Christian. It's too hard being a Christian when you're young." This is one of Satan's traps. Don't delay your decision to follow Jesus, the way the white whale delays its departure to colder water. Ask Jesus today to help you not get caught in Satan's trap.

THE PEEPERS

Ye shall know them by their fruits. Matthew 7:16.

The peeper frog is so small that it fits on the thumb nail of an adult human. One of the smallest frogs in existence, it's about an inch long. You may have heard its bell-like call, for when peepers are in concert they sound like sleigh bells and can be heard up to a half mile away. New England folklore states that whatever you're doing when you hear the first peeper, that's what you'll be doing when you die. Another belief is that there will be three more freezes after the first peeper is heard in the spring. It's interesting how people try to determine the future by the habits of various wild creatures.

The peeper's mouth and nostrils are closed when it makes its noise. It inflates a large vocal sac, which acts as a resonator in its throat. As air passes back and forth from the peeper's lungs to its mouth and over the vocal cords, the vocal sac resonates the sound. Another interesting feature of the peeper is that it has an X-shaped cross on its back. This helped it get the species name of *crucifer*. And it has suction pads at the tips of its toes, enabling it to climb.

Although they belong to the tree frog family, peepers are not found in trees. They live in low plants along the water's edge, and when something disturbs them they shut right up or dive under the water. And like a chameleon, they can color themselves according to their surroundings. They change their coloration in response to variations in temperature, light, or humidity, but the process may take as long as an hour. Changing color helps the little frogs escape from their enemies—herons, snakes, and larger frogs. And though she is tiny, a female peeper may lay up to 1,000 eggs in the water.

As these frogs are known by their music, so we as Christians should be known by our lifestyle. Just as Jesus did, we should treat people with kindness and respect, and help those in need. Ask God to help you look out for kids who don't quite fit in, and give you wisdom to know how to be their friend. Ask God to help you be known by your Christian lifestyle, patterned after Jesus.

November 7

RABIES

Their poison is like the poison of a serpent; they are like the deaf cobra that stops its ear. Psalm 58:4, NKJV.

I'm sure that you've heard of rabies, a terrible disease that affects the nervous system. It's been given the name of lockjaw, as the throat muscles are usually paralyzed. You've probably heard of mad dogs, too, but other animals also carry it. The germs are in the animal's saliva and are usually transmitted to the victim in a bite wound. If it's not treated, rabies will be fatal. If a person is bitten by a dog, a farm animal, or wild animal and rabies is suspected, several things must be done. First, the bite wound must be thoroughly cleaned with much soap and water. (One physician said that that was almost as important as the rabies vaccine.) Then, of course, get to a doctor.

Second, the biting animal must be captured and put under surveillance. If after 10 days it's proved not to have rabies, it is usually turned loose. If it has rabies, it is put to sleep. Third, if rabies is suspected, the victim must start a series of rabies vaccine shots immediately. Years ago the series of shots were given in the abdomen and were quite painful. Today the first injection is given at the wound site, and the others are put in a large muscle, depending upon the case. If it is proved that the animal does not have rabies, the shots can be stopped.

Today few dogs and cats are found with rabies, because they have been immunized against it. The upswing of the disease now is among wild animals. Skunks, even pet skunks, seem to be the most common carriers. Bats, raccoons, some foxes, and coyotes carry rabies too. It was once thought that rodents were great carriers of rabies, but it has been found that they are not. It is dangerous to approach a wild animal that appears sick, for rabies is a real possibility.

David, speaking about wicked, unconverted folk, talked about their poisonous influence. Ask God today to protect you from the poisonous influence of those who are not Christians.

A Rare Species

Whoever confesses Me before men, him the Son of man also will confess before the angels of God. But he who denies Me before men will be denied before the angels of God. Luke 12:8, 9, NKJV.

The black-footed ferret, a cousin to the weasel, is considered to be the rarest mammal in North America. They were never very plentiful, but as poison has been put out to kill off the abundant prairie dogs, the ferret has largely disappeared. Prairie dogs are the chief source of food for the ferret.

The black-footed ferret used to range from Canada to Texas, especially in the central United States, where there were a lot of prairie dogs. Now the only protected reserve is in Meeteetse, Wyoming, with 240 captive breeders (90 male and 150 female). About 500 now live in the wild in Montana, Wyoming, Arizona, South Dakota, Colorado, and Utah, with some in Chihuahua, Mexico. Ferrets are 20 to 24 inches long and weigh about one and a half pounds.

The black-footed ferret usually comes out only at night. It is rarely seen, except in the wintertime when there is snow. It is buff in color, with a mask on the face similar to the raccoon, and it has black feet. By the summer of 1983 about 18 had been seen in the colony in Wyoming. Six of these were caught, and radio transmitters were attached to them to help researchers study their habits. There are usually three or four kits in a litter.

Just as these black-footed ferrets hide from people all of the time, there are many Christians who are ashamed to let others know of their belief in God and their love for Him. So they too go into "hiding," not telling anyone of Jesus' love for them. Do you go around hiding, ashamed to let people know that you are a Christian?

Jesus said that He would confess us if we confess Him. He will be willing to represent us in heaven if we will represent Him here on earth. What is your response? Ask Him today to help you be willing to be His representative here on earth. What a thrill to be a representative of the King of the universe!

GOING, GOING, GONE

"The wolf and the lamb will feed together, and the lion will eat straw like the ox, but dust will be the serpent's food. They will neither harm nor destroy in all my holy mountain," says the Lord. Isaiah 65:25, NIV.

Almost every day on the radio and television news we hear about some part of our environment that is in danger of being damaged or destroyed, or that some wild animal or plant is in danger of extinction. For many years the federal government has had an endangered species list, and it is against the law to harass, capture, or kill any plant or animal on that list.

On the list updated in 1983, two kinds of Great Lakes fish and one bird that had been on the list were no longer on it—the blue pike and the long-jaw cisco, and the Santa Barbara song sparrow, of California. Evidently they are extinct. The Florida cougar was almost extinct, though its numbers have increased when Texas cougars were placed in their habitat for crossbreeding.

Other creatures have almost been wiped out for one reason or another, such as the black-footed ferret we talked about yesterday. The numbers of many species are dwindling for various reasons. Most of them are becoming endangered because of problems caused by humans. Hunting, poisoning, trapping, and acid rain are some of the reasons that they are becoming extinct. Almost 2,100 cougars are killed by hunters yearly.

I enjoy going outdoors and observing what God created. Whether it is in the mountains, on the beach, in the desert, or in the woods, there is beauty everywhere. The world was originally created for our enjoyment. We can't enjoy some of the creation if we don't have it, can we?

From our text today we know that there will be animals in heaven. I am happy that God has chosen to have wildlife in heaven. Can you imagine what it would be like if there were no wildlife to observe or play with? God has given us the opportunity to enjoy and take care of His creation now. Ask Him to help you enjoy it more and preserve our world as much as possible.

LICORICE

Woe unto you, scribes and Pharisees, hypocrites! For you pay tithe of mint and anise and cummin, and have neglected the weightier matters of the law: judgment and mercy and faith. These you ought to have done, without leaving the others undone. Matthew 23:23, NKJV.

I was happy to note that In His talks to people Jesus mentioned anise, a licorice-flavored plant. Of all the candies, licorice is my favorite. When I was a boy, there were several licorice-smelling plants where my family lived, and I enjoyed chewing on their stems.

There are four licorice scent- and taste-related plants, but licorice stands alone. The other three are related and used extensively in cooking for the flavor. Anise, fennel, and star anise are the others. Licorice is an herb from the legume family, and it is claimed that pieces of the licorice root were found in King Tut's tomb in Egypt. The licorice root is very sweet, and it is reported that even when it is diluted in water 20,000 times its volume, it can still be tasted.

Fennel and anise are members of the carrot family, which includes other plants that are rich in essential oils: dill, parsley, celery, coriander, and caraway. Fennel and anise have been used for a long time as flavorings. Star anise was discovered by some British sailors; they introduced it into candymaking. The Chinese use it heavily in making candy. They also use it to flavor nuts and many of their meats—chicken, beef, ham, cold cuts. The substance called anethole is what gives the taste of licorice to these different plants.

Jesus was talking to the people of His day about doing some things and not others. He told them it was good that they should tithe (returning to God one tenth of our earnings), but that they should not forget to be just and merciful to others and have faith in God and obey His law. Tell God today that you are willing to tithe your income, to be merciful and just to your friends, and to have faith in Him and obey His law. It will make Him very happy to hear that.

HUMPBACK WHALES

And he said, It is not the voice of them that shout for mastery, neither is it the voice of them that cry for being overcome: but the noise of them that sing do I hear. Exodus 32:18.

As I stood on the porch of the condominium where my family was staying on the island of Maui, in the Hawaiian Islands, I saw several big humpback whales come up out of the water. I could not understand why they were coming up out of the ocean and splashing back down. I have since learned that even scientists do not know why the humpbacks do this breaching. Some have speculated that it may be a form of communication, or an attempt to dislodge the barnacles or crustaceans that live on the whales' flippers and undersides. Whatever the reason, when one does it, several may follow, and it is an interesting sight to watch. One report records a humpback breaching 40 times in a row.

Male humpback whales are singers, and their underwater songs have been recorded. Each singer follows a similar pattern. They perform alone, within 150 feet of the surface of the water. When they sing, the head is down, flippers are outstretched, and the body is inclined to a 45-degree angle. After a while they stop singing and swim to join the other whales.

Several groups of scientists have been studying humpback whales, taking tape recordings of their singing and at the same time taking pictures of their bodies. The scientists then trade the pictures and the tapes for study. It has been found that the whales of Baja California go to southern Alaska for the summer and the humpbacks of Hawaii go to the Aleutian Islands.

Joshua and Moses were listening to the sound of people, and Moses recognized it as singing. God wants us to be happy. Singing is one way of not only showing our happiness but also of communicating a message. This is why it is so important to make sure that we sing and listen to music that is uplifting and inspiring. The lyrics of some of today's music are clearly violent, and portray a harmful lifestyle. Our music should be not human-centered but Christ-centered. We can communicate with God through music. Try that today. Ask God to help you choose good music so that you can communicate with Him through song.

BLUEFIN TUNA

Go ye therefore, and teach all nations, baptizing them in the name of the Father, and of the Son, and of the Holy Ghost: teaching them to observe all things whatsoever I have commanded you: and, lo, I am with you alway, even unto the end of the world. Matthew 28:19, 20.

One of the largest of fish in the ocean is the bluefin tuna. It is also one of the fastest fish, capable of bursts of speed up to 55 miles an hour. It is built for speed, as three fourths of its body is pure muscle. It has ramjet ventilation and a strong heart, and it is hydrodynamically designed. No predators except the killer whale and mako shark can catch it. Tuna glide through the water like a bird glides through the air.

Some say that their name in the Greek language means "rush," and that is just what they do. Their fins are set into grooves in the body so that they can glide through deep water without any resistance. They must swim to breathe, and they must keep their mouth open all the time to get sufficient oxygen. Sea water contains only about 2.5 percent as much oxygen as the air we breathe. The bluefin takes in water and forces it through the gills to remove the oxygen in a procedure called ramjet ventilation.

The bluefin has an exceptionally muscular heart, which pumps a large volume of blood. It also has the ability to conserve and regulate heat to the extent that it can feed in the northern seas where the temperature is 40°F(4°C), and spawn in the tropical waters, where the temperature is 85°F (29°C). Their muscle temperatures average about 88°F (31°C).

Many bluefin have been tagged and later found all around the world. They are great long-distance travelers. When they are caught by fishermen, their meat is sold and shipped all around the world for special meals of royalty and in very expensive restaurants.

Jesus wants us as Christians to be found all over the world spreading the good news of His salvation and love. Ask Him today in your prayer to help you, right where you live and go to school, to share the gospel with others today. That is your world.

BABIRUSA

And the pig, though it has a split hoof completely divided, does not chew the cud; it is unclean for you. Leviticus 11:7, NIV.

The domestic pig has been declared unclean by God, unfit for food. However, on the Indonesian island of Sulawesi and on a few smaller surrounding islands, there lives a piglike creature called the babirusa. This name means "deer hog," because it eats leaves and other foliage like a deer. It not only has divided hoofs, but also chews its cud. The babirusa has a long snout, and growing from that snout are curved tusks.

The babirusa is attracting much attention because it eats cellulose-heavy foods, such as leaves, which a real pig cannot. And it has an extra sac that resembles the stomach of the sheep. Scientists are not quite sure of the function of this sac, but they speculate that it acts like the extra stomach that cows and sheep have. Another word for chewing the cud is rumination, a form of food processing in which the animal eats the food and swallows it, then at a later time regurgitates the food and chews it again for digestion.

These 200-pound animals are rugged and seemingly resistant to diseases. This would make them a welcome addition in the tropics, where there is much disease, especially since they eat vegetation and not expensive grain.

God gave us instructions as to what is all right to eat and what is not. God had His reasons, and today scientists are finding out that creatures such as the pig and other scavengers are unfit to eat. Could the babirusa be fit to eat? Scientists are not sure about that yet. But God has given us so many good things—fruits, vegetables, nuts, grains—to eat for firsthand nutrition. We don't need secondhand food, such as meat—beef, animals, birds, fish. Thank God for providing for your physical needs when He created the earth.

BIRDS THAT WALK ON WATER

And he said, Come. And when Peter was come down out of the ship, he walked on the water, to go to Jesus. Matthew 14:29.

The western grebe is about the size of a mallard duck. When one grebe meets another grebe, they perform a ceremony called rushing, walking on top of the water at great speed. They will do this for a while, then they dive down into the water. If a male and female are doing this with each other, they may come back up out of the water with some reeds in their beaks. They perform another little ritual with their beaks in the air and the reeds hanging from them. Then they paddle toward each other, bump breasts, and swim off to a clump of reeds and begin to build their nest.

The male helps the female stamp down the reeds for the nest. He is very faithful to the female and the family during the time the young are being raised. He helps the female incubate the eggs, which are a pale bluish-white. As these three or four chicks hatch, they climb up onto the backs of the parents into a feather pouch that is between the wing and the body. Usually the female carries them. As she swims out of the bulrushes with her brood, the male swims on ahead. He will spear or catch some fish and feed it to his offspring.

Grebes have calls for each other. The male or female will pick out their mate's call from among many calls and swim toward it, even if it is coming from a tape recorder.

Jesus gave Peter the invitation to walk on the water, and Peter accepted the opportunity. Peter got along fine until he took his eyes off Jesus, and then he began to sink. Jesus invites us to come to Him. He may not invite us to walk on the water to come to Him, but He does invite us to come in other ways. Today in your prayer to God, tell Him that you will be happy to accept His invitation and go to Him and live eternally with Him.

PRAIRIE DOGS

For I [Paul] long to see you, that I may impart unto you some spiritual gift, to the end ye may be established. Romans 1:11.

If you study all of the breeds of dogs that there are in the world, you will not find the prairie dog among them, because it is not a dog. It is a squirrel. The American Indians heard the shrill barks of the prairie dogs and thought they were dogs—that's how they got their name. Lewis and Clark, in their reports about the explorations of the West, called them "barking squirrels."

Prairie dogs do not live in trees like many other squirrels, but in holes in the ground. Their burrows go down 10 feet or more and then run horizontally. The entrance tunnel drops straight down, but it may have a small ledge just below the ground surface. The prairie dog can go there and listen for danger, just before exiting.

These little dogs of the plains are about a foot long and yellowish brown. A town of prairie dogs may consist of a group of mounds each a foot or two high and 25 to 75 feet apart. It is reported that one such town stretched almost 240 miles long and 100 miles wide and contained about 400 million prairie dogs. Can you imagine the noise they must have made when they all were barking?

Several sentries are stationed at their respective holes to watch for danger. When they see an owl, hawk, coyote, or other enemy approaching, they sound the alarm with a bark or series of barks up to 40 times a minute. All of the residents of the town scurry to their holes for safety. When the danger is gone, the sentries will sound the all-clear bark.

As Christians we need to let our friends know of the dangers of sin and try to help save them from the enemy. Jesus told us to love and care for one another. You may have a friend today who needs your help. Ask Jesus to help you be a good sentry and sound the alarm for your friend when you see that he or she is approaching the danger of sinning. Jesus will help you.

SUNFLOWER

I will make your offspring like the dust of the earth, so that if anyone could count the dust, then your offspring could be counted. Genesis 13:16, NIV.

When I was a boy riding my bike to school, I used to stop by a little store and purchase some bags of sunflower seeds. I liked to crack the seeds open with my teeth, spit out the hull, and eat the inner part. Today you can buy these seeds already shelled and salted.

Sunflowers are an interesting plant. The state of Kansas is called the Sunflower State because the sunflower is its state flower. Many sunflowers are grown throughout the central part of the United States. Early Native Americans discovered that by boiling sunflower seeds they could skim off oil that they could then use in cooking. This process has been passed down to us, and we still use it today. Sunflower oil is used for cooking and for salads. It's used in margarine, many other foods, and even in paints.

The sunflower plant can be 15 feet tall. A city radio station sponsors a sunflower-growing contest every year to see who can grow the tallest plant, and supplies sunflower seeds to anyone who requests them. Thus far the record for the tallest sunflower plant is about 19 feet. Though some sunflower plants have many stems and are covered with small flowers, the giant sunflower plant produces a very large head, about 12 to 15 inches across. The head is filled with tightly packed seeds that often are gathered, pressed into oil, ground into meal for cattle feed, and processed for human food. It is very nutritious. Finches and other birds like them too.

Russia claims to have developed the first commercial processing of sunflower seed for oil, and through research they have increased production of the oil content by 45 percent. Bees are the principal pollinator of the sunflowers plants.

God told Abraham that his descendants would be numberless as the dust of the earth. The seeds of the sunflowers are also very plentiful and are almost impossible to count. God made a promise to Abraham, which He kept. God's promises are still valid today. He will keep His promises, so claim a promise today and ask God to fulfill it in your life.

GEOTHERMAL ENERGY

Then Nebuchadnezzar flew into a rage with Shadrach, Meshach and Abednego, and his face was distorted with anger. He gave orders that the furnace should be heated up to seven times its usual heat. Daniel 3:19, NEB.

Can you imagine the rage that King Nebuchadnezzar had against these three young Hebrew men because they wouldn't follow his orders? The heat of that furnace must have been intensely hot to kill the men who had been commanded to throw the three youths into the fire.

In Iceland are some important volcanoes that have been put to good use by the people who live there. Put a volcano to good use, you ask? Yes, that's right. Many years ago some of the people living in Iceland discovered that if they poured water on the smoldering volcanoes it produced steam. So a system was invented whereby sea water was brought in and dumped on the smoldering volcanic fires. The steam is trapped and piped into the cities, where it is used to heat houses. Iceland also has some underground hot springs from which water is piped. About 28 cities in Iceland use this hot water for heat. In the capital city of Reykjavik half of the island's population of 300,000 use hot water from hot springs.

The government has gone to a lot of expense to pipe this water into the homes as well as as into greenhouses, where vegetables are raised. This geothermal energy, as it is called, is used not only for heat but also to make electricity and power industrial factories. Some companies have even started mining the residue that comes up with the steam and hot water from the volcanoes.

Down through the years people have learned to do many things with the natural resources found on this earth. Heat has been a very important need. Gas, coal, oil, and other resources have been used to produce heat. And at the end of this world God will use heat and fire to cleanse the earth for the new world He will bring into being here. Nothing will survive.

Ask Him today to help you be a citizen in that new clean world. He'll help you.

Shrews

But the tongue can no man tame; it is an unruly evil, full of deadly poison. James 3:8.

There are only two mammals known that poison their prey, the platypus and some shrews. About 30 species of shrews live in North America. These mouse-sized creatures are feisty and afraid of almost nothing. They will tackle a rat or other rodent almost twice their size, and usually win!

Just to stay alive, a shrew must eat more than its own body weight every day. Shrews have a very high metabolic rate. Their heartbeat ranges from 700 beats a minute when calm to 1,200 beats a minute when frightened. One species is reported to breathe 850 times a minute. Because shrews are so small, they need to breathe very rapidly to keep their body temperature up, as they have no fat. Some shrews can starve to death in about seven hours if they don't have food. They are constantly eating insects, rodents, frogs, worms, mollusks, and some small amphibians.

Though they are active both during the day and night, shrews are rarely seen by humans. During the winter months they're usually under leaves or in burrows made by other animals. They have very poor eyesight, so they have to depend on their keen senses of touch and smell. Shrews are really their own worst enemy, although they occasionally fall prey to other predators. They may become frightened from a clap of thunder and drop dead. Shrews are constantly looking for something to eat, which usually means killing.

The apostle James has told us that our tongue can be like poison. It may not kill, but it surely can hurt. God gave us tongues to help us eat and enjoy our food, and to talk. Ask God to help you use your tongue nicely today as you visit with your friends. They will appreciate your not cutting them down. God will help you; just ask Him. You'll be glad you did.

DIGGING IN TO SURVIVE

For in the time of trouble he shall hide me in his pavilion: in the secret of his tabernacle shall he hide me; he shall set me up upon a rock. Psalm 27:5.

The great Mojave Desert in California is a most fascinating place. So many things happen on this desert that it is a paradise for those interested in studying God's created world. The temperature may change as much as 80 degrees in a day. Rain may fall suddenly and cause flash flooding. Beautiful flowers can adorn certain areas while adjacent areas show no signs of life. And hundreds, if not thousands, of creatures make the desert their home.

The burly tortoise is one of these creatures. Tortoises don't live on the desert as much as they live in it. They are a very hefty and hardy species, able to survive the changes in temperature, the torrential rains, and all of the other natural changes that occur. They dig burrows or tunnels and live in them most of the year. During the winter months they hibernate in their tunnel, living off the fat that their bodies have stored up.

Although there is not much water available to these tortoises, they do drink deeply when water is available, and they get some water from the foliage they eat, some of which is stored in their bladder. You have noticed, I am sure, that turtles or tortoises have a hard leatherlike skin. This helps them retain water in the body and protects against evaporation.

The tortoise has a hard shell to protect it from its enemies, but David knew that his *only* protection from Satan was God. So he put himself in God's hands and allowed Him to take care of him. Like David, we need for God to hide us under His almighty arms of protection. If you want God to hide you from the devil today, just kneel down and ask Him to do so, and He will. When you give yourself totally and unreservedly to God, the devil cannot touch you.

SNOWSHOE HARE

Therefore, if anyone is in Christ, he is a new creation; the old has gone, the new has come! 2 Corinthians 5:17, NIV.

Another marvel of nature is the snowshoe hare. This little creature is unusual in that it changes its color of hair twice a year. It has brown hair for the spring, summer, and fall, and snow-white hair for the winter, when snow is on the ground. The snowshoe hare lives in the northern parts of North America, where there is usually a lot of snow.

Some have thought that the snowshoe hare turns white because of the amount of snow. This is not true. As the rays of the sun pass through the eyes of the hare, they activate the pituitary gland, which regulates the amount of pigment that goes into the hare's new coat. Over a period of about a month small patches of white begin to appear among the brown. Eventually the hare is all white, except the black tips of its ears. The change of color is usually affected by the length of daylight.

These creatures have long back legs. They can run at speeds up to about 25 miles an hour and jump a distance of 10 feet. When running, they have the ability of zigzagging. Sometimes they can throw a predator off their trail by the amount of zigging and zagging they do. However, this is generally not enough to escape, and many of these little creatures fall prey to larger animals, especially the lynx. During the winter months the snowshoe hare has extra hair on its feet that enables it to walk on top of soft snow. Few other animals, including the lynx, can do that without sinking in.

As the Lord has provided the wherewithal for the snowshoe hare to change his fur color, God has given us the wherewithal to change our lifestyle. When we come to Him, He will change our lives, and we can become new creatures. Ask God to change your life today, as it may need to be changed.

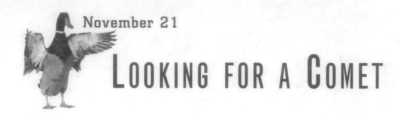

LOOKING FOR A COMET

He determines the number of the stars and calls them each by name. Psalm 147:4, NIV.

Halley's Comet was named after a British astronomer named Edmund Halley, who calculated that the comet would return to visibility from earth every 76 years. No one had seen the famous Halley's Comet since 1910, until it made its scheduled appearance in 1986. Astronomers had been looking into the heavens and studying them, year after year, looking for a trace of Halley's Comet and any other celestial body that might be of interest to them. From the latter part of 1982 there was an astronomers' race on to find Halley's Comet first.

A group of astronomers at the McDonald Observatory in Texas slept in the daytime and worked at night, searching for some evidence of Halley's Comet. They would set the large telescope by the computer, then begin to search the heavens. When they would find something they thought might be the comet, they would take pictures of it, then move the telescope a slight bit and take more pictures. They would then develop the photos and examine them to see if they really had Halley's Comet on film. They were not sure until it appeared in 1986. Then it was sure.

Comets are made of frozen lumps of gas and rock. The comet has no light of its own, and is seen only when it passes close to the sun and heats up. The center (nucleus) is very dark. In fact, it is one of the darkest objects in our solar system. The next sighting of Halley's Comet is expected in 2062. Hopefully we'll be in heaven by then and see God's wonders up close.

Some astronomers do not give God the credit for creating the heavens. They believe that things just happened. They keep trying to put the pieces of their theories together and they always come up empty-handed. Much of what people see won't make sense until they realize that God created the heavens and the earth. God knows all about them; He even knows the number of stars and their names. Put your faith and confidence in God, knowing that He knows everything, and thank Him today for knowledge about the heavenly bodies that He created.

MOOSE

You are a people holy to the Lord your God. Out of all the peoples on the face of the earth, the Lord has chosen you to be his treasured possession. Deuteronomy 14:2, NIV.

Moose are among the beautiful animals of the forest, meadows, and water. They belong to the deer family and are the largest animal in that family. Even though they are large, they are very fleet-footed. They can run at good speed through shallow water and can swim quite rapidly in deep water.

Moose can make themselves at home in alpine meadows, dense forests, frozen tundra, and sprawling marshlands. Usually where they live, in the northern latitudes from Maine to Washington and Wyoming to Alaska, springs are brief, summers are short, and winters are harsh.

Throughout the winter the young calves may stay with their mother, but when spring comes she chases them off in preparation for new calves. Since the winters are so harsh and foliage is scarce, the moose become very malnourished. But as spring comes and the snow melts, the moose eat a lot. A large bull will eat from 50 to 60 pounds of food a day. Young calves, which weigh about 25 pounds at birth, will gain about 150 pounds in one season. Moose do not have any upper incisors (teeth). They must use their lower teeth and upper lip to take foliage from trees and eat grass.

As spring approaches, the bulls begin to grow their large antlers anew, as they have lost them in the winter. By the end of the summer they have rubbed off the velvet from the antlers, and as fall approaches they begin the rutting season. In the rutting season the bulls fight for territory and females.

As moose are quite different from the rest of the deer family, so God's family is to be different from the rest of the world. God wants His own special people, and those who accept Him and follow Him are His chosen and special people. Thank God today that you, as a special person to God, have been chosen by Him as part of His special people.

BALANCED ROCKS

And Jesus said unto them, See ye not all these things? verily I say unto you, There shall not be left here one stone upon another, that shall not be thrown down. Matthew 24:2.

Naturally balanced rocks have been found in many places in the world. It has been a marvel to millions of people as to how these rocks got the way they did, and what keeps them from falling. Geologists explain that in most cases, the rock underneath has been worn away by glaciers, wind, or running water, leaving a harder rock in place above.

In the country of Zimbabwe on the African continent, just south of the capital city of Marare, is a very famous pair of balancing rocks called the Rocks of Epworth. According to history, these two rocks have been balancing there for centuries and are among the oldest and first of the balancing rocks found. These rocks appear to be an easy pushover. However, many tourists and others, visiting these rocks, have tried to push them over, but in vain. They seem to have a perfect balance, and no one has been able to move them off of their perch.

Famous balancing rocks are found in England (the Dartmoor); Australia (the Yellowdine); Argentina (the Tandil); and the United States (many, including the Red Rocks and the Garden of the Gods in Colorado, Monument Valley in Arizona and Utah, and elsewhere).

As people admire these rocks, they stand in awe. "How did it happen?" they ask. Of course, we believe what the Bible teaches about the Flood, so we understand how these rocks got there in the first place. With all of its destruction, the Flood left some marvels for us to admire and contemplate. God is a God of might and power!

As Jesus was talking to His disciples about the beautiful Temple in Jerusalem, He told them about the great tribulation coming, when not one stone of the Temple would be left standing upon another. He linked that time with the end of the world and His second coming. I hope that you are looking forward to Jesus' return, and that you will ask Him just now to help you be ready so that you can be in His heavenly family for all eternity.

BROOK LAMPREY

The people which sat in darkness saw great light; and to them which sat in the region and shadow of death light is sprung up. Matthew 4:16.

While living in the Commonwealth of Massachusetts some years ago, I heard about a fish that wasn't really a fish. There had been discovered in the inland waters a species of lamprey, different from the kind found in the coastal tributary waters. The inland lamprey is the brook lamprey; the coastal one, the sea lamprey.

With an electric shocking mechanism the researchers were able to catch a few of the brook lamprey. Very few of them had been seen, so not much was known about them. They discovered that the brook lamprey is not a true fish. It has a primitive skeleton of cartilage, but no jaws, ribs, shoulder girdle, pelvic girdle, or paired fins.

These brook lampreys have a life span of about five to six years. They grow to be about six to eight inches long, and are not parasites, as are the larger sea lampreys. The brook lampreys are blind, toothless, and have a fleshy hood over the mouth. They spend most of their life in the bottom mud and muck of the streams and come out from the muck only when they mature, when they are about 5 years old.

When the adult females spawn, they make nests of gravel for their eggs. (They get their name from the Latin *lampetra*, which means "sucker of rocks.") After laying their eggs, they die, and the new generation takes over in the muck of the streams. The eggs hatch in five days, and the larvae burrow into the silt and muck, where they live for the next five years of their life.

As the brook lampreys live in darkness, so those who continue to sin are constantly in spiritual darkness. Jesus does not want any to sit in the darkness of sin. Matthew says that those who were sitting in darkness received light when Jesus came. Those who invite Jesus into their life will have a life of light, not darkness. Invite Jesus to come into your life today and thank Him that you don't have to live a life in darkness, like the lampreys.

THE NAMIB DESERT

But I scattered them with a whirlwind among all the nations whom they knew not. Thus the land was desolate after them, that no man passed through nor returned: for they laid the pleasant land desolate. Zechariah 7:14.

In both the part of the country of Israel that this text talks about and in other parts of neighboring countries, it is very desolate. Other desolate areas are found around the world, also. One of these is the Namib Desert, on the southwestern tip of the continent of Africa, in what is now known as Namibia. This desert is about 1,200 miles long

Marks made by humans passing through the area and by other smaller creatures that live there remain for many years. As rain is rare, these lines and marks are not erased easily.

Creatures of the Namib have learned to adapt to the situation of no rain and hot weather. The temperature may go as high as 150°F (66°C) in the hot part of the day. Two kinds of beetles have learned to survive in this barren desert, the head-stander beetle and the button beetle.

The head-stander beetles crawl up to the top of the sand dunes and wait for the heavy fog that comes about 60 times a year. They point their abdomen into the air, and as the fog condenses on their shell the moisture runs down and they catch it with the mouth. The button beetle has a different method. It digs furrows in the sand parallel to the top of the sand dune. As the heavy fog settles it drops into these furrows, and they get wetter than the rest of the sand. The button beetles then go under the sand and drink the water there.

There is very little vegetation, so most creatures live on the water and seeds, with the predators living on the smaller creatures. Apparently there are no large animals living in this area, because of the lack of food and water.

Although God scattered the Israelites into desolate areas, He is planning a beautiful home for His faithful children. Ask God to help you prepare and be ready to join His heavenly family when Jesus comes. Plan for that today; it will be a beautiful life.

FIRE BLIGHT

The Lord of hosts has purposed it, to bring to dishonor the pride of all glory.
Isaiah 23:9, NKJV.

Fire blight is not known to many people. It is basically pear farmers and other agricultural people who are aware of the blight and the damage it does. When the early settlers came to the United States, they brought from Europe some very fine pear, apple, and quince trees. These had produced well for them in the Old World, so they decided to try them in their new homeland.

The trees grew fine for the first several years; then they started to show black splotches on the leaves, trunk, and fruit. After years of wondering what was happening, it was discovered that this black stain was caused by a bacterial infection to the tree. The disease was named fire blight because the blossoms, young fruit, and shoots wither up and drop off of the tree, blackened as though they had been in a fire.

Most of the pear trees on the east and west coasts of the United States have been wiped out by this blight. Most of the pear crops now being produced are in the midwestern areas of the United States. The colder climate keeps the bacteria from spreading very fast, and in some areas the severe cold actually kills the bacteria.

These little bacteria are so tiny that when their image is enlarged about 30,000 times by an electron microscope they appear only about an inch long. Under the magnification of the microscope there can be seen hairlike flagella, which propel the bacteria. One of the effective carriers of this bacteria is the honeybee. The bees land on the flower to take out the sweet nectar and then fly to another tree. They pollinate the trees in this way, which is a must, but they also carry the bacteria from tree to tree, spreading the disease as they go.

The lives of those people who deny Christ will be stained by the blight of sin. This will cause them to lose their life when Jesus comes, unless they confess their sins and change their lifestyle. Ask God today to purify your life so that it will not be stained by the blight of sin.

337

MY HORSE BACH

Whatever your hands find to do, do with your might. Ecclesiastes 9:10, NRSV.

From the time I was a small boy I had wanted a horse, but until I was in seventh grade my family always lived where there was no place to keep one. Finally we moved to a small farm near Boulder, Colorado, and we had a place to keep a horse. I kept reminding my dad that I wanted a horse, but Dad always said, "We just can't afford one now, son."

One day I was riding with one of my friends on his horse, and we happened to pass our bachelor neighbor's farm, where he was working in his garden beside the road. As he saw us boys come riding by on the one horse, he looked up and said, "Hey, I have a horse I'd like to sell. Maybe you could buy him and you wouldn't have to ride double. His name is Bach. I want only $10 for him." I told him I'd tell my dad. You can be assured that when Dad came home that night I told him about Bach. Well, Dad thought we might be able to afford that, so we drove over to our neighbor's house. Not only did my dad buy Bach, but we bought two sets of harnesses, a harrow, a small walking plow, and a couple of other useful items, all for $20.

I was excited as I put the bridle on Bach and began to ride him home. The only problem was that Bach had one stiff front knee, so naturally he couldn't run. Even though Bach was not perfect, I had my horse. He was a workhorse, not a saddle horse, but that didn't make any difference to me. Dad would put the harness on him and hook him up to the plow or harrow, and Bach worked right along as best he could. Whatever job Dad had for him, he would do it as well as he could, even though he was not as fast as a horse with four good legs. Although just a horse, Bach taught me many lessons.

The one he taught me that has meant the most to me was to do my job well, whatever I was asked to do. My dad helped instill that lesson in me too. This is counsel from God, to do well whatever we do. Ask Him to help you do good work in whatever you need to do today.

NATURAL ARCHES

Listen to me, you that pursue righteousness, you that seek the Lord. Look to the rock from which you were hewn. Isaiah 51:1, NRSV.

Among the many interesting natural phenomena around the world are the natural arches. Some of them disappear after many years, because of erosion, but others withstand the weathering of time.

There is one national park in the state of Utah that is set aside just for the purpose of preserving natural arches. It is called the Arches National Park. In this park is the famous Landscape Arch, the world's longest natural arch. It measures 291 feet. In Panama City, Panama, is another natural arch, the flattest natural arch in the world. Israel has a number of natural arches too. Then in the state of Virginia is the famous limestone Natural Bridge. Natural arches are found where there is a lot of sandstone, as this type of rock lends itself to the making of natural arches.

Natural arches and bridges seem to abound where there is pink-tinted sandstone. This rock takes its color from minute particles of quartz and makes a very beautiful sight. In the Arches National Park a famous arch is one called the Delicate Arch. It looks so fragile that people wonder why it doesn't fall, but it is quite solid. There is also one section in the park called the window section. People can look through at the arches and give them their own name. The tall Courthouse Towers and Fiery Furnace are named as such because of their soil color and formation.

Some years ago when we were in Hawaii, we saw along the ocean a beautiful natural arch, and I took pictures of it. Two years later when we returned, the arch was gone. The ocean water had washed away all the sandstone, and it had collapsed. We could see only where it had been.

Paul says that Jesus is our rock of salvation; we are made in His image. He is the foundation rock upon which we should build our lives. Thank Him today that He made you and that He is the solid rock of your salvation.

THE MIGHTY AMAZON RIVER

A river watering the garden flowed from Eden; from there it was separated into four headwaters. Genesis 2:10, NIV.

The Amazon River in South America is one of the natural wonders of this earth. I was happy to have had the opportunity to live on the bank of the Amazon in both Brazil and Peru. The Amazon is not the longest river; that distinction belongs to the Nile River. But the Nile is not much longer than the Amazon. The Amazon River is about 4,000 miles long and is the biggest of all the rivers in the world. It is said that it would make about 12 Mississippi Rivers.

The Amazon begins up in the Andes of Peru, just about 100 miles from the Pacific Ocean. Little trickles run down through the small valleys, then pick up more water, get larger, and continue to grow, until in Peru the Ucayali and Maranon (mar-RAN-yon) rivers are formed. These join up just east of the city of Iquitos, where we lived for six years. Flowing another 500 miles, this "Amazon River," called as such by the Peruvians, meets other rivers from Colombia and forms the Solimões (sol-LEE-moings) River until it reaches the Brazilian city of Manaus (man-OUS). Just south of Manaus the Solimões merges with the Rio Negro ("Black River"), and the two form the "Brazilian" Amazon. From the point where the two rivers come together, there is a line between the muddy and the black waters that continues for many miles downriver until they finally merge into the muddy Amazon.

Since the Amazon does not have much fall to it, the ocean tides from the Atlantic Ocean affect the height of the Amazon River upstream for more than 600 miles. The water from the Amazon that empties into the Atlantic Ocean is "sweet," not salty, for many miles out.

God created a river to water the Garden of Eden. He divided it into four heads, but the Amazon, with all of its water, flows from many heads and goes into one. We who are God's children are many, but we are united in Jesus. Thank Jesus today that you belong to a united family. Tell Him that you want to stay under His guiding hand.

AUSTRALIAN SINKHOLES

They that dwell under his shadow shall return; they shall revive as the corn, and grow as the vine. Hosea 14:7.

In the southeastern part of Australia are underground caverns called sinkholes. It is not a very glamorous name for them, but in essence that is what they are. Picaninnie Chasm, a large cavern, water-filled, goes down almost 200 feet. This chasm is located in the largest sinkhole, called Picaninnie Pond. The water is very clear and presents divers with a beautiful picture of the underground world. One diver said that swimming in that water reminded her of just floating in space. It was almost like flying.

The rock is all limestone. It is suggested that if you could cut off a slice of this the way you would cut off a piece of cake, it would look like a piece of Swiss cheese. There are about 20,000 sinkholes in this region of Australia, although many of them are dry.

Because many divers have lost their lives in these sinkholes, now all divers are required to obtain diving permits and to use special equipment. Some of the older divers, who actually discovered many of the sinkholes, are not allowed to dive because of the new regulations.

In the sinkholes named Ewens Ponds are lovely green plants. Water comes in through springs at the bottom at the rate of about 36,000 gallons a minute, which creates quite a current. However, the plants are not disturbed. Watercress and other edible plants abound in these ponds. A person could make a giant salad with all of the greens that grow there. The rapid movement of water prohibits stagnation, and the amount of plant growth on the bottom prevents silt from muddying up the water.

From down under comes the lesson to us that when we are prepared properly, and under the shadow of guidelines and regulations, life will be safer. The same is true under the guidelines and care of Jesus. Thank Him today for His guidelines (the Bible), which He has given us for our safety and future eternal life.

NATURAL HOUSES

The holy portion of the land shall be for the priests the ministers of the sanctuary, which shall come near to minister unto the Lord: and it shall be a place for their houses, and an holy place for the sanctuary. Ezekiel 45:4.

Sandstone has been a favorite building material for many because it can be easily worked. Many beautiful buildings have been made of sandstone blocks of varying colors. You may have even seen some in your town. And around the world people have made houses of sandstone. We'll talk about two of these today.

In the central part of Turkey, in the city of Urgup, which is about 150 miles southeast of the capital city of Ankara, are found some unique houses. Many years ago the people noticed the sandstone columns of the area and decided that they would make good houses, so they began to carve into them. These houses are still in use today. In the larger columns churches were carved, and the people worshipped in them. More than 300 churches have been found.

We find something interesting right here in North America, in the state of Colorado. The Pueblo Indians built themselves villages and communities under large overhanging rocks, actually part of a large open cave. These rocks were so large and flat that they were named Mesa Verde, Spanish for "green table." The Pueblo Indians cut out the sandstone, formed blocks, and built their dwellings in the cliffs, under the overhanging rocks. This is the largest assemblage of Indian ruins anyplace in the United States. This mesa is about 20 miles long and 15 miles wide.

God gave instructions as to how the people in Israel should build and locate their houses and the sanctuary. No doubt some of their technology has come down through their descendants to our day. Provisions were made in every community for some type of religious services.

God is preparing a home for us in heaven, more expensive than sandstone, and we will worship our God throughout all eternity. There is no expense for the mansion that God is preparing for each one of us. He wants us to prepare ourselves for that by giving our hearts to Jesus. Get ready today by asking Jesus to help you prepare for eternity in heaven with Him.

QUEENEY THE COW

And he said, "Who are You, Lord?" Then the Lord said, "I am Jesus, whom you are persecuting. It is hard for you to kick against the goads." Acts 9:5, NKJV.

When I was a boy, we had a little farm near Boulder, Colorado. Dad bought a number of milk cows both to provide milk for us and to sell the milk for income. Dad went out and bought the cows, bringing them back one or two at a time in a trailer and unloading them into our corral. It was fun to help him until he brought home Queeney. When Dad and I unloaded her from the trailer, she went to the feed trough. Shortly she whirled around, saw me, and made a beeline for me. I ran and jumped up onto the corral fence, and she stopped just short of me.

That scared me, and I was always careful not to get in her way. But when she saw me coming toward the corral, she'd come toward me. As I had the fence between us, I'd tease her. Evidently that's what had happened at her previous home, too, and she didn't like boys.

Some months later a load of pipe rolled off the truck and pinned my dad to the ground, breaking his ankle. It was put in a cast, and he had to stay off of it for many weeks. This meant that Mother, Grandpa, and I had to do the milking. All of the cows were gentle, but we had to put hobbles on Queeney. Mother milked the cows in the morning, and I was supposed to milk them in the evening. That first time I went carefully from cow to cow, milking them. But when I sat on my stool to milk Queeney she immediately realized that she had a different milker. She looked around, saw me, and even with the hobbles began kicking. I sailed under two nearby cows. Boy, could she kick! I was happy I was not hurt. Mother finished milking Queeney, and I never touched her after that.

Saul was persecuting the Christians, but God finally stopped him and asked him why he was doing it. He told Saul that he shouldn't kick against Him. Queeney could kick against me, because I was human, but we can't kick against God. God invites us, as He did Saul, to come to Him and accept Him. Accept His invitation today.

Cocoons

The Lord is good to those who wait for him, to the soul that seeks him. It is good that one should wait quietly for the salvation of the Lord. Lamentations 3:25, 26, NRSV.

Cocoons are one of the most fascinating objects of the natural world. It is astonishing to know that a little caterpillar can change its whole life in a short time inside one of these cocoons.

No doubt you have seen a cocoon. It all begins by a butterfly or moth laying some eggs on a leaf. (Depending on the species, each caterpillar uses a different leaf.) After a certain period of time the eggs hatch, and out of each egg crawls a caterpillar. Immediately it starts eating the leaves of the tree on which it is hatched. As the caterpillar grows and gets fat, it comes to a time in its life, again designated by species, that it begins to spin its cocoon. Certain glands in the caterpillar secret a liquid that hardens in the air. The caterpillar wraps this silky substance around itself, working until it has itself completely enclosed and sealed off from the outside world.

Inside its cocoon the caterpillar becomes an immobile pupa. Through the process of metamorphosis, its entire body is changed into that of a beautiful butterfly or moth. When it is time for the newly formed butterfly or moth to come out of the cocoon, it chews open a hole and tries to get out. It must struggle and struggle, and all the while it is struggling, it is developing its strength to fly. It eventually gets out, unfolds its wings, lets them dry, and flies away. If for any reason the struggling cycle of the butterfly or moth coming out of the cocoon is cut short, it will never make a butterfly or moth and flit around in God's natural world. It needs to struggle to complete the entire cycle that God created for it.

God has a developing plan for each one of us, and each one is developing in a different way. Some of us see our friends developing faster, and we want to develop faster too, but that may not be God's plan for you. We need to accept God's plan and be patient and wait for the Lord. There is a reward for those who wait on the Lord, who knows no haste or delay. Ask Him today to help you be patient in your life and wait on Him, like the emerging butterfly or moth.

EUROPEAN ALPS

Then they shall begin to say to the mountains, Fall on us; and to the hills, Cover us.
Luke 23:30.

The Alps of Europe extend in an arc through the seven countries of France, Italy, Switzerland, Austria, Germany, Yugoslavia, and Liechtenstein. These mountains are high and rugged. The Flood and subsequent geological forces were really active in this part of the world. Those geologists who do not believe in anything relating to Creation or God have said that it took more than 180 million years for the Alps to form. Fortunately, the Bible tells us that mountains actually came to be as the result of the Flood.

Altogether these mountains are about 750 miles long and contain some of the most beautiful sights in the world. The Matterhorn, the Jungfrau, and Mont Blanc are some of the famous peaks in the Alps. Two famous glaciers, the Aletsch and the Gorner, provide water for the croplands below. Famous rivers such as the Danube, Rhine, Po, and Rhone have their headwaters in the Alps.

The Alps form a climatic barrier between the warmer airs of the Mediterranean and the colder temperatures of Northern Europe. They are the highest in the west and south, and slope downward to the east and north. Climbers have looked up at those tall peaks for many years. In 1786 two Frenchmen succeeded in climbing Mont Blanc for the first time. It is the tallest peak, at 15,781 feet. Tourism is very popular now in the Alps, as people want to vacation amid the beautiful scenery.

The day that Jesus will be coming back to this earth is soon approaching. There are many people who will not want to see Him come, because everything they love is the opposite of what He taught. The light shining from Jesus when He comes will be blinding, and those who are not His followers will run from it. The Bible tells us that they will call for the rocks and mountains to fall on them. Pray today that you will not be in that group. Ask God to help you be in the group that awaits and looks forward to Jesus' coming.

WALLEYE FISH

Now he who supplies seed to the sower and bread for food will also supply and increase your store of seed and will enlarge the harvest of your righteousness.
2 Corinthians 9:10, NIV.

One of the biggest fish-management programs in many Midwestern and Northern states in the United States is the stocking of streams and lakes with walleye fish. I'd always heard about trout, bass, and other fish which I used to fish for, but I was a grown man before I heard of walleye. They were not in the area where I grew up. Walleye are one of the fisherman's dream fish. They are not really strong fighters, but they do put up some resistance. They are a fleshy fish, and may weigh up to 20 pounds.

One of the reasons that the state departments of natural resources like these fish is that they help keep the lakes and streams clean. They are not scavengers, like catfish, but they are a predatory fish and so help to keep nature in balance. With all of the pollutants in the water now, the walleye help manage the streams and lakes in a remarkable way.

People working for state natural resources catch female and male walleyes in their spawning run. They milk the ripe females of their eggs and fertilize them with male milt. This has to be done in 60 to 90 seconds to produce more small fry. Literally hundreds of millions of these walleye fry are returned into the streams. Many of the fry are eaten by fish or other creatures, so the vast number small fry placed in the water does not necessarily mean a large population of walleye adults. A single female walleye may lay 20,000 eggs at a time. These hatch in 12 to 16 days. As the little fry hatch out, they eat on their egg sack for several days, and then with enough strength they begin to look for food on their own. Neither parent looks after them once the eggs are laid.

You and I serve a God who is interested in us. He does not just let us go and develop the best we can. He is willing to be by our side through the Holy Spirit and help us develop in the right way. Pray today, asking God to send the Holy Spirit to be by your side right there with your guardian angel.

PELICANS

[Pharoah] dealt craftily with our race and forced our ancestors to abandon their infants so that they would die. Acts 7:19, NRSV.

Pelicans are interesting birds. Among the largest of the flying birds, an adult pelican is between four and five feet long and weighs up to 16 pounds. The brown pelicans that people in the United States are familiar with are maritime birds. They are well insulated against cold weather, as they have heavy, thickly feathered bodies and numerous air spaces beneath the skin and also in the bones.

They are tremendous fliers, soaring to great heights by using thermal currents, or updrafts of warmer air. When migrating or looking for fishing grounds, they usually do so in flocks. By using the thermal currents, they arrive at their destination with a minimum of effort.

The diet of pelicans is almost totally fish. When they see a fish, they dive toward the water. Just before the pelican reaches the surface, it straightens out its curved neck and hits the water straight in. Its mouth opens, the pouch on its lower bill expands as water is forced through it, and it scoops up the fish. The pelican comes back to the surface and the water drains out, so the pouch returns to its normal size. The upper bill is tightly closed, and the fish trapped inside is swallowed whole. Contrary to some cartoons, the pouch is not used to carry fish, only for catching them, and after a dive they rarely come up empty.

The one to four young hatch from eggs after about 35 to 37 days of incubation, which both parents take part in. Both parents also feed the young. These young cannot walk for about three weeks, and cannot fly for about two months.

Our text this morning is referring to the time Moses was born. Pharaoh had ordered that all the male children be killed. Today also there is much evil going on because of sin. Thank God that He will never forsake you, because He loves you. Ask Him to be with you today.

SILK

I clothed you in embroidered cloth and gave you sandals of badger skin; I clothed you with fine linen and covered you with silk. Ezekiel 16:10, NKJV.

People have been making silk clothing and other goods for thousands of years. I don't know how the process was first discovered. For centuries the Chinese have used silkworms to produce silk for them, and then it is processed and made into beautiful garments and tapestries. The Chinese are not the only leaders in the silk fabric business today. Japan, India, Russia, South Korea, Italy, Spain, and France are also involved in the silk fabric business. China is the largest producer of white silk fiber. India produces a golden silk.

Silk is the result of a caterpillar, not a worm. The silkworm caterpillar ejects a smooth, lustrous protein mixture that hardens with the exposure to air. Each silkworm caterpillar has two three-inch glands that produce this liquid silk. As the silk passes through the pink midsection of the gland it is coated with a sticky substance that gives the cocoon cohesiveness. When these fibers hit the air, they harden, and the caterpillar wraps these around itself until it has a fine, tightly woven cocoon. These silk fibers may be 2,000 to 3,000 feet long. The cocoons are harvested, soaked in hot water, and the silk strands unraveled. Five or six strands are used as a thread.

The cocoons used for silk are put into a hot room, which kills the caterpillars so they will not eat their way out of the cocoon as they turn into moths. When a pupa turns into a moth, it emits a liquid that softens the cocoon, thus making it easy to come out. But that partially destroys the silk fibers. Naturally, some cocoons are allowed to mature, and the adult moths come out to reproduce more caterpillars.

Thank God that He provided for your needs by creating such creatures as the silkworm, and that you have a part in enjoying and benefiting from this creation.

GROWING FOR 17 YEARS

And have put on the new man, which is renewed in knowledge after the image of him that created him. Colossians 3:10.

The female cicada uses her saw toothed ovipositor at the rear end of her body to cut a slit in the branches of trees. There she lays her eggs—400 to 600, depending on her species. Shortly afterward she drops from the branch and dies. The eggs hatch into nymphs, and the nymphs develop into adults. This is the interesting life cycle of the cicada, which is described below.

Some people call the cicadas locusts, but they are not. There are about 3,000 species of cicadas in the world. The dog-day cicada has a two-year life cycle, but the periodical cicadas have a 13-year or 17-year cycle. The nymphs of the 17-year cicada, smaller than a grain of rice, hatch from the eggs after a six- or seven-week incubation period. They drop from the branch and burrow 18 to 24 inches into the ground close to some nice tree roots. There they will set up their special little house where they remain during the next 17 years, sucking liquid from the tree or shrub. During that time they molt and change their body shell several times. Since it takes them so long to mature, and they stay in the nymph stage so long, there are some animals that dig down and eat them.

Once they have matured, the entire brood—billions of them—comes up out of the ground at the same time. They cover everything. Many animals like to eat the cicadas, and so many of the new adult cicadas never take part in the great population explosion. Scientists have numbered the broods of the cicada. The 17-year broods carry the numbers I to XVII, and so on, and the 13-year broods numbers XVIII through XXX. In this way, scientists can keep track of the years and know which ones are about to come out.

Just as the cicadas remain in the ground, we will remain in this sin-darkened world until the right time. Jesus promised to give us a new life if we turn our life over to Him. Ask Jesus today to come soon and take you out of this world of darkness and into the world of light, where you'll live eternally.

BUSH BABY

But the angel of the Lord by night opened the prison doors, and brought them forth.
Acts 5:19.

Most of us sleep at night, and we have very little concept of what goes on in the world while we are asleep. The world is almost a different place at night, and I'm not talking about all of the people who stay up at night—many of them working to keep things going for the rest of us.

Many of God's creatures are nocturnal by nature. They sleep in the daytime and roam and hunt at night. One of these lives in the rain forest belt of West Africa—the bush baby. This little creature is smaller than most house cats, but it often has better eyesight than the house cat. It has a light-reflecting tapetum located behind the retina of the eye,

These animals are basically insectivorous (they eat insects for food), but will eat a variety of fruits and nuts. During the nighttime hours bush babies also look for gum from the acacia trees. This gives them calcium that they don't get from eating small rodents and insects. The gum flows from the acacia trees when wood-boring larvae of two kinds of beetles and one kind of moth form galleries in the tree branches. When the gum is exposed to oxygen, it starts to flow. As it flows, the bush baby eats it. Once a gum lick is established, the bush baby will visit it frequently. One adult bush baby might visit up to 300 trees during a night looking for the gum.

During the day bush babies usually sleep in groups. At night they hunt alone. The female bush baby gives birth to two litters of young a year, usually with two in a litter. The gestation period is about 120 days.

God and His angels work at night as well as in the daytime. God opened the prison doors for His servants at night, and Jesus wrestled with Jacob at night. He wants the best for us, and sometimes that must be done at night. Thank God that He is always on duty, day or night, watching out for your best good.

THE SHARPSHOOTER

Let your eyes look straight ahead, fix your gaze directly before you. Proverbs 4:25, NIV.

Have you ever been under the water at the beach or in a pool and tried looking at the sky or the shore? Without a mask or goggles, things look distorted. As you look down into the water from above, the position of things is distorted, too. This is what is known as light refraction.

There is a kind of fish that is a tremendous sharpshooter with a stream of water. This fish is called the archerfish. It has a God-given optical system that allows it to adjust for distance and compensates in some unknown way for the bending of light rays by water. If the archerfish is within about four or five feet of a small object, it can shoot a stream of water under pressure that knocks the object right off its perch and into the water.

This is how it works. The archerfish has been so designed by God that it is able to form a canal with its tongue up against the groove in the roof of its mouth. With the pressure made by closing its gills, it can shoot a stream of water through the canal a distance of five feet. As the archerfish sees a bug or something else on a branch hanging low over the water, it can come up to the surface and with just its snout sticking out of the water get ready, take aim, and fire! It almost never misses. The bug falls into the water, and bingo! It is eaten by the fish.

According to reports, the archerfish does not have to depend on this method to get the food it eats. It can also live out in the coastal waters and survive. There are no low-hanging branches there decorated by tasty bugs just waiting to be shot, so no doubt the archerfish has another method of obtaining food. Some researchers say they shoot their stream just for sport. What fun, eh?

Yes, God is a lover of the unique and unusual. He has certainly proved that. Jesus tells us through the psalmist to keep looking at the direction we are going and make sure that our eyesight is straight, not curved. We must have a straight view of God. Ask Him to help you have a straight and clear view of His words today.

NEW ZEALAND'S SADDLEBACK BIRD

The Lord is my rock, and my fortress, and my deliverer. 2 Samuel 22:2.

Between the years A.D. 750 and 1300 a group of Polynesian settlers named Maori were the first to migrate to the island now called New Zealand and settle there. They found the island heavily forested and rich in insects and birds. There were only two species of mammals there, both bats. So the Maoris began to import other animals onto the island.

They brought dogs, cats, pigs, goats, cattle, hedgehogs, ferrets, opossums, wallabies, and weasels. The opossums were brought in with the idea of starting a fur business, but it never materialized. As time went on, new settlers brought in even rats, hoping that with the dogs they would get rid of the wingless moa bird. They also cut down more than 70 percent of the trees to make room for agriculture. But this destroyed the habitats of some birds, one of them being the North Island saddleback, known to the Maori people as tieke.

Tieke are black with a reddish-brown saddle on their backs and have a fleshy, usually orange, wattle in the corner of their beaks. According to a Maori legend, the god Maui and his brothers once snared the sun and beat it. They told the sun to move slower so as to give people a longer day. Maui was hot and thirsty and asked the tieke to bring him some water. The bird refused, so Maui seized the bird and flung it away from him, leaving two scorched marks from his hot hands on the hot bird's back. The Maori believe this is how the saddleback got the two brownish marks, which look like a saddle, on its back. Legends can be fun to hear, but isn't it nice to believe in a Creator?

To save the tieke and other birds from extinction, New Zealanders set aside several nearby rocky uninhabited islands as bird sanctuaries. The North Island saddlebacks have started to increase again, after being almost extinct.

Jesus is our rock and our salvation. We can depend on Him because He is solid and never changes. Put your trust in Jesus, the Solid Rock. You'll always have a firm foundation with Him.

ROSS ICE SHELF

Then the Lord opened the eyes of Balaam, and he saw the angel of the Lord standing in the way, and his sword drawn in his hand: and he bowed down his head, and fell flat on his face. Numbers 22:31.

In the Antarctic is a vast amount of ice. In fact, most of Antarctica is covered with ice. And in 1841 a British explorer named James Clark Ross was searching for the south magnetic pole when he happened to come upon an extremely large ice pack. It was so large that he and his men spent many days and then weeks trying to get around it, but they failed. Ross was not aware that this is the largest ice pack in the world, measuring about 500 miles wide, 200 feet high, and 600 miles long. It covers an area of about 200,000 square miles, or an area about the size of Texas.

Many icebergs break off from this massive ice shelf, and some of these floating islands are 20 to 30 miles long or longer. Despite the losses of these large icebergs, and there are many of them, the Ross Ice Shelf, named in honor of the explorer, continues to stay about the same size. As the snow that falls in the Antarctic continues to pile up, this adds to the ice pack, so actually it does not lose any of its size. Some scientists say that the Ross Ice Shelf is moving toward the ocean at a speed of about six feet per day. Of course, the ice that gets into the warmer water or air begins to melt, and so icebergs are born.

The ice barrier stopped Ross, but it helped Roald Amundsen and Robert F. Scott, the first two men to reach the South Pole. Today on this large ice shelf the countries of the United States and New Zealand have year-round research stations. They are located at the western end, on McMurdo Sound.

The Ross Ice Shelf stopped the British explorer, but others succeeded. In our Christian experience we need to be stopped from doing some things and helped in doing others. We need to be sure that we are doing what God wants us to do; then we will succeed. Ask God to help you follow His will today, and you will succeed.

THE RHINE RIVER

This is what the Sovereign Lord says to the mountains and hills, to the ravines and valleys: I am about to bring a sword against you, and I will destroy your high places. Ezekiel 6:3, NIV.

The Rhine River is not the longest river in the world, but it is a very important river for the European countries that it serves. It is probably the busiest river in the world, even busier than the Mississippi. Like the Amazon River, the Rhine starts high up in the mountains. The Swiss mountains provide the bulk of the water for the Rhine, but it picks up water from other rivers as it flows 833 miles toward the North Sea. The Rhine is one of the few rivers that flow *north*. Most rivers flow south.

The Rhine begins in Switzerland under the name of Rein. As the two rivers, the Vorder Rhein and the Hinter Rhein, come together at the town of Reichenau, they form the upper Rhine. It passes through Austria and Liechtenstein and into the Lake of Constance. There it leaves the silt that it has brought from the mountains and goes on as a virtually clear river. By the time the river reaches Basel, it has traveled only 233 miles and dropped 7,000 feet in elevation. In its final 600 miles the river drops only about 800 feet.

At Basel the Rhine heads north into the Black Forest area of Germany. Once past the town of Bingen, the river passes through the area of the castles of the old monarchs and other important people of days gone by. After leaving the city of Bonn, the river leaves the mountains and becomes darker in color, and many more ships travel on it. The river enters the North Sea at Rotterdam, Holland, which is a very deep seaport.

The Rhine is important in history for all of its charm and splendor. In the new earth God will reestablish even more beautiful scenery, with more fashionable mansions for us than the castles seen along the Rhine River.

Pray that you will be able to enjoy the outdoor beauty and the mansion that God has planned for you throughout all eternity. Thank Him for it. It's something you will not want to miss.

SEA STACKS

Moses then wrote down everything the Lord had said. He got up early the next morning and built an altar at the foot of the mountain and set up twelve stone pillars representing the twelve tribes of Israel. Exodus 24:4, NIV.

The oceans are often rough and always moving. In some areas this creates beaches, and in other areas it creates cliffs or rocky shorelines. Coastal areas are almost always scenic and beautiful, although some are rugged and even dangerous.

Certain coastal areas are made of sandstone, and the constant battering of the waves wears away the rock. In some places the water has chewed the shoreline back for many hundreds of feet, as the rock has crumbled and washed away. Along some coasts you see pillars standing out in the water. The constant washing of waves has weakened the rock. Boring creatures have made holes in the soft rock. And the combination of waves and boring has caused the cliffs to deteriorate, leaving pillars of the stronger rock standing in the water. These pillars are called sea stacks.

One of the most noted areas of sea stacks and cliffs is in Australia. Called the Port Campbell National Park, it has 20 miles of these sea stacks and cliffs. A number of arches are also in this area, including the London Bridge, an arch with a tower at each end. At another spot are 12 sea stacks. They're named after the 12 apostles.

You can see sea stacks off the island of Bermuda, and with the background of emerald water they are a striking sight. Stacks are also found off the coasts of Oregon, California, Washington, the Hawaiian Islands, Portugal, Spain, Ireland, England, and elsewhere.

Moses built an altar with 12 pillars signifying the 12 tribes of Israel. In the walls of the New Jerusalem there will be 12 gates and 12 foundations of precious stones, one for each tribe. Today, thank God for His love and for His preparations to make a wonderful world for you that will last forever.

KILLER CATERPILLARS

And the chief priests and scribes sought how they might kill him; for they feared the people. Luke 22:2.

The inchworm, or measuring worm, is known as the killer caterpillar. These caterpillars eat flies. How can an inchworm caterpillar catch a fly? Is the caterpillar that fast? You've probably tried many times to catch a fly, and now you wonder how a slowmoving caterpillar can do it.

Mimicry (impersonation) is part of this caterpillar's hunting technique. It bites off and spits out parts of a leaf. Then it crawls into the hole it has made in the leaf and waits. As a fly approaches and lands on the leaf, the caterpillar continues to wait patiently. Then all of a sudden it swings around and with its six feet grabs the fly. It may not eat all of the fly, but it will eat most of it. Different species of inchworms also mimic twigs, thorns, and scales.

Inchworms are just that, about an inch long. The female lays each of her eggs individually, each one with a silk thread attached to it. She may lay up to 100 eggs, which hatch in about 14 days. The larvae will molt four times in their growing process. They split their tight skins, wiggle out, and in a half hour they are ready again to go after their prey. After the third molting they spin a doilylike cocoon. About three weeks later they molt for the fourth time, appearing as a moth.

These moths mimic the fern leaf. They appear in two colors, brown and green. Scientists are not quite sure how they get their color. Do they just molt into a color, or are they influenced by the environment? It's another of God's interesting mysteries.

Jesus was once a victim of the jealous priests. They didn't like the way He did things, because it challenged their traditional ways. Jesus didn't conform to tradition, He taught about the love of God in simple ways, and He went about helping people in their time of need. Give your life over to Jesus, invite Him into your life today, and He'll show you real love, not make-believe.

KIWI

Blindly they wandered through the streets, so defiled with blood that no one was able to touch their garments. Lamentations 4:14, NRSV.

New Zealand is the only place the kiwi bird is found. Therefore, it has become the national symbol of New Zealand. Its picture is on their coins, stamps, clothing, and even cans of shoe polish. The kiwi doesn't really look like a bird, but it is.

Kiwis don't have typical bird feathers. Their feathers are coarse and something like fur. They don't have wings, either. People are their only enemies, and since the kiwi is the country's national symbol, they are protected from being hunted.

About the size of chickens, kiwis have very poor eyesight. They can make out shadows, but objects must be very close if they are actually to be seen. The nose of the kiwi is at the tip of its bill. Fine hairs at the base of the bill act as feelers, and it is said that the kiwi has the keenest sense of smell of any bird. Kiwis come out and hunt at night for their favorite meal, the earthworm. If they cannot find enough earthworms, they will eat snails, insects, and even some berries. Kiwis have keen hearing also, and they run at the slightest noise. They are fast runners, and run along like a spear thrower, with their nose straight out.

The kiwi lays a very large egg, one of the largest of any bird egg. It is about five inches long and weighs about one pound. The male will incubate the egg, not eating for a week at a time. It takes 75 to 80 days for the one egg to hatch. When the chick hatches, it is covered with a fuzzy down, and in a few hours it is foraging for itself. Then the parents lay another egg and start another chick on its way.

God doesn't want us to wander around like the wicked, as though we were blind. He wants us to have good eyesight. The way to have that good spiritual eyesight is to continue to study the Word of God, which gives us the insights into our present and future life. Ask God to help you have good eyesight today.

GYPSUM

He did not spare the ancient world when he brought the flood on its ungodly people, but protected Noah, a preacher of righteousness, and seven others. 2 Peter 2:5, NIV.

God told Noah what to do and what He would do if Noah was faithful. Noah was faithful, and God fulfilled His promise. A worldwide flood destroyed the earth, and Noah and his family were saved. Under the waters of that flood great upheavals of earth occurred, and many natural resources were buried. Today many of those natural resources are being discovered. One of them is gypsum.

Though you may not realize it, we depend a lot on gypsum. There is gypsum in toothpaste. Gypsum is also used in matches; in molds to make sterling-silver handles for knives, forks, and spoons; in plaster of Paris for splints; in the making of plates, saucers, cups, and other dishes; and in casts used by dentists in making dentures. Many of the houses that we live in have gypsum wallboard in one form or another. Gypsum wallboard is the biggest and most lucrative part of the gypsum business, which consumes more than 30 million tons a year in the United States. Gypsum is also found all over Canada, and most of Nova Scotia's gypsum is exported to the United States.

The early Assyrians, Egyptians, and Greeks all used gypsum. The Assyrians used it in their cuneiform scripts, and the Egyptians used it in making vessels, boxes, and sculptures. It was also used in constructing the Egyptian family pyramids. The Greek word for this substance is *gypsos*, meaning "chalk." Gypsum in its natural state is white and chalky. It is soft and can be scratched easily. Gypsum is the only product that can be softened with water and then when it is dry takes back its original hard form. This is why plaster of Paris is so good for casts—it dries quickly and gets hard.

God has a plan for everything that He does, and He gives us the wisdom to know how to use the natural resources He has provided. Thank God today for His foresight in your behalf. He is a God of love, and thank Him for that, too.

HORSETAILS

People were eating, drinking, marrying and being given in marriage up to the day Noah entered the ark. Then the flood came and destroyed them all. Luke 17:27, NIV.

In the coal layers under the earth, geologists have found fossil prints of the leaves of the plants that today we call horsetails. Apparently before the Flood they were very large bushes and are responsible for much of the coal that is mined today.

Horsetails are found on every continent except Australia. They will grow anywhere, and that is beneficial to us, because they will cover areas where no other vegetation grows, and so keep back the erosion of soil. In many areas horsetails grow up to three feet tall, but the most common height is from 18 inches to two feet.

The horsetail shoots up a stem that is jointed every so often. It is from these joints that the leaves grow. The leaves have a glasslike deposit of silica in some of their cells that works well for scouring. Native Americans and early foreign settlers in America used these weeds to scour their pots and pans. Some researchers are wondering if people in remote areas may still be using horsetails for that purpose.

There are 15 varieties of horsetails in North America, extending down into northern Mexico. The aerial shoots of the plants are of two types: (1) vegetative branches that have tufts at the nodes, and (2) reproductive branches that have small cones on their tips. The cones release spores that have four attached threadlike elators that coil and straighten rapidly, according to the moisture content of the air. These movements help release the spores, which reproduce new plants in June and July of each year.

Horsetails that have become coal are among the resources God has made for our use. Let us use our natural resources wisely. Ask God to help you be a good steward of our natural resources today.

GEODES

See, I lay a stone in Zion, a tested stone, a precious cornerstone for a sure foundation; the one who trusts will never be dismayed. Isaiah 28:16, NIV.

You may find a geode's beautiful inside difficult to imagine just by looking at it from the outside. But crack open this lumpy dull rock, and you will see crystals of different sizes and colors—some of the most beautiful crystal formations in the world.

Geodes are found usually in deserts, volcanic ash beds, or areas containing limestone. You must know what to look for, however. Rock hounds say that one cannot judge the beauty of a geode by the exterior appearance. To some they look like petrified cauliflower heads. However, one rock hound said that when he sees an ugly rock he knows that there is going to be a beautiful crystal formation inside.

Geodes come in all sizes, and scientists disagree on how they originated. There are many different theories. Many types of crystals form geodes. In the state of Indiana, where a lot of geodes are found, 20 different minerals have been identified in them. They are found in sedimentary rocks, such as limestone; rarely are they found in shale, siltstone, and sandstone.

Geodes are composed of a thin layer of a kind of quartz called chalcedony, which is very beautiful and is named as one of the 12 foundation stones for the wall of the New Jerusalem.

While some people are trying to determine how geodes are made, others are trying to do away with the importance of the Cornerstone, Jesus. Christians know that Jesus is the true cornerstone upon whom we should build our life. Ask Jesus to help you build your life on Him today; He is the only sure foundation that will not crumble when everything else gives way. He is always there to hold you up.

GOATSBEARD

And you have been given fullness in Christ, who is the head over every power and authority. Colossians 2:10, NIV.

G oatsbeard. Do you know what it is? "Sure, it's the beard on a goat." Wrong!

"Oh, I know; it's a big dandelion."

Wrong again. "Well, tell me what it is."

You were on the right track when you thought that it looked like a dandelion, but it is much bigger than a dandelion and is not related. Goatsbeard is a beautiful yellow flower, slightly larger than dandelion flowers, found in meadows and woods. It is not mistaken for a dandelion, as the flower is entirely different, having long pointed green bracts.

We are told that the goatsbeard came from somewhere in Europe. It is mostly a biennial herb, and is definitely a wildflower. The flower looks like an aster, sunflower, and daisy all in one. Its green leaves sweep up from the base of the flower. The flower itself is made up of many little flowers at its center, surrounded by spikelike clusters radiating out from the main flower stalk. These are called ray flowers.

I have seen goatsbeard beside the road as I've traveled, and I think they are beautiful. I am especially fond of them when the yellow flower has disappeared and they turn to a large white seedhead similar to the dandelion. This is why, at a quick glance, you might think they are dandelions. The large, delicate pappus ball at the end of the stem is striking. Many people do not see the yellow flower because it closes at noon, earning it the nicknames of sleep-at-noon, noontide, Jack-go-to-bed-at-noon, meadow salsify, Joseph's flower, star of Jerusalem, noonflower, and bucksbeard.

Jesus has many names too. He is referred to as the Morning Star, Prince of Peace, Counselor, Lamb of God, Son of man, Son of God, Lord of lords, King of kings, and Savior. He truly is our Savior and Lord, and we should thank Him today for that.

MANTA RAY

These see the works of the Lord, and his wonders in the deep. Psalm 107:24.

Manta rays are the largest of the ray family, which includes stingrays and eagle rays. The manta ray is a graceful, perfectly harmless creature with very small teeth and no stinging tail. It feeds on plankton as it swims in the ocean. It has big "wings" that flap in the water, and it can swim up to 25 miles an hour by wafting its wings.

A group of divers and underwater photographers were filming underwater in the Sea of Cortes in Mexico when they saw a very large creature floating toward them. They discovered it to be a manta ray with a wingspan of about 18 feet across and a body about 10 feet long. It measured three feet between its eyes.

The manta ray stopped right underneath one of the divers. He let go of the rope he was resting on and dropped to the back of the manta ray. As he grabbed hold of the ray's shoulders it surged forward. With the diver on his back the manta sailed through the water to a depth of about 160 feet. The diver described it as "reality becoming fantasy and fantasy becoming real." He was able to see beautiful fan corals and other sea creatures, which in addition to the thrill of the ride made it a delightful trip.

Other divers also rode on the back of this large manta ray. They were ecstatic over this opportunity. They found that a rope was tied around its body and after several tries they finally cut it loose. The manta seemed to want to say Thank you, so it continued to come back for more riders. Why some creatures act the way they do we won't know until we reach heaven. Some creatures almost seem human in their reaction to the treatment they receive.

David said that those who went out to sea would see the wonderful works of the Lord. Certainly these divers saw them that day. Pray to God today, asking Him to help you be faithful so that you will have that opportunity.

CORDILLERA BLANCA

A man will be as a hiding place from the wind, and a cover from the tempest, as rivers of water in a dry place, as the shadow of a great rock in a weary land.
Isaiah 32:2, NKJV.

The Cordillera Blanca, the white mountains in the Andes of Peru, is one of my favorite places. I have flown over it many times, and each time I did I took pictures. It was always a special part of my trip. There are more than 30 jagged peaks in this range and they always have snow on them. The highest one is Huascarán (waz-CAR-ron), 22,205 feet high.

The Cordillera Blanca is about 125 miles long and only about 100 miles from the Pacific Ocean. The western side of this range drops into the valley of the Rio Santa ("holy river"). On the eastern side the streams flow into the Amazon River. Although the Cordillera Blanca is only a few hundred miles south of the equator, snow still remains on the peaks that rise above 15,000 feet in elevation. It is sort of a perpetual ice cap. Also, some glaciers have formed, which empty into some beautiful and picturesque lakes.

When I flew between Iquitos, on the Amazon, in the jungles of Peru, to Lima, the capital city, the plane always flew to the south of Huascarán, but I wanted to see the north side. On one trip our airplane captain took us north of Huascarán. I was very excited and took some good pictures. I didn't know that a few years later an earthquake would cause much of that side of Huascarán to tumble down into the valley below. It destroyed a city or two and many lives. I was saddened to hear the news of that event.

Many thought that Huascarán was a good hiding place, a place they were safe. But they found out that it was not a secure one. The prophet Isaiah told us that "a man" who would be the hiding place for us would come. We can depend on this hiding place, because it is the Rock, Jesus. If we will allow Him to do so, He will shelter and protect us forever. Place your trust in Him again today, and tell Him about your desire to be in His abiding care.

RED-SIDED GARTER SNAKE

But I fear, lest somehow, as the serpent deceived Eve by his craftiness, so your minds may be corrupted from the simplicity that is in Christ. 2 Corinthians 11:3, NKJV.

In the province of Manitoba, Canada, one of the world's strangest displays of wildlife behavior is staged from April to May each year. It happens near the community of Inwood, about 60 miles north of the city of Winnipeg.

This bizarre event takes place in the lime pits, when the red-sided garter snakes come out of hibernation. Amid the crawling, squirming mass of thousands of snakes, the mating ceremony takes place, involving all of the snakes. After the ceremony is completed, the snakes leave the lime pits and wriggle their way to their summer homes in the marshes and fields, up to 10 miles away. There they spend the next three months living on frogs, leeches, worms, slugs, and occasionally small rodents.

In August the females give birth to the young. Shortly thereafter the young snakes disappear and are not seen for a year, when they return to the lime pits. Where they go no one seems to know for sure, but it is guessed that they live in abandoned anthills and rodent burrows—which may *not* have been abandoned until the snakes arrived.

The town of Inwood has many tales about these red-sided garter snakes. The people seem content to have all of these snakes around. They don't want government health department officials coming around and inspecting their stores for fear that they will declare them "infested" and close them. Outsiders have wanted to reactivate the lime pits for commercial purposes, but the townspeople do not want their snakes harmed. They have learned to live with the red-sided garter snakes, and enjoy them as part of their environment.

The apostle Paul was concerned that God's people would be deceived in their minds, as Eve was. Only as we keep in close contact with Christ can this be avoided. Ask Jesus to occupy your mind today. If He does, the devil will not be able to get in and try to deceive you.

SEA UNICORNS

We want each of you to show this same diligence to the very end, in order to make your hope sure. We do not want you to become lazy, but to imitate those who through faith and patience inherit what has been promised. Hebrews 6:11, 12, NIV.

Five sixths of Greenland, the world's largest island, is covered with ice. In many remote areas of the island the people live on what they can hunt. In the northwest corner of the island, in an area called the Thule region, the native Inuit eke out an existence.

During the very short summer the ice melts, and the minerals suspended in the melting water help produce millions of the microscopic plankton that are eaten by halibut. Halibut fish are the favorite food of the narwhal whale, so these whales watch for the melt. If they arrive ahead of the melt, they patiently swim and wait, knowing they will be rewarded with halibut dinners.

When the narwhals arrive, the Inuit get busy. The law allows the hunting of these whales only from kayaks. The sealskin kayaks are ready, the hunting gear strapped to the tops. At the sight of the narwhals, the hunters go into action to harpoon them. When they have killed one, which usually takes several men, the first harpooner gets the skin, called *muhtuk*, and the tusk. The second harpooner gets the second-largest share, and so on, everyone getting something for their help. The Inuit store this *muktuk* for the winter in rock-lined holes in the ground.

A left tooth in the male narwhal grows long, protruding as much as 10 feet from the front of the whale. This tusk or tooth is straight but spirally grooved. A nice tusk will sell for about $800, which buys heating fuel and other necessities. The tusk makes the whale look like a unicorn; therefore, the nickname "sea unicorn."

As the Inuit wait for the return of the narwhals, so we should wait for the return of Jesus. If we wait patiently He will come, just at the right time. God promised, and He keeps His promises. God is seldom early, but never late.

Thank God for His promises today.

U.S. NATIONAL CHRISTMAS TREE

When you lay siege to a city for a long time . . . do not destroy its trees by putting an ax to them, because you can eat their fruit. Deuteronomy 20:19, NIV.

The Sierra redwoods, or *Sequoia gigantea*, which live only in California, are immensely big, beautiful, graceful trees. In the King's Canyon National Park stands the second-largest of these trees, named the General Grant. This tree was first discovered by Joseph Hardin Thomas in the 1860s and given its name by Lucretia Parker, of Porterville, California, in 1867. In 1924 R. J. Senior, a resident of nearby Sanger, California, was looking up at the gigantic General Grant tree and admiring it when a little girl passed by with her father and asked if it would take a lot of lights to make it their Christmas tree. Senior overheard this and later mentioned the possibility of making it Sanger's Christmas tree. Charles Lee, who was from the Sanger Chamber of Commerce, wrote a letter to Calvin Coolidge, who was the U.S. president at the time, suggesting that the General Grant be made the nation's Christmas tree. Within four months the U.S. Department of the Interior named the General Grant the "official national Christmas tree." It was dedicated as the national Christmas tree on April 28, 1926. It was officially made a national shrine by an Act of Congress.

A special Christmas celebration was held in 1926 at the tree, and has been repeated the second week of each December ever since, when a wreath is laid at the foot of the tree. One man who attended the first celebration did so every year until he died.

The General Grant tree is estimated to be about 3,500 years old, is 267 feet high, and measures more than 100 feet around at the base and 33 feet in diameter. It is estimated that it contains more than 550,000 board feet of lumber, weighs about 5,000 tons, and would fill 28 railroad boxcars.

God told the people in Bible times to save the trees. Today God is telling us to work to save the people. God loves trees, but He loves people much more, because He created us in His image. Thank God today because He reminds us of His creation. He is a peopleoriented God.

BIRDS ON CHRISTMAS ISLAND

And the wild beasts of the islands shall cry in their desolate houses, and dragons in their pleasant palaces: and her time is near to come, and her days shall not be prolonged. Isaiah 13:22.

Christmas Island is a tiny island 1,334 miles south of the Hawaiian Islands in the South Pacific. It is the largest coral atoll in the world, which means that the coral is like a horseshoe around a shallow lagoon. No one lived on this island until 1925, when people were brought there from the Gilbert Islands, about 2,500 miles west, to work on coconut plantations. During World War II the United States set up a military base on Christmas Island. During the 1950s and 1960s both the United States and Great Britain tested atomic bombs in the area, although no bombs were dropped directly on the island.

The atomic bomb testings didn't seem to seriously affect the bird life on Christmas Island. About 18 different seabird species congregate there, and it is the home for an estimated 16 million birds.

Several of the birds have unique habits. The fairy terns build no nests, but lay their eggs in slight depressions on the bare ground. The frigate birds catch fish. When one is carrying home it's catch, the others try to take it away. They jockey in the air and clown around. The red-footed boobies build their nests in the branches of bushes. The blue-faced boobies, which have clownlike faces, lay two eggs but take care of only one. If the one hatches, they forget the other. If the baby bird dies, the parents try to incubate the other egg. This extra egg is called the insurance egg. The tropic birds cannot walk, but they are fantastic aerial acrobats. When one lands, it does so on a bush, then falls to the ground and shuffles along on its breast. They can hover, fly backward, and do many other startling maneuvers, but they cannot walk.

The islands of the seas are often wild but beautiful, and full of all types of wildlife. God hears the cries of these creatures, and He will hear your cry for help. Turn to Him today and ask Him to help you with a problem you may have. He'd love to hear from you.

INK

Write, therefore, what you have seen, what is now and what will take place later.
Revelation 1:19, NIV.

Have you ever wondered what people used to write with back in Bible times? Did they make their own ink? God told John the revelator to write what he had seen. What did he use?

When I was a small boy, we had holes in our school desks called inkwells. A small ink bottle fit in the hole. We had both straight pens and fountain pens. We had to dip the straight pens into the ink bottle often, as the point didn't hold much ink, but the fountain pens had a rubber reservoir inside them that held maybe a teaspoon of ink until it was all used up. One day our teacher said that we would make our own ink. She went with us into a field by the woods where our school was situated, and we picked pokeberries. The early Native Americans used the pokeberries to dye cloth, and they cooked the soft shoots of the plant the way asparagus would be cooked. The roots and the seeds of the berries are poisonous.

We brought the berries into the school, put them into a kettle, and boiled them. Then the softened berries were put into cheesecloth and the juice squeezed out. The berry pulp and seeds were discarded. After cooking the berry juice another half hour, the teacher told us that this was our ink. It was the color of crimson. (She also added alum to keep the ink from fading.) We learned that the more berries we used, the darker would be the color of the ink. As soon as the ink cooled, the teacher allowed us to dip our pens into it and write. What fun we had drawing and writing with the ink we had made.

John wrote as he was instructed. Because he obeyed, we have the book of Revelation. Jesus is the center of Revelation, and it contains many prophecies for us to study and understand. They help us know the reason for what is happening in the world today. If we are obedient and follow the commands of Jesus, we will have a successful future, as did John. Ask Jesus today to help you be obedient to His commands.

QUICK-CHANGE FLEA

Being then made free from sin, ye became the servants of righteousness. Romans 6:18.

How would you like to be born just for the purpose of being eaten? Such is the life of the quick-change flea. The water flea is not much bigger than a small grain of rice, and is a common resident of most of the ponds in North America. Its chief enemy is the young aquatic fly larva called a midge. And if no midges are around, there is usually some other predator to eat the water flea. It seems that its only purpose is to be eaten. However, it does have a strong defensive strategy. As one scientist said of quick-change fleas: "They don't take this whole matter lying down."

When the baby water fleas are born, they look quite different from their parents. In fact, some scientists have said that they look almost like a different species. According to the season of the year in which they are born, their outer skin may be all armor. If they are born when the midge-fly larvae are active, the water fleas will come equipped with neck teeth or a special spine spike that makes them hard to eat.

It has been discovered that midge larvae secrete some kind of a fluid as they swim around looking for their water flea meal. When the female water flea detects the presence of the midge larvae, she is able to produce her young fleas with these defensive barbs. This cuts the mortality rate by 50 percent. Researchers have also found that longer and warmer days cause the female water flea to produce her young with the special armor. The water flea is quite active and a fast swimmer. A quick sprint may keep it away from a midge larvae so that it will not be a meal for a while. But inevitably it is eaten.

The youth who has made his or her life right with God is no longer a prey of the devil, as the water flea is for the midge larvae. We take on the armor by accepting Jesus as our personal Savior and by studying the Bible to know His will. Pray and invite Jesus into your life today.

THE SILVER DOME

The devil took him to a very high mountain and showed him all the kingdoms of the world and their splendor. Matthew 4:8, NIV.

If the mountain that Satan took Jesus to was in Palestine, it was not high as the world's mountains go. The Flood has left many high peaks and mountains around the world.

In the country of Tanzania, on the African continent, stands a very famous mountain called Mount Kilimanjaro. It is the highest mountain in Africa. The highest peak of the mountain is called Kibo, and it is 19,340 feet above sea level. The area around this peak is glacial. Because of the constant ice and snow, the early native Africans called the peak the Silver Dome. As the bright African sun hit the ice caps and reflected down to where the people lived, it no doubt looked silver.

Kilimanjaro means "mountain of greatness" or "mountain of caravans," depending on which dialect you use. Kilimanjaro has three volcanoes within it, but only one—the Kibo Crater—is the youngest. On a clear day Kilimanjaro can be seen for about 100 miles. It rises nearly four miles into the air and is located about 180 miles from the East African coast.

Although Kilimanjaro is so noticeable, the early explorers seemed to ignore it. Not until May 1848 was it discovered by two German missionaries named Johannes Rebmann and Ludwig Krapf. Today people come from all over the world to climb Kilimanjaro. Although it is somewhat difficult to climb and the air at the top is very thin, there are rewards for those who conquer the climb. One can see much beautiful country round about.

Satan took Jesus up on a high mountain and showed Him the bright kingdoms of the world spread out below. Satan told Jesus that all would be His if He would worship him—the devil. Be thankful that Jesus didn't fall for the devil's bargain, and that He is your loving Savior and Lord today. Thank Him for His love and His decision to reject the devil's invitation.

HOATZIN, THE WORLD'S STRANGEST BIRD

A little while, and the wicked will be no more; though you look for them, they will not be found. Psalm 37:10, NIV.

One of the strangest, most interesting, and remarkable birds of today lives in the jungles of South America and is called the hoatzin (what-sin) bird. These birds grow to about 25 inches long and weigh almost two pounds. The feathers are an olive brown barred with white on top and cream to rusty color below. The head is very small, with a strange-looking crest about four inches long. The eyes are scarlet red and surrounded with a light-blue skin with no feathers. The male and female look alike.

These hoatzins build a flat nest that is just a pile of sticks thrown together. They usually built far out on a limb, four to 15 feet above water, because their main enemies, the capuchin monkeys, are afraid to go out too far. Both parents will sit on the nest and incubate the eggs, which take about four weeks to hatch. The parents feed almost exclusively on leaves and fruit, another oddity for most birds, and the regurgitated food from the parents keeps the baby chicks alive for the first three to four months. The small hoatzins grow and develop slowly. The chicks have four clawed digits when they hatch, two at each wing bend, which help them climb a branch or tree. When they are old enough to fly, the claws drop off.

When danger comes near the nest, the chicks drop to the water below and swim for quite a distance under the surface. When the danger is past, they swim back to the tree and climb back to their nest, using their claws. From one week old hoatzin chicks are good swimmers. Adult hoatzins are not good flyers and do not fly more than about 500 feet from the nesting area. Only about 50 percent of the hoatzins have a clutch of chicks, and only half of the chicks live to be adult birds.

As the hoatzin chick escapes the wicked enemy, with the help of Jesus we can escape our enemy, Satan. Jesus is coming to put an end to all the wickedness. Thank Him today for that.

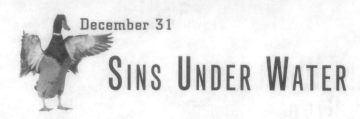

Sins Under Water

You will cast all our sins into the depths of the sea. Micah 7:19, NKJV.

A camp counselor wanted to teach his campers a spiritual lesson about God's great forgiving love. He loaded his unit of boys into several canoes, and they paddled out into the lake to a spot where he had been told the lake was the deepest. He asked the boys to put the points of their canoes into a circle right over that spot. After the boys brought the points of their canoes to the place their counselor was and tied the canoes together, he began his worship talk.

"Fellows, we are over the deepest part of this lake. I am told it is about 60 feet deep here. You know, I read that in the Mariana Trench near the island of Guam in the Pacific Ocean, there is a spot nearly seven miles deep. That is almost 37,000 feet. The Bible tells us that God will cast our sins into the depths of the sea. Just think, if God would literally cast our sins into the deepest hole in the ocean, they'd be under 37,000 feet of water. Isn't that neat?

"I hold a rock here in my hand. Let's pretend this rock is our sins. I invite you fellows to confess to God a sin that you'd like to get rid of from your life right now. Then we'll ask God to take away these sins, according to 1 John 1:9: 'If we confess our sins, he is faithful and just to forgive us our sins, and to cleanse us from all unrighteousness.' We'll drop this rock, representing our confessed sins, into this lake, and it will drop 60 feet."

Each of the boys confessed a sin or two he wanted to get rid of, and, after prayer, the rock was dropped.

"Can you see the rock, boys?" the counselor asked.

"No" was the reply.

"That, fellows, is the meaning of the promise in Micah 7:19. Aren't you glad your sins have been forgiven! Let's all sing 'I am so glad that Jesus loves me.' "

When you have sins in your life that you want to get rid of, you only have to confess them to Jesus, asking Him to forgive those sins. He will, and He figuratively throws them deep into the sea. Ask Him, as you begin a new year tomorrow, to help you start with a clean life.

TOPICAL INDEX

SOAR INTO A TRUE WILD ADVENTURE!

Rick, Tim, and Marcus can't stop dreaming of becoming mission pilots and buying the ultimate mission plane— a yellow Super Cub. The only problem is that at the rate their allowance is coming in, it will take 63.9 years to raise enough money! As they set out to raise funds, the boys meet up with lots of surprises —from an angry skunk to slashed bike tires, a fire in the woods, and a reckless hang-glider flight. You won't believe the mishaps they encounter—and the lessons they learn along the way—as they set out to earn cash for the plane of their dreams.

JUST PLANE CRAZY

Melanie Scherencel **BOCKMANN**

0-8280-1919-3

3 Ways to Shop
• Visit your local Adventist Book Center®
• Call 1-800-765-6955
• Order online at AdventistBookCenter.com

REVIEW AND HERALD®
PUBLISHING ASSOCIATION
Since 1861 | www.reviewandherald.com

A Horse Called . . .

Meet five remarkable horses—Mayonnaise, Blackberry, Poppyseed, Tamarindo, and Saskatoon. As you read these exciting stories, you'll learn information that will help you earn Pathfinder honors in Horsemanship and Horse Husbandry.

Book One 0-8280-1131-1
A Horse Called **Mayonnaise**
JoAnne Chitwood Nowack

Book Two 0-8280-1090-9
A Horse Called **Blackberry**
JoAnne Chitwood Nowack

Book Three 0-8280-1307-1
A Horse Called **Poppyseed**
JoAnne Chitwood Nowack

A Horse Called **Tamarindo**
JoAnne Chitwood Nowack
Book Four 0-8280-1499-X
Sequel to *A Horse Called Poppyseed*

A Horse Called **Saskatoon**
JoAnne Chitwood Nowack
Book Five 0-8280-1562-7
Sequel to *A Horse Called Tamarindo*

REVIEW AND HERALD®
PUBLISHING ASSOCIATION
Since 1861 | www.reviewandherald.com

Ways to Shop
ABC **3**
• Visit your local Adventist Book Center®
• Call 1-800-765-6955
• Order online at AdventistBookCenter.com

LORI PECKHAM, editor
BOOK CLUB
Guide's Greatest
MYSTERY STORIES

Guide's Greatest Mystery Stories
Collected from more than 50 years of Guide
magazine, these mystery stories, filled with
suspense and excitement, will keep you on
the edge of your seat.
978-0-8280-2038-1

unbelievable
true stories

Read these other amazing true stories in
the *Guide's Greatest* Series:

HELEN LEE ROBINSON, editor
0-8280-1880-4
Guide's Greatest
ANGEL STORIES

HELEN LEE, editor
0-8280-1575-9
Guide's Greatest
MIRACLE STORIES

HELEN LEE ROBINSON, editor
0-8280-1802-2
Guide's Greatest
CHRISTMAS STORIES

HELEN LEE ROBINSON, editor
Guide's Greatest
SABBATH STORIES

HELEN LEE, editor
Guide's Greatest
PRAYER STORIES

HELEN LEE, editor
Guide's Greatest
ESCAPE FROM CRIME STORIES
0-8280-1753-0

LORI PECKHAM, editor
Guide's Greatest
ANIMAL STORIES
0-8280-1944-4

0-8280-1814-6

0-8280-1647-X

3 Ways to Shop
• Visit your local Adventist Book Center®
• Call 1-800-765-6955
• Order online at AdventistBookCenter.com

R REVIEW AND HERALD®
PUBLISHING ASSOCIATION
Since 1861 | www.reviewandherald.com

War
of the
Ages
Series
by Sally Pierson Dillon

It's the ultimate battle.

It rages while you sleep, sit in school, talk on your cell, or watch DVDs.

And it's being fought over you.

1. War of the Invisibles
The amazing story of the great controversy
0-8280-1549-X.

2. Victory of the Warrior King
The story of the life of Jesus
0-8280-1604-6.

3. Survivors of the Dark Rebellion
God's Heroes from Adam to David
0-8280-1686-0.

4. Exile of the Chosen
God's Heroes From Solomon to Malachi
0-8280-1703-4.

5. Champions of the King
The Story of the Apostles
0-8280-1610-0.

3 **Ways to Shop**

- Visit your local Adventist Book Center®
- 1-800-765-6955
- www.AdventistBookCenter.com

FR REVIEW AND HERALD®
PUBLISHING ASSOCIATION
Since 1861 | www.reviewandherald.com

Meet Four Amazing Adventist Girls

You'll be swept back in time with these true stories about six generations of Adventist girls. The exciting series weaves through changing times, beginning with Ann, born in 1833, and ending with Erin, who is a teenager today. Read *Hannah's Girls* because every girl has a special story, a rich history, and a great heritage as a daughter of God.

The first four books of a six-book series

Ann (1833-1897)
0-8280-1951-4

Marilla (1851-1916)
0-8280-1952-1

Grace (1890-1973)
0-8280-1953-8

Ruthie (1931-)
0-8280-1954-5

Paperback.

Ways to Shop
• Visit your local Adventist Book Center®
• Call 1-800-765-6955 (ABC)
• Order online at www.AdventistBookCenter.com

Price and availability subject to change.

REVIEW AND HERALD®
PUBLISHING ASSOCIATION
Since 1861 | www.reviewandherald.com

WHAT WOULD YOU DO TO FIT IN?

JENNIFER WILL DO WHATEVER IT TAKES.

When Jennifer moves to Milwaukee, she finds herself in a new world of crushes, going steady, pranks, cheerleaders, and rebellion. As she struggles to launch from wallflower status to super-popular girl, she is sure that being cool will fill the emptiness within her. But as Jennifer's reality crashes down, it becomes clear that only God can fill the aching hole in her heart.

Paperback. **978-0-8127-1913-2.**

3 WAYS TO SHOP

- Visit your local Adventist Book Center®
- Order online at AdventistBookCenter.com
- Call your ABC at 1-800-765-6955

REVIEW AND HERALD®
PUBLISHING ASSOCIATION
Since 1861 | www.reviewandherald.com

More Great
Junior Devotional Books

0-8280-1140-0
Paperback, 376 pages.

0-8280-1573-2
Hardcover, 373 pages.

0-8280-1574-0
Hardcover, 384 pages.

0-8280-1699-0
Hardcover, 384 pages.

REVIEW AND HERALD®
PUBLISHING ASSOCIATION
Since 1861 | www.reviewandherald.com

3 Ways to Shop
• Visit your local Adventist Book Center®
• Call 1-800-765-6955
• Order online at AdventistBookCenter.com